iPhone® 4S

Guy Hart-Davis

John Wiley & Sons, Inc.

Teach Yourself VISUALLY™ iPhone® 4S

Published by
John Wiley & Sons, Inc.
10475 Crosspoint Boulevard
Indianapolis, IN 46256

www.wiley.com

Published simultaneously in Canada

Wiley also publishes its books in a variety of electronic formats and by print-on-demand. Some content that appears in standard print versions of this book may not be available in other formats. For more information about Wiley products, visit us at www.wiley.com.

Library of Congress Control Number: 2011939642

ISBN: 978-0-470-94219-2

Manufactured in the United States of America

10 9 8 7 6 5 4 3 2 1

Trademark Acknowledgments

Contact Us

For general information on our other products and services please contact our Customer Care Department within the U.S. at 877-762-2974, outside the U.S. at 317-572-3993, or fax 317-572-4002.

For technical support please visit www.wiley.com/techsupport.

WILEY **Sales** | Contact Wiley at (877) 762-2974 or fax (317) 572-4002.

Credits

Acquisitions Editor
Aaron Black

Sr. Project Editor
Sarah Hellert

Technical Editor
Dennis R. Cohen

Copy Editor
Scott Tullis

Editorial Director
Robyn Siesky

Business Manager
Amy Knies

Sr. Marketing Manager
Sandy Smith

Vice President and Executive Group Publisher
Richard Swadley

Vice President and Executive Publisher
Barry Pruett

Project Coordinator
Patrick Redmond

Graphics and Production Specialists
Joyce Haughey
Andrea Hornberger
Jennifer Mayberry
Heather Pope

Quality Control Technician
Lauren Mandelbaum

Proofreader
Susan Hobbs

Indexer
Broccoli Information Mgt.

Screen Artists
Ana Carrillo
Cheryl Grubbs
Jill A. Proll

Illustrator
Ronda David-Burroughs

Cover Photo
Pink Plumeria copyright
© Sandy Smith

About the Author

Guy Hart-Davis is the author of *Teach Yourself VISUALLY iMac, 2nd Edition*, *iMac Portable Genius, 2nd Edition*, *iLife '11 Portable Genius*, and *iWork '09 Portable Genius*.

Author's Acknowledgments

My thanks go to the many people who turned my manuscript into the highly graphical book you are holding. In particular, I thank Aaron Black for asking me to write the book; Sarah Hellert for keeping me on track and guiding the editorial process; Scott Tullis for skillfully editing the text; Dennis Cohen for reviewing the book for technical accuracy and contributing helpful sugggestions; and Ana Carrillo, Ronda David-Burroughs, Cheryl Grubbs, and Jill Proll for creating the pictures.

How to Use This Book

Who This Book Is For

This book is for the reader who has never used this particular technology or software application. It is also for readers who want to expand their knowledge.

The Conventions in This Book

1 Steps

This book uses a step-by-step format to guide you easily through each task. **Numbered steps** are actions you must do; **bulleted steps** clarify a point, step, or optional feature; and **indented steps** give you the result.

2 Notes

Notes give additional information — special conditions that may occur during an operation, a situation that you want to avoid, or a cross-reference to a related area of the book.

3 Icons and Buttons

Icons and buttons show you exactly what you need to click to perform a step.

4 Tips

Tips offer additional information, including warnings and shortcuts.

5 Bold

Bold type shows command names or options that you must click or text or numbers you must type.

6 Italics

Italic type introduces and defines a new term.

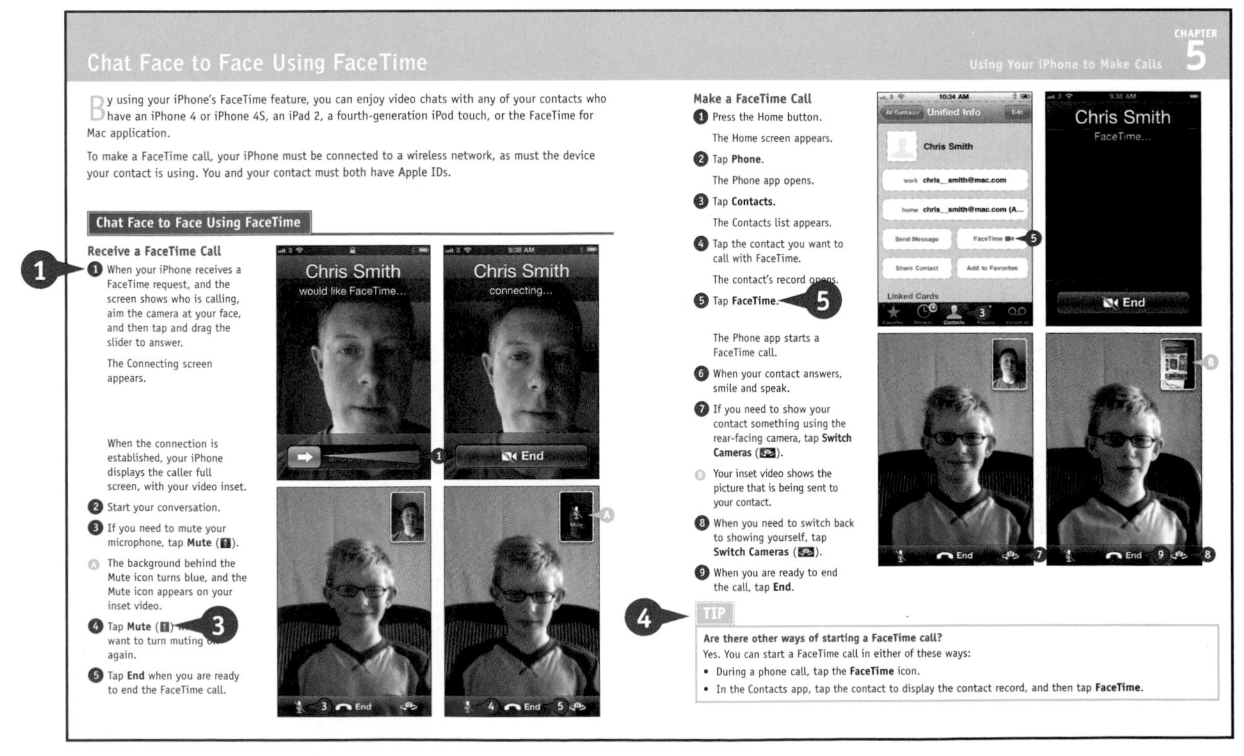

Chat Face to Face Using FaceTime

CHAPTER 5

Using Your iPhone to Make Calls

By using your iPhone's FaceTime feature, you can enjoy video chats with any of your contacts who have an iPhone 4 or iPhone 4S, an iPad 2, a fourth-generation iPod touch, or the FaceTime for Mac application.

To make a FaceTime call, your iPhone must be connected to a wireless network, as must the device your contact is using. You and your contact must both have Apple IDs.

Chat Face to Face Using FaceTime

Receive a FaceTime Call

1 When your iPhone receives a FaceTime request, and the screen shows who is calling, aim the camera at your face, and then tap and drag the slider to answer.

The Connecting screen appears.

When the connection is established, your iPhone displays the caller full screen, with your video inset.

2 Start your conversation.

3 If you need to mute your microphone, tap **Mute** ( ).

A The background behind the Mute icon turns blue, and the Mute icon appears on your inset video.

4 Tap **Mute** ( ) [illegible] want to turn muting [illegible] again.

5 Tap **End** when you are ready to end the FaceTime call.

Make a FaceTime Call

1 Press the Home button.

The Home screen appears.

2 Tap **Phone**.

The Phone app opens.

3 Tap **Contacts**.

The Contacts list appears.

4 Tap the contact you want to call with FaceTime.

The contact's record opens.

5 Tap **FaceTime**.

The Phone app starts a FaceTime call.

6 When your contact answers, smile and speak.

7 If you need to show your contact something using the rear-facing camera, tap **Switch Cameras** ( ).

B Your inset video shows the picture that is being sent to your contact.

8 When you need to switch back to showing yourself, tap **Switch Cameras** ( ).

9 When you are ready to end the call, tap **End**.

TIP

Are there other ways of starting a FaceTime call?

Yes. You can start a FaceTime call in either of these ways:

- During a phone call, tap the **FaceTime** icon.
- In the Contacts app, tap the contact to display the contact record, and then tap **FaceTime**.

Table of Contents

Chapter 1 Getting Started with Your iPhone

Chapter 2 Choosing Which Data to Sync

Chapter 3 Personalizing Your iPhone

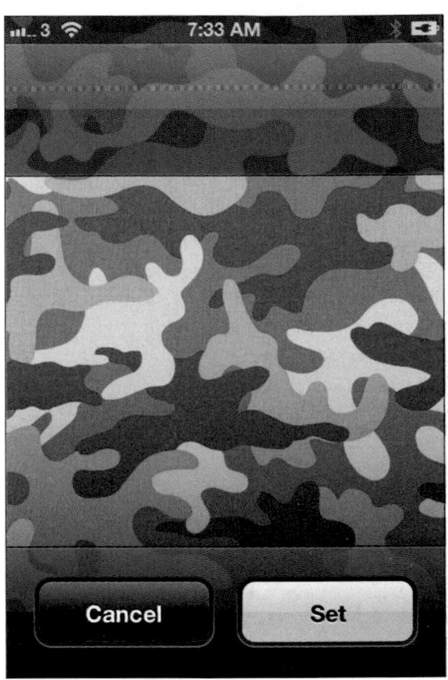

Chapter 4 Setting Up Mail, Contacts, and Calendar

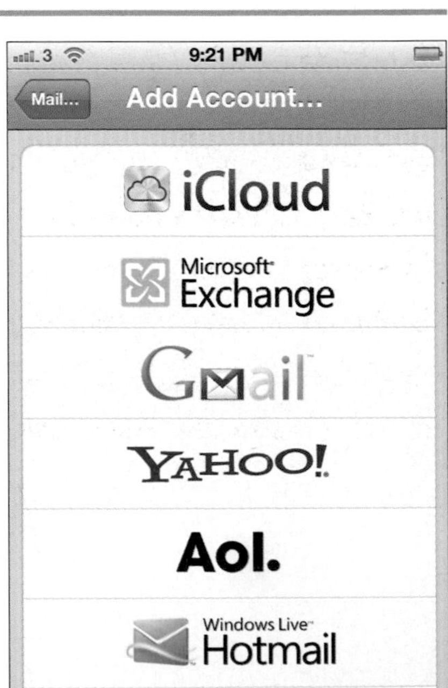

Table of Contents

Chapter 5 Using Your iPhone to Make Calls

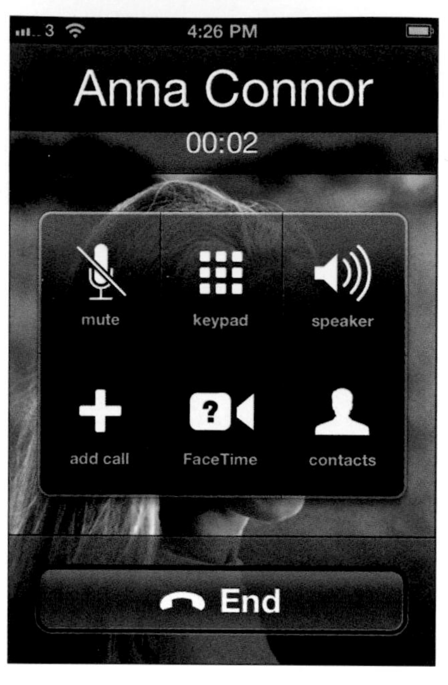

Chapter 6 Networking with Cellular and Wi-Fi

Chapter 7 Working with Apps

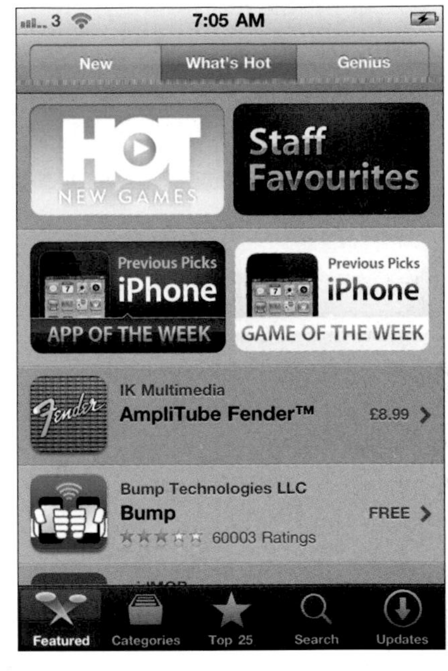

Chapter 8 Browsing the Web and Sending Email

Table of Contents

Chapter 9 Working with Contacts and Calendars

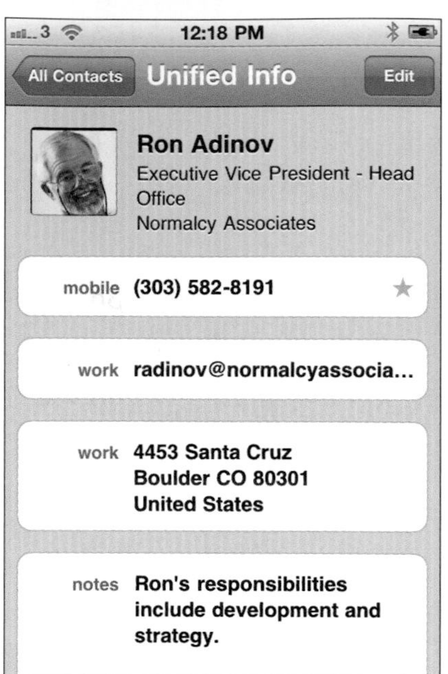

Chapter 10 Playing Music and Videos

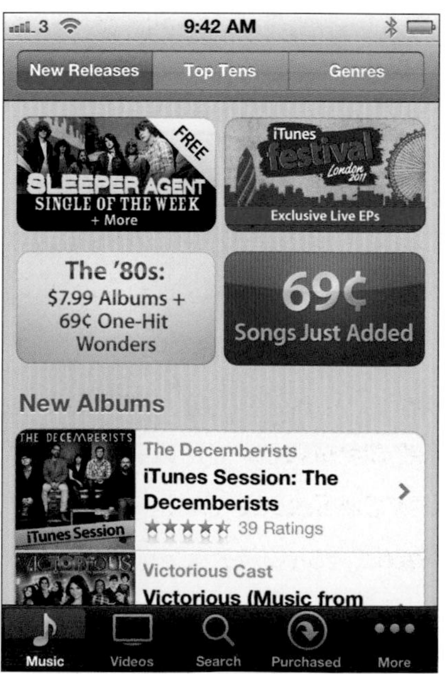

Chapter 11 Working with Photos and Books

Chapter 12 Using the Bundled Apps

Table of Contents

Chapter 13 Taking Photos and Videos

Chapter 14 Using Advanced Features

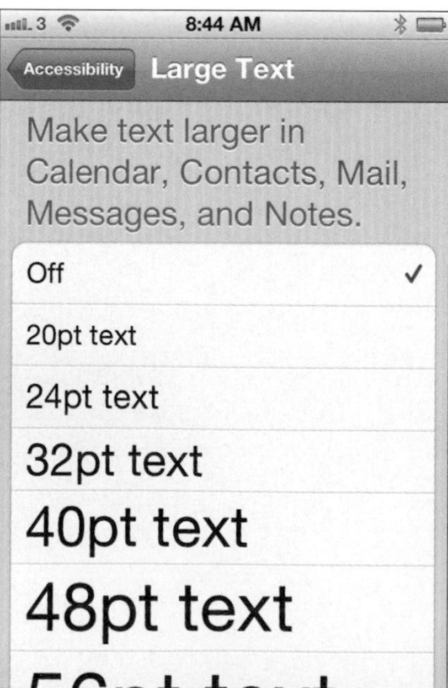

Chapter 15 Troubleshooting Your iPhone

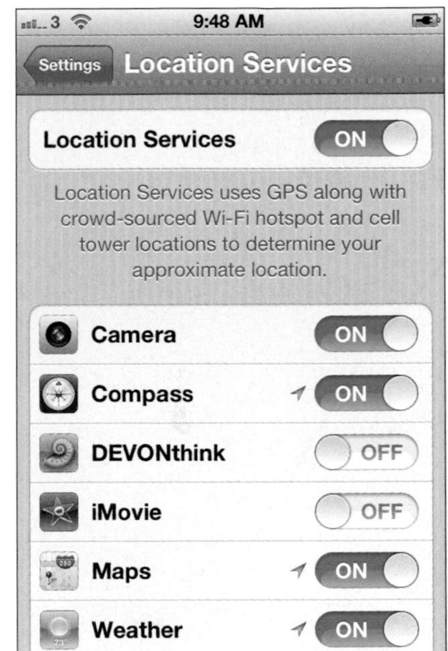

CHAPTER 1

Getting Started with Your iPhone

In this chapter, you learn how to set up your iPhone to work with your computer or your account on Apple's iCloud online service. You install iTunes on your computer if necessary, choose which items to sync, and learn to use the iPhone's interface.

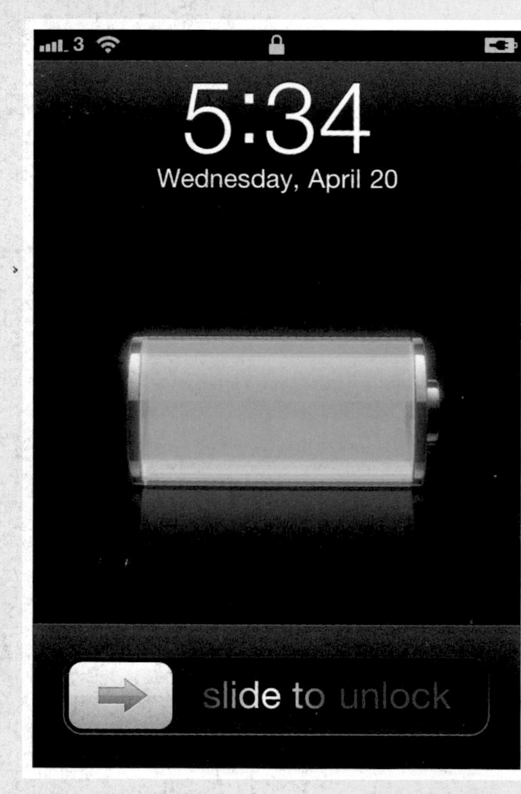

Unbox the iPhone and Charge It

Once you have gotten your iPhone, your first move is to unbox it, identify the components, and set the iPhone to charge.

To get the best battery life out of your iPhone, you should first fully charge the battery, even if it came partly charged. So no matter how eager you are to set up your iPhone, sync it with iTunes or iCloud, and start using it, take a few hours to charge it fully first.

Unbox the iPhone and Charge It

1. Open the iPhone's box and remove its contents.
2. Make sure you have the iPhone itself and the following components:

   A The headset.

   B The USB cable.

   C The power adapter.

3. Peel the protective stickers off the front and back of the iPhone.

4 Connect the small end of the USB cable to the power adapter.

5 Plug the power adapter into a power socket.

6 Connect the large end of the USB cable to the iPhone.

Note: The side of the cable with the symbol goes on the same side as the iPhone's screen.

A Charging readout appears on-screen.

7 Leave the iPhone to charge until the battery readout shows that the battery is fully charged.

TIP

Can I charge the iPhone from my computer's USB port instead of using the power adapter?

Yes, you can. Charging from the USB port offers the convenience of charging the iPhone at the same time as syncing data with it. You must make sure that the USB port provides enough power to the iPhone; some USB ports on keyboards, other external devices, and even some older computers do not provide enough.

For the first charge, using the power adapter is better than charging from a USB port. This is because the power adapter delivers a more consistent power feed, which charges the iPhone as fast as possible.

Turn On the iPhone and Meet the Hardware Controls

After charging your iPhone, turn it on and meet its hardware controls. For essential actions, such as turning on and controlling volume, the iPhone has a Power/Sleep button, a Ringer On/Off switch, a Volume Up button and a Volume Down button, together with the Home button below the screen.

Most stores and carriers insert a SIM card in your iPhone for you. But in some cases, you may need to insert a suitable SIM card yourself.

Turn On the iPhone and Meet the Hardware Controls

1. Press and hold the Power/Sleep button on top of the iPhone for a couple of seconds.

   The top of the iPhone also contains:

A. The microphone.

B. The headphone socket.

As the iPhone starts, the Apple logo appears on the screen.

Above the iPhone's screen:

C. The front-facing camera.

D. The receiver speaker, which plays phone calls into your ear when you hold the iPhone up to your face.

E. Below the iPhone's screen is the Home button, which you press to display the Home screen.

2 Turn the iPhone so that you can see its left side.

3 Move the Ringer On/Off switch to the rear, so that the orange background appears, when you want to turn off the ringer.

Note: Turn the ringer off when you do not want the iPhone to disturb you or the peace. Move the Ringer On/Off switch back to the front when you want to turn the ringer back on.

4 Press the Volume Up (+) button to increase the ringer volume.

Note: When the iPhone is locked, you can press the Volume Up (+) button to take a picture with the camera.

5 Press the Volume Down (–) button to decrease the ringer volume.

6 When the lock screen appears, tap the **Slide to Unlock** slider, and then drag your finger to the right.

The iPhone unlocks, and the Home screen appears.

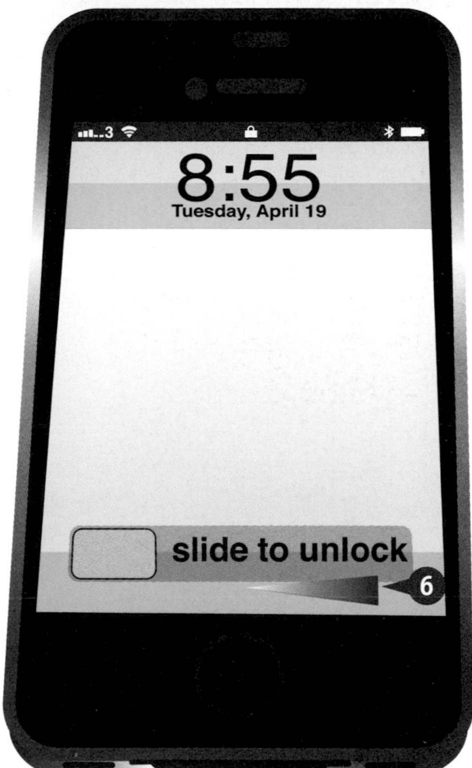

TIP

How do I insert a SIM card in my iPhone?

If the store or carrier has not inserted a SIM card, insert the SIM removal tool (A) in the SIM hole (B) on the right side of the iPhone. Push gently until the tray (C) pops out, and then pull it with your fingernails. Insert the SIM in the tray (D), and then push the tray in fully.

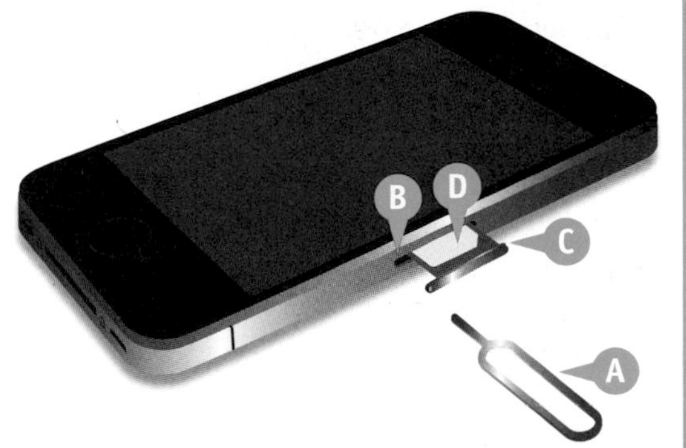

Download, Install, and Set Up iTunes

To sync your iPhone with your computer, you use Apple's iTunes application. iTunes comes preinstalled on every Mac but not on PCs; to get iTunes for Windows, you download it from the Apple website and then install it on your PC.

If you do not have a computer, or you do not want to sync your iPhone with your computer, you can set up and sync your iPhone using Apple's iCloud service, as described later in this chapter.

Download, Install, and Set Up iTunes

1. On your PC, open the web browser, Internet Explorer in this example.
2. Click the Address box, type **www.apple.com/itunes/download**, and then press Enter.

   The Download iTunes Now web page appears.
3. Deselect the check boxes (☑ changes to ☐) unless you want to receive email from Apple.
4. Click **Download Now.**

   The File Download – Security Warning dialog box opens.
5. Click **Save.**

   The Save As dialog box appears.
6. Select the download location — for example, your Downloads folder — and then click **Save.**

   The download starts.
7. In the Download Complete dialog box, click **Run.**

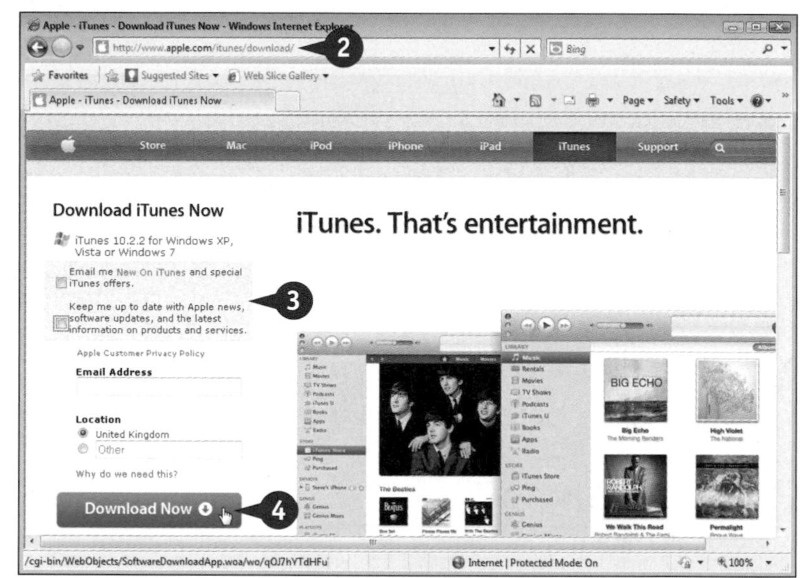

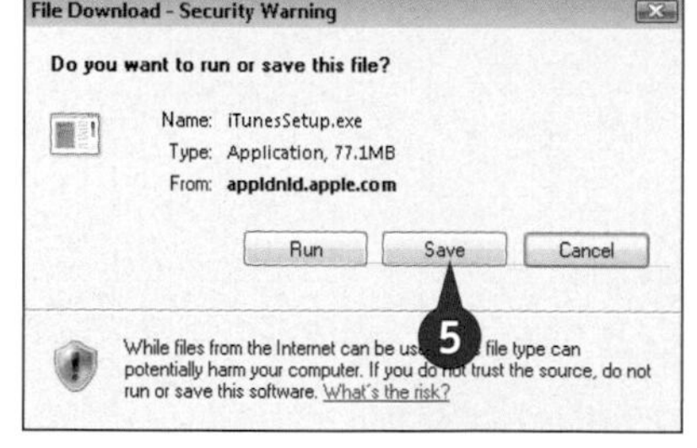

The iTunes + QuickTime Installer opens.

8 Click **Next**, and then follow through the steps of the installer.

Note: You must accept the license agreement in order to install iTunes. On the Installation Options screen, click the **Add iTunes and QuickTime shortcuts to my desktop** check box (☑ changes to ☐) unless you need these shortcuts.

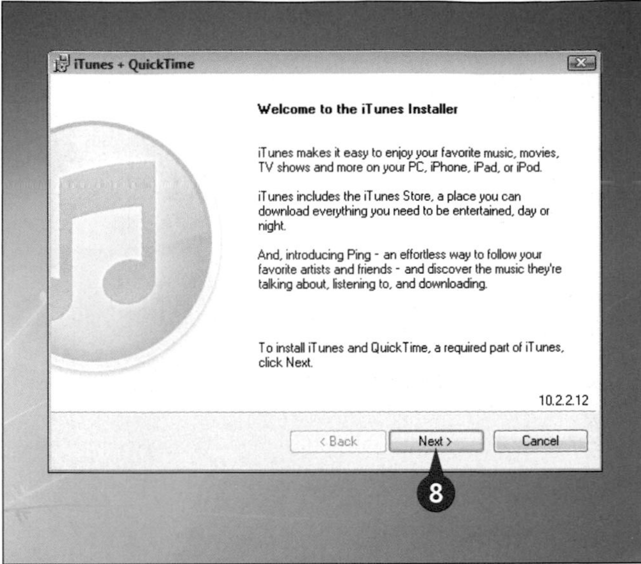

When the installation finishes, the installer displays the Congratulations screen.

9 Click **Finish**.

The installer closes.

10 If the installer prompts you to restart your PC, restart it as soon as is convenient.

TIP

How do I set up iTunes on a Mac?

If you have not run iTunes already, click the **iTunes** icon (🎵) that appears on the Dock by default. If the Dock contains no iTunes icon, click the desktop, choose **Go** and then **Applications** from the menu bar, and then double-click the iTunes icon in the Applications folder. The iTunes Setup Assistant launches. Follow through the steps to set up iTunes.

Authorize and Set Up Your iPhone Using iTunes

Before you can use your iPhone, you must authorize it and set it up. You can authorize the iPhone through iTunes, as described in this task, or by using iCloud, as explained later in this chapter.

Authorization involves registering the iPhone with Apple's servers and providing registration information. Setup involves choosing which items to sync automatically with the iPhone. You can choose other sync options as described in the next task.

Authorize and Set Up Your iPhone Using iTunes

1. Turn on the iPhone by pressing and holding the power switch for a couple of seconds until the Apple logo appears on-screen.
2. When the initial iPhone screen appears, tap the slider and drag it to the right.

   The iPhone unlocks and begins the setup routine.
3. If the Language screen shows the language you want to use, tap **Next**. Otherwise, tap **Show More**, tap the language on the screen that appears, and then tap ➡.
4. If the first Country or Region screen shows the right country or region, tap **Next**. Otherwise, tap **Show More**, tap the country or region on the second Country or Region screen, and then tap **Next**.

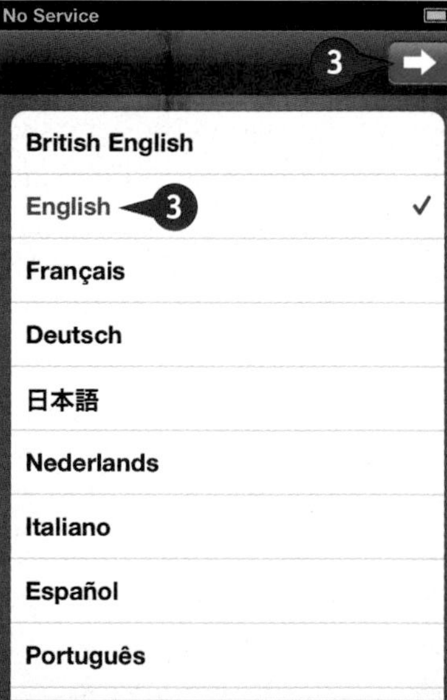

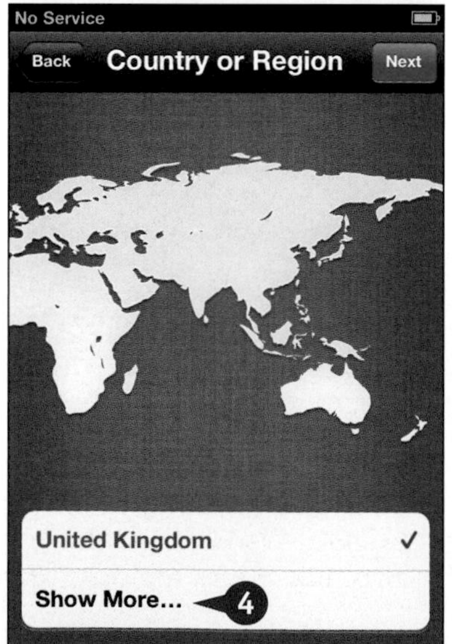

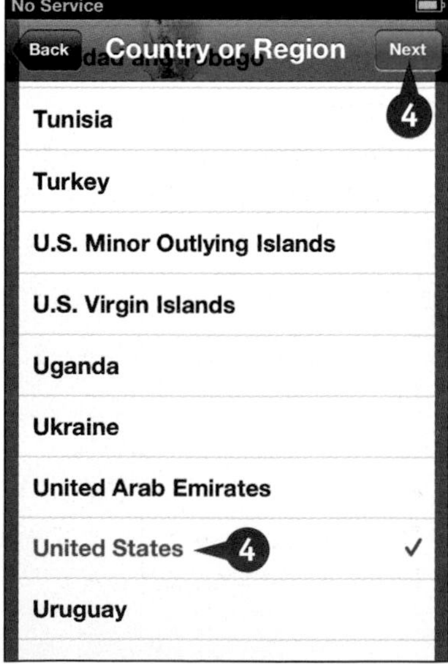

The Location Services screen appears.

5. Tap **Enable Location Services** or **Disable Location Services.**

Note: Location Services can be helpful for finding businesses and services near your current location.

6. Tap **Next.**

7. On the Wi-Fi Networks screen, tap **Connect to iTunes.**

8. Connect your iPhone to your computer using the USB cable.

   The iTunes window appears.

9. On the Set Up Your iPhone screen, change the name as needed.

10. Select **Automatically sync contacts, calendars, bookmarks, notes, and email accounts** (☐ changes to ☑) to sync all these items.

Note: To control which items you sync, deselect this check box (☑ changes to ☐) and see the next task.

11. Select **Automatically sync applications** (☐ changes to ☑) to sync new apps automatically. Syncing apps automatically is usually helpful.

12. Click **Done.**

    iTunes syncs your iPhone.

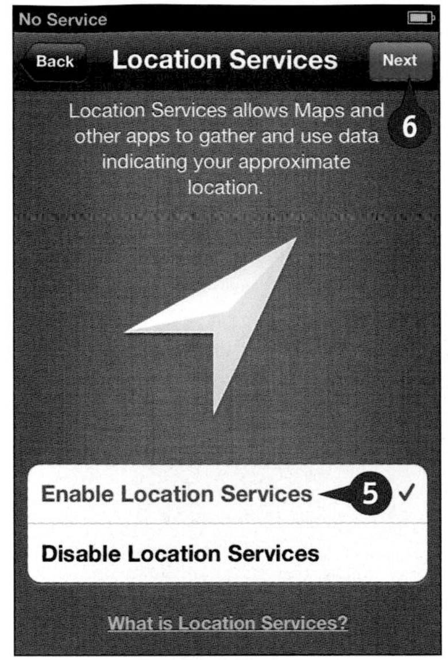

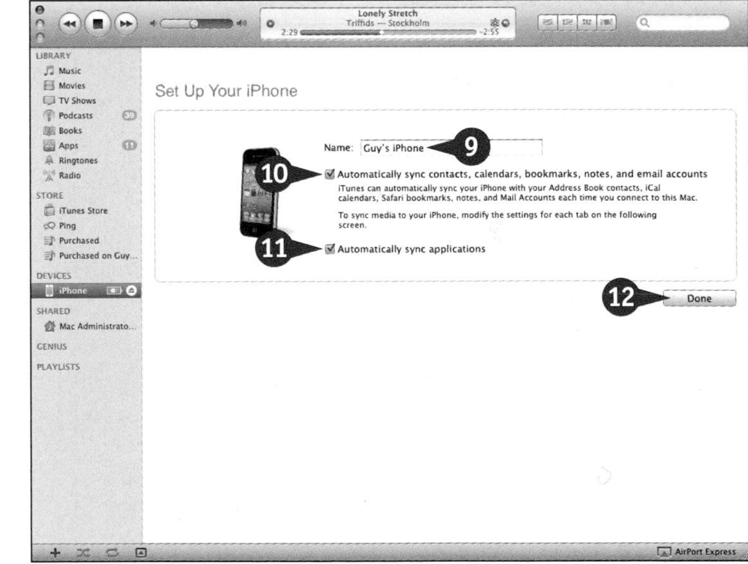

TIP

What should I do if iTunes does not open when I connect my iPhone?

If iTunes does not open automatically, launch iTunes manually. In Mac OS X, click **iTunes** ( ) on the Dock or in the Applications folder. In Windows, click **Start** and then **iTunes**.

Choose Which Items to Sync

After authorizing and setting up your iPhone, you can choose which items to sync to it. You can sync a wide range of items, ranging from your contacts, calendars, and email accounts to your music, movies, books, and photos. This task shows you how to sync the items you will most likely need at first: contacts, calendars, email, music, movies, and photos. This task shows Mac OS X screens; the Windows screens are similar, but some items have different names.

Choose Which Items to Sync

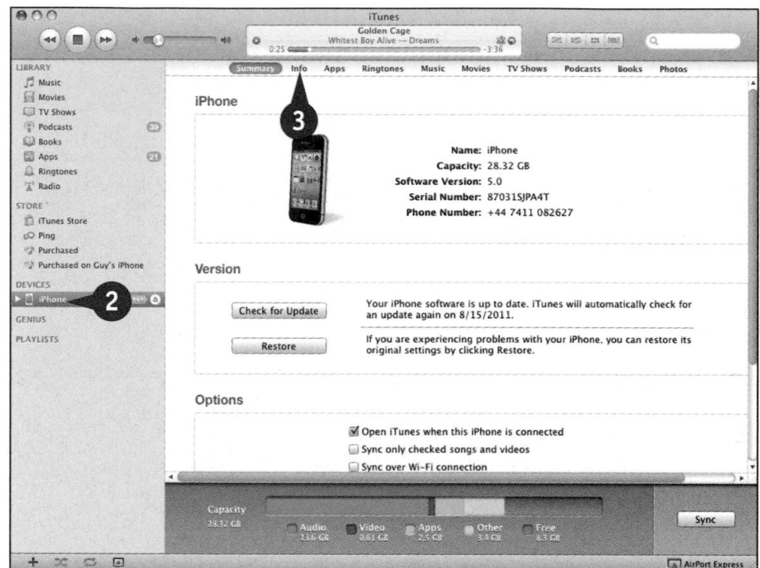

1. Connect your iPhone to your computer.

   The iTunes window appears.

2. Click your iPhone.

Note: Your iPhone appears in iTunes with the name you gave it.

   The iPhone's control screens appear.

3. Click **Info**.

   The Info tab appears.

4. Click **Sync Address Book Contacts** (☐ changes to ☑) if you want to sync contacts.

Note: In Windows, you can sync contacts from Windows Contacts, Google Contacts, Outlook, or Yahoo! Contacts. You can sync calendars with Outlook.

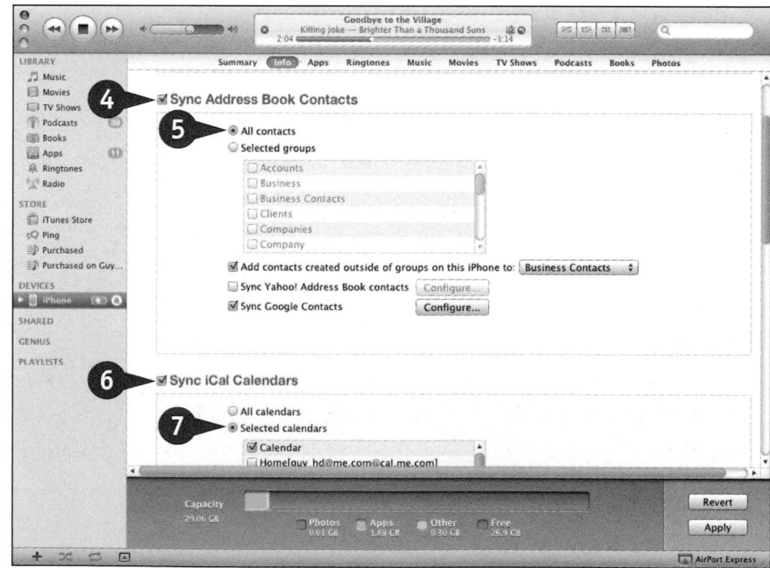

5. Choose which contacts to sync. For example, click **All contacts** (○ changes to ◉).

6. Click **Sync iCal Calendars** (☐ changes to ☑) if you want to sync calendars.

7. Choose which calendars to sync. For example, click **Selected calendars** (○ changes to ◉) and then click the check box (☐ changes to ☑) for each calendar to sync.

8 Click **Sync Mail Accounts** (☐ changes to ☑) if you want to sync email accounts. Then click the check box (☐ changes to ☑) for each email account to sync.

9 Click **Sync Safari bookmarks** (☐ changes to ☑) if you want to sync bookmarks.

Note: In Windows, you can sync email from Outlook or Outlook Express. You can sync bookmarks from Internet Explorer or Safari.

10 Click **Sync notes** (☐ changes to ☑) if you want to sync notes.

11 Click **Apps**.

The Apps tab appears.

12 Click **Sync Apps** (☐ changes to ☑).

13 Select the check box for each app you want to sync to the iPhone.

14 Select **Automatically sync new apps** (☐ changes to ☑) if you want to sync new apps automatically. This is usually helpful.

15 Click **Music**.

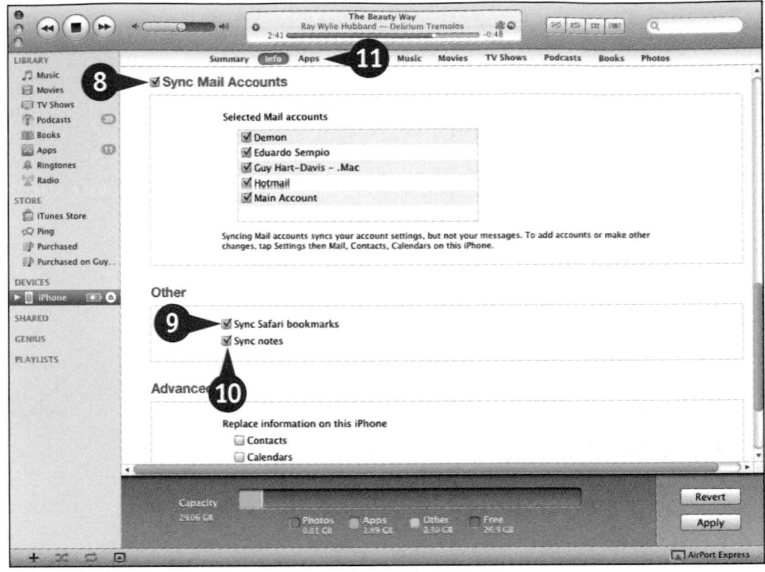

TIP

Should I sync my entire music library to my iPhone?

This depends on how big your music library is, how high your iPhone's capacity is, and how much other data you need to put on the iPhone. In iTunes, click **Music** in the left column, and then click **All** in the Genres box, **All** in the Artist box, and **All** in the Albums box. The readout at the bottom of the iTunes window shows you how much space the items occupy, enabling you to judge whether they will all fit on the iPhone.

continued ►

Choose Which Items to Sync (continued)

When you have chosen all the items to sync, you click the **Apply** button to run the sync. The initial sync normally takes much longer than subsequent syncs — often several hours, or even overnight. This is because iTunes must transfer large amounts of data, such as your music files, to the iPhone. Subsequent syncs typically involve much less data and so go much faster.

Choose Which Items to Sync (continued)

The Music tab appears.

16 Click **Sync Music** (☐ changes to ☑).

17 Use the controls in the Sync Music box, Playlists box, Artists box, Genres box, and Albums box to specify which music to sync.

A Click **Automatically fill free space with songs** (☐ changes to ☑) if you want to put as much music as possible on your iPhone.

18 Click **Movies**.

The Movies tab appears.

19 Click **Sync Movies** (☐ changes to ☑).

20 Choose which movies to sync.

B To sync only movies you have not watched, click **Automatically include** (☐ changes to ☑), open the pop-up menu, and choose a suitable setting — for example, **5 most recent unwatched** movies.

21 Click **Photos**.

The Photos tab appears.

22 Click **Sync Photos** (☐ changes to ☑).

Note: In Windows, click **Sync Photos with** (☐ changes to ☑), and then choose the folder in the drop-down list.

23 In the pop-up menu, choose the source of the photos — for example, iPhoto.

24 Choose which photos to sync. For example, click **Selected albums, events, and faces, and automatically include** (○ changes to ◉), and then choose which albums, events, and faces to include.

25 Click **Apply**.

iTunes syncs the items to your iPhone.

C The readout shows you the sync progress.

D If you need to stop the sync, click ⊗.

26 When the sync finishes, disconnect your iPhone.

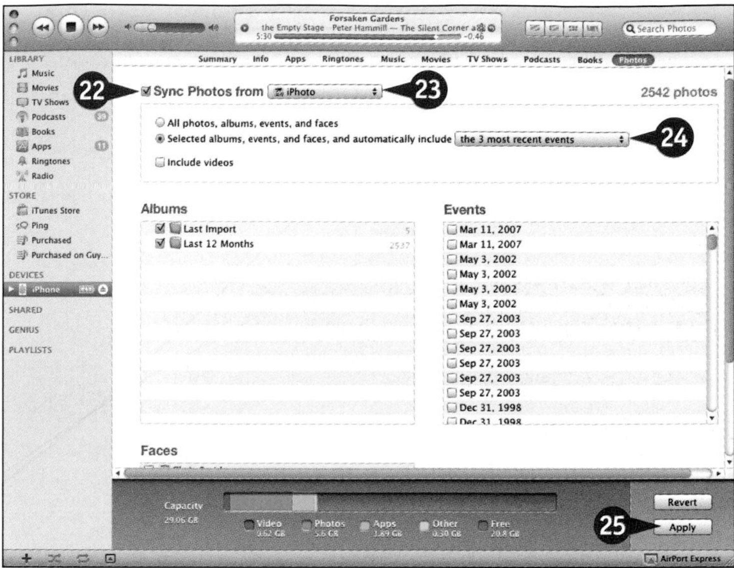

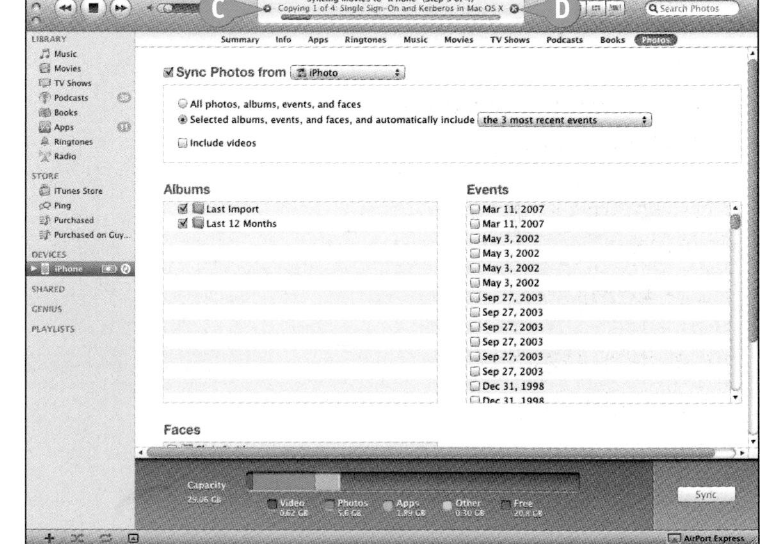

TIP

How do I sync ringtones, TV shows, podcasts, and books?

To sync ringtones, TV shows, podcasts, and books, click the appropriate tab in iTunes, and then use the controls to specify which items you want. For example, for TV shows, you can click **Sync TV Shows** (☐ changes to ☑) and then choose a setting such as **Automatically include the 3 newest unwatched episodes of all shows**.

Sync Your iPhone with iTunes via Wi-Fi

The normal way to sync your iPhone with iTunes is by using the USB cable to connect the iPhone to your computer. But if you connect both your computer and your iPhone to the same network, you can sync the iPhone with iTunes wirelessly. This is called syncing "over the air."

To use wireless sync, you must first enable it in iTunes. You can then have the iPhone sync automatically when it is connected to a power source and to the same wireless network as the computer. You can also start a sync manually from the iPhone even if it is not connected to a power source.

Sync Your iPhone with iTunes via Wi-Fi

Set Your iPhone to Sync with iTunes via Wi-Fi

1. Connect your iPhone to your computer with the USB cable.

   The iTunes window appears.

2. Click your iPhone.

Note: Your iPhone appears in iTunes with the name you gave it.

   The iPhone's control screens appear.

3. Click **Summary**.

   The Summary tab appears.

4. Click **Sync over Wi-Fi connection** (☐ changes to ☑).

5. Click **Apply**.

   iTunes applies the change.

6. Disconnect your iPhone from your computer.

Perform a Manual Sync via Wi-Fi

1. Press the Home button.

   The Home screen appears.

2. Tap **Settings**.

   The Settings screen appears.

3. Tap and drag up to scroll down until the third box of settings appears.

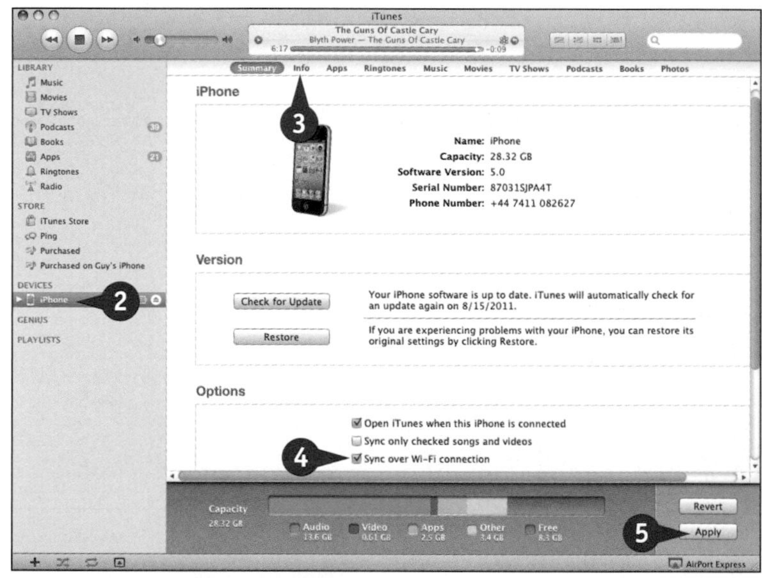

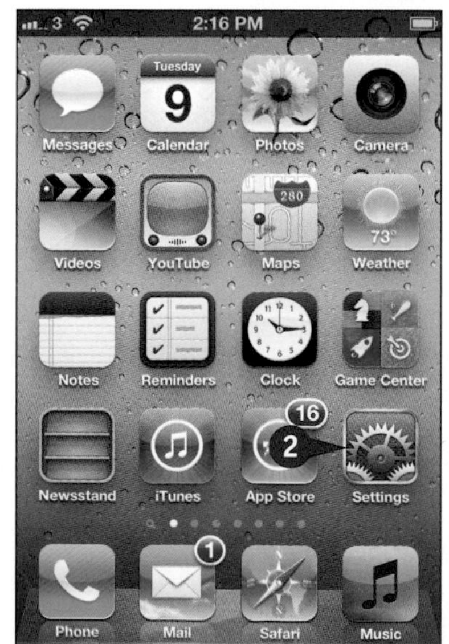

4 Tap **General**.

The General screen appears.

5 Tap **iTunes Wi-Fi Sync**.

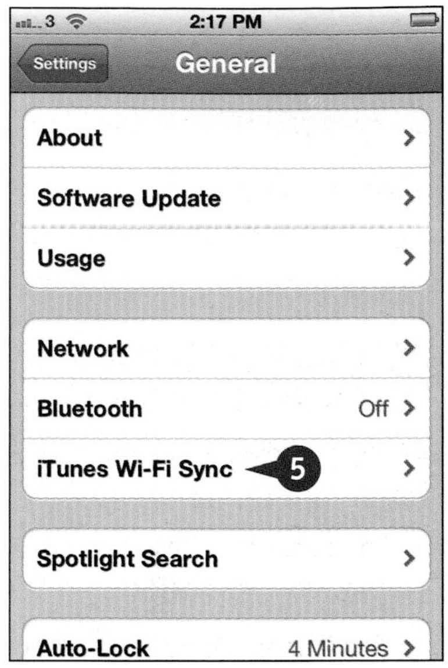

The iTunes Wi-Fi Sync screen appears.

6 Tap **Sync Now**.

The sync runs.

TIP

Can I sync my iPhone automatically via Wi-Fi?

To sync your iPhone automatically via Wi-Fi, connect your iPhone to a power source — for example, the iPhone Power Adapter. Make sure your computer is on and connected to your network, and that iTunes is running. Your iPhone automatically connects to your computer across the wireless network. iTunes syncs the latest songs, videos, and data.

Authorize and Set Up Your iPhone Using iCloud

Instead of using iTunes and your computer to set up and sync your iPhone, you can set it up and sync it without a computer using Apple's iCloud online service. To do this, you need an Apple ID. You can create an Apple ID using either your existing email address or a new iCloud account that you create during setup.

Authorize and Set Up Your iPhone Using iCloud

1. Follow steps **1** to **6** of the task "Authorize and Set Up Your iPhone Using iTunes" to begin setting up your iPhone.
2. On the Wi-Fi Networks screen, tap your wireless network, type the password, and then tap **Next.**

   The Apple ID screen appears.
3. Tap **Create a Free Apple ID.**

   The Birthday screen appears.
4. Move the spin wheels to your birthday or the date you want to claim is your birthday.
5. Tap **Next.**

   The Name screen appears.
6. Tap the First Name box and type your first name.
7. Tap the Last Name box and type your last name.
8. Tap **Next.**

   The Create Apple ID screen appears.
9. Tap **Get a free iCloud email address.**
10. Tap **Next.**

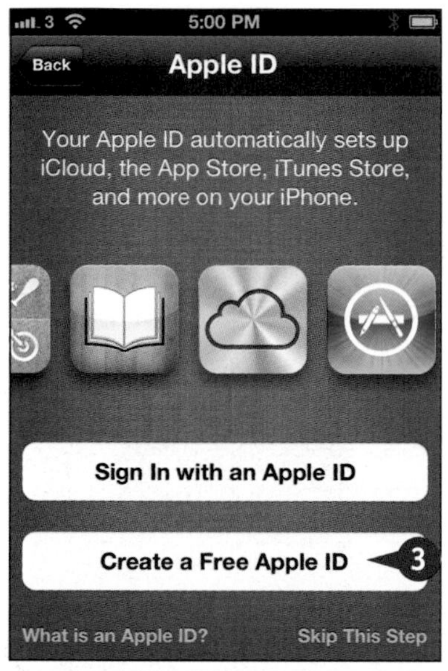

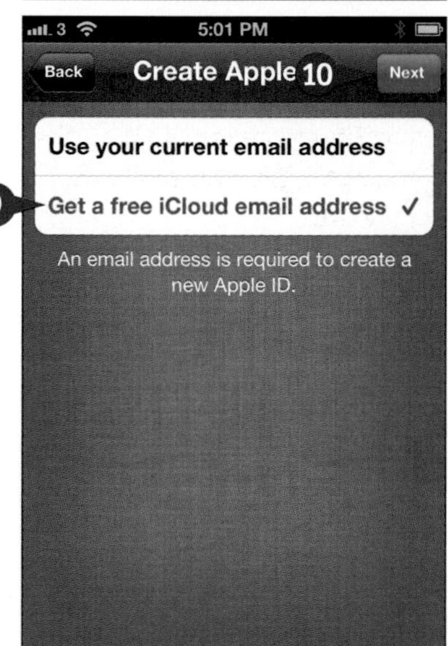

The iCloud Email screen appears.

11 Type the address you want to use.

12 Tap **Next**.

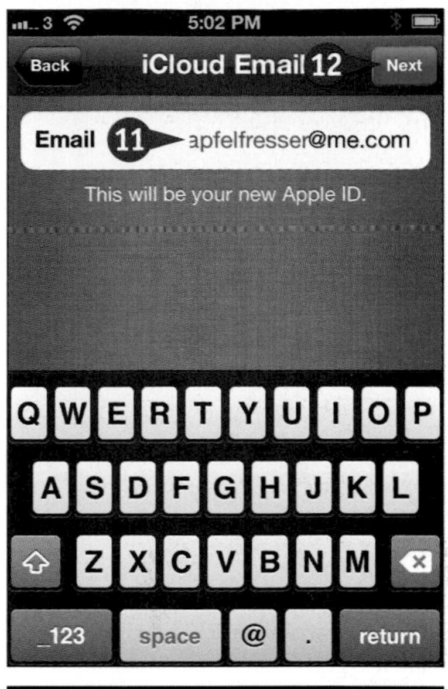

The Security Info screen appears.

13 Tap the question you want to use. You can use a custom question for added security.

14 Tap the Answer box and type the answer to your question.

15 Tap **Next**.

Note: If the Apple ID you are requesting is already in use, the iPhone prompts you to choose another ID.

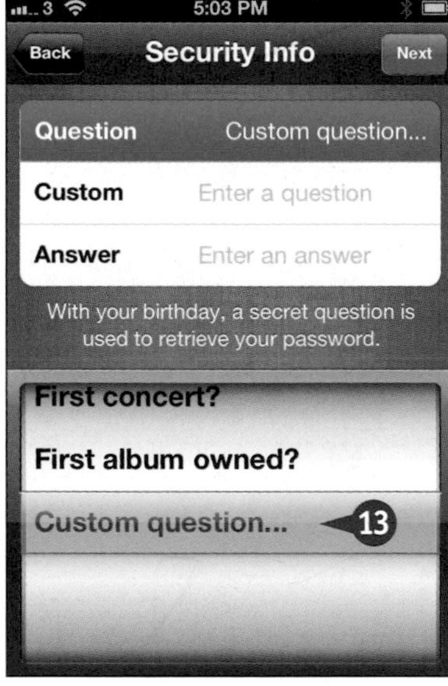

TIP

Should I sync my iPhone with iCloud rather than with my computer?

If you have a main computer that you use most of the time, you will probably be better off syncing your iPhone with the computer than with iCloud. You can keep all your music and videos on your computer, organize them with iTunes, and then sync the items you want with your iPhone, as discussed earlier in this chapter.

If you do not have a computer you use regularly, sync with iCloud. For example, if you use an iPad as your main computer, you must sync your iPhone with iCloud because you cannot sync the iPhone directly with the iPad.

continued ▶

By using iCloud, you can synchronize your songs, videos, apps, and documents with other devices running Apple's iOS operating system. For example, if you have an iPad or an iPod touch, you can use iCloud sync to keep that device's contents synced with your iPhone's contents, and vice versa.

Authorize and Set Up Your iPhone Using iCloud (continued)

The Email Updates screen appears.

16 Tap the **Email Updates** switch and move it to Off if you do not want to receive email updates from Apple.

17 Tap **Next**.

The Terms and Conditions screen appears.

18 Read the terms and conditions, and then tap **Agree** if you want to proceed.

The Terms and Conditions dialog appears.

19 Tap **Agree**.

The Creating Apple ID screen appears while your iPhone creates your Apple ID.

20 Make sure the iCloud switch is set to On.

21 Tap **Next**.

The iCloud Backup screen appears.

22 Tap **Back Up to iCloud**.

23 Tap **Next**.

The Find My iPhone screen appears.

24 Make sure the Find My iPhone switch is set to On if you want to use the Find My iPhone feature.

25 Tap **Next**.

The Diagnostics screen appears.

26 Tap the **Send Diagnostics** switch and move it to On if you want to send anonymous diagnostic and usage data to Apple to help improve its products and services.

27 Tap **Next**.

The Thank You screen appears.

28 Tap **Start Using iPhone**.

The Home screen appears, and you can start using the iPhone, as discussed in the following task.

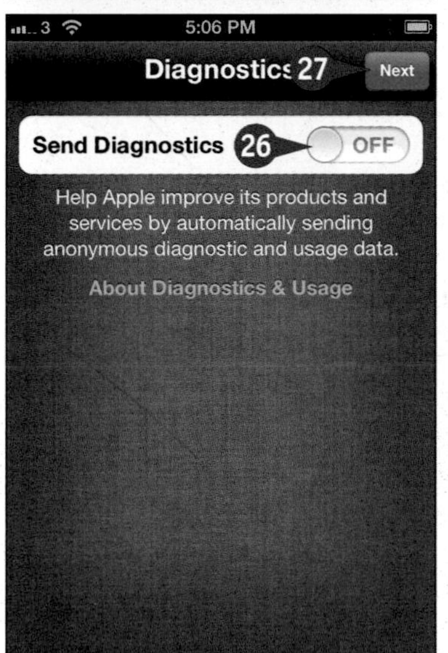

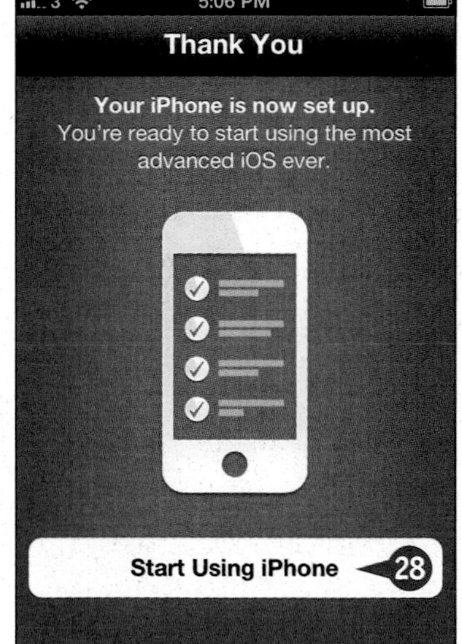

TIP

Should I use the Find My iPhone feature, or is it a threat to my privacy?
The Find My iPhone feature can help you locate your iPhone if you have mislaid it or if someone has removed it.

To use Find My iPhone, you log in to iCloud using your Apple ID. You can then give the command to locate your iPhone.

Unless you share your Apple ID with others, no one but you can use Find Your iPhone, so it is not a privacy threat worth worrying about.

Explore the iPhone's User Interface and Launch Apps

After you sync the iPhone or set it up with iCloud, you are ready to start using the iPhone. When you press the Power/Sleep button to wake the iPhone from sleep, it displays the lock screen. You then unlock the iPhone to reach the Home screen, which contains icons for running the apps installed on the iPhone.

You can quickly launch an app by tapping its icon on the Home screen. From the app, you can return to the Home screen by pressing the Home button. You can then launch another app as needed.

Explore the iPhone's User Interface and Launch Apps

1. Press the Power/Sleep button.

   The iPhone's screen lights up and shows the Lock screen.

2. Tap the slider and drag it to the right.

   The iPhone unlocks, and the home screen appears.

- A The iPhone has two or more Home screens, depending on how many apps are installed. The gray dots at the bottom of the Home screen show how many Home screens there are. The white dot shows the current Home screen. The leftmost item in the row of dots is a magnifying glass representing Spotlight, the search feature.

3. Tap **Notes**.

   The Notes app opens.

Note: If you chose to sync notes with your iPhone, the synced notes appear in the Notes app. Otherwise, the list is empty until you create a note.

4. Tap **New** (+).

   A new note opens, and the on-screen keyboard appears.

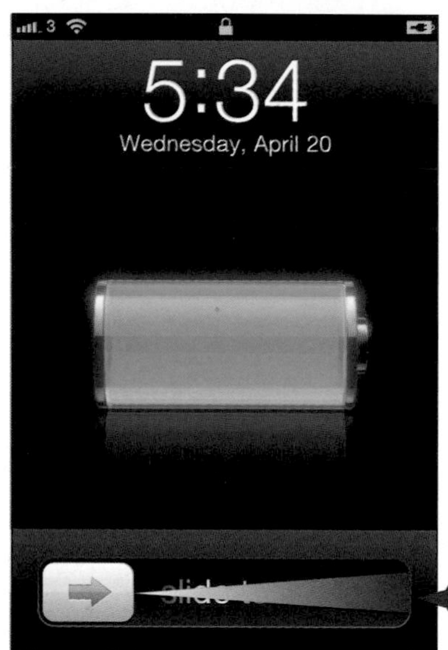

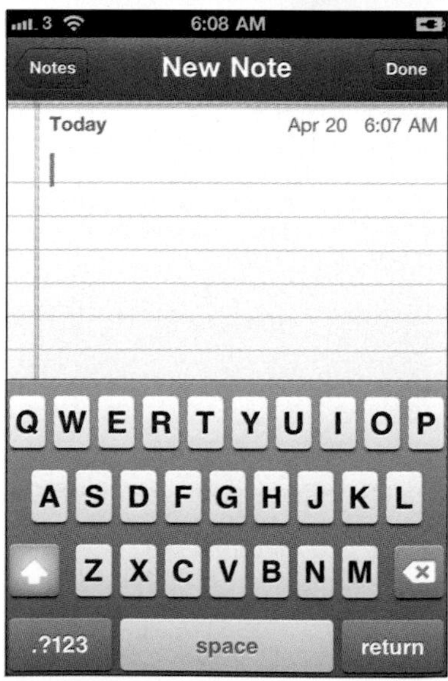

5 Type a short note by tapping the keys.

B If a pop-up bubble suggests a correction, tap **space** to accept it. Tap × on the bubble to reject it.

6 Tap **Done**.

The on-screen keyboard closes.

7 Tap **Notes**.

C The Notes list appears, with your note in it.

8 Press the Home button.

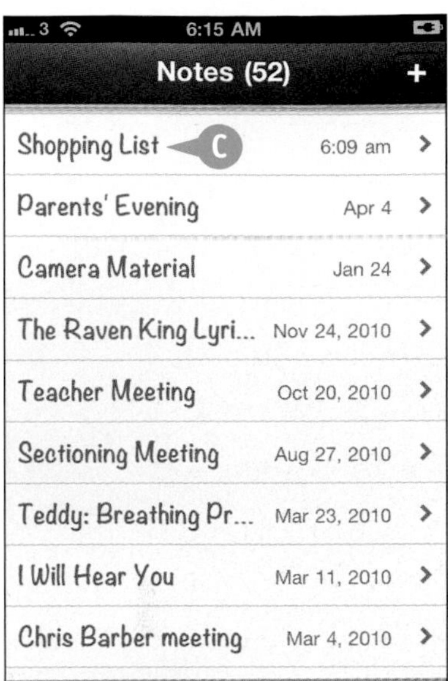

The Home screen appears.

9 Tap and drag to the left to display the second Home screen.

You can now launch another app by tapping its icon.

10 Press the Power/Sleep button.

Your iPhone goes to sleep.

TIP

Where do I get more apps to perform other tasks?

You can find an amazingly wide selection of apps — both free and ones you pay for — on Apple's App Store. See Chapter 7 for instructions on finding and downloading the apps you need.

CHAPTER 2

Choosing Which Data to Sync

In this chapter, you learn to sync your contacts, calendars, mail accounts, notes, and other essential data with your iPhone using iTunes. You also learn to put photos, books, and audiobooks on the iPhone, and to transfer other types of files to the iPhone using the iTunes File Sharing feature.

Sync Contacts with Your iPhone

To put your contacts on the iPhone, you can sync them from your PC or Mac. iTunes and the iPhone then keep the contacts synced, so that when you change contact information on one device, the changes appear on the other as well. You can choose between syncing all your contacts and syncing only particular groups — for example, only family and friends.

If you have an iCloud account and use it to sync your contacts with your iPhone, do not also synchronize them as described here. If you do, you may get duplicated contacts on the iPhone.

Sync Contacts with Your iPhone

1. Connect the iPhone to your PC or Mac.
2. In iTunes, click your iPhone.
3. Click **Info**.
4. Click **Sync Address Book Contacts** (☐ changes to ☑).

Note: In Windows, click **Sync contacts with** (☐ changes to ☑). Then select the program that contains the contacts — for example, Outlook.

5. To sync only some contacts, click **Selected groups** (○ changes to ◉).
6. Click the check box for each contacts group you want to sync (☐ changes to ☑).
7. Click **Add contacts created outside of groups on this iPhone to** (☐ changes to ☑).
8. Click ⬍ and then click the contacts group to which you want to add contacts created outside the iPhone.
9. If you need to sync Google contacts, click **Sync Google Contacts** (☐ changes to ☑).

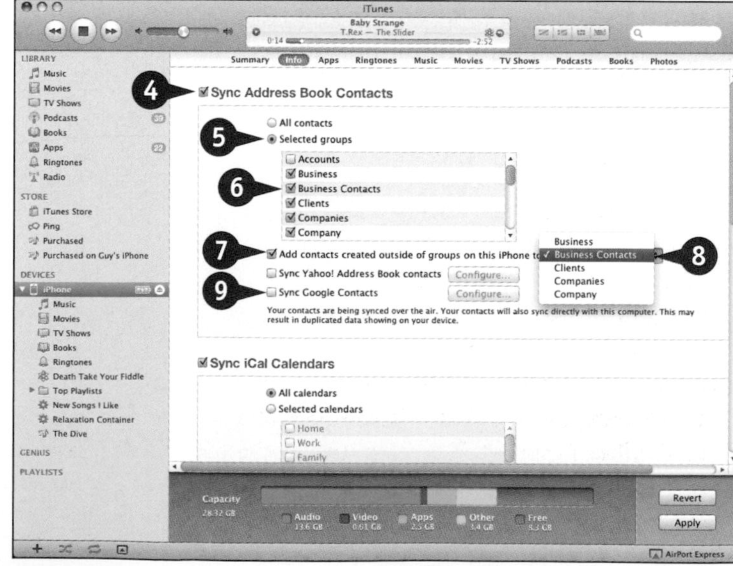

Note: If you want to sync Yahoo! contacts, click **Sync Yahoo! Address Book contacts** (☐ changes to ☑). Follow through the procedure for setting up iTunes to access your Yahoo! account.

A Google Contacts dialog box containing an agreement opens.

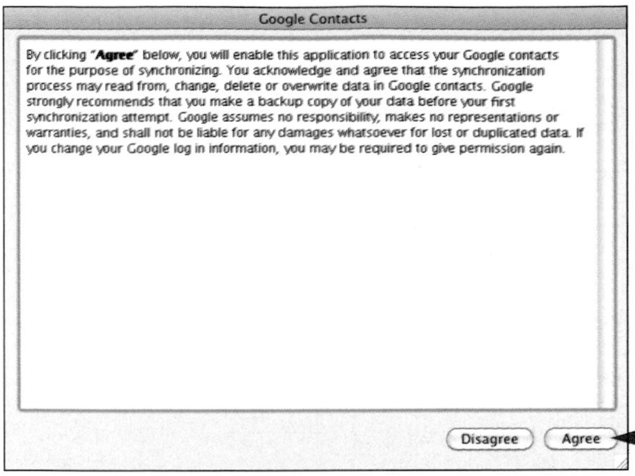

10 Read the agreement, and then click **Agree**.

Another Google Contacts dialog box opens.

11 Type your Google ID.

12 Type your password.

13 Click **OK**.

The Google Contacts dialog box closes.

14 Click **Apply**.

iTunes syncs your chosen contacts with the iPhone.

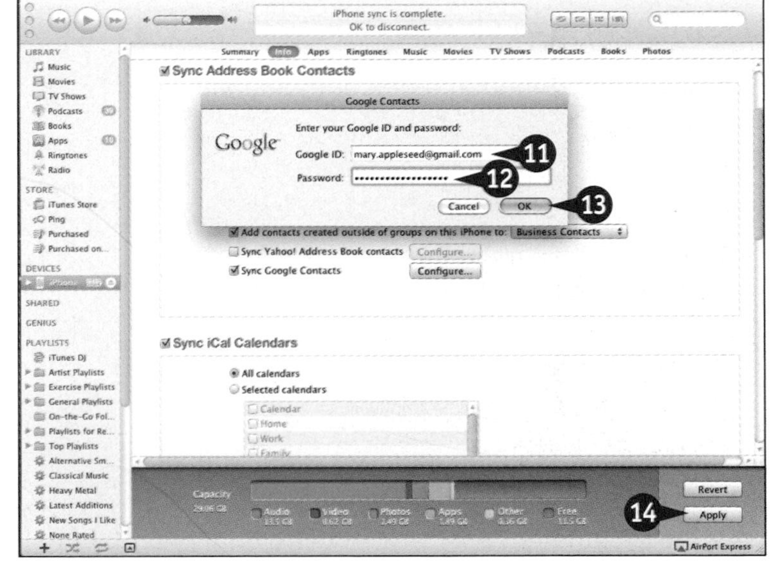

TIP

What happens if I change the same contact on my computer and my iPhone?

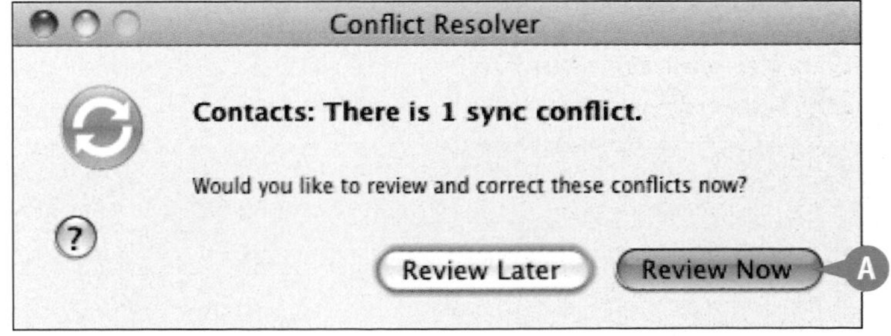

If you change contact information on your computer or your iPhone, iTunes syncs the changes for you. But if you change the same information on both computer and iPhone between syncs, you create a sync conflict. When iTunes detects a sync conflict, it displays the Conflict Resolver dialog box. Click **Review Now** (A) to expand the Conflict Resolver dialog box to see the details. You can then click the correct version of each contact record that has a conflict. Click **Done** to close the Conflict Resolver dialog box.

Choose Which Calendars to Sync

To keep the same appointments and events on your iPhone as on your PC or Mac, you can sync one or more calendars between your computer and the iPhone. From the PC, you can sync the Outlook calendar; from the Mac, you can sync the iCal calendar.

If you have an iCloud account or a MobileMe account and use it to sync your calendars with your iPhone, do not also synchronize them directly as described here. If you do, you may get duplicated calendar events on the iPhone.

Choose Which Calendars to Sync

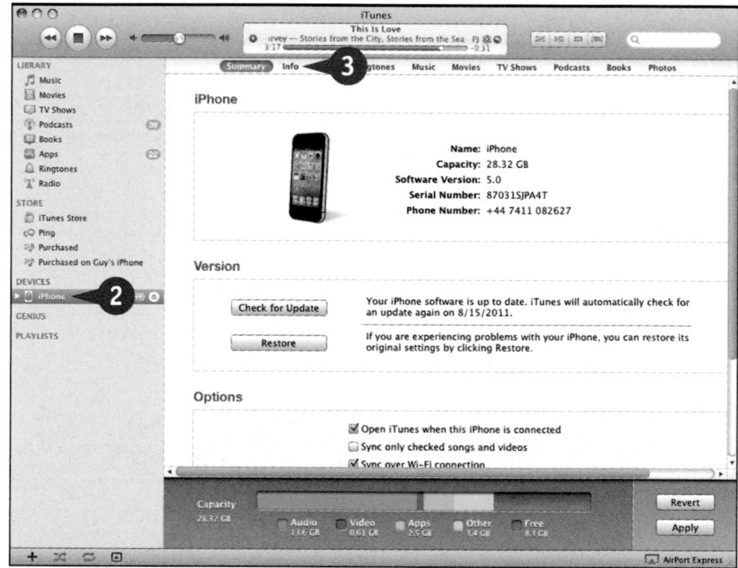

1 Connect the iPhone to your PC or Mac.

iTunes launches or becomes active, and the iPhone appears in the Devices list.

2 Click your iPhone.

The iPhone's control screens appear, with the Summary screen at the front.

3 Click **Info**.

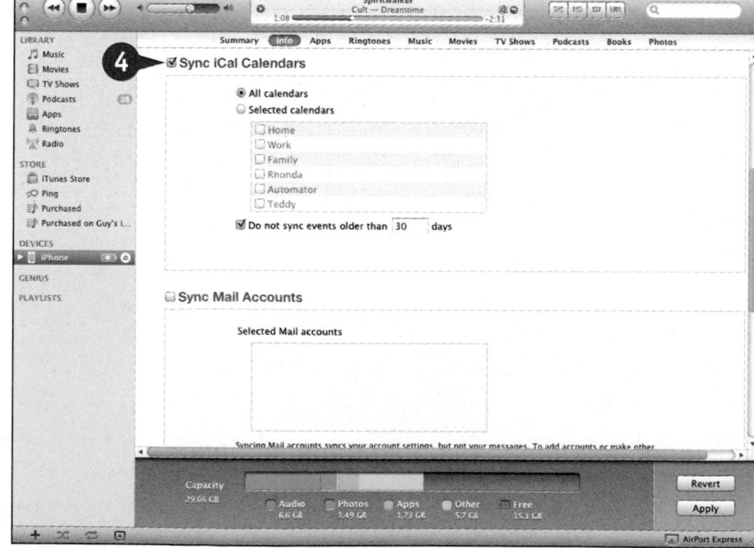

The Info screen appears.

4 Click **Sync iCal Calendars** (☐ changes to ☑).

Note: In Windows, click **Sync calendars with** (☐ changes to ☑). You can then choose the program with which you want to sync — for example, Outlook.

5. To sync only some calendars, click **Selected calendars** (○ changes to ◉).

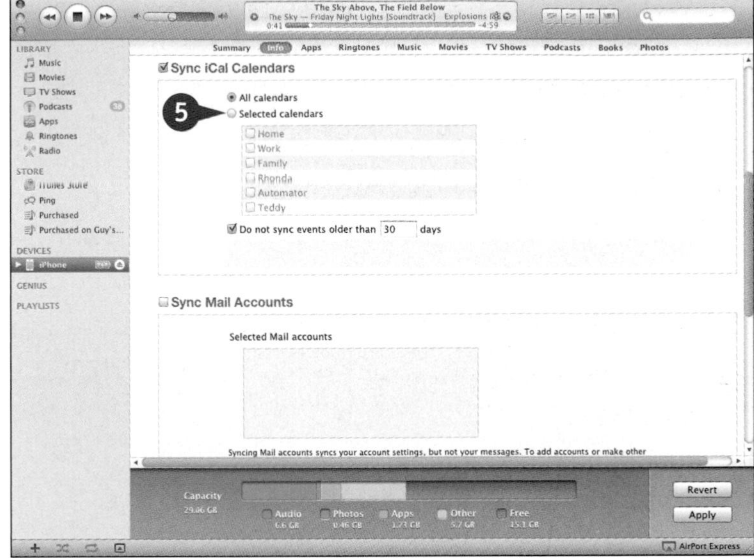

The controls in the Selected Calendars box become available.

6. Click the check box for each calendar you want to sync (☐ changes to ☑).
7. To limit the number of days of calendar data, click **Do not sync events older than *N* days** (☐ changes to ☑). Leave the default number, 30, or type a different number in the box.
8. Click **Apply**.

iTunes syncs your chosen calendars to the iPhone.

TIP

Why should I choose not to sync events older than a certain number of days?

If your calendars contain many events, it is usually a good idea to use the Do not sync events older than *N* days option to limit the amount of data you sync between the iPhone and your computer. You may want to change the number of days from the default, 30 — for example, set 90 days to sync around the last three months' worth of events. Limiting the number of days reduces the amount of data that iTunes must sync, which makes syncing faster. But if your calendars contain few events, or you need to carry details of your old events with you on the iPhone, syncing all your calendar events is fine.

Sync Mail Accounts with Your iPhone

If you need to be able to access your email on your iPhone, you can quickly sync one or more email accounts from your PC or Mac. The iPhone can access most types of email accounts, including Gmail, Hotmail and Windows Live, iCloud, MobileMe, Yahoo!, and Microsoft Exchange accounts.

Sync Mail Accounts with Your iPhone

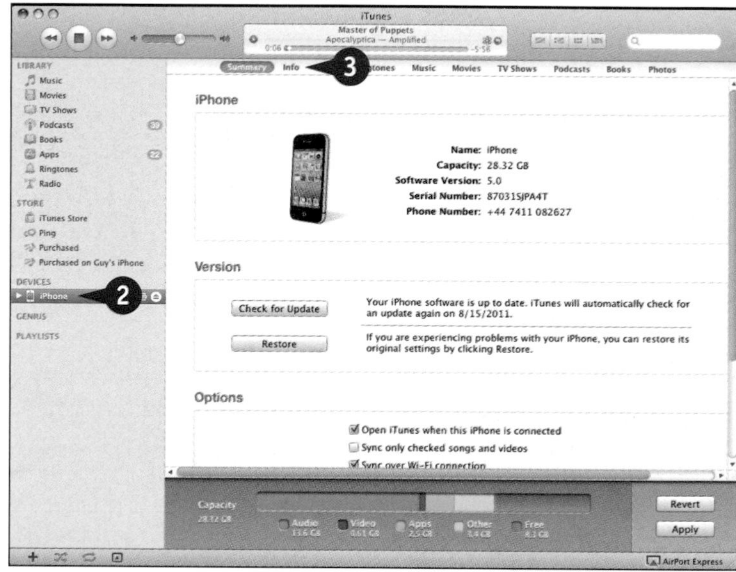

1. Connect the iPhone to your PC or Mac.

   iTunes launches or becomes active, and the iPhone appears in the Devices list.

2. Click your iPhone.

   The iPhone's control screens appear, with the Summary screen at the front.

3. Click **Info**.

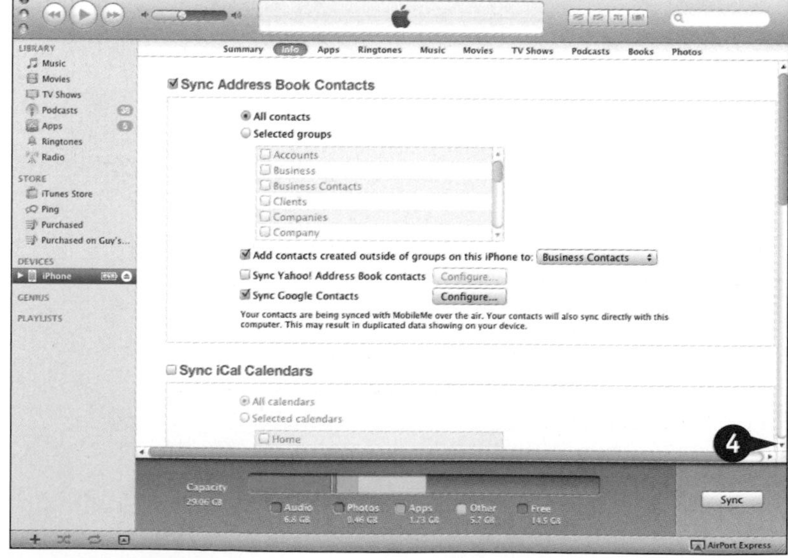

The Info screen appears.

4. Scroll down.

The Mail box appears with a list of accounts.

5 Click **Sync Mail Accounts** (☐ changes to ☑).

Note: In Windows, click **Sync selected mail accounts from** (☐ changes to ☑). Click the drop-down button, and then click the program.

6 Click the check box for each mail account you want to sync (☐ changes to ☑).

7 Click **Apply**.

iTunes syncs the mail account details with the iPhone.

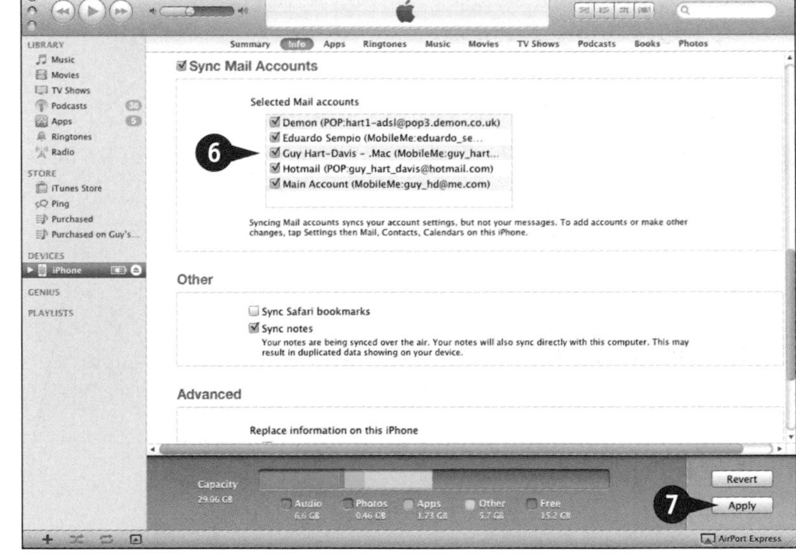

TIPS

Can I add to the iPhone an email account that is not on my computer?

Yes. You can set an email account directly on the iPhone. See Chapter 4 for instructions on how to set up an email account.

Do I need to sync with iTunes to get my email on my iPhone?

No. You need only sync with iTunes to put the details of your email accounts on the iPhone. Once you have done that, you can get your email directly on the iPhone without involving your computer.

Sync Bookmarks and Notes with Your iPhone

To make browsing on the iPhone faster and easier, you can sync your bookmarks from your computer's browser. Similarly, you can sync your notes from Outlook in Windows or from the Mail app on a Mac to the iPhone's Notes app.

If you have a MobileMe account and use it to sync your notes with your iPhone, do not also synchronize them directly as described here. If you do, you may get duplicated notes on the iPhone.

Sync Bookmarks and Notes with Your iPhone

1. Connect the iPhone to your PC or Mac.

   iTunes launches or becomes active, and the iPhone appears in the Devices list.

2. Click your iPhone.

   The iPhone's control screens appear, with the Summary screen at the front.

3. Click **Info**.

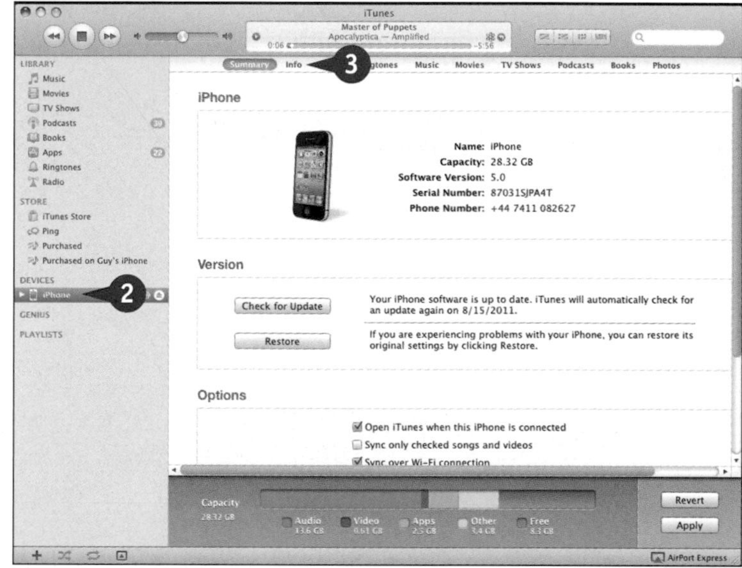

   The Info screen appears.

4. Scroll down.

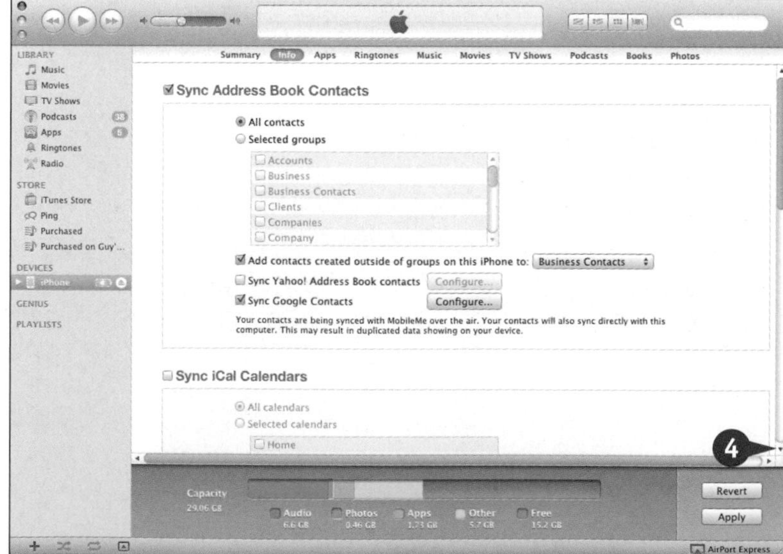

The Other box appears.

5. Click **Sync Safari bookmarks** (☐ changes to ☑).
6. Click **Sync notes** (☐ changes to ☑).
7. Click **Apply**.

iTunes syncs the bookmarks and notes with the iPhone.

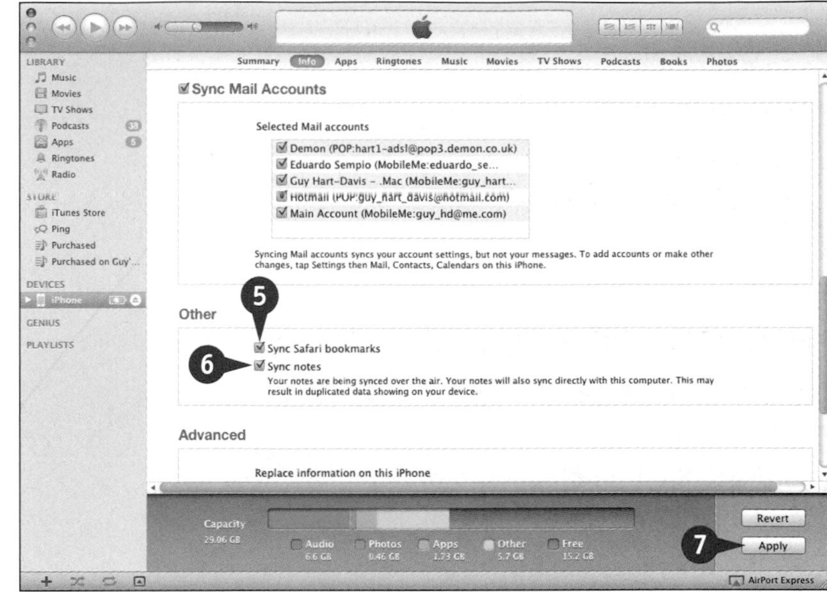

TIP

What do the options in the Advanced box on the Info screen do?

Advanced

Replace information on this iPhone

☐ Contacts
☐ Calendars
☐ Mail Accounts
☐ Bookmarks
☐ Notes

During the next sync only, iTunes will replace the selected information on this iPhone with information from this computer.

The options in the Advanced box enable you to control which information iTunes overwrites on the iPhone when syncing.

Normally, when you first set up an iPhone to sync items such as notes, bookmarks, or email accounts, you do not need to overwrite the data on the iPhone. But if the data on the iPhone becomes corrupted, you can select the check boxes in the Advanced box (☐ changes to ☑) to overwrite the iPhone's data during the next sync. After overwriting the data, iTunes clears these check boxes (☑ changes to ☐) so that it does not overwrite the data again.

Put Photos on Your iPhone

As well as taking photos with the iPhone's camera, you can load your existing photos on the iPhone so that you can take them with you. You can then show the photos either on the iPhone's screen or on a TV or an external monitor to which you connect the iPhone.

iTunes enables you to copy all your photos to the iPhone, but if you have many photos, they can take up all the free space on the iPhone. So normally it is best to copy only selected photos to the iPhone.

Put Photos on Your iPhone

1. Connect the iPhone to your PC or Mac.

   iTunes launches or becomes active, and the iPhone appears in the Devices list.

2. Click your iPhone.

   The iPhone's control screens appear, with the Summary screen at the front.

3. Click **Photos**.

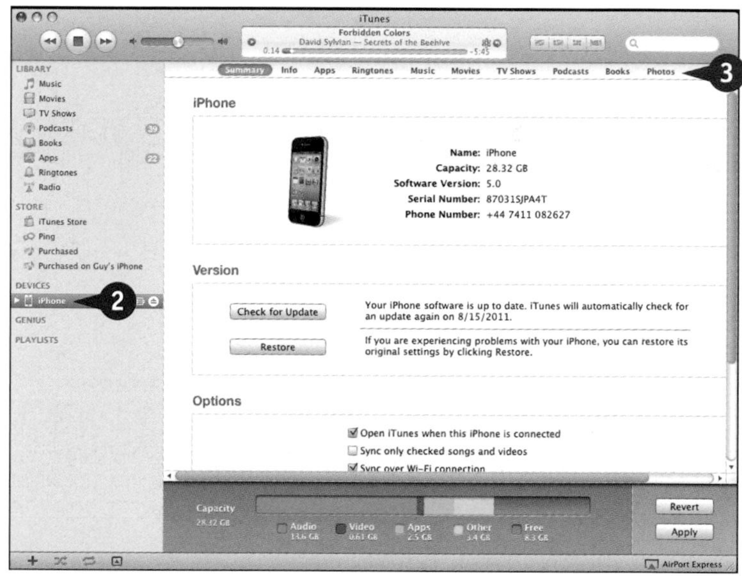

The Photos screen appears.

4. Click **Sync Photos from** (☐ changes to ☑).
5. Open the pop-up menu and choose the source of the photos.

Note: In Windows, click **My Pictures** to sync with the My Pictures folder, or click **Choose Folder** and then select the folder. In Mac OS X, click **iPhoto** to sync with your iPhoto library, or click **Choose Folder** and then select the folder.

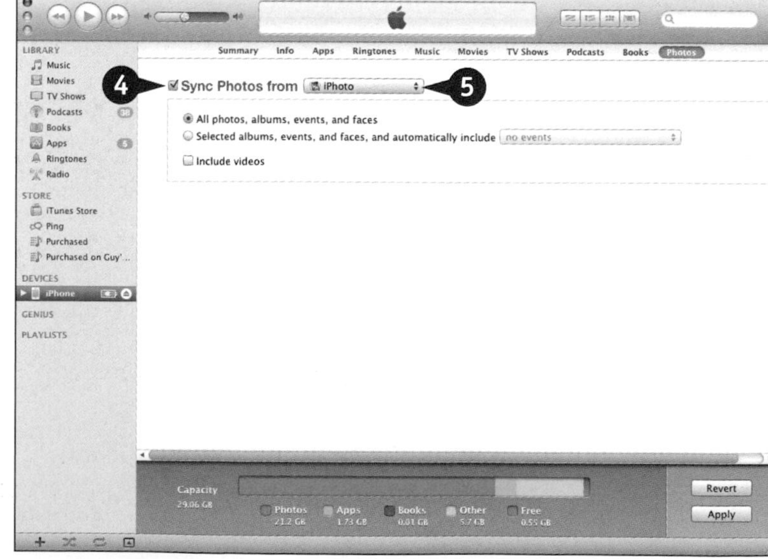

6 Click **Selected albums, events, and faces, and automatically include** (○ changes to ◉).

7 Click the pop-up menu and then click an events option — for example, **the 3 most recent events.**

A Click **Include videos** (☐ changes to ☑) if you want to include videos you have added to your iPhoto library. These are normally videos you have taken with your iPhone or digital camera.

8 Click the check box (☐ changes to ☑) for each album you want to include.

9 Click the check box (☐ changes to ☑) for each event you want to add.

10 Scroll down.

The Faces box appears.

11 Click the check box (☐ changes to ☑) for each Face you want to sync.

12 Click **Apply**.

iTunes syncs the photos to the iPhone.

TIP

How can I tell how much space the photos will take up on the iPhone?

Look at the readout at the bottom of the iTunes window. As you select different combinations of photos, albums, events, and faces, the readout changes to show how much space (A) your current choices will occupy.

Put Books, Audiobooks, and PDF Files on Your iPhone

You can quickly install the free iBooks app on your iPhone and use it to read books in formats such as the widely used ePub format. You can also open Portable Document Format (PDF) files in iBooks.

If you prefer to listen to your reading material, you can put audiobooks on the iPhone instead, and then listen to them using the Music app.

Put Books, Audiobooks, and PDF Files on Your iPhone

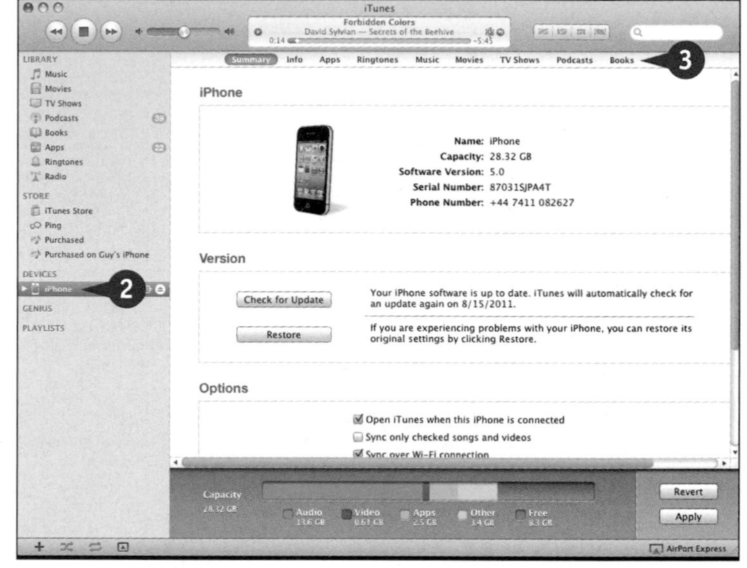

1. Connect the iPhone to your PC or Mac.

   iTunes launches or becomes active, and the iPhone appears in the Devices list.

2. Click your iPhone.

   The iPhone's control screens appear, with the Summary screen at the front.

3. Click **Books**.

   The Books screen appears.

4. Click **Sync Books** (☐ changes to ☑).

   The controls in the Sync Books box and the Books box become enabled.

5. To sync only some books, click **Selected books** (○ changes to ◉).

6. Click the check box (☐ changes to ☑) for each book or PDF file you want to sync.

A. If you have many books and PDF files, click the left pop-up menu and click **Only Books** or **Only PDF Files** to shorten the list.

7. Scroll down.

The Audiobooks area appears.

8 Click **Sync Audiobooks** (☐ changes to ☑).

The controls in the Sync Audiobooks box become available.

9 To sync only some audiobooks, click **Selected audiobooks** (○ changes to ◉).

10 Click the check box (☐ changes to ☑) for each audiobook you want to include.

11 Click the check box (☑ changes to ☐) for each part you want to omit.

12 Scroll down.

The Include Audiobooks from Playlists box appears.

13 Click the check box (☐ changes to ☑) for each playlist of audiobooks to include.

14 Click **Apply**.

iTunes syncs the books and audiobooks.

TIP

How do I make book files appear in the Audiobooks list?

In iTunes, select the audio files you want to mark as audiobooks, and then click **File** and **Get Info**. If iTunes confirms that you want to edit information for multiple items, click **Yes**. In the Multiple Item Information dialog box, click **Options** (A). Click the **Media Kind** pop-up menu and then click **Audiobook** (B). Click **OK**.

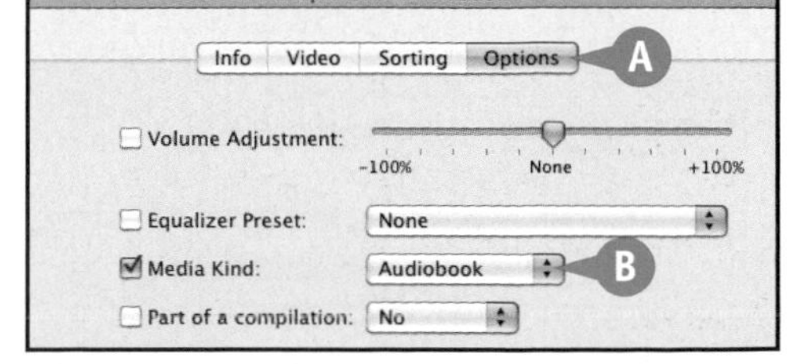

Put Files on MobileMe iDisk from Your Computer

If you have an account with Apple's MobileMe service, you can upload files to your iDisk storage area on the MobileMe servers. You can then access the files from your iPhone by using the iDisk app.

iDisk is a useful storage tool, but Apple has announced that it will terminate MobileMe on June 30, 2012. Apple is replacing MobileMe with the iCloud service, but iCloud does not include a replacement feature for iDisk. So if you use iDisk, you must plan to use an alternative online storage account from July 2012 onward — for example, with the Dropbox service (www.dropbox.com).

Put Files on MobileMe iDisk from Your Computer

1 Open your web browser.

2 Click the address box.

3 Type **www.me.com** and press Enter in Windows or Return on a Mac.

The MobileMe Sign In page appears.

4 Type your MobileMe username.

5 Type your MobileMe password.

A Click **Keep me signed in for 2 weeks** (☐ changes to ☑) if you want your computer to log you in automatically for two weeks.

6 Click **Sign In**.

The browser opens your MobileMe account and displays the last screen of MobileMe you used — for example, MobileMe Gallery.

7 Click **Switch Apps** (▭).

The Switch Apps bar appears.

8 Click **iDisk**.

The iDisk screen appears.

9 Click **Upload a file or files.**

The Uploads window appears.

10 Click **Choose.**

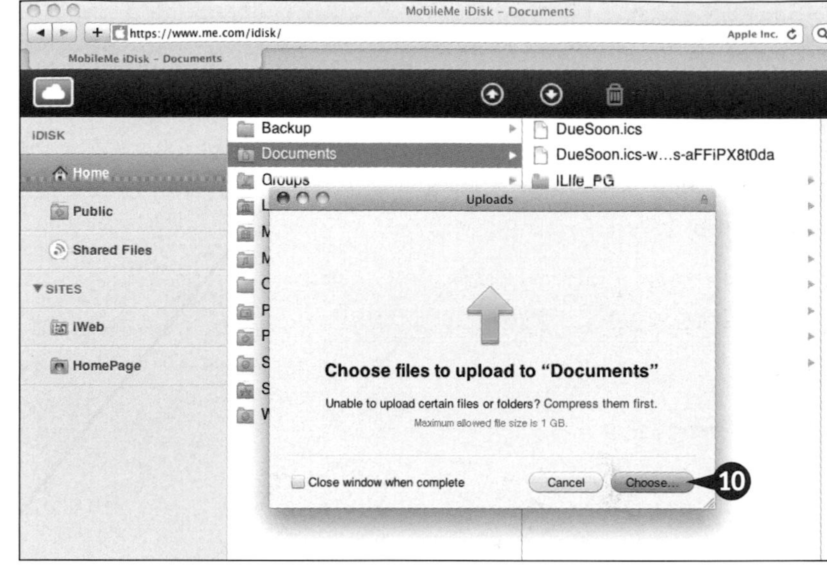

The Select File(s) to Upload dialog box opens.

11 Click the file or select the files.

12 Click **Open.**

Your browser uploads the files to your iDisk.

13 In the Uploads window, click **Done.**

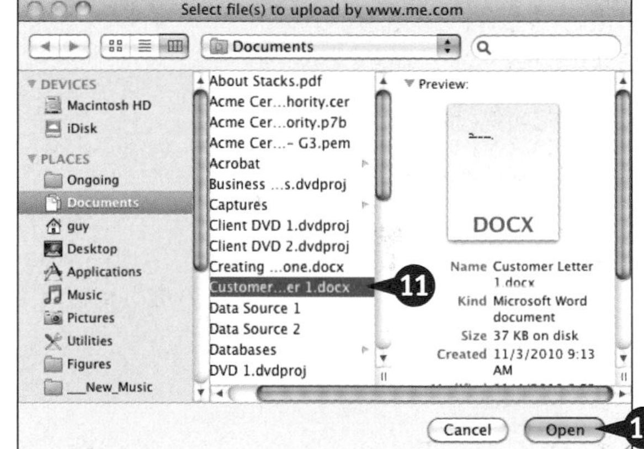

TIP

How do I access my iDisk using the iPhone?

To access your iDisk using the iPhone, install the free MobileMe iDisk app.

1 Press the Home button.

2 Tap **App Store.**

3 Tap **Search.**

4 Type **MobileMe iDisk.**

5 Tap the **MobileMe iDisk** search result.

6 Tap **Free.**

7 Tap **Install.**

8 After the app installs, tap **iDisk** on the Home screen. You can then log in to your iDisk.

Transfer Files to the iPhone Using iTunes File Sharing

When you need to transfer files to the iPhone, you can use the File Sharing feature built into iTunes. This feature enables you to transfer files to the iPhone's storage area devoted to a particular app. For example, when you need to use a file with the DocsToGo app on the iPhone, you transfer to the DocsToGo area using File Sharing.

Only some apps can transfer files, and you must install an app capable of transferring files via File Sharing before you can use File Sharing as described on these pages.

Transfer Files to the iPhone Using iTunes File Sharing

1. Connect the iPhone to your PC or Mac.

   iTunes launches or becomes active, and the iPhone appears in the Devices list.

2. Click your iPhone.

   The iPhone's control screens appear, with the Summary screen at the front.

3. Click **Apps**.

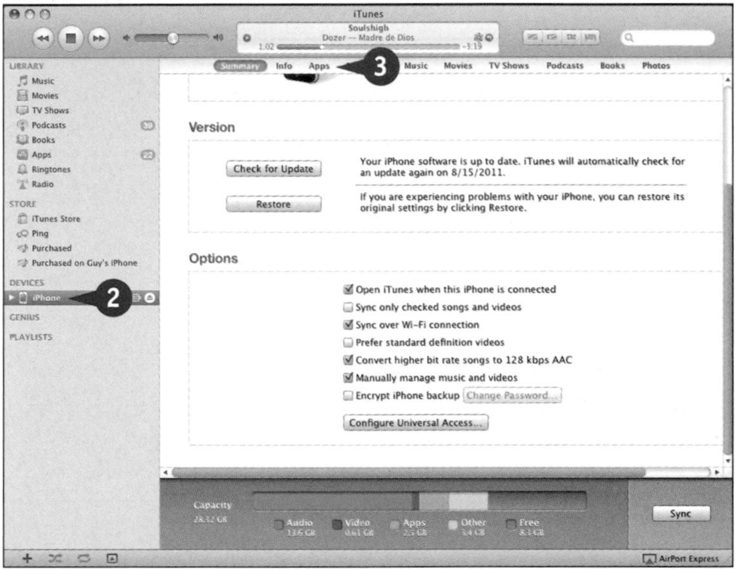

   The Apps screen appears.

4. Scroll down.

The File Sharing area appears.

5 Click **Add**.

The iTunes dialog box opens in Windows, or the Choose a File: iTunes dialog box opens on a Mac.

6 Click the file you want to copy to the iPhone.

Note: You can copy multiple files at once by selecting them. For example, click the first file, and then Shift-click the last file to select a range of files.

7 Click **Open** in Windows or **Choose** on a Mac.

iTunes copies the file or files to the iPhone.

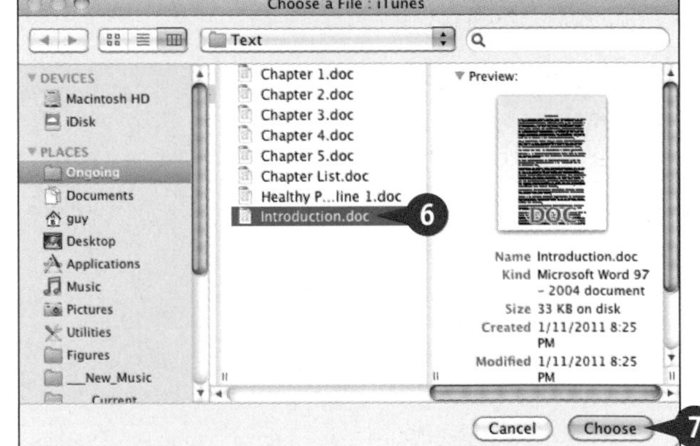

TIP

How do I copy a file from the iPhone to my computer?

1 Open File Sharing as discussed on these pages.

2 In the Apps box, click the app that contains the file.

3 In the Documents box, click the file.

4 Click **Save To**. The iTunes dialog box opens in Windows or the Choose a Folder: iTunes dialog box opens on a Mac.

5 Click the folder to save the file in.

6 Click **Select Folder** in Windows or **Choose** on a Mac. iTunes copies the file.

CHAPTER 3

Personalizing Your iPhone

To make your iPhone work the way you prefer, you can configure its many settings. This chapter shows you how to access the most important settings and use them to personalize the iPhone. You learn how to control notifications, audio preferences, screen brightness, and other key aspects of the iPhone's behavior.

Find the Settings You Need

To configure the iPhone, you work with its settings using the Settings app. This app contains settings for the iPhone's system software, the apps the iPhone includes, and third-party apps you have added. To reach the settings, you first display the Settings screen, and then display the category of settings you want to configure. Some apps provide access to settings through the apps themselves. So if you cannot find the settings for an app on the Settings screen, look within the app. In this task, you learn how to open the Settings screen and see the main categories of settings it contains.

Find the Settings You Need

Display the Settings Screen

1. Press the Home button.

   The Home screen appears.

2. Tap **Settings**.

The Settings screen appears.

3. Tap and drag the screen up to scroll down to display other settings.

Display a Settings Screen

1. On the Settings screen, tap the button for the settings you want to display. For example, tap **Sounds** to display the Sounds screen.
2. Tap **Settings** when you are ready to return to the Settings screen.

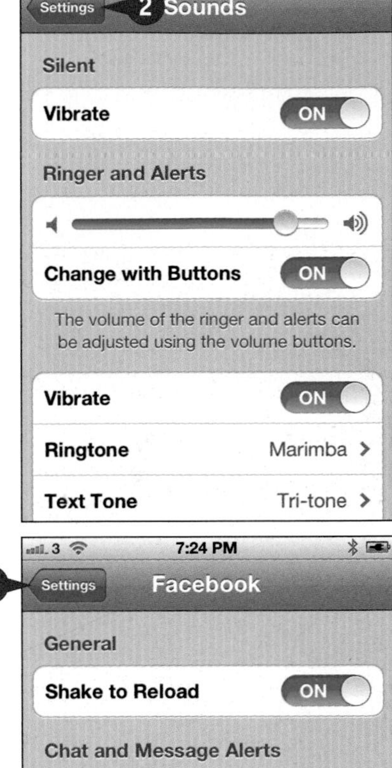

Display the Settings for an App

1. On the Settings screen, scroll down toward the bottom.
2. Tap the button for the app whose settings you want to display. For example, tap **Facebook** to display the Facebook settings.
3. Tap **Settings** when you are ready to return to the Settings screen.
4. Press the Home button.

   The Home screen appears again.

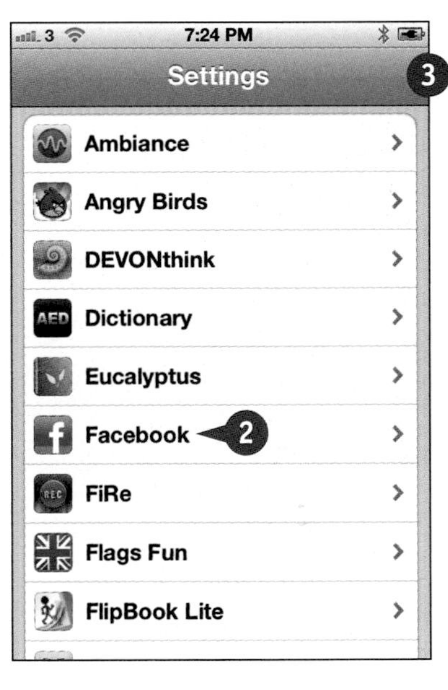

TIP

Why do only some apps have a Settings entry?

The Settings screen contains entries for only those apps that have settings you can configure. For example, the Nike + iPod app's settings include choosing your PowerSong, specifying your weight, and configuring the movement sensor. Other apps have no settings you can configure and so have no entry on the Settings screen.

Choose Which Apps Can Give Notifications

Some iPhone apps can notify you when you have received messages or when updates are available. You can choose which apps give which notifications, or prevent apps from showing notifications altogether. You can also choose the order in which the notifications appear in the Notifications Center and control which notifications appear on the lock screen.

iPhone apps use three types of notifications. A *badge* is a red circle or rounded rectangle that appears on the app's icon on the Home screen and shows a white number indicating how many notifications there are. An *alert* is a text message that appears in front of the running app; you can also display an alert as a banner across the top of the screen. A *sound* notification plays a sound to get your attention.

Choose Which Apps Can Give Notifications

Display the Notifications Screen

1. Press the Home button.

   The Home screen appears.

   A. A badge notification shows how many new items an app has.

2. Tap **Settings**.

   The Settings screen appears.

3. Tap **Notifications**.

   The Notifications screen appears.

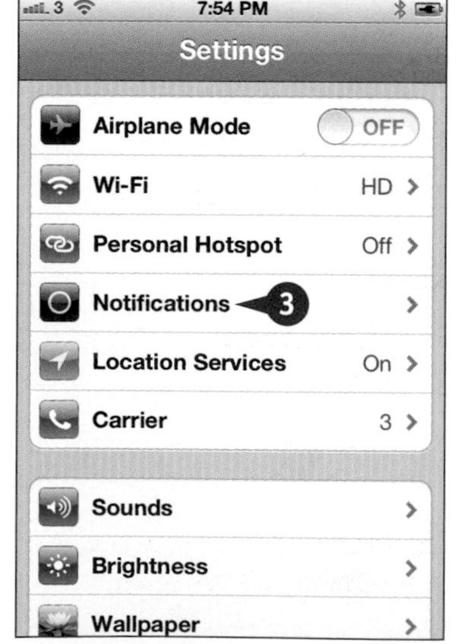

Choose How to Sort Apps That Give Notifications

1. Tap **Manually** to use manual sorting for apps that give notifications. Tap **By Time** to have Notification Center sort the apps by the times of their notifications.

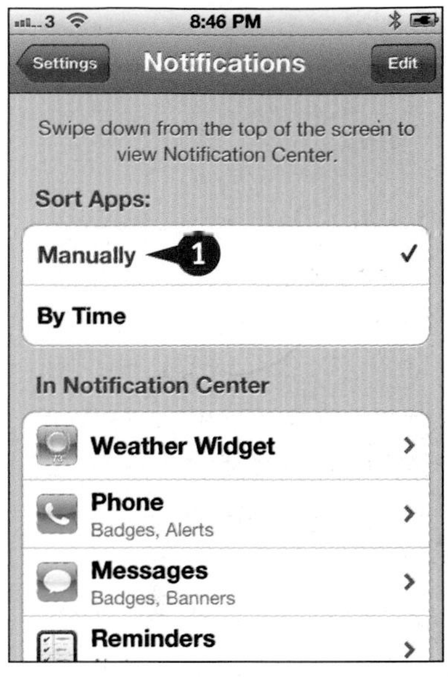

Choose Which Notifications Each App Can Give

1. On the Notifications screen, tap the app's name.
2. On the Notifications screen for that app, move the **Notification Center** switch to On to have the app's notifications to appear in Notification Center. Move the switch to Off if you do not want the notifications in Notification Center.
3. Tap **Show**, tap the number of recent items to display in Notification Center on the Show screen, and then tap the app's name button to return.
4. Tap **Alerts** to display alerts, **Banners** to display banners, or **None** to suppress alerts.
5. Move the **Badge App Icon** to On to show badges or Off to hide them.
6. Move the **Sounds** switch to On or Off.
7. Move the **View in Lock Screen** switch to On or Off.
8. Tap **Notifications** to return to the Notifications screen.

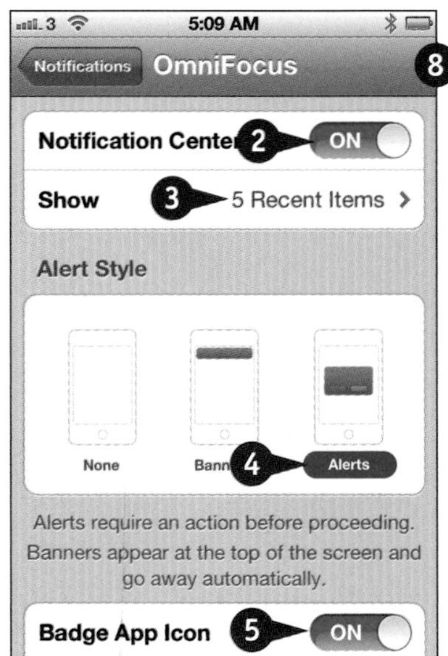

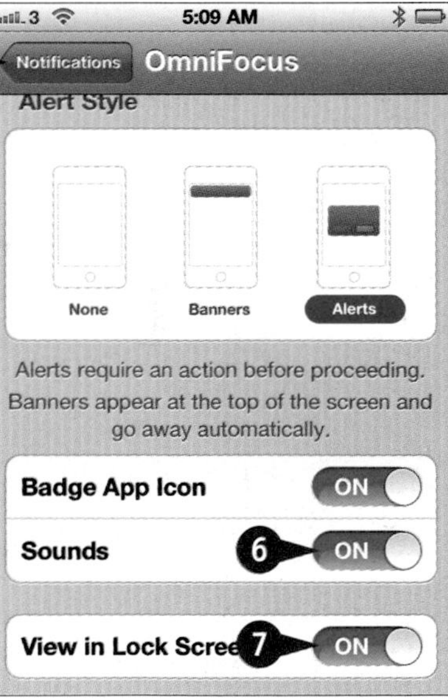

TIP

How do I view notifications?

To view notifications, open the Notification Center by tapping the bar at the top of the screen and dragging it down. You can then touch a notification to display its details in the app that produced it. Tap the handle at the bottom of the screen and drag it back up when you are ready to close the Notifications Center.

Choose Sounds Settings

To control how the iPhone gives you audio feedback, choose settings on the Sounds screen. Here, you can choose whether to have the iPhone vibrate always to signal incoming calls, or vibrate only when the ringer is silent. You can set the volume for the ringer and for alerts, choose your default ringtone and text tone, and choose whether to receive alerts for voicemail, email, and calendar items.

Playing lock sounds helps confirm that you have locked or unlocked the iPhone as you intended. Playing keyboard clicks confirms each key press on the iPhone's keyboard.

Choose Sounds Settings

Display the Sounds Screen

1. Press the Home button.

   The Home screen appears.

2. Tap **Settings**.

   The Settings screen appears.

3. Tap **Sounds**.

   The Sounds screen appears.

Choose Ringer and Vibration Settings

1. In the Silent area, tap the **Vibrate** switch and move it to On or Off, as needed.

Note: The Vibrate switch in the Silent area controls whether the iPhone vibrates when you have turned off the ringer.

2. Tap and drag the **Ringer and Alerts** slider to set the volume.

A. As long as the **Change with Buttons** switch is set to On, you can also press the ringer buttons on the side of the iPhone to change the Ringer and Alerts volume.

3. Tap the **Vibrate** switch and move it to On or Off, as needed.

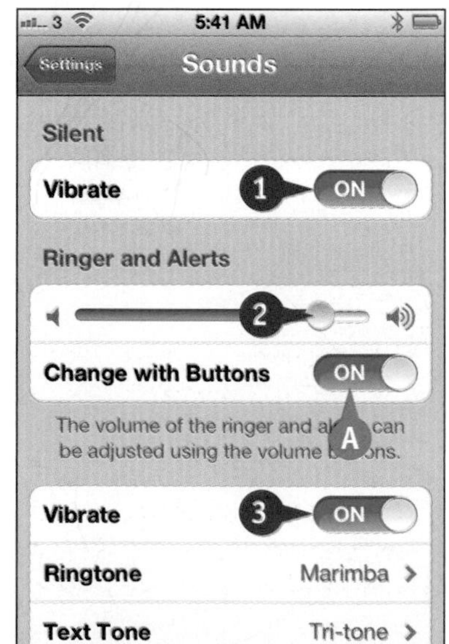

Choose Ringtones and Alerts

1. Tap **Ringtone**.

   The Ringtone screen appears.

2. Tap the ringtone you want to hear.
3. Tap **Sounds**.
4. Tap **Text Tone**.
5. Tap the text tone you want to hear.
6. Tap **Sounds**.

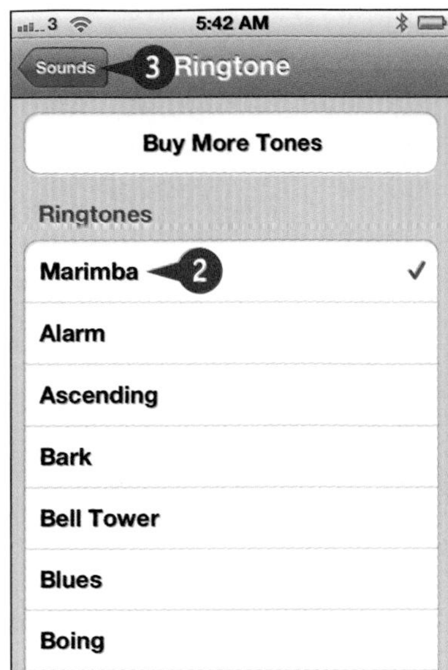

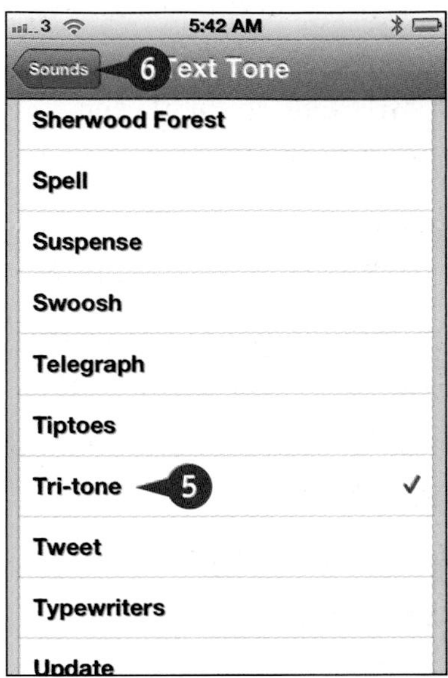

Choose Alerts, Lock Sounds, and Keyboard Clicks

1. Scroll down to the lower part of the Sounds screen.
2. Choose alerts for the **New Voicemail**, **New Mail**, **Sent Mail**, **Sent Tweet**, **Calendar Alerts**, and **Reminder Alerts** items by tapping the item name, choosing the alert type on the resulting screen, and then tapping **Sounds**.
3. Tap the **Lock Sounds** switch and move it to On or Off, as needed.
4. Tap the **Keyboard Clicks** switch and move it to On or Off, as needed.

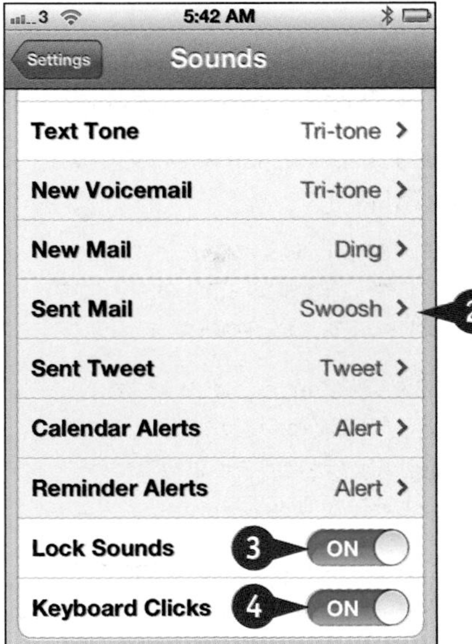

TIP

How do I use different ringtones for different callers?
The ringtone and text tone you set in the Ringtone area of the Sounds screen are your standard tone for phone calls, FaceTime calls, and messaging calls. To set different tones for a contact, press the Home button and then tap **Contacts**. In the Contacts app, tap the contact and then tap **ringtone**. On the Ringtone screen, tap the ringtone, and then tap **Save**. Tap **text tone**, tap the text tone to use, and then tap **Save**.

Set Screen Brightness and Wallpaper Backgrounds

To make the screen easy to see, you can change its brightness. You can also have the iPhone's Auto-Brightness feature automatically set the screen's brightness to a level suitable for the ambient brightness that the iPhone's light sensor detects.

To make the screen attractive to your eye, you can choose which picture to use as the wallpaper that appears in the background. You can set different wallpaper for the lock screen — the screen you see when the iPhone is locked — and for the Home screen.

Set Screen Brightness and Wallpaper Backgrounds

Set Screen Brightness

1. Press the Home button.

   The Home screen appears.

2. Tap **Settings**.

   The Settings screen appears.

3. Tap **Brightness**.

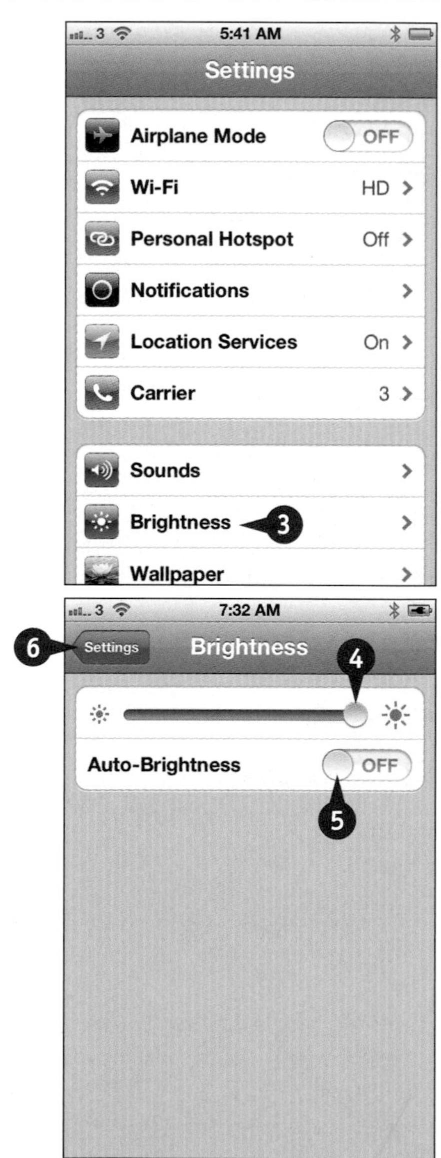

   The Brightness screen appears.

4. Tap the **Brightness** switch and drag it left or right to set brightness.
5. Tap the **Auto-Brightness** switch and move it to On or Off, as needed.
6. Tap **Settings** to return to the Settings screen.

Set Wallpaper Backgrounds

1. From the Settings screen, tap **Wallpaper**.

   The Wallpaper screen appears.

Note: The Wallpaper screen shows the lock screen wallpaper on the left and the Home screen wallpaper on the right.

2. Tap anywhere in the white button containing the wallpaper pictures.

   The list of picture categories appears.

3. Tap **Wallpaper**.

A. To choose a picture from a different picture category, tap that category. For example, tap **Camera Roll** to display pictures you have taken with the iPhone's camera.

   The Wallpaper category screen appears.

4. Tap the wallpaper you want.
5. Tap **Set**.
6. Tap **Set Lock Screen**, **Set Home Screen**, or **Set Both**.
7. Tap **Back**.
8. Tap **Wallpaper**.
9. Tap **Settings**.

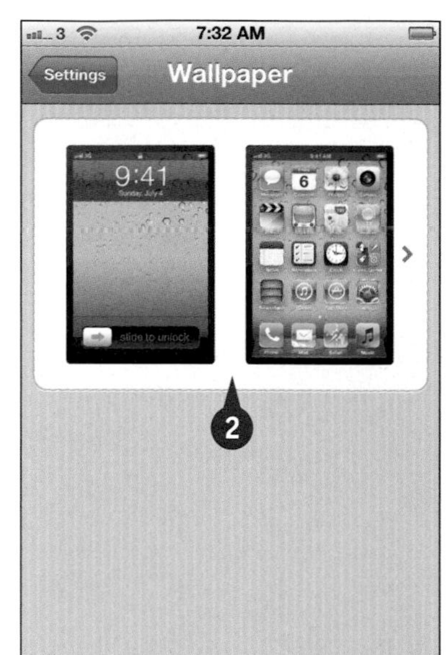

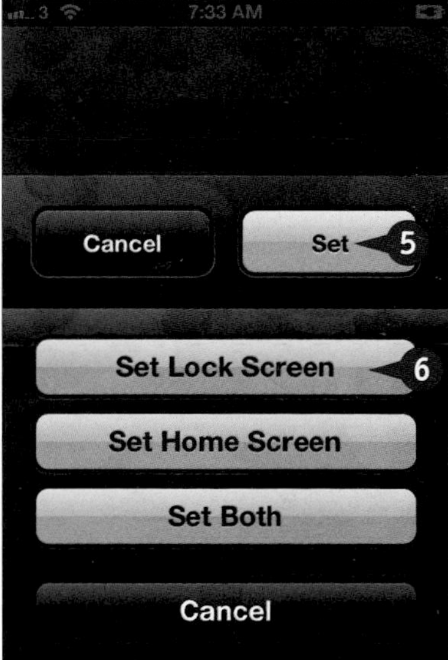

TIP

How do I use only part of a picture as the wallpaper?

The iPhone wallpapers are the right size for the screen, so you do not need to resize them. But when you use a photo for the wallpaper, you usually need to choose which part of it to display. When you choose a photo as wallpaper, the iPhone displays the screen for moving and scaling the photo. Pinch in or out to resize the photo, and tap and drag to move the picture around. When you have chosen the part you want, tap **Set**.

Choose Which Apps Can Learn Your GPS Location

The iPhone includes a Global Positioning System, or GPS, feature that can pinpoint where you are to within a few yards. GPS lets you learn where you are or where to find stores or services near you.

GPS can compromise your privacy, so it is a good idea to review the list of apps using GPS location services and turn off any that do not have a good reason to do so.

Choose Which Apps Can Learn Your GPS Location

1. Press the Home button.

   The Home screen appears.

2. Tap **Settings**.

   The Settings screen appears.

3. Tap **Location Services**.

The Location Services screen appears.

4 If you need to turn location services off completely, tap the **Location Services** switch and move it to Off.

5 Tap the switch for an app, and move it to On or Off, as needed. For example, tap the **Camera** switch and move it to On.

6 Scroll down to the bottom of the screen and tap **System Services**.

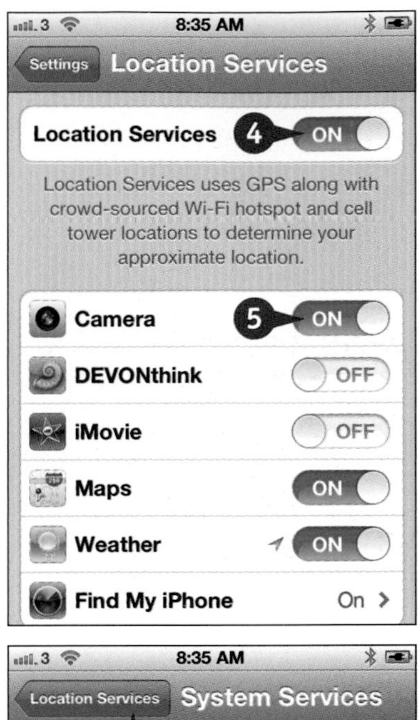

The System Services screen appears.

7 Tap the switch for a system service, and move it to On or Off, as needed. For example, tap the **Location-Based iAds** switch and move it to Off.

8 Tap **Location Services**.

The Location Services screen appears.

9 Tap **Settings**.

The Settings screen appears.

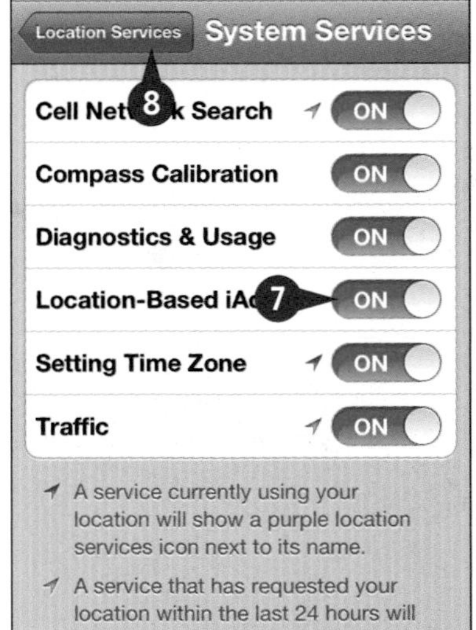

TIP

Why do some apps need to use location services?

Some apps and system services need to use location services to determine where you are. For example, the Maps app needs to use location services so that it can display your location, and the Compass service needs to learn your position in order to display accurate compass information.

If you allow the Camera app to use location services, it stores GPS data in your photos. You can then sort the photos by location in applications such as iPhoto on Mac OS X. Other apps use location services to provide context-specific information, such as information about nearby restaurants. It is a good idea to review which apps are using GPS and to turn off any that do not have a compelling reason for doing so.

Configure Spotlight Search to Find What You Need

The iPhone can put a huge amount of data in the palm of your hand, and you may often need to search to find what you need.

To make your search results more accurate and helpful, you can configure the iPhone's Spotlight Search feature. You can turn off searching for items you do not want to see in your search results, and you can change the order in which Spotlight displays the items it finds.

Configure Spotlight Search to Find What You Need

1. Press the Home button.

   The Home screen appears.

2. Tap **Settings**.

   The Settings screen appears.

3. Scroll down a little way, and then tap **General**.

   The General screen appears.

4. Tap **Spotlight Search**.

The Spotlight Search screen appears.

5 Tap to remove the check mark from each item you do not want to search.

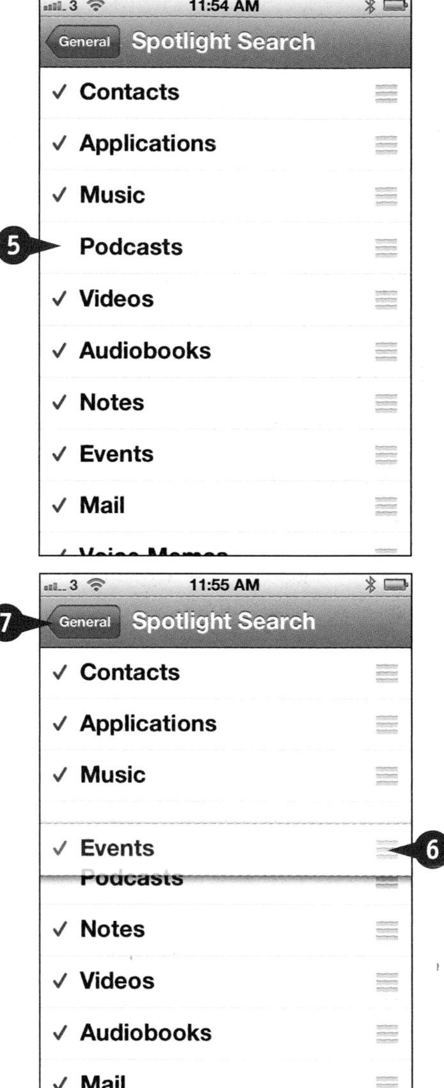

6 Tap a movement handle and drag an item up or down the search order.

Note: Spotlight displays the search results in descending order, starting with the first item on the list.

7 Tap **General** to go back to the General screen.

8 Tap **Settings** to go back to the Settings screen.

TIP

Which items should I make Spotlight search?
This depends on what you need to be able to search for. For example, if you do not need to search for music, videos, or podcasts, remove the check marks for the Music, Podcasts, and Videos item on the Spotlight Search screen to exclude them from Spotlight searches. For normal use, you may want to leave all the check marks in place but move the items most important to you to the top of the Spotlight Search list.

Choose Locking and Sleep Settings

To avoid unintentional taps on the screen, the iPhone automatically locks itself after a period of inactivity. After locking itself, the iPhone turns off its screen and goes to sleep to save battery power.

You can choose how long the iPhone waits before locking itself. Setting the iPhone to lock quickly helps preserve battery power, but you may prefer to leave the iPhone on longer so that you can continue work. You can then lock the iPhone manually.

Choose Locking and Sleep Settings

1. Press the Home button.

   The Home screen appears.

2. Tap **Settings**.

   The Settings screen appears.

3. Scroll down a little way, and then tap **General**.

The General screen appears.

4 Tap **Auto-Lock**.

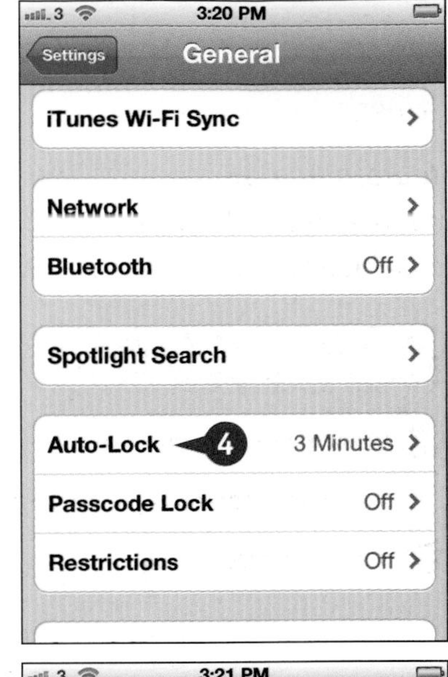

The Auto-Lock screen appears.

5 Tap the interval — for example, **3 Minutes**.

6 Tap **General**.

The General screen appears.

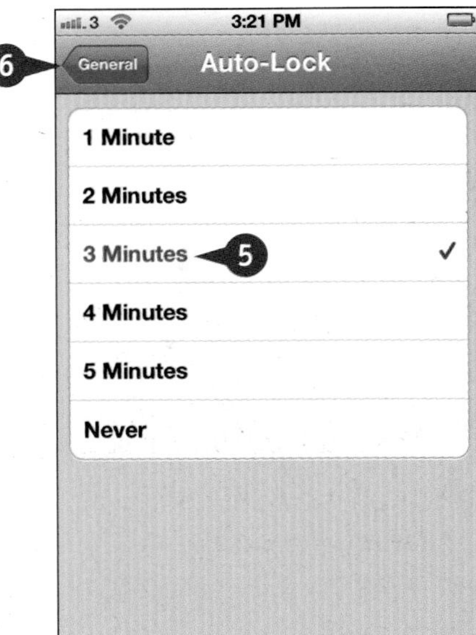

TIPS

How do I put the iPhone to sleep manually?

You can put the iPhone to sleep at any point by pressing the Power button for a moment.

Putting the iPhone to sleep as soon as you stop using it helps to prolong battery life. If you apply a passcode, as discussed later in this chapter, putting the iPhone to sleep also starts protecting your data sooner.

When should I use the Never setting for Auto-Lock?

Choose the **Never** setting for Auto-Lock if you need to make sure the iPhone never goes to sleep. For example, if you are demonstrating an iPhone app at a tradeshow, turning off auto-locking like this may be helpful.

Secure Your iPhone with a Passcode Lock

To prevent anyone who picks up your iPhone from accessing your data, you can lock the iPhone with a passcode. This is a code that takes effect when you lock your iPhone, or it locks itself. When you unlock the iPhone, you must provide the passcode.

For added security, you can set the iPhone to automatically erase its data after ten failed attempts to enter the passcode. You can also choose between a standard, four-digit password and a longer password in which you can use numbers, letters, and other characters.

Secure Your iPhone with a Passcode Lock

1. Press the Home button.

   The Home screen appears.

2. Tap **Settings**.

   The Settings screen appears.

3. Scroll down a little way, and then tap **General**.

   The General screen appears.

4. Tap **Passcode Lock**.

   The Passcode Lock screen appears.

5. To follow this example, make sure the **Simple Passcode** switch is On. If not, tap and move it to On.

6. Tap **Turn Passcode On**.

   The Set Passcode screen appears.

Note: The iPhone shows dots instead of your passcode digits in case someone is watching.

7. Type your passcode.

   The iPhone displays the Set Passcode screen again, this time with the message "Re-enter your passcode."

8. Type the passcode again.

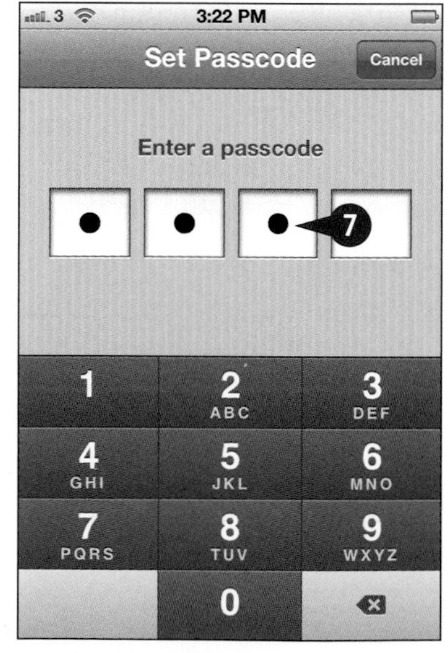

The Passcode Lock screen appears.

9 Tap **Require Passcode**.

The Require Passcode screen appears.

10 Tap the button for the length of time you want.

Note: Tap **Immediately** on the Require Passcode screen for the tightest security: You then must provide the passcode even after locking the iPhone for a second. Tap **After 1 minute** or **After 5 minutes** for relatively tight security.

11 Tap **Passcode Lock**.

The Passcode Lock screen appears.

12 If you want the iPhone to erase all its data after ten failed passcode attempts, tap the **Erase Data** switch and move it to On.

The iPhone displays a confirmation dialog box.

13 Tap **Enable**.

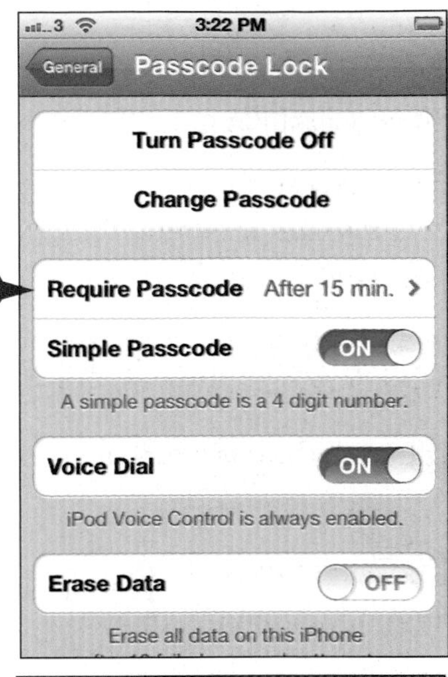

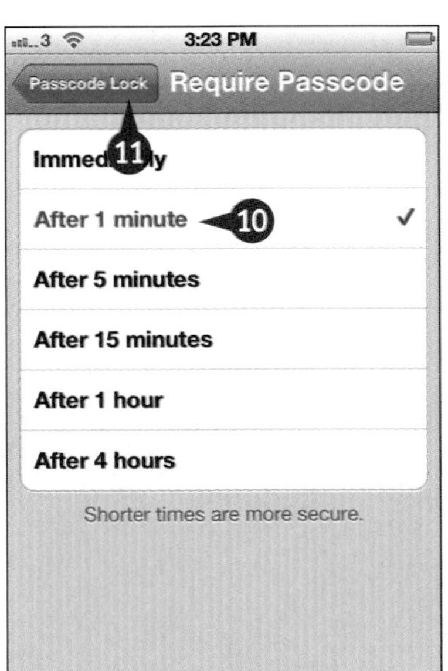

TIPS

How can I make my passcode even more secure?
If you feel a four-digit passcode is not secure enough, tap the **Simple Passcode** switch on the Passcode Lock screen and move it to Off. When you tap **Turn Passcode On**, the Set Passcode screen lets you set a passcode of any length.

How do I turn the passcode lock off again?
Press the Home button, tap **Settings**, and then tap **General**. Tap **Passcode Lock**, tap **Turn Passcode Off**, and then type the current passcode.

Like any other computer than can access the Internet, the iPhone can reach vast amounts of content not suitable for children or business contexts.

You can restrict the iPhone from accessing particular kinds of content. You can use the restrictions to implement parental controls — for example, preventing the iPhone's user from buying content in apps or watching adult-rated movies.

Configure Restrictions and Parental Controls

1. Press the Home button.

   The Home screen appears.

2. Tap **Settings**.

   The Settings screen appears.

3. Scroll down a little way, and then tap **General**.

   The General screen appears.

4. Tap **Restrictions**.

   The Restrictions screen appears.

5. Tap **Enable Restrictions**.

   The Set Passcode screen appears.

Note: The passcode you set to protect restrictions is different from the passcode you use to lock the iPhone. Do not use the same code.

6. Type the passcode.

Note: The iPhone shows dots instead of your passcode digits in case someone is watching.

   The iPhone displays the Set Passcode screen again, this time with the message "Re-enter your Restrictions Passcode."

7. Type the passcode again.

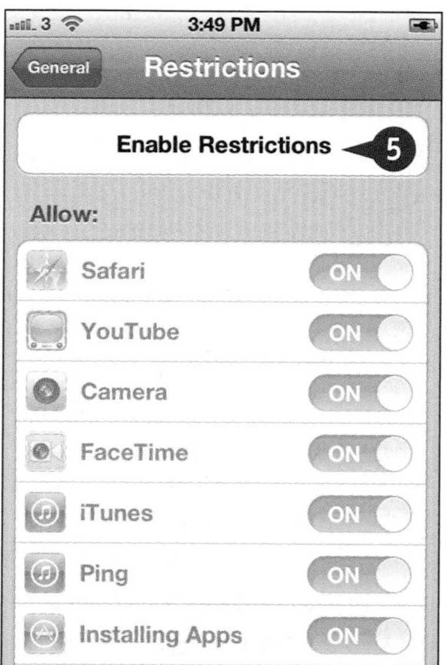

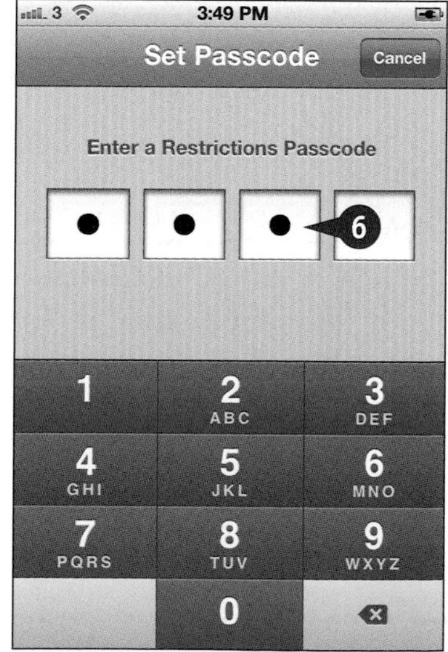

The Restrictions screen appears with the controls in the Allow box now available.

8 In the Allow box and Allow Changes box, move each switch to On or Off, as needed.

9 Scroll down to display the Allowed Content area and the Game Center area.

10 Move the In-App Purchases switch to Off if you want to prevent the user buying items from within apps.

11 If you need to change the country used for rating content, tap **Ratings For**. On the Ratings For screen, tap the country, and then tap **Restrictions**.

12 In the Allowed Content box, choose settings for Music & Podcasts, Movies, TV Shows, and Apps. See the tip for details.

13 In the Game Center box, move the **Multiplayer Games** switch and the **Adding Friends** switch to On or Off, as needed.

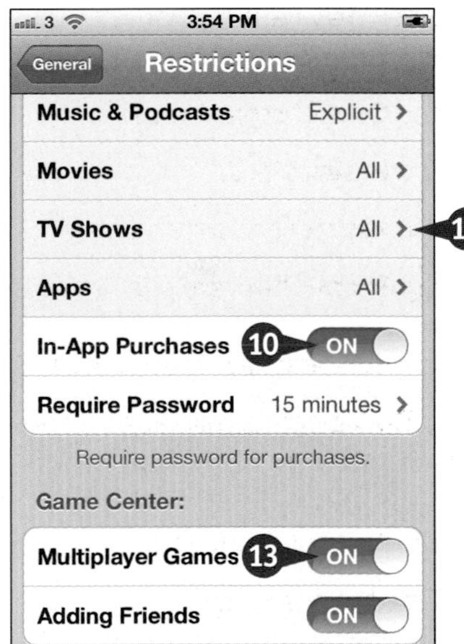

TIP

How do I control which movies and TV shows a user can watch?

Press the Home button, tap **Settings**, and then tap **Restrictions**. Type your passcode on the Enter Passcode screen, and then scroll down to the Allowed Content box and tap **Movies**. Tap the highest rating you will permit. For example, tap **PG-13** (A) to turn off R and NC-17. Or tap **Don't Allow Movies** to ban all movies. Tap **Restrictions**, tap **TV Shows**, and then either tap the highest rating you will permit or tap **Don't Allow TV Shows**.

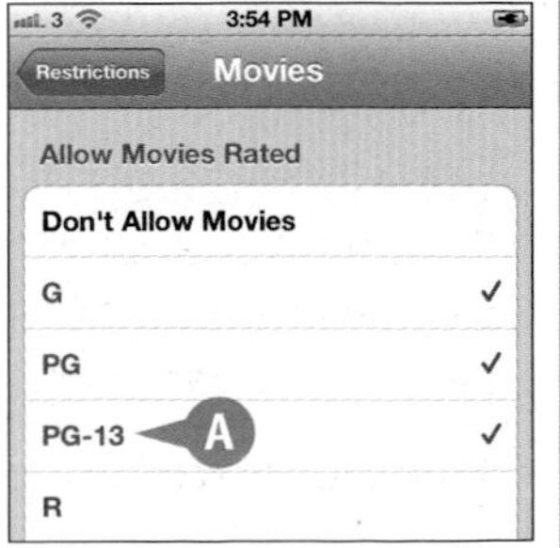

Choose Date, Time, and International Settings

To keep yourself on time and your data accurate, you need to make sure the iPhone is using the correct date and time.

To make dates, times, and other data appear in the formats you prefer, you may need to change the iPhone's International settings.

Choose Date, Time, and International Settings

Choose Date and Time Settings

1. Press the Home button.

   The Home screen appears.

2. Tap **Settings**.

   The Settings screen appears.

3. Scroll down a little way, and then tap **General**.

   The General screen appears.

4. Scroll down to the bottom.

5. Tap **Date & Time**.

   The Date & Time screen appears.

6. Tap the **24-Hour Time** switch and move it to On if you want to use 24-hour times. Otherwise, make sure the switch is set to Off.

7. If you want to set the date and time manually, tap the **Set Automatically** switch and move it to Off.

   The Date & Time screen displays Time Zone and Set Date & Time controls. Use these controls to specify the time zone, date, and time.

8. Tap **General**.

   The General screen appears.

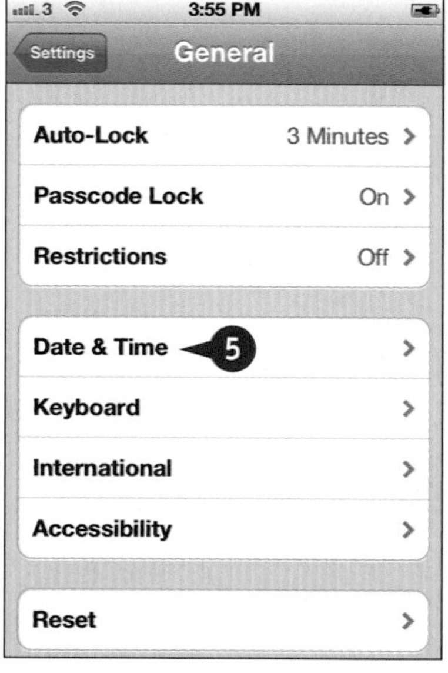

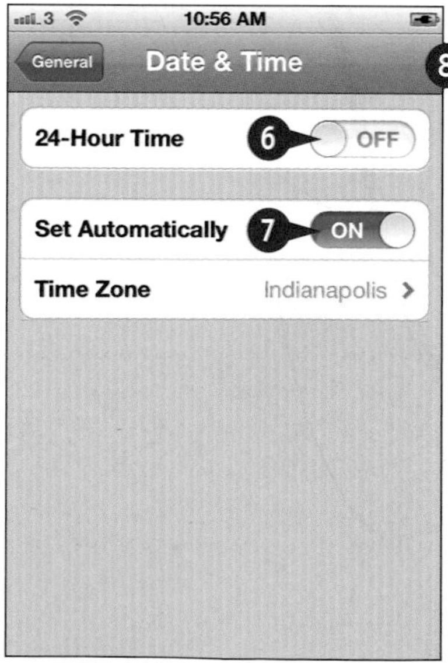

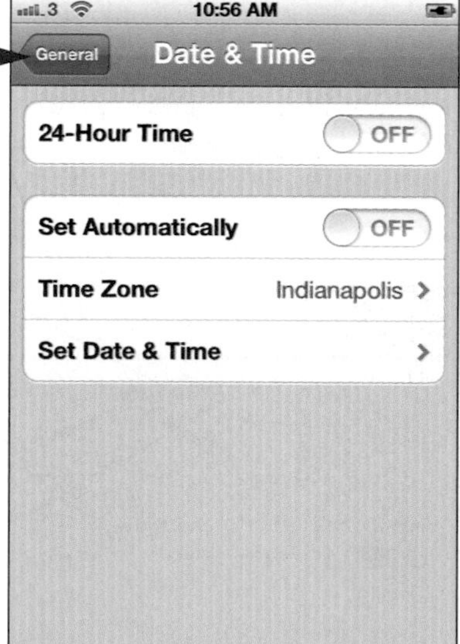

Choose International Settings

1. From the General screen, tap **International**.

   The International screen appears.

2. Tap **Region Format**.

   The Region Format screen appears.

3. Touch the region you want, placing a check mark next to it.

4. Touch **International**.

   The International screen appears.

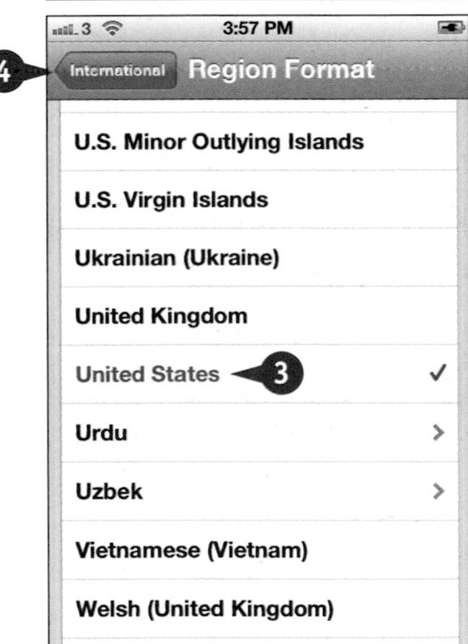

Note: From the International screen, you can also change the language used for the iPhone's user interface and the language used for voice control.

TIP

How does the iPhone set the date and time automatically?

The iPhone sets the date and time automatically by using time servers, computers on the Internet that provide date and time information to computers that request them. The iPhone automatically determines its geographical location so that it can request the right time zone from the time server.

CHAPTER 4

Setting Up Mail, Contacts, and Calendar

In this chapter, you learn how to add your email accounts to the Mail app, and choose options for your contacts, calendars, and notes.

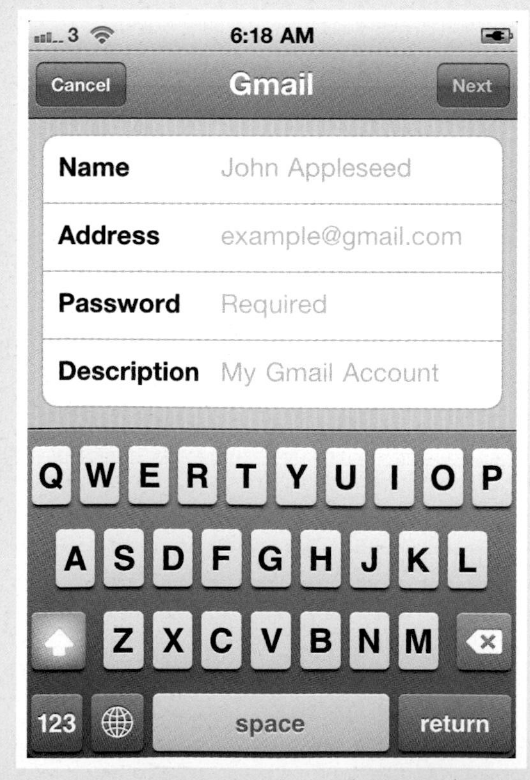

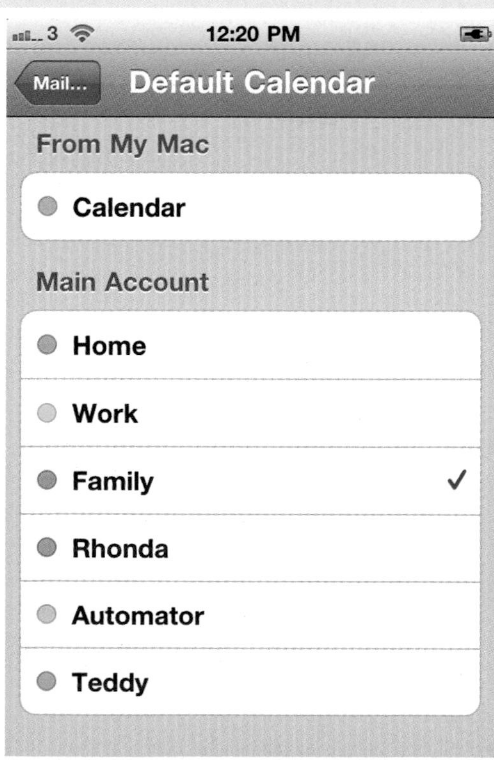

Set Up Your Mail Accounts

The easiest way to set up an email account on your iPhone is to synchronize the details from your PC or Mac, as discussed in Chapter 2. But if the email account is not set up on the computer with which you synchronize the iPhone, you can set the account up directly on the iPhone as explained in this task.

To set up an email account, you will need to know the email address, password, and the email provider. You may also need to know the addresses of the mail servers the account uses. For Microsoft Exchange, you must know the domain name as well.

Set Up Your Mail Accounts

1. Press the Home button.

   The Home screen appears.

2. Tap **Settings**.

   The Settings screen appears.

Note: If you have not yet set up an email account on the iPhone, you can also open the Add Account screen by tapping **Mail** on the iPhone's Home screen.

3. Tap and drag up to scroll down until the third group of buttons appears.

4. Tap **Mail, Contacts, Calendars**.

   The Mail, Contacts, Calendars screen appears.

5. Tap **Add Account**.

Note: This example uses a Gmail account. Setting up a Yahoo! account or an AOL account uses the same fields of information. For details on setting up an iCloud account, see the tip section. For an iCloud account, you enter only the email address and password.

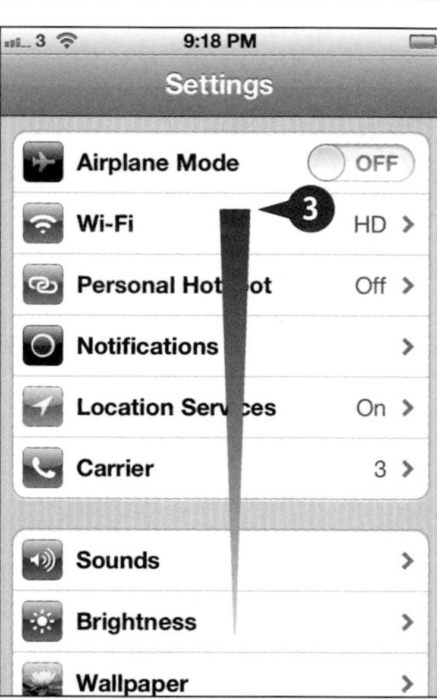

The Add Account screen appears.

6 Tap the kind of account you want to set up.

The screen for setting up that type of account appears.

7 Tap **Name** and type your name as you want it to appear in messages you send.

8 Tap **Address** and type the email address.

9 Tap **Password** and type the password.

10 Tap **Description** and type a descriptive name for the account.

11 Tap **Next**.

The configuration screen for the account appears.

12 Make sure the **Mail** switch is set to On.

13 Tap the **Calendars** switch and move it to On or Off.

14 Tap the **Notes** switch and move it to On or Off.

15 Tap **Save**.

A The account appears on the Mail, Contacts, Calendars screen.

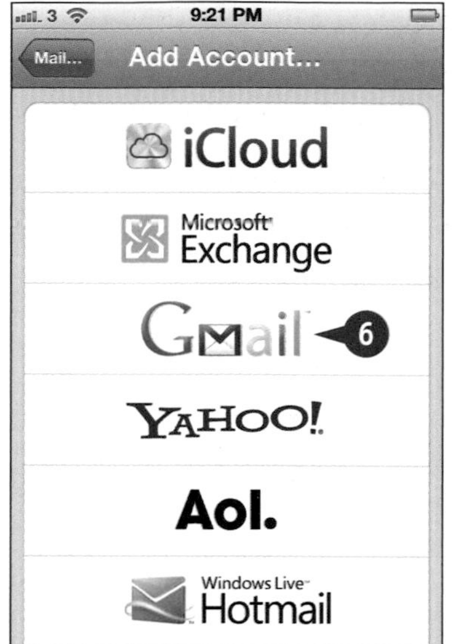

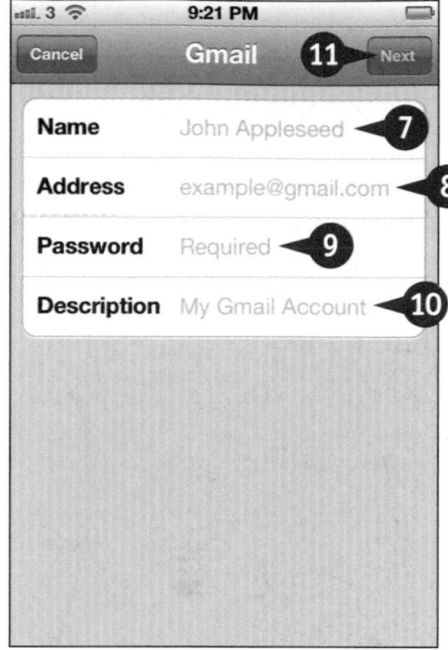

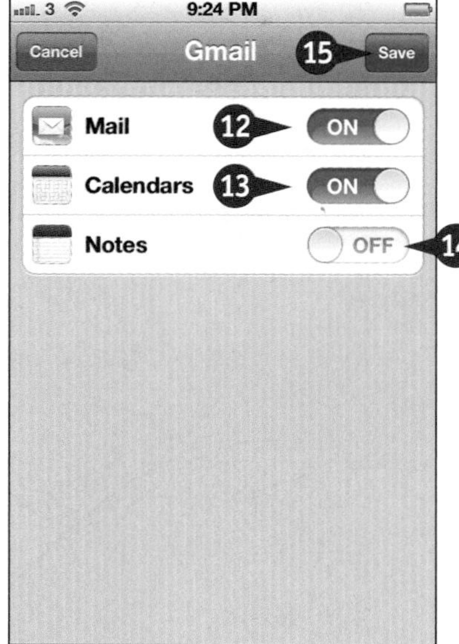

TIP

How do I change the name for an iCloud account?

When you set up an iCloud account, the iCloud screen prompts you for only your Apple ID, which is your email address, and password. The account appears under the name iCloud in the Accounts list on the Mail, Contacts, Calendars screen. To change the name, press the Home button and then tap **Settings**. Scroll down to display the third group of buttons and tap **Mail, Contacts, Calendars**. Tap the iCloud account and then tap **Account**. Tap **Description** and type the name to identify the account. Tap **Done** and then tap **Mail, Contacts, Calendars**.

Control How the iPhone Displays Your Email

To make the iPhone's Mail app easy to use, choose settings that suit the way you work. You can choose how many messages to show in each mailbox and how many lines to include in the preview. To make messages easy to read, you can change the minimum font size. You can also choose whether to load remote images in messages.

Control How the iPhone Displays Your Email

1. Press the Home button.

   The Home screen appears.

2. Tap **Settings**.

   The Settings screen appears.

3. Tap and drag up to scroll down until the third group of buttons appears.

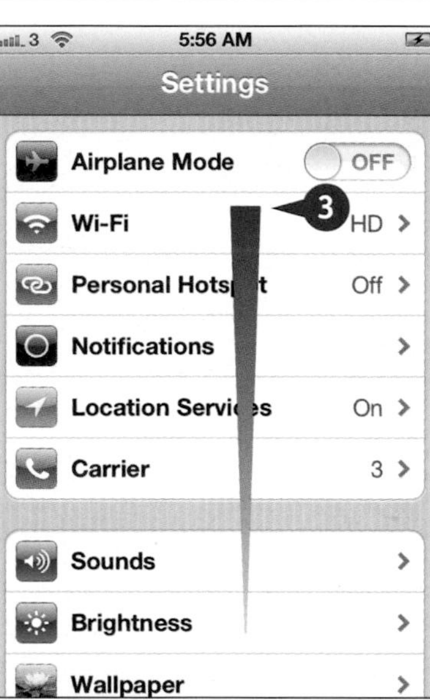

4. Tap **Mail, Contacts, Calendars.**

   The Mail, Contacts, Calendars screen appears.

5. Tap and drag up to scroll down.

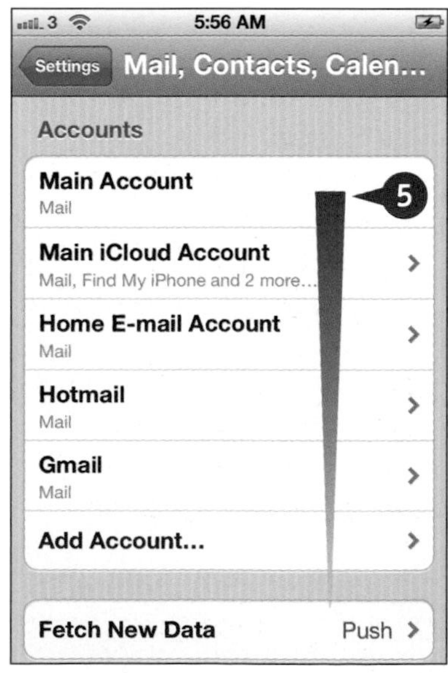

The Mail options appear.

6. Tap **Show**.
7. On the Show screen, tap the number of messages you want.
8. Tap **Mail, Contacts, Calendars**.
9. On the Mail screen, tap **Preview**.
10. On the Preview screen, tap the number of lines you want to see in previews.
11. Tap **Mail, Contacts, Calendars**.
12. On the Mail screen, tap **Minimum Font Size**.
13. On the Minimum Font Size screen, tap the font size you want.
14. Tap **Mail, Contacts, Calendars**.
15. On the Mail screen, tap the **Show To/Cc Label** switch and move it to On or Off.
16. Tap the **Load Remote Images** switch and move it to On or Off.
17. Tap **Settings**.

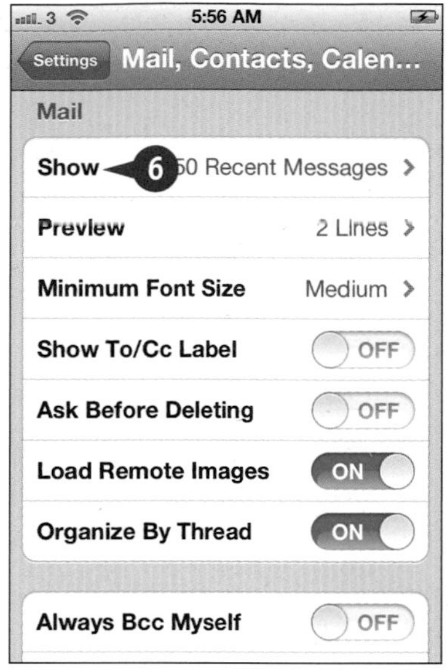

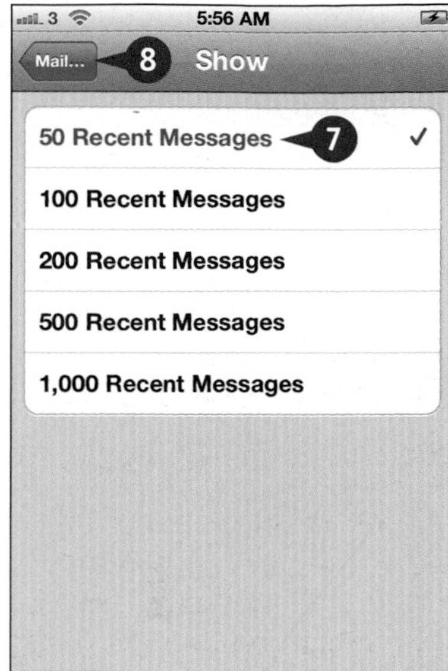

TIPS

Why may I want to turn off the Load Remote Images feature?
Loading a remote image enables the sender to learn that you have opened the message. When Mail requests the remote image, the server that provides the image can log the date and time and tie it to the message sent to you. The server can also learn your Internet connection's IP address and determine your approximate location.

What is the Always Bcc Myself setting useful for?
Most email services automatically put a copy of each message you send or forward into a folder with a name such as Sent, so that you can easily review the messages you have sent. If your email service does not use a Sent folder, move the Always Bcc Myself switch to On to send a bcc copy of each message to yourself. You can then file these messages in a folder of your choosing — for example, a folder named Sent — to keep a record of your sent messages.

Organize Your Email Messages by Thread

The Mail app gives you two ways to view email messages. You can view the messages as a simple list, or you can view them with related messages organized into threads, which are sometimes called conversations.

Having Mail display your messages as threads can help you navigate your Inbox quickly and find related messages easily.

Organize Your Email Messages by Thread

Set Mail to Organize Your Messages by Thread

1. Press the Home button.

   The Home screen appears.

2. Tap **Settings**.

   The Settings screen appears.

3. Tap and drag up to scroll down until the third group of buttons appears.

4. Tap **Mail, Contacts, Calendars**.

   The Mail, Contacts, Calendars screen appears.

5. Tap and drag up to scroll down.

   The Mail options appear.

6. Tap the **Organize By Thread** switch and move it to the On position.

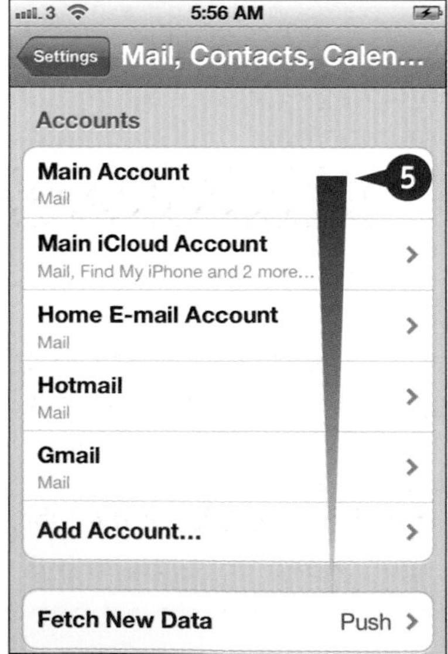

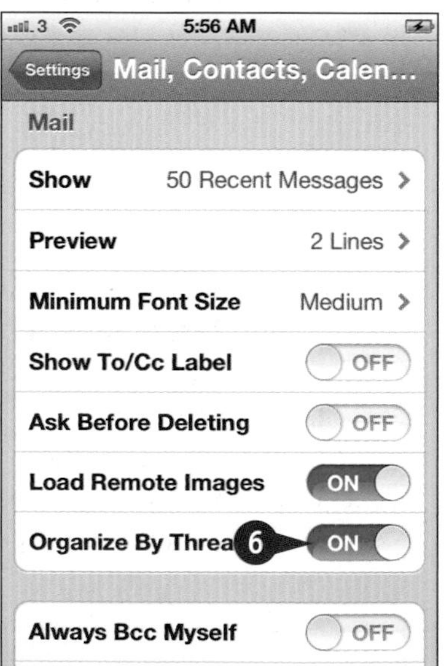

Read Messages Organized into Threads

1. Press the Home button.

   The Home screen appears.

2. Tap **Mail**.

   The Mailboxes screen appears.

3. Tap the mailbox.

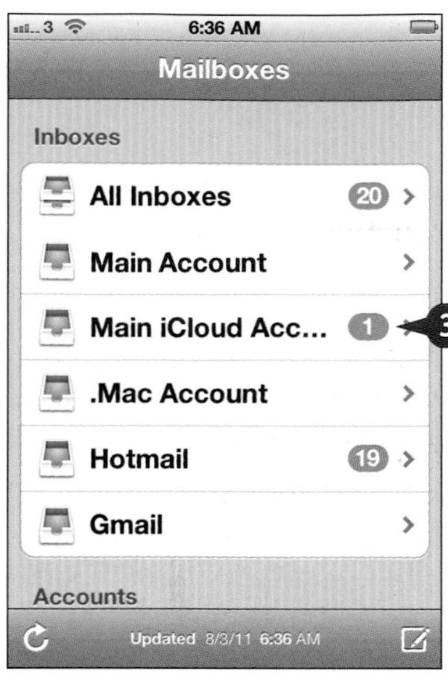

The Inbox for the account appears.

Ⓐ A number on the right indicates a threaded message.

4. Tap the threaded message.

   A screen showing the threaded message appears.

5. Tap the message you want to display.

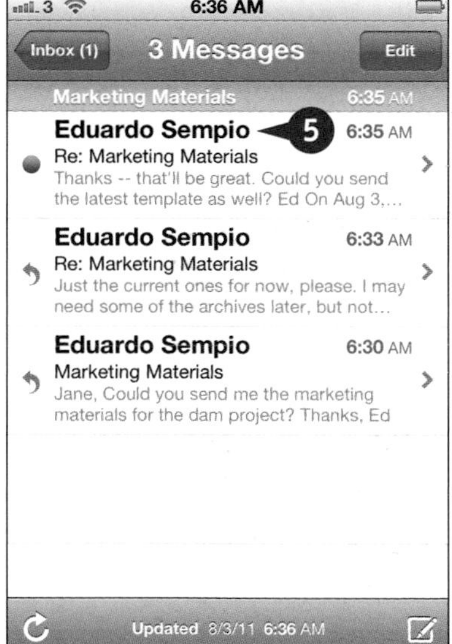

TIP

Should I turn threading on or off?

If you tend to have long email conversations, turning threading on helps make your Inbox easier to navigate by reducing the number of messages you see at once. But if you tend to have shorter correspondences with many people, or if you quickly move messages out of your Inbox into other folders, you may prefer to turn off threading. The related messages then appear as individual entries in the Inbox.

Create an Email Signature

You can set the Mail app to automatically add a *signature*, a block of text at the end of each email message you send. For example, you can add your name, position, and contact details for reference or a motivational quote for interest.

The iPhone's default setting is to use a signature that says "Sent from my iPhone." This is occasionally suitable, but you will normally want to change it — or simply to remove it.

Create an Email Signature

1. Press the Home button.

   The Home screen appears.

2. Tap **Settings**.

   The Settings screen appears.

3. Tap and drag up to scroll down until the third group of buttons appears.

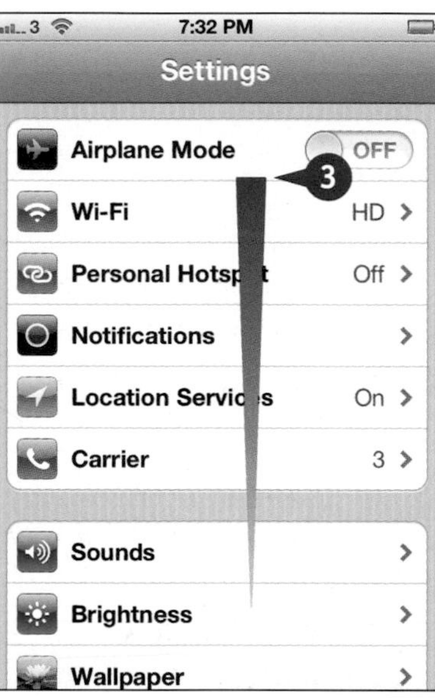

4. Tap **Mail, Contacts, Calendars.**

   The Mail, Contacts, Calendars screen appears.

5. Tap and drag up to scroll down until the third box of controls appears.

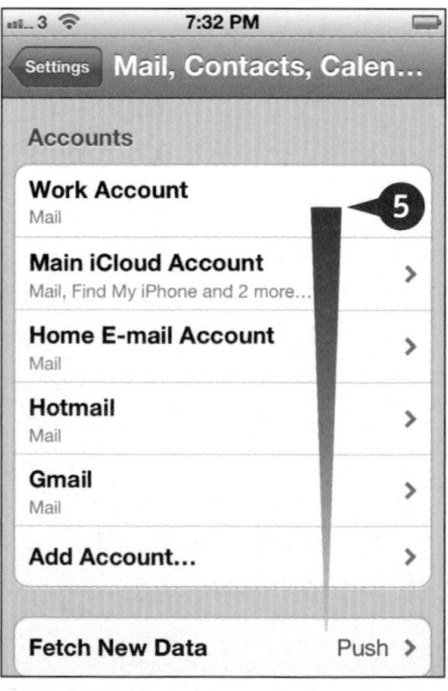

6 Tap **Signature**.

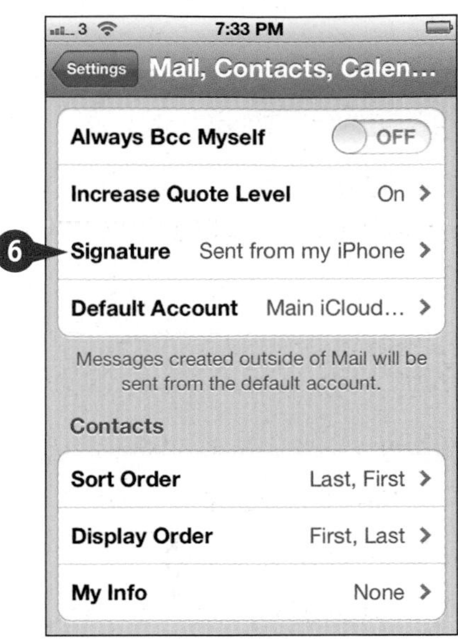

The Signature screen and on-screen keyboard appear.

7 Type or paste the signature text.

A If there is an existing signature, you can tap **Clear** to delete it.

8 Tap **Mail, Contacts, Calendars**.

The Mail, Contacts, Calendars screen appears.

TIPS

How can I use an email signature only on some messages?
If you want to use an email signature on most of the messages you send, set up the signature as described in this task, and delete it from the messages that do not need it. If you want to add an email signature to only a few messages, type or paste the signature as needed. If you want to paste in the signature, store its text in a note in the Notes app.

Can I include a picture in my email signature?
At this writing, there is no way to include a picture in your email signature on the iPhone.

Set Your Default Email Account

If you set up two or more email accounts on the iPhone, make sure that you set the right email account to be the default account. The default account is the one from which the Mail app sends messages unless you choose another account, so choosing the appropriate account is important.

Set Your Default Email Account

1. Press the Home button.

   The Home screen appears.

2. Tap **Settings**.

   The Settings screen appears.

3. Tap and drag up to scroll down until the third group of buttons appears.

4. Tap **Mail, Contacts, Calendars**.

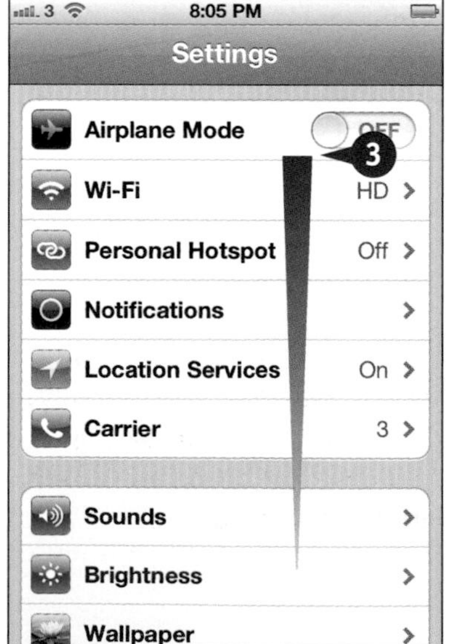

The Mail, Contacts, Calendars screen appears.

5 Tap and drag up to scroll down until the fourth box of controls appears.

6 Tap **Default Account**.

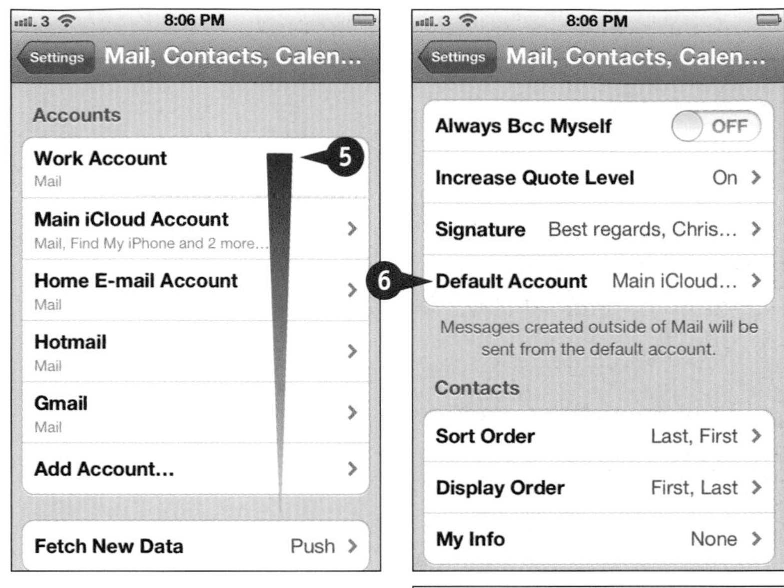

The Default Account screen appears.

7 Tap the account you want to make the default.

A A check mark appears next to the account you tapped.

8 Tap **Mail, Contacts, Calendars**.

The Mail, Contacts, Calendars screen appears.

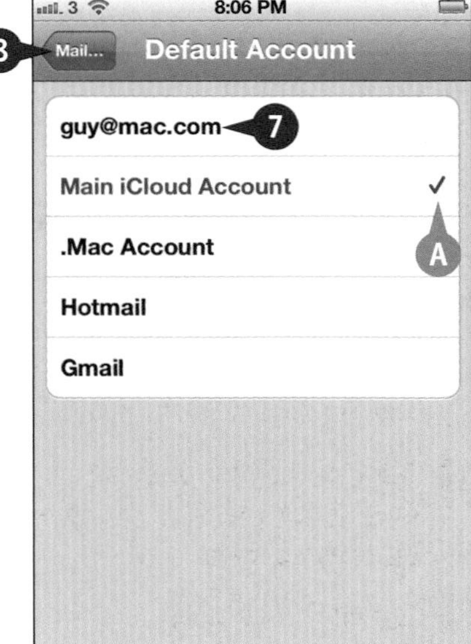

TIP

How do I use a different account when sending a new message?

When you create a new message, the Mail app automatically makes your default email account the sender. To change the email account, tap the **From** button and hold down until a spin wheel showing your email addresses appears. Then tap the address you want to use.

Choose How the iPhone Displays Your Contacts

To find the contacts you need swiftly and easily, you can set the iPhone to sort and display your contacts in your preferred order.

The iPhone can sort contacts either by first name or by last name. Whichever way you sort the contacts, the iPhone can display them in alphabetical order either by first name or by last name. By entering data only in the Company field for a business, you can make business names sort correctly whether you sort people's names by first name or last name.

Choose How the iPhone Displays Your Contacts

1. Press the Home button.

   The Home screen appears.

2. Tap **Settings**.

   The Settings screen appears.

3. Tap and drag up to scroll down until the third group of buttons appears.

4. Tap **Mail, Contacts, Calendars**.

The Mail, Contacts, Calendars screen appears.

5 Scroll down until the Contacts box appears.

6 Tap **Sort Order.**

The Sort Order screen appears.

7 Tap **First, Last** to sort by first name and then last name, or tap **Last, First** to sort by last name and then first name.

8 Tap **Mail, Contacts, Calendars.**

The Mail, Contacts, Calendars screen appears.

9 Tap **Display Order.**

The Display Order screen appears.

10 Tap **First, Last** to display the first name and then the last name, or tap **Last, First** to display the last name and then the first name.

11 Tap **Mail, Contacts, Calendars.**

The Mail, Contacts, Calendars screen appears.

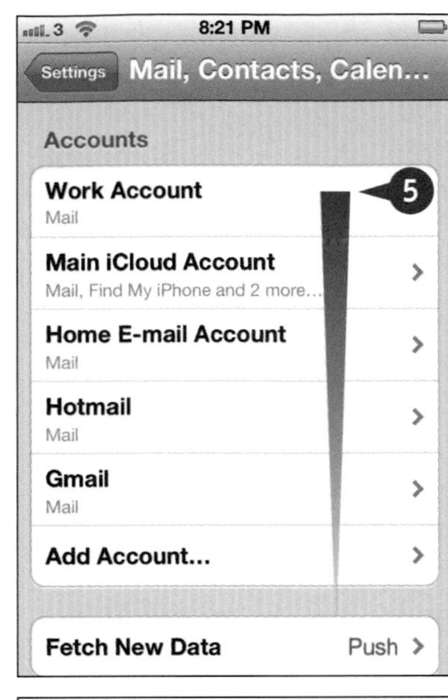

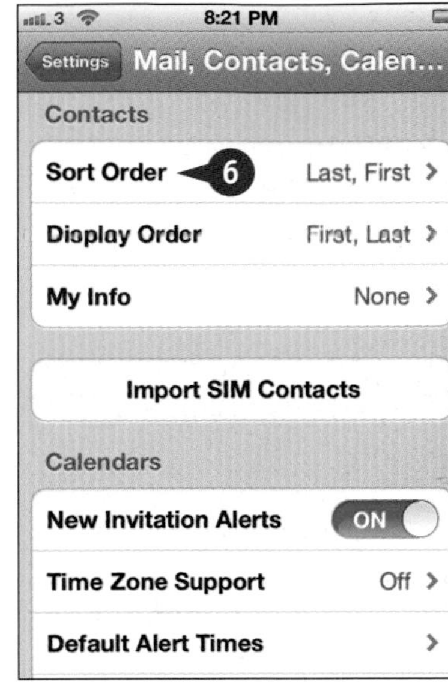

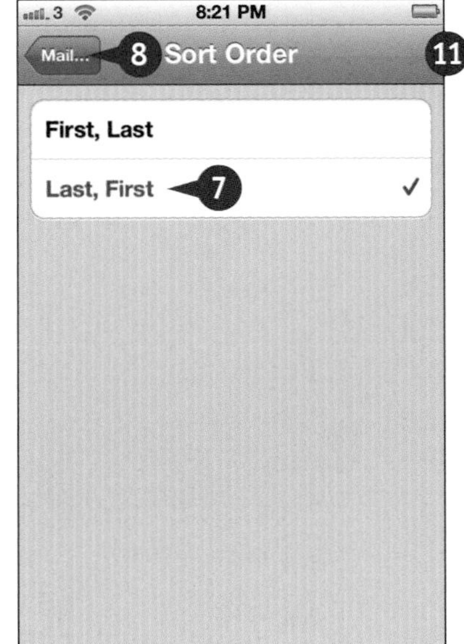

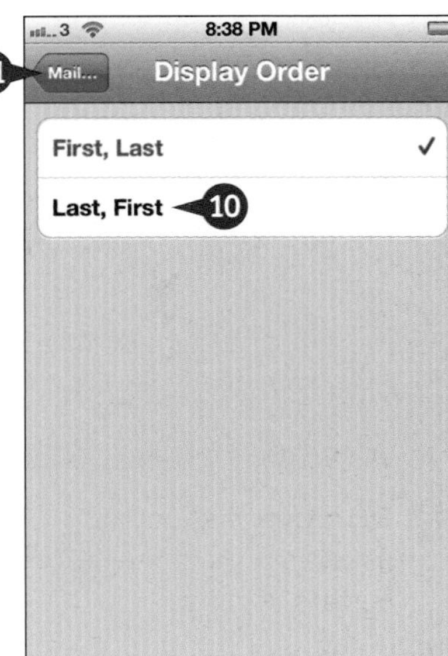

TIP

What is the best way to sort and display my contacts?

How to sort and display your contacts is really up to you. If you tend to think of your contacts primarily by their first names, choosing the First, Last sort order may help you locate your contacts more quickly. If you are more comfortable identifying the contacts by their last names, use the Last, First sort order. For either sort order, the First, Last display order is usually best because Mr. John Smith is easier to grasp than Mr. Smith John.

Import Contacts from a SIM Card

If you have stored contacts on a SIM card, you can import them into the iPhone. For example, you may have contacts stored on a SIM card from your previous cell phone. You can put that SIM card in the iPhone temporarily and import the contacts. You can also insert the iPhone's SIM card in an unlocked cell phone, copy the contacts to the SIM card, and then put the SIM card back in the iPhone.

Import Contacts from a SIM Card

1. Press the Home button.

   The Home screen appears.

2. Tap **Settings**.

   The Settings screen appears.

3. Tap and drag up to scroll down until the third group of buttons appears.

4. Tap **Mail, Contacts, Calendars**.

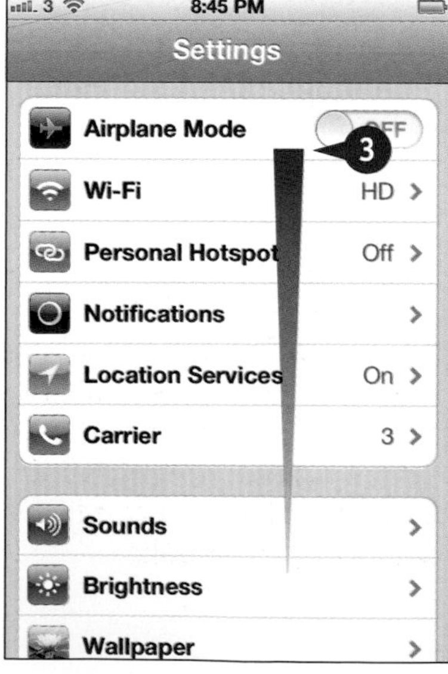

The Mail, Contacts, Calendars screen appears.

5 Tap and drag up to scroll all the way to the bottom of the screen.

The bottom part of the Mail, Contacts, Calendars screen appears.

6 Tap **Import SIM Contacts**.

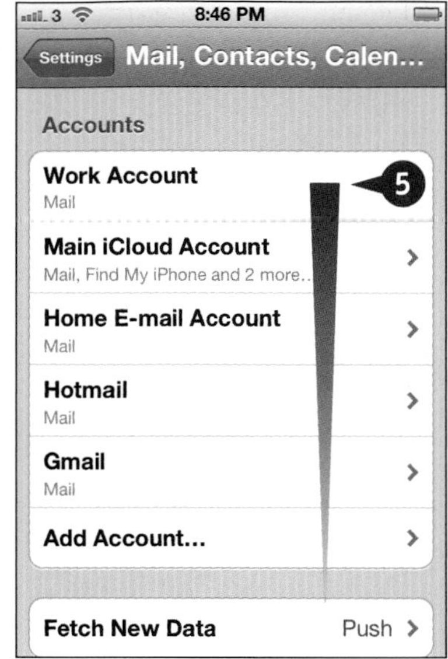

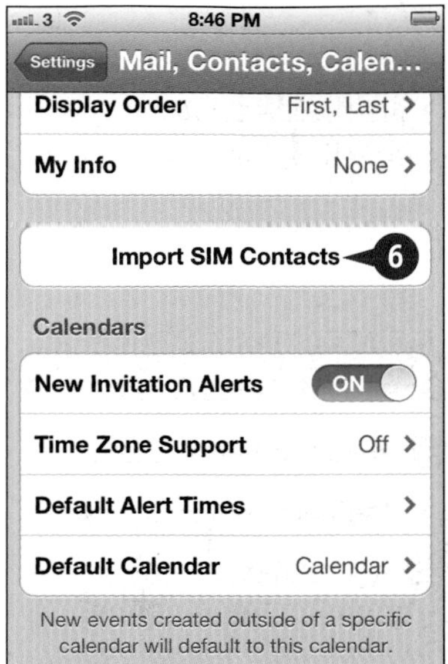

The screen shows the Importing from SIM message as it imports the contacts.

7 Tap **Settings**.

The Mail, Contacts, Calendars screen appears.

TIP

Is there another way to copy contacts from my old phone to the iPhone?

If your previous phone takes a larger SIM card than the iPhone's micro-SIM, you cannot insert the SIM card in the iPhone. Instead, you can take out the iPhone's micro-SIM, put it in a SIM card adapter or *SIM shim*, insert the shim in the previous phone, and transfer the contacts to the SIM. Then put the micro-SIM back in the iPhone and import the contacts. If this approach is not possible, see if the previous phone can export the contacts as vCard files, virtual business card files. Then add the vCard files to the address book you synchronize with the iPhone, and perform a synchronization.

Choose Alerts Options for Calendar Events

By synchronizing your calendars from your PC or Mac with your iPhone, you can keep details of your events in the palm of your hand.

To keep yourself on schedule, you can set the iPhone to alert you to new invitations you receive. You can also set default alert times to give you the warning you need before a regular event, an all-day event, or a birthday.

Choose Alerts Options for Calendar Events

1. Press the Home button.

   The Home screen appears.

2. Tap **Settings**.

   The Settings screen appears.

3. Tap and drag up to scroll down until the third group of buttons appears.

4. Tap **Mail, Contacts, Calendars**.

The Mail, Contacts, Calendars screen appears.

5 Tap and drag up to scroll down to the bottom of the screen.

The bottom part of the Mail, Contacts, Calendars screen appears.

6 Tap the **New Invitation Alerts** switch and move it to On or Off, as needed.

7 Tap **Default Alert Times**.

The Default Alert Times screen appears.

8 Tap the event type you want to set the default alert time for. For example, tap **Events**.

The Events screen, Birthdays screen, or All-Day Events screen appears.

9 Tap the amount of time you want as the warning.

10 Tap **Default Alert Times**.

The Default Alert Times screen appears again.

11 Set default alert times for other event types by repeating steps **8** to **10**.

12 Tap **Mail, Contacts, Calendars**.

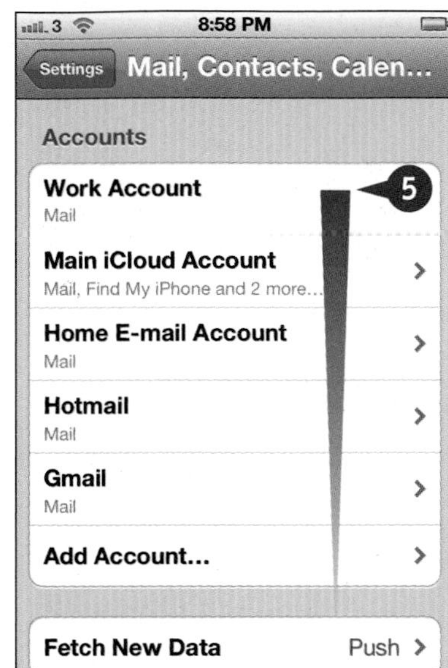

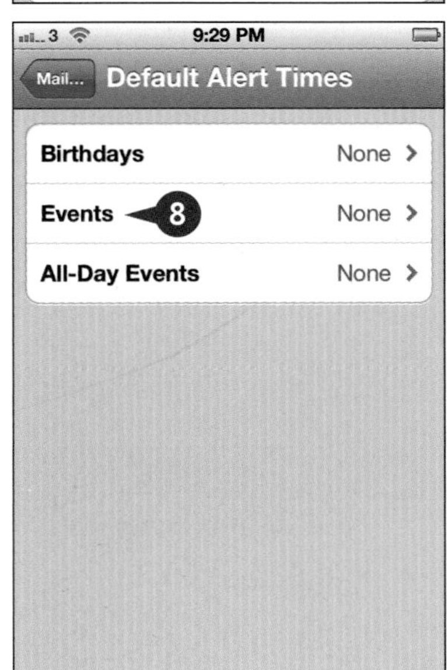

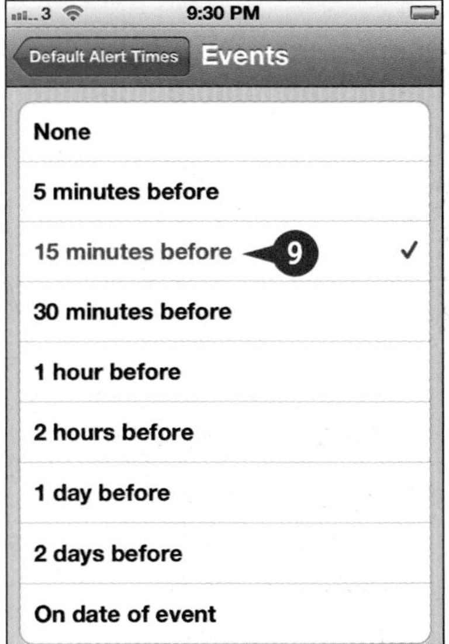

TIP

How do I add events to my calendars directly?

You can add events to your calendars directly by using the Calendar app. Press the Home button to display the Home screen, and then tap **Calendar**. You can also add events to your calendars on the iPhone by adding them to the calendars you synchronize with the iPhone. For example, on a Mac, you can add events in the iCal application, and then sync them to the iPhone.

Choose Your Default Calendar and Time Zone

When you use multiple calendars on the iPhone, you need to set your default calendar. This is the calendar that receives events you create outside any specific calendar. For example, if you have a Work calendar and a Home calendar, you can set the Home calendar as the default calendar.

If you travel to different time zones, you may need to specify which time zone to show event dates and times in. Otherwise, Calendar uses the time zone for your current location.

Choose Your Default Calendar and Time Zone

1. Press the Home button.

   The Home screen appears.

2. Tap **Settings**.

   The Settings screen appears.

3. Tap and drag up to scroll down until the third group of buttons appears.

4. Tap **Mail, Contacts, Calendars**.

   The Mail, Contacts, Calendars screen appears.

5. Tap and drag up to scroll all the way to the bottom of the screen.

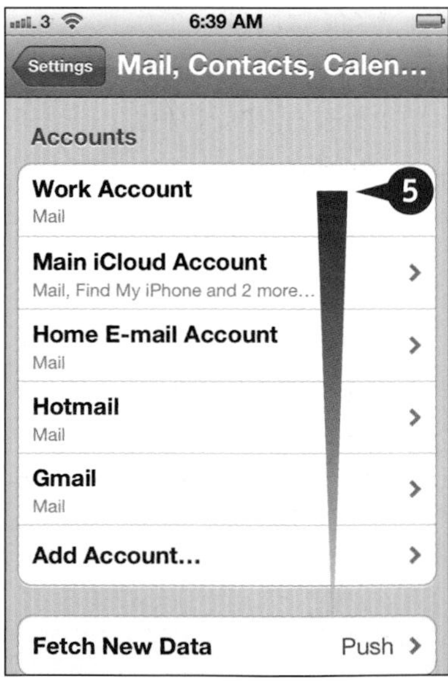

The bottom part of the Mail, Contacts, Calendars screen appears.

6 Tap **Time Zone Support**.

The Time Zone Support screen appears.

7 Tap the **Time Zone Support** switch and move it to On.

8 Tap **Time Zone**.

The Time Zone screen appears.

9 Type the start of the time zone.

10 Tap the search result you want.

11 Tap **Time Zone Support**.

12 Tap **Mail, Contacts, Calendars**.

13 Tap **Default Calendar**.

The Default Calendar screen appears.

14 Tap the calendar you want to make the default.

A A check mark appears next to the calendar.

15 Tap **Mail, Contacts, Calendars**.

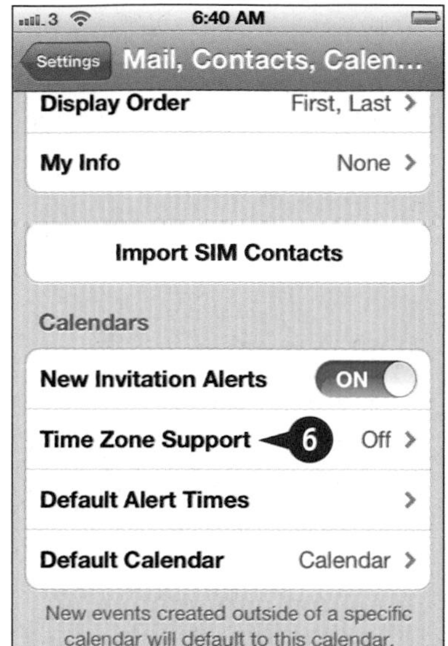

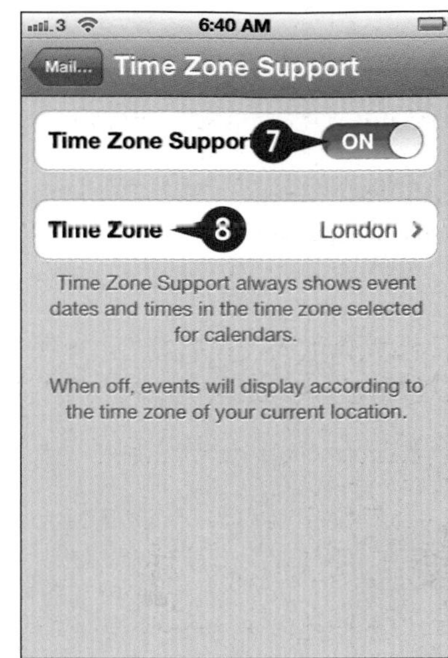

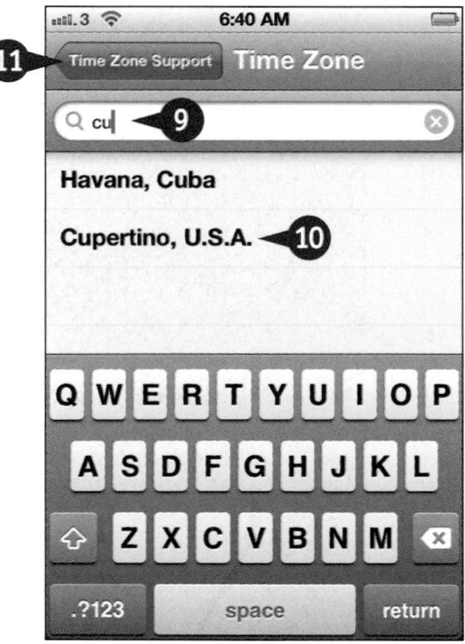

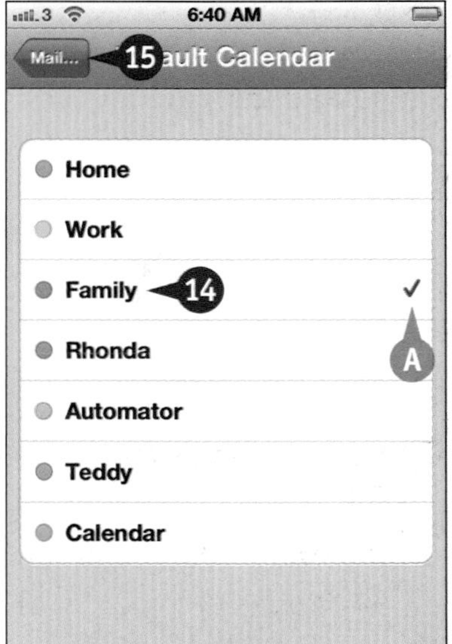

TIP

How do I choose which calendars to display in the Calendar app?

You choose the calendars in the Calendar app rather than on the Mail, Contacts, Calendars settings screen. Press the Home button to display the Home screen, tap **Calendar**, and then tap **Calendars**. On the Calendars screen, tap to place a check mark on each calendar you want to display. Tap to remove a check mark from a calendar you want to hide. Then tap **Done**.

Set Your Default Account for Notes

As described earlier in this chapter, you can set up multiple email accounts on the iPhone. Each email account can synchronize notes.

You can set the default account for notes to tell the iPhone which email account it should store new notes in unless you specify storing them elsewhere.

Set Your Default Account for Notes

1. Press the Home button.

   The Home screen appears.

2. Tap **Settings**.

   The Settings screen appears.

3. Scroll down to display the third group of buttons.

4. Tap **Notes**.

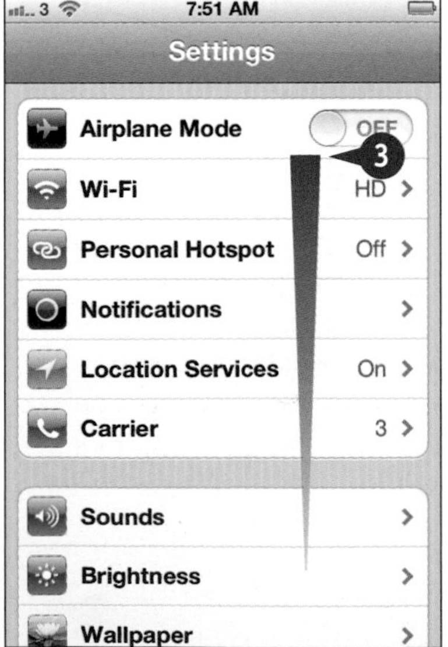

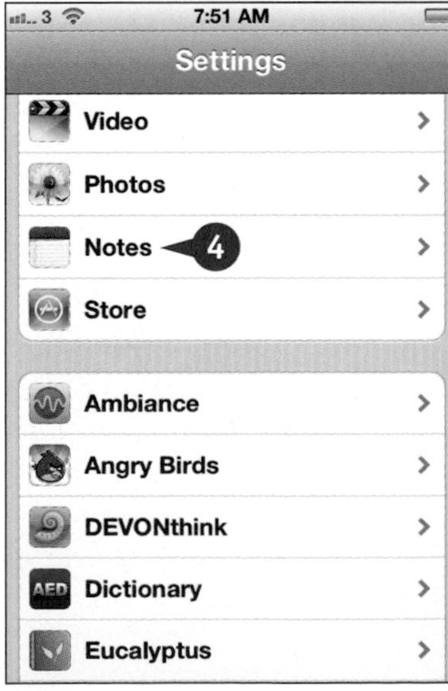

The Notes screen appears.

5 Tap **Default Account**.

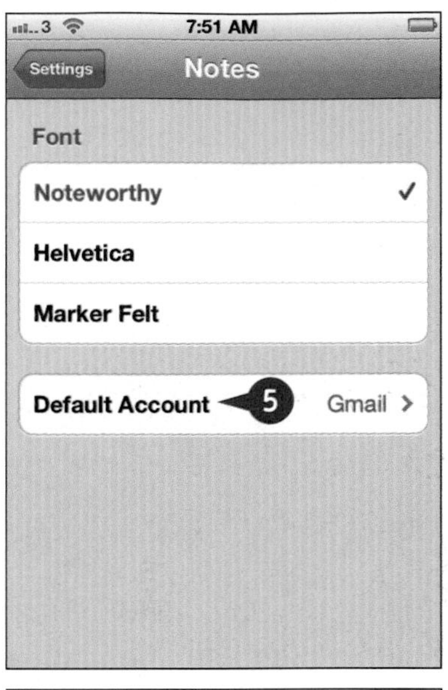

The Default Account screen appears.

6 Tap the account you want to make the default.

A A check mark appears next to the account you tapped.

7 Tap **Notes**.

The Notes screen appears.

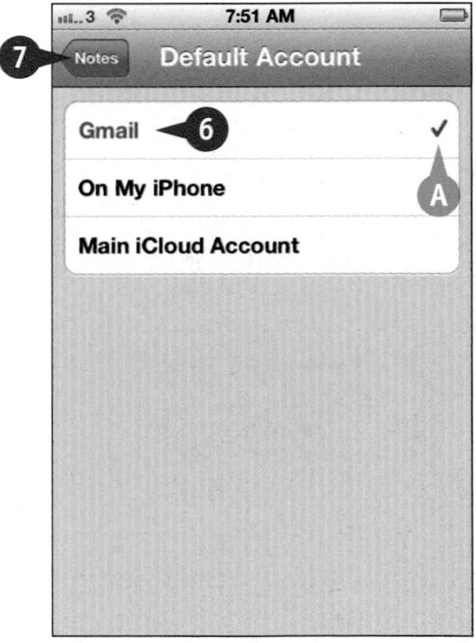

TIPS

Why does the Default Account setting not appear on the Notes screen on my iPhone?

The Default Account setting appears on the Notes screen in the Settings app when you have set up two or more email accounts to synchronize notes. If you add multiple email accounts to the iPhone, but set up only one account to synchronize notes, the Default Account setting does not appear because the only notes account is the default account.

How do I change the font used for notes?

On the Notes screen in the Settings app, tap **Chalkboard**, **Helvetica**, or **Marker Felt** in the Font area.

CHAPTER 5

Using Your iPhone to Make Calls

You can make calls by holding the iPhone to your face, by using the speakerphone capabilities, or by using the iPhone's headset or a wireless headset. You can put a call on hold or mute it, or easily turn it into a conference call. You can also make calls quickly using Favorites and recent numbers, retrieve your messages from the timesaving Visual Voicemail system, and chat face to face using the FaceTime feature.

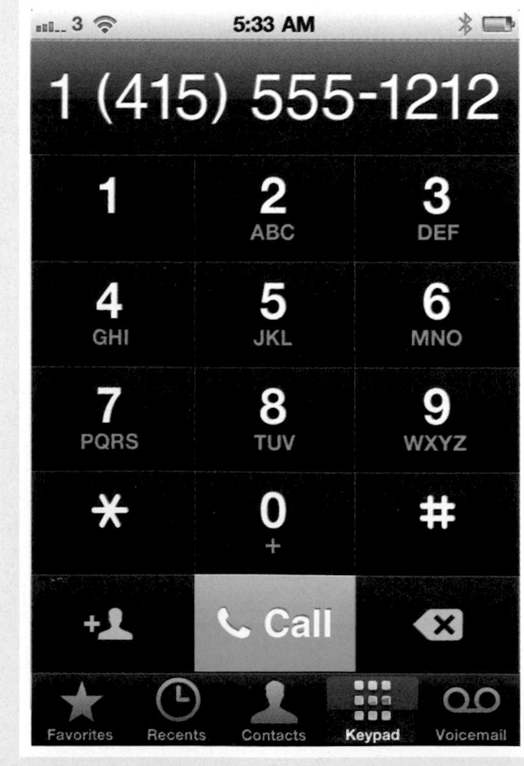

Make Phone Calls

With your iPhone, you can make phone calls anywhere you have a connection to the cellular network. You can make a phone call by dialing the phone number using the iPhone's keypad, but if the person you want to call is one of your contacts, you can place the call more easily by touching the appropriate phone number.

When you need other people near you to be able to hear the phone call you are making, you can switch on your iPhone's speaker.

Make Phone Calls

Open the Phone App

1. Press the Home button.

   The Home screen appears.

2. Tap **Phone**.

   The Phone app opens and displays the screen you used last — for example, the Contacts screen.

Note: You can also place a call to a phone number that the iPhone has identified — for example, by tapping an underlined phone number on a web page.

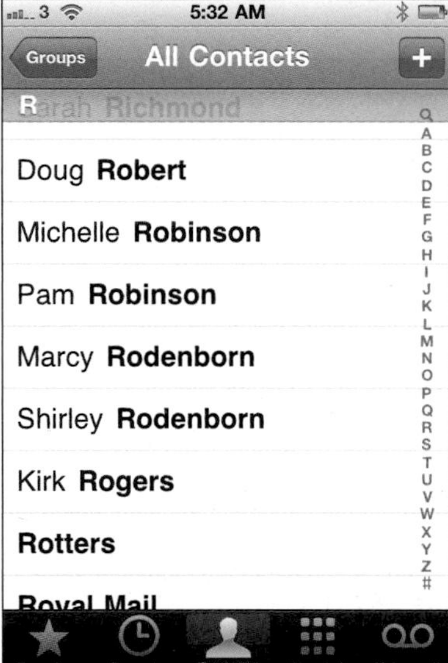

Dial a Call Using the Keypad

1. Tap **Keypad**.

   The Keypad screen appears.

2. Tap the number keys to dial the number.

3. Tap **Call**.

   Your iPhone makes the call.

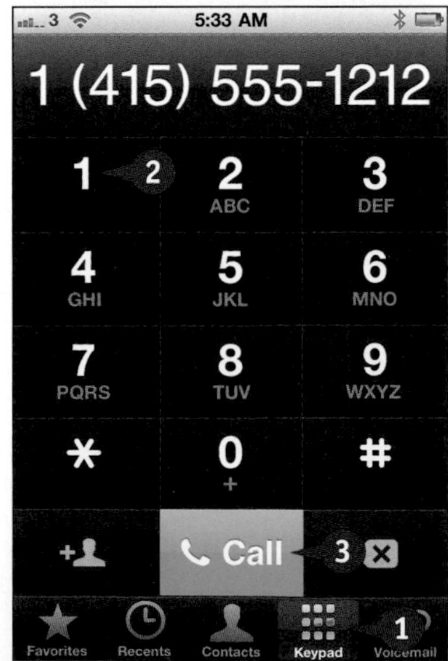

Dial a Call to a Contact

1. Tap **Contacts**.

   The All Contacts list appears.

2. Tap the contact you want to call.

   The contact's info appears.

3. Tap the phone number you want to call.

   Your iPhone makes the call.

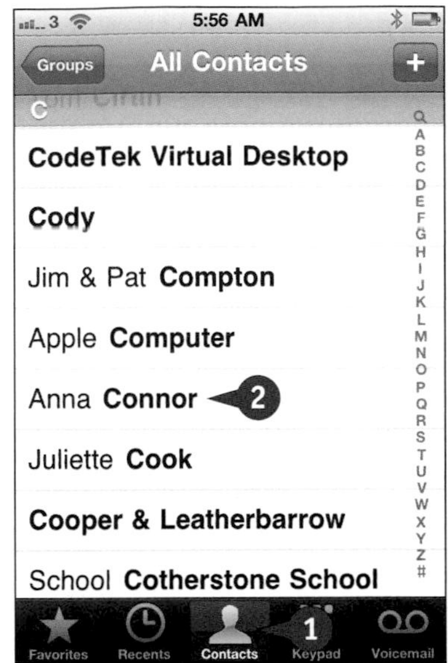

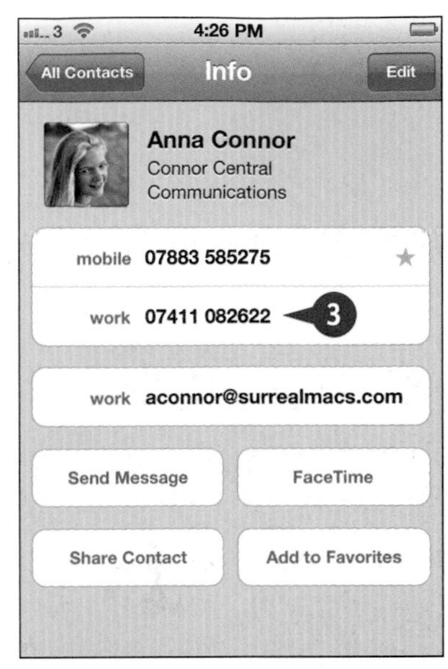

End a Phone Call

1. Tap **End**.

   Your iPhone ends the call.

   The Call Ended screen appears for a moment.

   Your iPhone then displays the screen from which you placed the call.

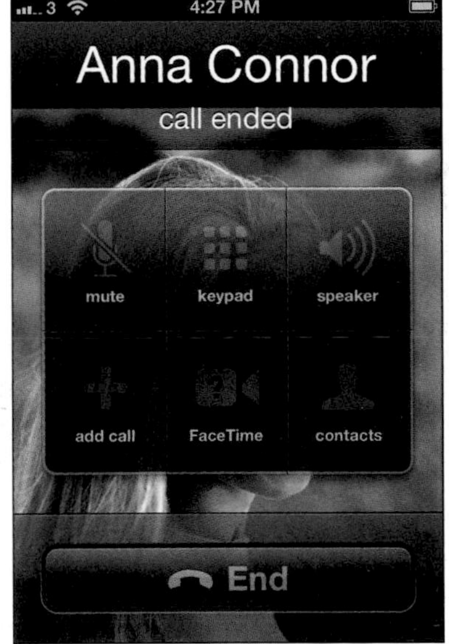

TIP

Can I use the iPhone as a speaker phone?

Yes. All you need do is tap **Speaker** (A) on the control panel that appears while you are making a phone call. The iPhone starts playing the phone call through the speaker on the bottom rather than the small speaker at the top.

Tap **Speaker** again when you want to switch off the speaker.

Use the Headset to Make and Take Calls

Your iPhone includes a headset that you can use not only for listening to music but also making and taking phone calls. The control box on the headset's wire includes a microphone, a clicker switch for answering and hanging up phone calls, and Volume Up and Volume Down buttons.

Using the headset is convenient not only when you are out and about but also when you are listening to music. Your iPhone automatically pauses the music when you receive a phone call.

Use the Headset to Make and Take Calls

Make a Call Using the Headset

1. Connect the headset to your iPhone if it is not already connected.

Note: You can dial a call by activating the Voice Control feature and speaking the number or the contact's name. See Chapter 14 for instructions on using Voice Control.

2. Press the Home button.

   The Home screen appears.

3. Tap **Phone**.

   The Phone app opens.

4. Dial the call as usual using one of the techniques described in this chapter. For example, tap **Contacts**, tap the contact, and then tap the phone number.

5. If you need to change the volume, press the Volume Up button or the Volume Down button on the headset control box.

6. Press the clicker button on the headset when you are ready to end the call.

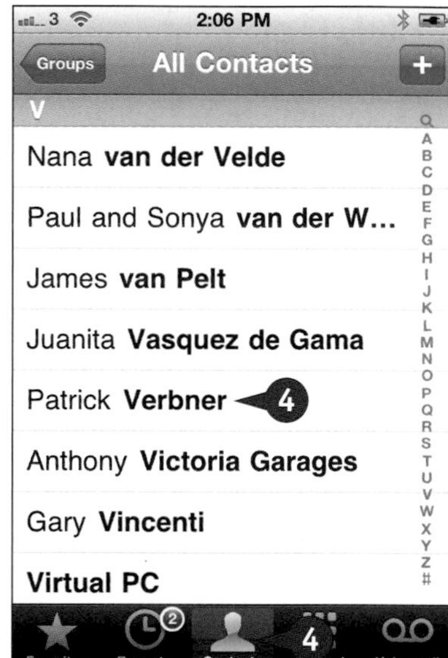

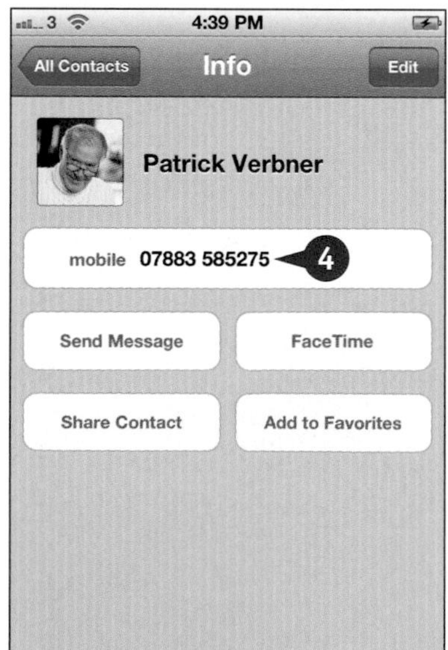

Take a Call Using the Headset

1. Connect the headset to your iPhone if it is not already connected.

   When you receive an incoming call, the phone ring plays in the headset and the screen comes on.

   The lock screen shows the caller's name and phone details — for example, Mobile or the phone number.

Note: If you are listening to music when you receive a call, your iPhone automatically fades and pauses the music. The same goes for video.

2. Press the clicker button on the headset to take the call.

   The lock screen shows the caller's name and the call's duration.

3. If you need to change the volume, press the Volume Up button or the Volume Down button on the headset control box.

4. Press the clicker button on the headset when you are ready to end the call.

   The lock screen appears again.

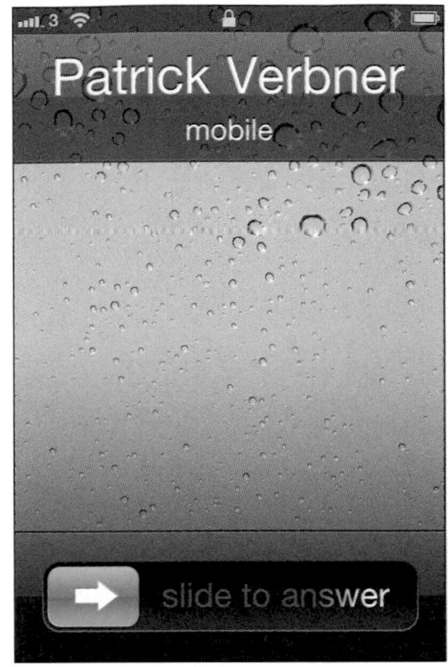

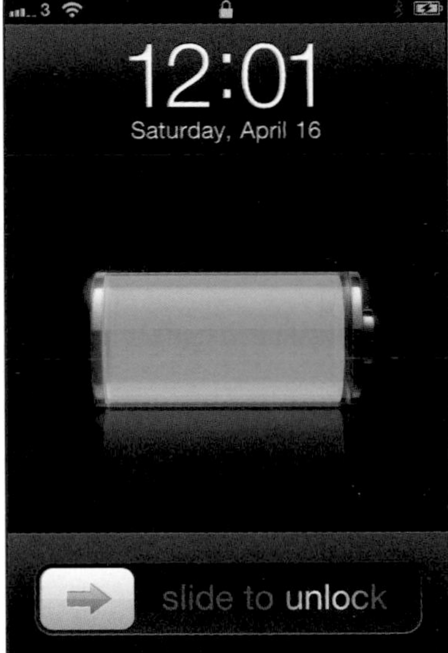

TIP

How do I access the phone controls when I am using the headset?

To access the phone controls, tap and drag the **Slide to Unlock** slider to the right. The Home screen appears with a green bar at the top. Touch this bar (A) to display the call screen.

Use a Wireless Headset or Car Kit

Instead of using the headset that came with your iPhone, you can use a Bluetooth headset. Similarly, you can use a car kit with a Bluetooth connection when using your iPhone in your vehicle.

You must first pair the Bluetooth headset or car kit with your iPhone as discussed in Chapter 6.

Use a Wireless Headset or Car Kit

1. Turn on the wireless headset or connection and make sure it works.
2. Press the Home button.

   The Home screen appears.
3. Tap **Phone**.

   The Phone app opens.
4. Dial the call as usual using one of the techniques described in this chapter. For example, tap **Contacts**, tap the contact, and then tap the phone number.

   Your iPhone starts to place the call.

   The dialog box for choosing the audio device appears.
5. Tap the headset or other device you want to use.

   The call begins.

Note: If you are playing audio or video on a Bluetooth headset when you receive a call, your iPhone automatically pauses the audio or video and plays the ringtone on the headset.

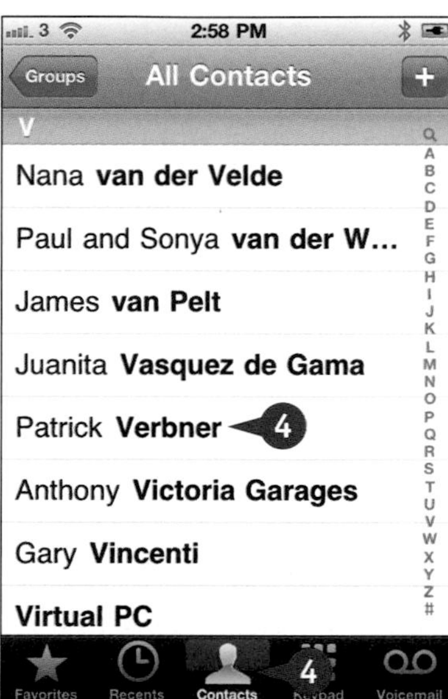

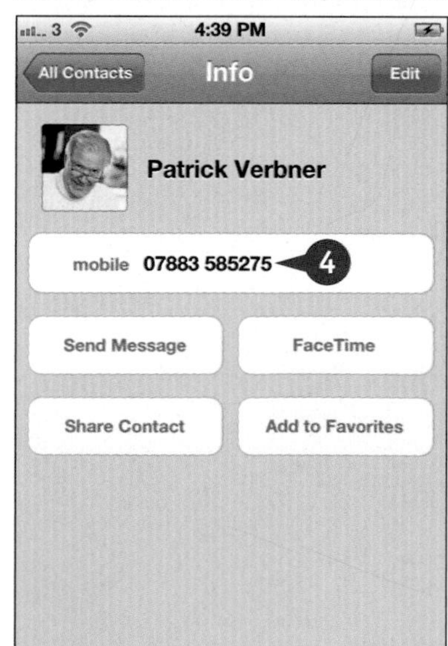

Mute a Call or Put a Call on Hold

When you are on a call, you may need to mute your iPhone's microphone so that you can confer with people near you without the person at the other end of the phone call hearing.

You may also need to put a call on hold so that you can make another call or take a break from the call.

Mute a Call or Put a Call on Hold

1. Establish the phone call as usual. For example, call a contact.
2. Tap **Mute**.

   The Mute button turns blue, and the iPhone mutes the call.
3. When you are ready to unmute the call, tap **Mute** again.
4. To put the call on hold, tap and hold **Mute** for several seconds.

   The Hold button appears in place of the Mute button, and turns blue.
5. When you are ready to take the call off hold, tap **Hold**.

Note: After placing a call on hold, you can make another call if necessary.

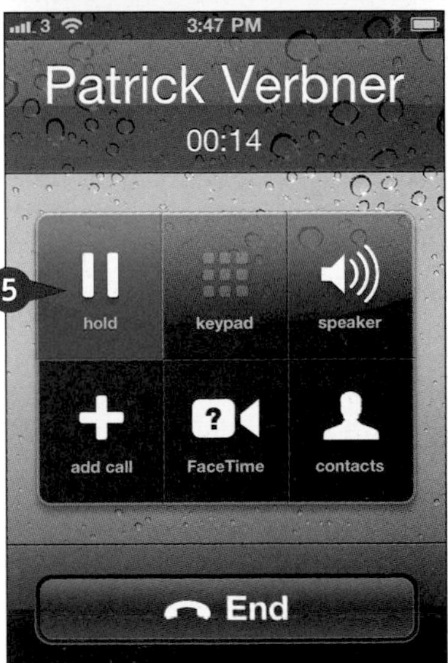

Make a Conference Call

As well as making phone calls to one other phone at a time, your iPhone can make conference calls to multiple phones. To make a conference call, you do not need to set it up with an operator in advance; instead, you call the first participant, and then add each other participant in turn.

During a conference call, you can talk in private to individual participants. You can also drop a participant from the call.

Make a Conference Call

Establish a Conference Call

1. Press the Home button.

   The Home screen appears.

2. Tap **Phone**.

   The Phone app opens.

3. Tap **Contacts**.

   The Contacts screen appears.

4. Tap the contact you want to call first.

   The contact's record appears.

5. Tap the phone number to use.

Note: You can also add a contact to the call by using Favorites, Recents, or the Keypad.

   Your iPhone makes the call.

6. Tap **Add Call**.

   The All Contacts screen appears.

7. Tap the contact you want to add.

   The contact's record appears.

8. Tap the phone number to use.

A The iPhone places the first call on hold and makes the new call.

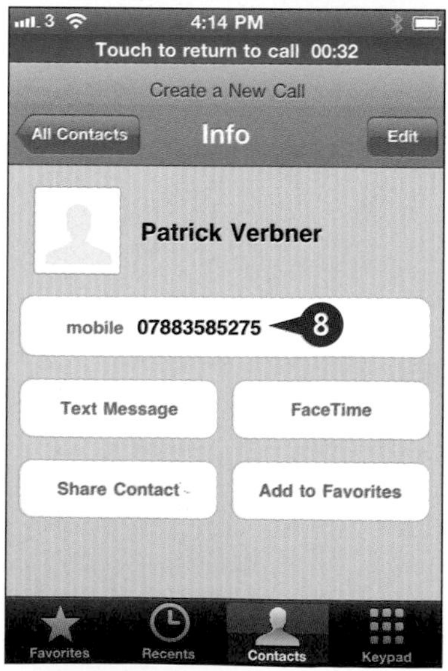

9 Tap **Merge Calls**.

The iPhone merges the calls and displays Conference at the top of the screen. You can now speak to both participants.

B You can add further participants by tapping **Add Call**, specifying the contact or number, and then merging the calls.

10 To speak privately to a participant, tap ⊙.

The Conference screen appears, showing a list of the participants.

11 Tap **Private** next to the participant.

The iPhone places the other callers on hold.

12 When you are ready to resume the conference call, tap **Back**, and then tap **Merge Calls**.

The iPhone merges the calls, and all participants can hear each other again.

13 When you finish the call, tap **End**.

The iPhone ends the call.

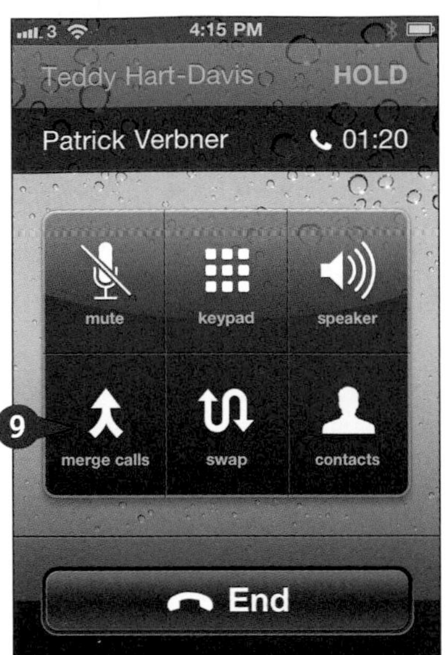

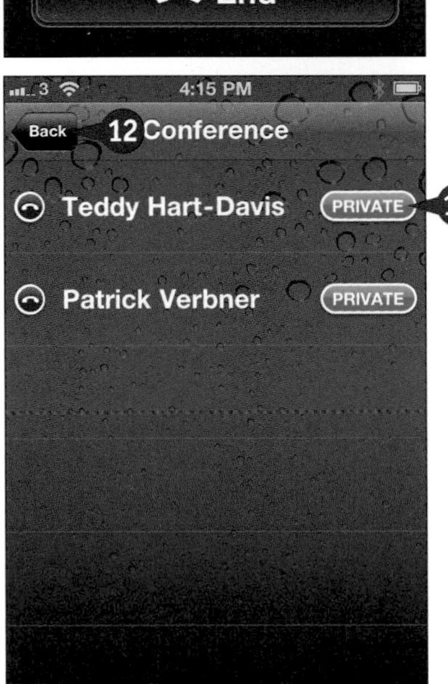

TIP

How do I drop a participant from a conference call?

Tap ⊙ to display the Conference screen. Tap ⊖ next to the participant you want to drop, and then tap **End** (A).

Save Time with Call Favorites and Recents

You can dial phone numbers easily from your Contacts list, but you can save further time and effort by using Favorites and Recents.

Favorites are phone numbers that you mark as being especially important to you. Recents are phone numbers you have called and received calls from recently.

Save Time with Call Favorites and Recents

Add a Contact to Your Favorites List

1. Press the Home button.

   The Home screen appears.

2. Tap **Phone**.

   The Phone app opens.

3. Tap **Contacts**.

   The Contacts list appears.

4. Tap the contact you want to add.

   The contact's record appears.

5. Tap **Add to Favorites**.

   The Add to Favorites dialog box opens.

6. Tap the phone number or email address you want to add to your Favorites list.

   The Add to Favorites as dialog box opens.

7. Tap **Voice Call** to create a favorite for voice calls.

A You can tap **FaceTime** to create a favorite for FaceTime calling.

Note: A star appears next to the item you made a Favorite.

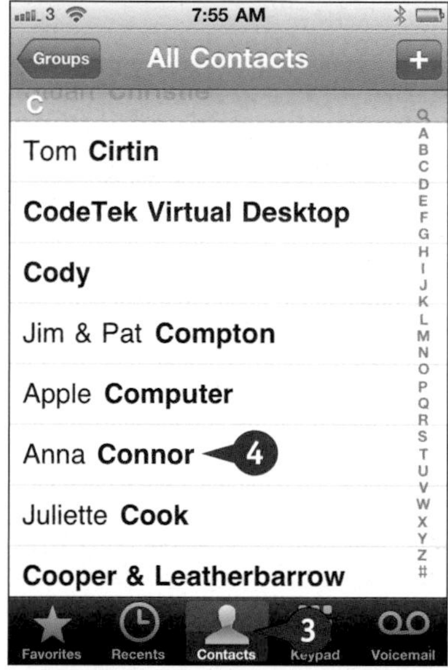

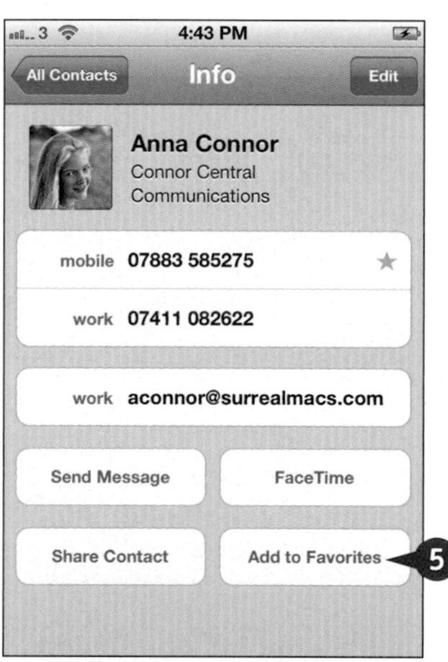

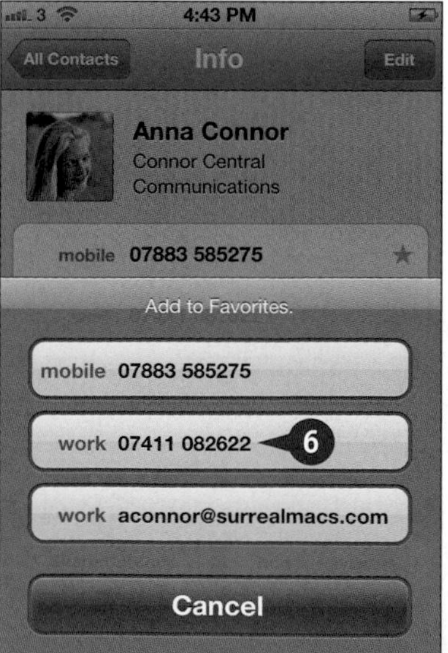

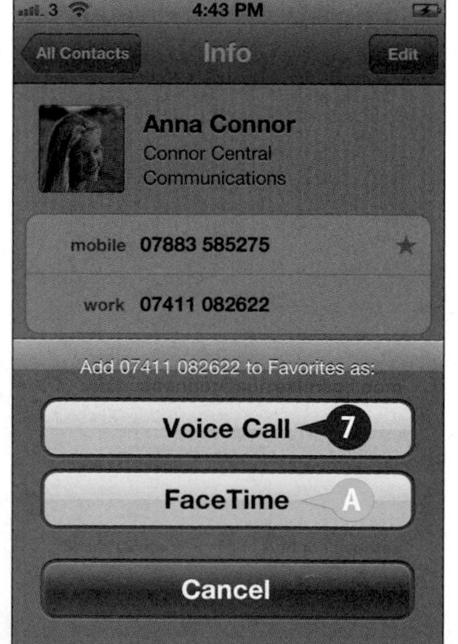

Call a Favorite

1. In the Phone app, tap **Favorites**.

   The Favorites list appears.

2. Tap the Favorite you want to call.

   Your iPhone places the call.

B To display the contact's record, tap ⊙ instead of tapping the contact's button. You can then tap a different phone number for the contact if necessary.

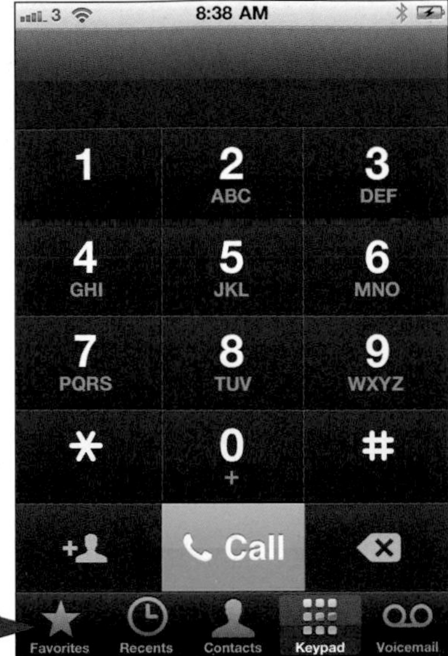

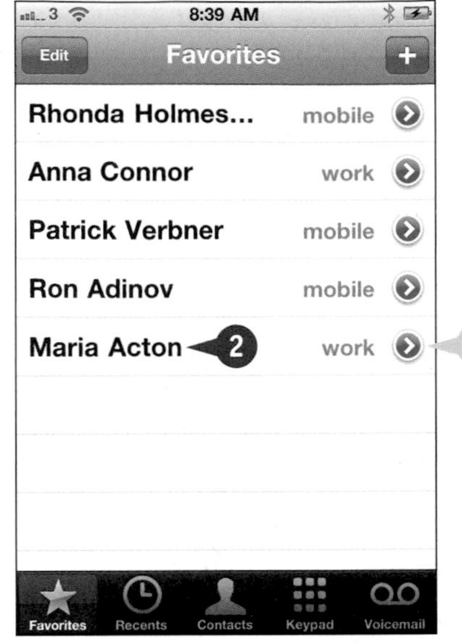

Call a Recent

1. In the Phone app, tap **Recents**.

   The Recents screen appears. Red entries indicate calls you missed.

C Tap **Missed** if you want to see only recent calls you missed.

2. Tap the recent you want to call.

   Your iPhone places the call.

D If you want to clear the Recents list, tap **Clear**. In the dialog box that opens, tap **Clear All Recents**.

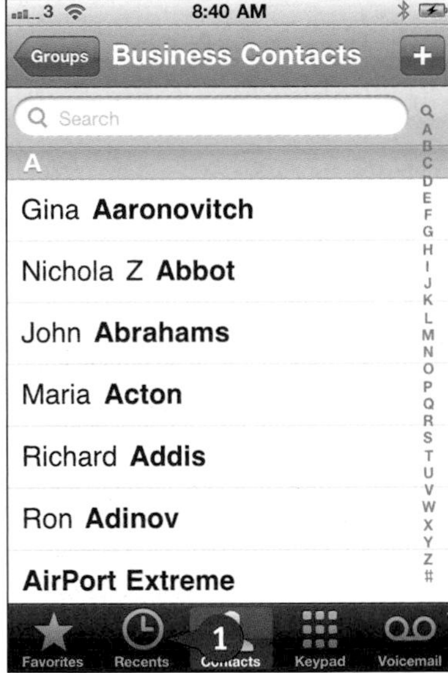

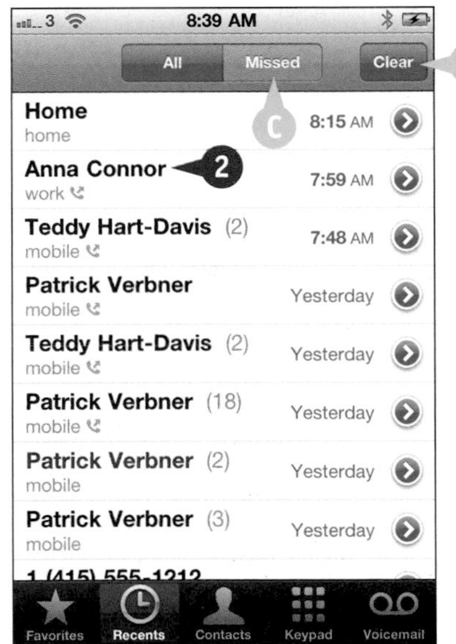

How do I remove a contact from my Favorites?

Tap **Favorites** to display the Favorites list, and then tap **Edit**. Tap ⊖ (A) next to the contact. You can also rearrange your favorites by tapping ≡ (B) and dragging up or down. Tap **Done** (C) when you have finished changing your favorites.

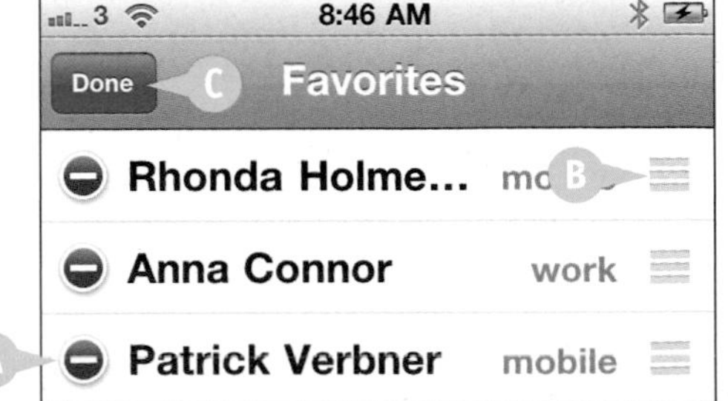

Set Up and Use Visual Voicemail

Your iPhone includes the Visual Voicemail system, which enables you to see a list of your voicemails and listen to those you want to hear instead of having to listen to them all in sequence.

Before you can use Visual Voicemail, you must set it up to work with your iPhone. Normally, recording a custom greeting is a good idea so that callers are certain they have reached the right voicemail box.

Set Up and Use Visual Voicemail

Set Up Visual Voicemail

1. Press the Home button.

   The Home screen appears.

2. Tap **Phone**.

   The Phone app opens.

3. Tap **Voicemail**.

   The first Voicemail screen appears.

   A. A red circle shows that Visual Voicemail is not yet set up.

4. Tap **Set Up Now**.

   The Password screen appears.

5. Type a four-digit password.
6. Tap **Save**.

   The password-confirmation screen appears.

7. Type the same password and tap **Save**.

   The first Greeting screen appears.

8. Tap **Custom**.
9. Tap **Record**.
10. Speak your greeting, and then tap **Stop**.

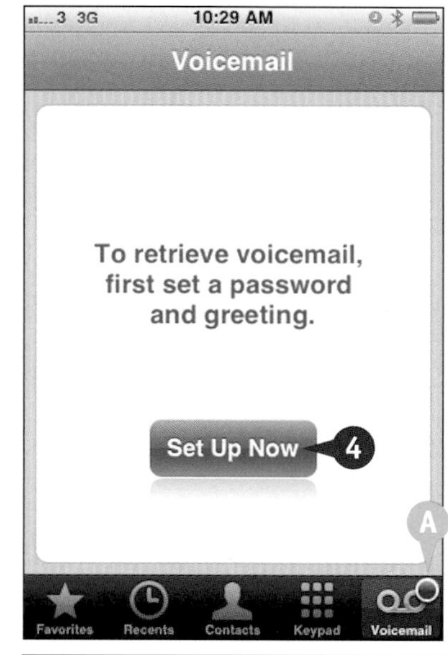

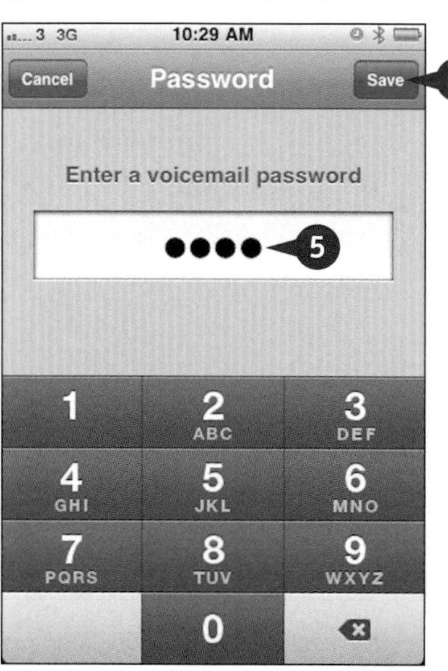

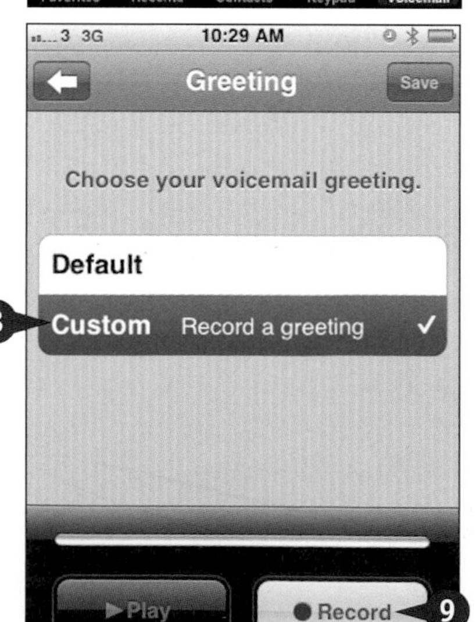

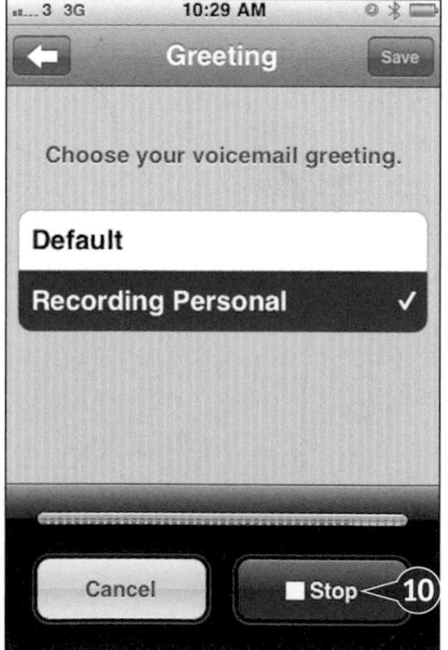

The Play button appears.

11 Tap **Play** and verify that your greeting is as you want it.

B To re-record your greeting, tap **Record**.

12 Tap **Save**.

Voicemail saves the greeting, and then displays the Voicemail screen.

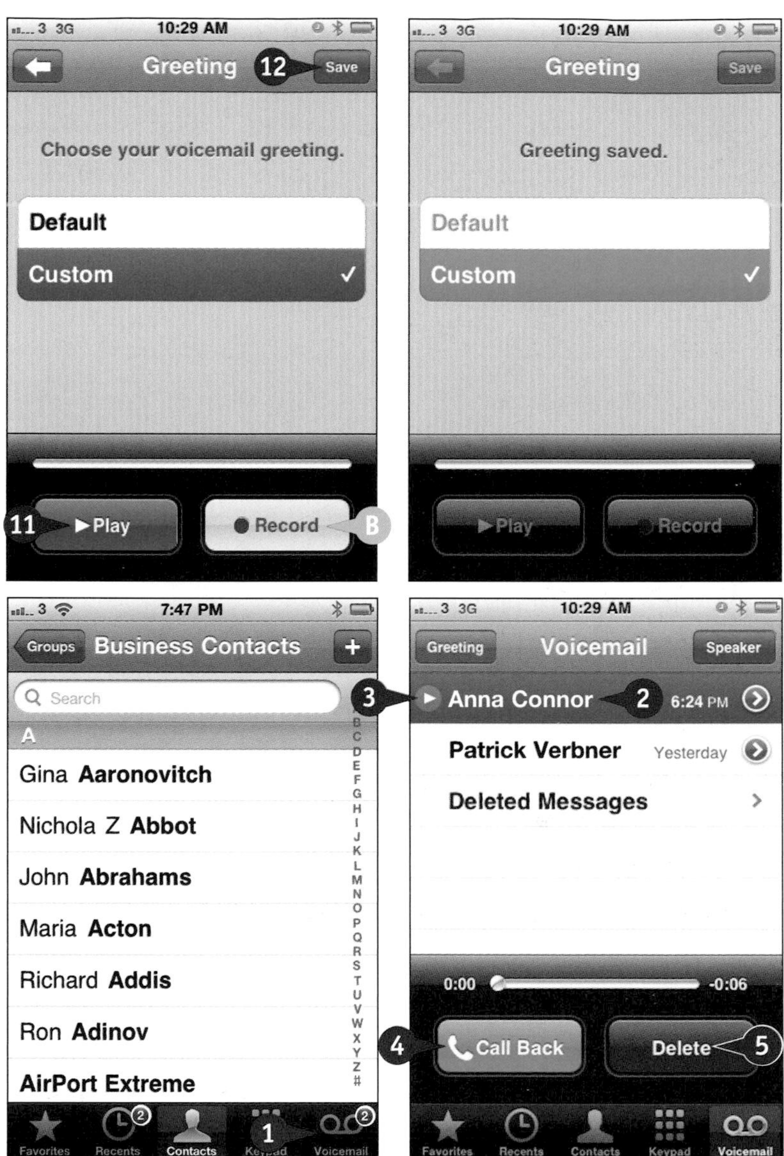

Use Visual Voicemail

1 In the Phone app, tap **Voicemail**.

The Voicemail screen appears.

2 Tap a message to select it.

3 Tap **Play** (▶) to play the message.

4 Tap **Call Back** if you want to call the phone that left the message.

5 Tap **Delete** to delete the message.

TIP

How do I turn on Visual Voicemail rather than regular voicemail?

If your iPhone does not display the Visual Voicemail screen when you tap the Voicemail button, but instead dials a voicemail service, your carrier does not provide Visual Voicemail. In this case, the only way to turn on Visual Voicemail is to switch to a carrier that does provide Visual Voicemail.

Send SMS and MMS Messages

When you need to communicate quickly with another phone user, but do not need to speak to him, you can send an SMS message or MMS message instead. SMS stands for Short Message Service; MMS stands for Multimedia Messaging Service.

An SMS message consists of only text, whereas an MMS message can contain text, videos, photos, sounds, or other data. When you start a message, the Messages app creates it as an SMS message. If you add a photo or video, Messages converts the message to an MMS message.

Send SMS and MMS Messages

1. Press the Home button.

   The Home screen appears.

2. Tap **Messages**.

   The Messages screen appears.

3. Tap **New Message** (✎).

Note: Before sending an SMS or MMS message, it is a good idea to make sure the recipient's phone number can receive such messages. Even some cell phones do not have messaging plans. Typically, you do not receive an alert if the message cannot be delivered.

   The New Message screen appears.

4. Tap ⊕.

   The Contacts list appears.

5. Tap the contact to whose phone you want to send the message.

Note: If the contact's record contains only one phone number, the iPhone adds the contact's name to the New Message screen without displaying the contact's record.

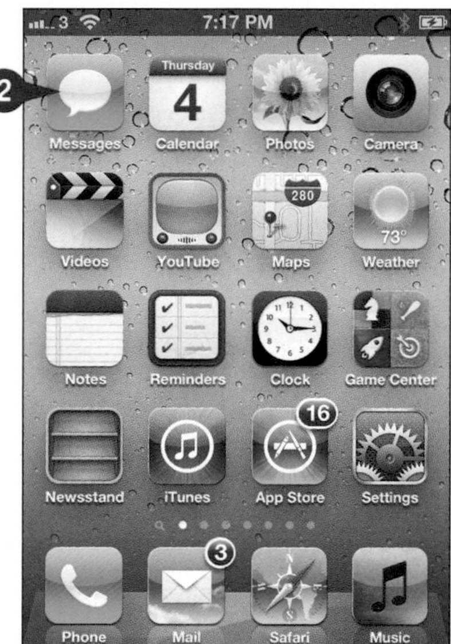

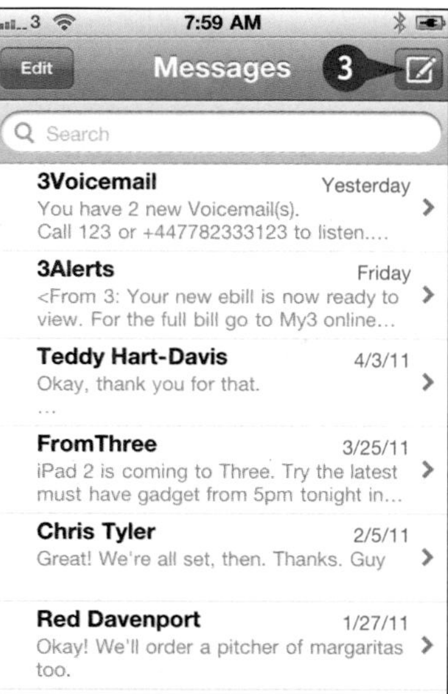

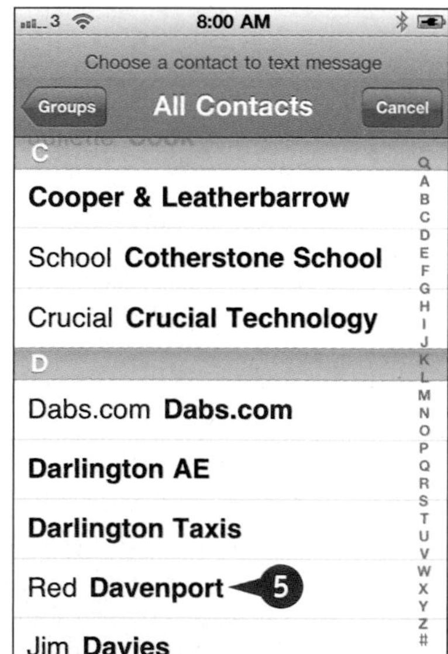

The contact's record opens.

6 Tap the phone number to use.

The contact's name appears in the To field of the New Message screen.

7 Tap in the text field, and then type your message.

8 To add a photo, tap .

9 In the dialog box that opens, tap **Choose Existing**. In this dialog box, you can tap **Take Photo or Video** to take a photo or video with the camera, and then send it with the message.

The Photo Albums screen appears.

10 Tap the album that contains the photo.

The album opens.

11 Tap the photo.

The photo opens.

12 Tap **Choose**.

The photo appears in the message.

Note: You can attach another photo or video by repeating steps **8** to **12**.

13 Tap **Send**.

The Messages app sends the message.

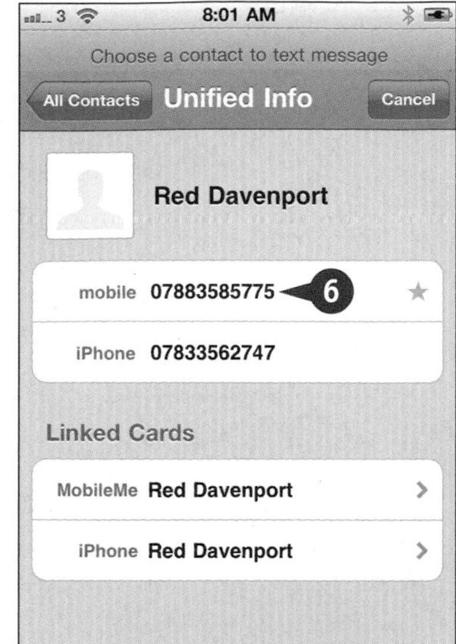

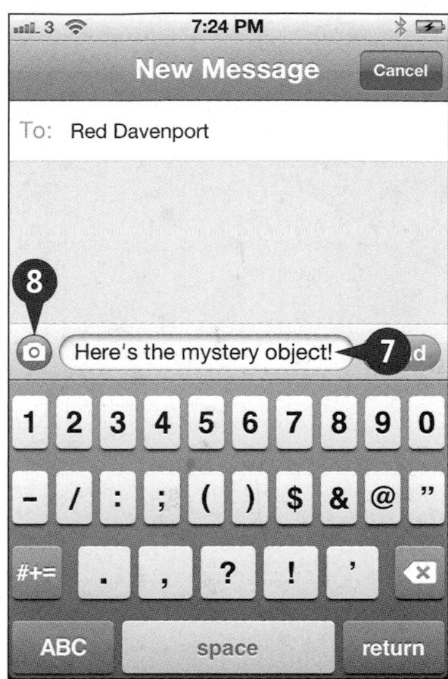

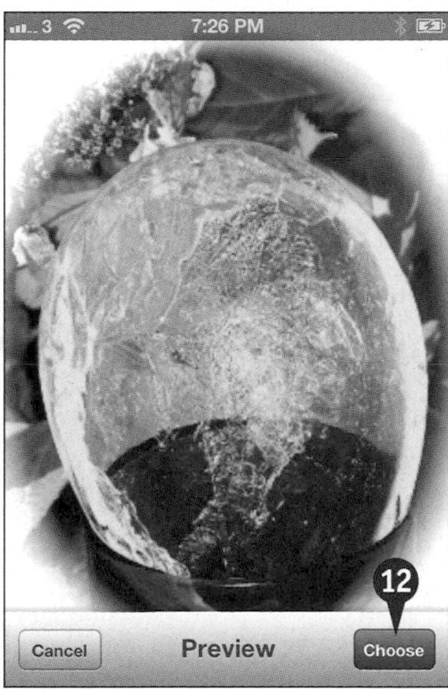

TIP

Is there another way to send a photo or video?

Yes. You can start from the Camera app or the Photos app. This way of sending a photo or video is handy when you are taking photos or videos or you are browsing your photos or videos. Tap the photo or video you want to share, and then tap . In the dialog box that opens, tap **MMS**. Your iPhone starts an MMS message containing the photo or video. You can then address and send the message.

Chat Face to Face Using FaceTime

By using your iPhone's FaceTime feature, you can enjoy video chats with any of your contacts who have an iPhone 4 or iPhone 4S, an iPad 2, a fourth-generation iPod touch, or the FaceTime for Mac application.

To make a FaceTime call, your iPhone must be connected to a wireless network, as must the device your contact is using. You and your contact must both have Apple IDs.

Chat Face to Face Using FaceTime

Receive a FaceTime Call

1. When your iPhone receives a FaceTime request, and the screen shows who is calling, aim the camera at your face, and then tap and drag the slider to answer.

   The Connecting screen appears.

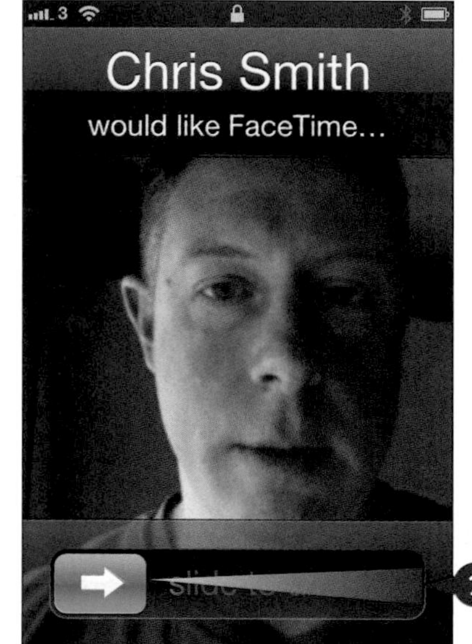

   When the connection is established, your iPhone displays the caller full screen, with your video inset.

2. Start your conversation.
3. If you need to mute your microphone, tap **Mute** (🎙).

Ⓐ The background behind the Mute icon turns blue, and the Mute icon appears on your inset video.

4. Tap **Mute** (🎙) when you want to turn muting off again.
5. Tap **End** when you are ready to end the FaceTime call.

Make a FaceTime Call

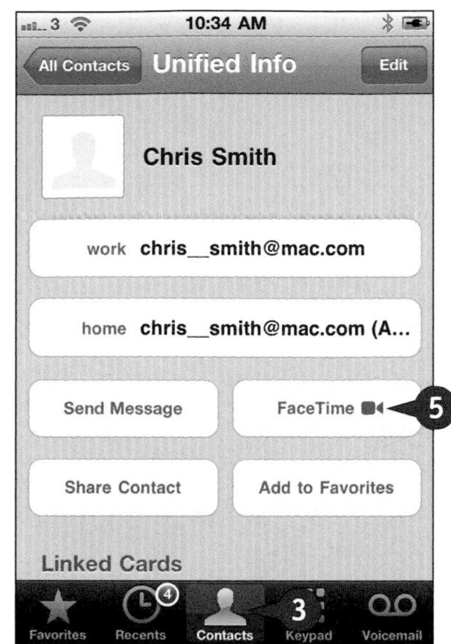

1. Press the Home button.

   The Home screen appears.

2. Tap **Phone**.

   The Phone app opens.

3. Tap **Contacts**.

   The Contacts list appears.

4. Tap the contact you want to call with FaceTime.

   The contact's record opens.

5. Tap **FaceTime**.

   The Phone app starts a FaceTime call.

6. When your contact answers, smile and speak.

7. If you need to show your contact something using the rear-facing camera, tap **Switch Cameras** (icon).

   B Your inset video shows the picture that is being sent to your contact.

8. When you need to switch back to showing yourself, tap **Switch Cameras** (icon).

9. When you are ready to end the call, tap **End**.

TIP

Are there other ways of starting a FaceTime call?

Yes. You can start a FaceTime call in either of these ways:

- During a phone call, tap the **FaceTime** icon.
- In the Contacts app, tap the contact to display the contact record, and then tap **FaceTime**.

Share Contacts via Email and MMS

Most likely, you will often need to share contact information with other people. From your Contacts list, you can quickly start an email message or an MMS message with a contact's record attached. The recipient can then import the contact's record into his or her contact-management application.

Similarly, when someone sends you a contact record, you can instantly add it to your Contacts list.

Share Contacts via Email and MMS

Open the Contact You Want to Share

1. Press the Home button.

   The Home screen appears.

2. Tap **Utilities**.

   The Utilities folder opens.

3. Tap **Contacts**.

   The Contacts app appears.

A. If you need to switch to a particular group of contacts, tap **Groups**. On the Groups screen, tap the group you want.

4. Tap the contact you want to share.

   The contact record opens.

5. If the contact record is long, tap and drag up to scroll down.

6. Tap **Share Contact**.

   The Share Contact Using dialog box opens.

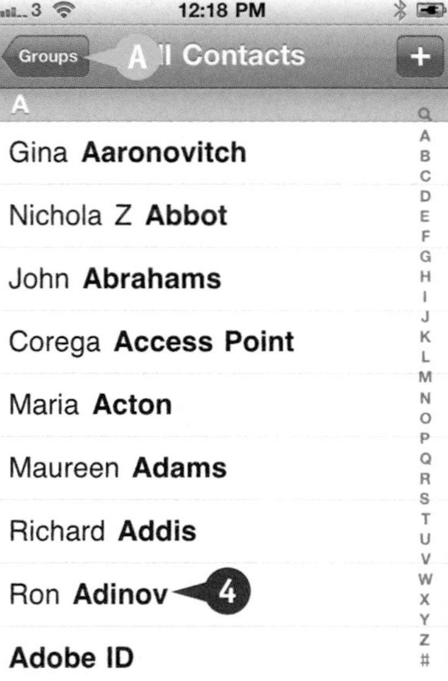

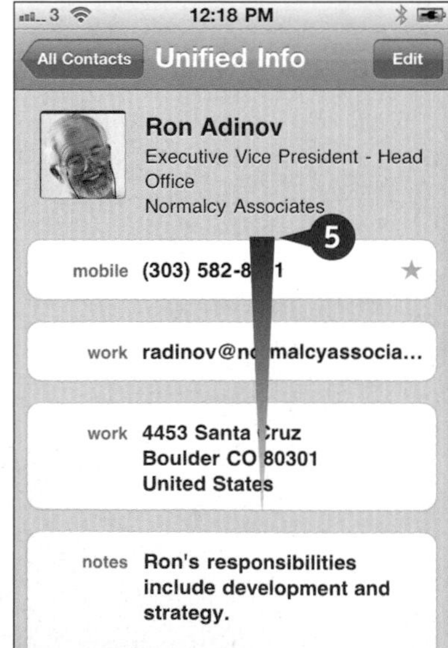

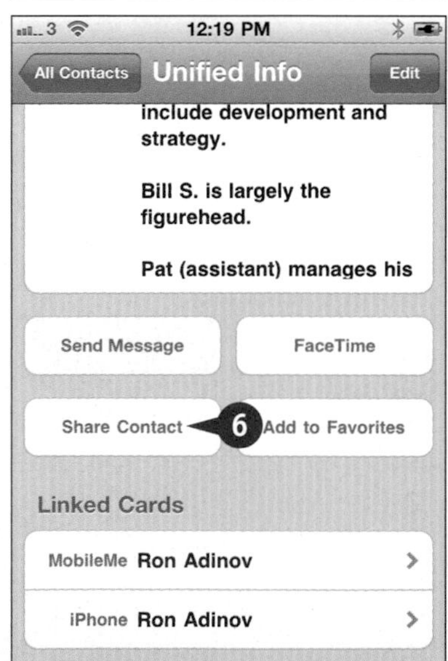

Share the Contact via Email

1. In the Share Contact Using dialog box, tap **Email**.

   B A new email message in the Mail app appears with the contact record attached.

2. Address the email message.
3. Type a subject in place of the default text, Contact.
4. Type any text needed.
5. Tap **Send**.
6. In the Photo Size dialog box that opens, tap the size of photo you want to send.

   Mail sends the message.

Share the Contact via MMS

1. In the Share Contact Using dialog box, tap **MMS**.

   C A new MMS message in the Messages app appears with the contact record attached.

2. Address the MMS message.
3. Type any text needed.
4. Tap **Send**.

   The Messages app sends the message.

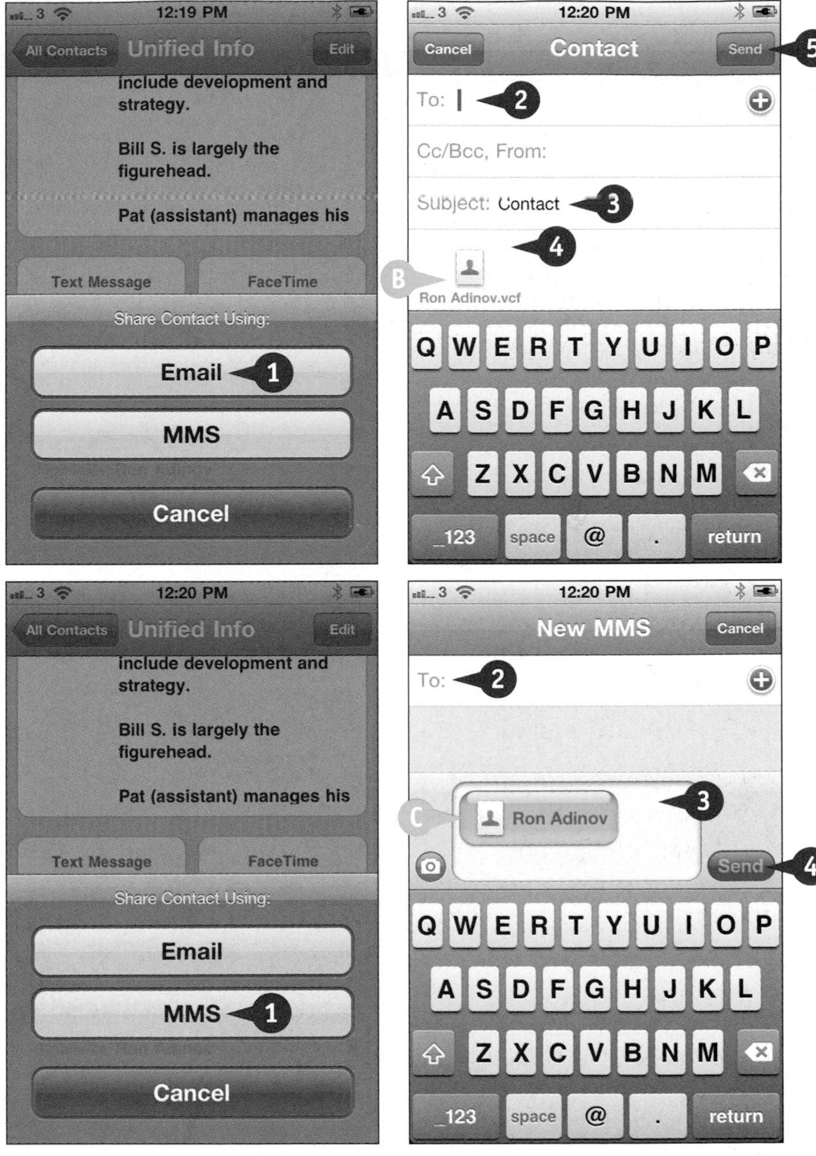

TIP

How do I add a contact record I receive to my Contacts list?

Tap the contact record in the email message or MMS message to display the Info screen. You can then tap **Create New Contact** to create a new contact from the contact record. If the contact record contains extra information for one of your existing contacts, tap **Add to Existing Contact**, and then tap the contact.

CHAPTER 6

Networking with Cellular and Wi-Fi

Your iPhone connects to a cellular network for phone calls and data. You can also connect it to wireless networks and Wi-Fi hotspots.

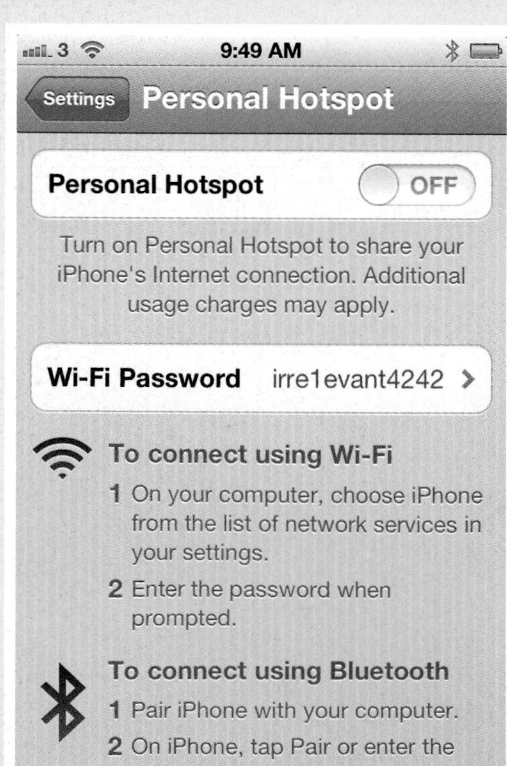

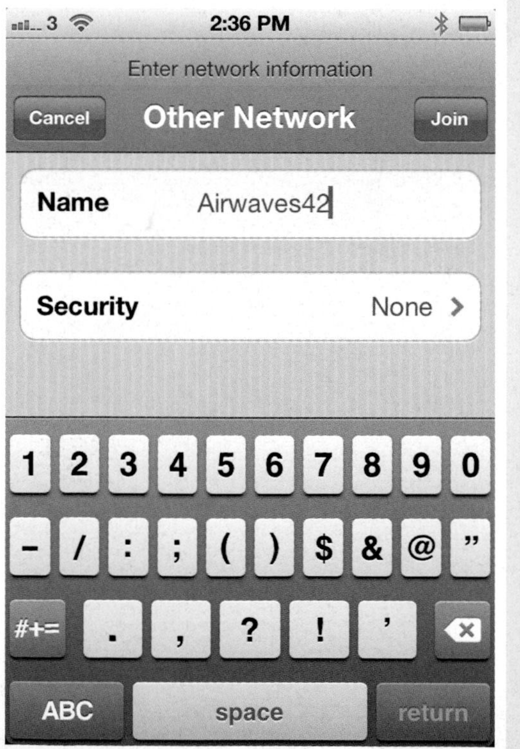

Turn Cellular and Wi-Fi Access On and Off

Normally, you will want to keep your iPhone connected to the cellular network so that you can make or receive phone calls and access the Internet. But when you do not need or may not use the cellular network, you can turn on the iPhone's Airplane Mode feature to cut off all connections.

Turning on Airplane Mode turns off Wi-Fi connections as well. But you can also turn Wi-Fi on and off separately when you need to.

Turn Cellular and Wi-Fi Access On and Off

1. Press the Home button.

   The Home screen appears.

2. Tap **Settings**.

   The Settings screen appears.

3. To turn Airplane Mode on, tap the **Airplane Mode** switch and move it to the On position.

Note: When your iPhone has a wireless network connection, it uses that connection instead of the cellular connection. This helps keep down your cellular network usage.

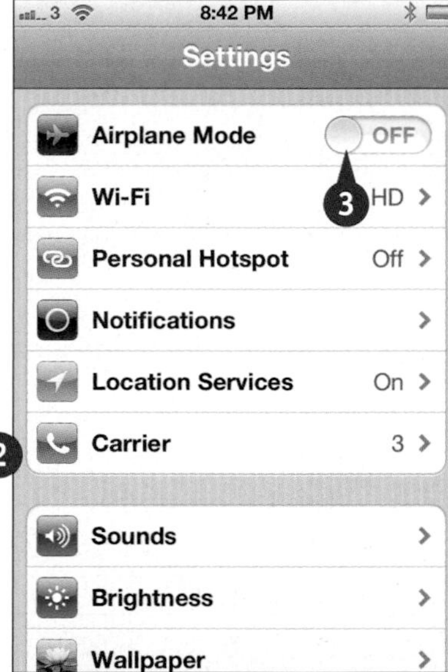

A. The iPhone turns off all cellular and Wi-Fi connections. An airplane icon appears in the status bar.

4. To turn on Wi-Fi, tap **Wi-Fi**.

   The Wi-Fi Networks screen appears.

5. Tap the **Wi-Fi** switch and move it to the On position.

   The list of available networks appears, and you can connect as described later in this chapter.

Monitor Your Cellular Network Usage

Most iPhone contracts include a certain amount of cellular network usage every month. If you use your iPhone extensively, you may need to monitor your usage of the cellular network to avoid incurring extra charges.

Monitor Your Cellular Network Usage

1. Press the Home button.

   The Home screen appears.

2. Tap **Settings**.

   The Settings screen appears.

3. Tap **General**.

   The General screen appears.

4. Tap **Usage**.

   The Usage screen appears.

5. Scroll down to the bottom of the screen.

A. The Usage readout shows your total phone usage since the last full charge.

6. Tap **Cellular Usage**.

   The Cellular Usage screen appears.

B. The Call Time box shows your phone usage.

C. The Cellular Network Data box shows how much data you have sent and received.

Note: To reset your usage statistics, tap **Reset Statistics** at the bottom of the Usage screen.

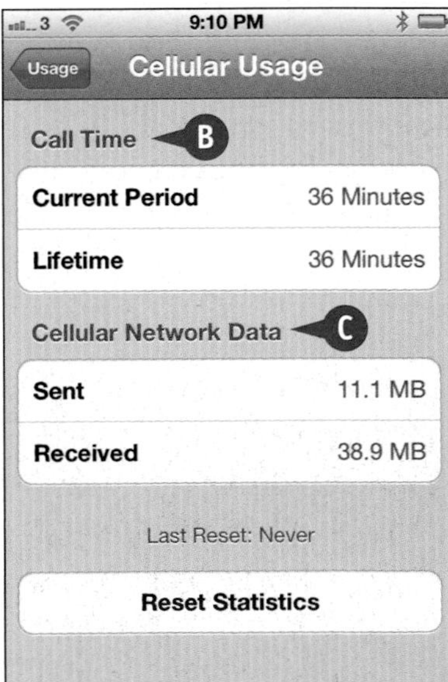

Connect Your iPhone to a Different Carrier

Your iPhone's SIM card makes it connect automatically to a particular carrier's network, such as the AT&T network or the Verizon network. When you go outside your carrier's network, you can connect the iPhone manually to a different carrier's network — for example, when you travel abroad.

To connect to a different carrier's network, you may need to set up an account with that carrier or pay extra charges to your standard carrier.

Connect Your iPhone to a Different Carrier

1. Press the Home button.

   The Home screen appears.

2. Tap **Settings**.

   The Settings screen appears.

3. Tap **Carrier**.

   The Network Selection screen appears.

4. Tap the **Automatic** switch and move it to Off.

   The list of available carriers appears.

5. Tap the carrier you want to use.

A. A check mark appears next to the carrier.

Note: When you want to switch back to your regular carrier, move the **Automatic** switch on the Network Selection screen to On.

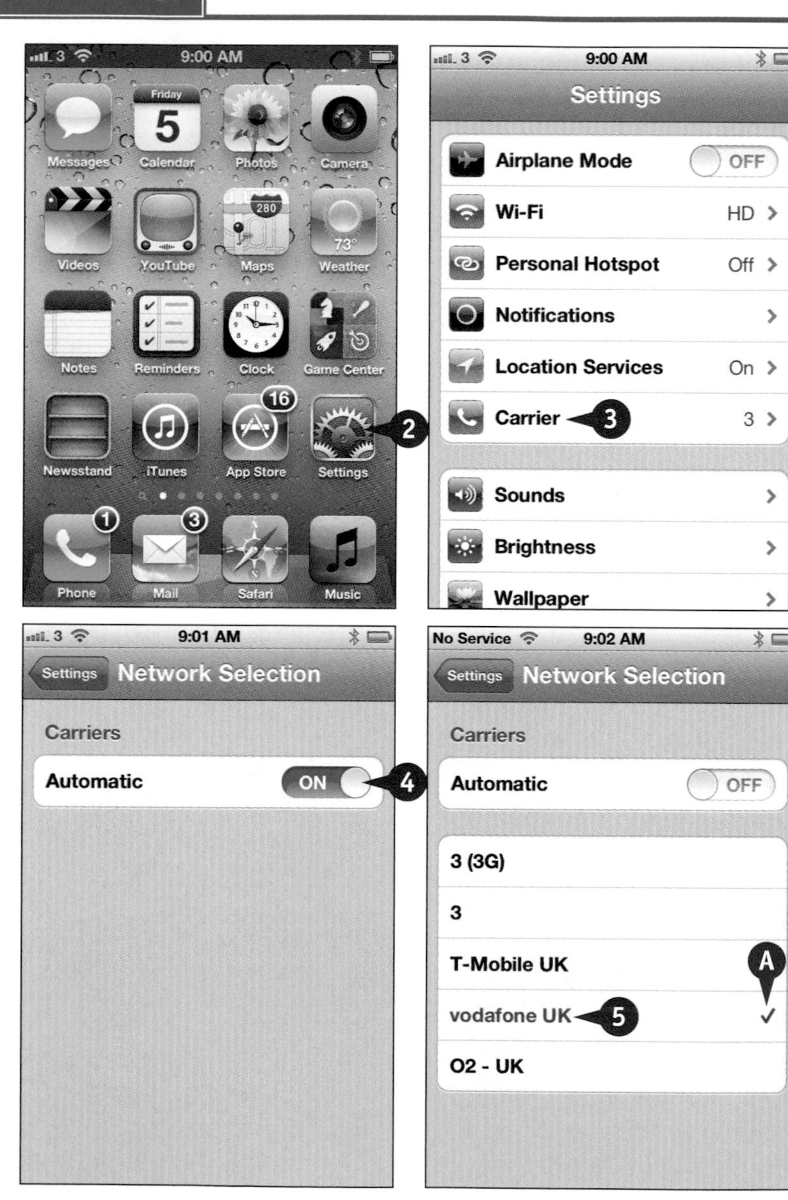

Turn Data Roaming On or Off

When you need to use your iPhone in a location where your carrier does not provide Internet service, you can turn on the iPhone's Data Roaming feature. Data roaming enables you to access the Internet using other carriers' networks. You can incur extra charges when using data roaming, especially when you use it abroad. For this reason, you may prefer to keep data roaming off most of the time and turn it on only when you need it. Normally, you will want to use data roaming only when no wireless network connection is available.

Turn Data Roaming On or Off

1. Press the Home button.

   The Home screen appears.

2. Tap **Settings**.

   The Settings screen appears.

3. Scroll down to the third box, and then tap **General**.

The General screen appears.

4. Tap **Network**.

   The Network screen appears.

A. On the Network screen, you can also turn off cellular data altogether by tapping the **Cellular Data** switch and moving it to Off.

5. Tap the **Data Roaming** switch and move it to On.

Note: When you need to turn data roaming off again, tap the **Data Roaming** switch on the Network screen and move it to Off.

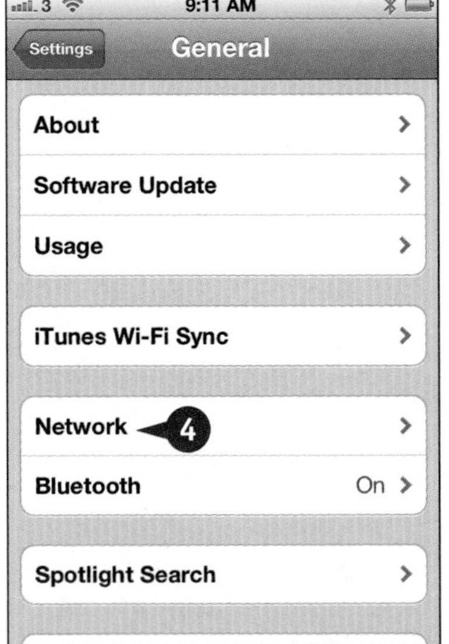

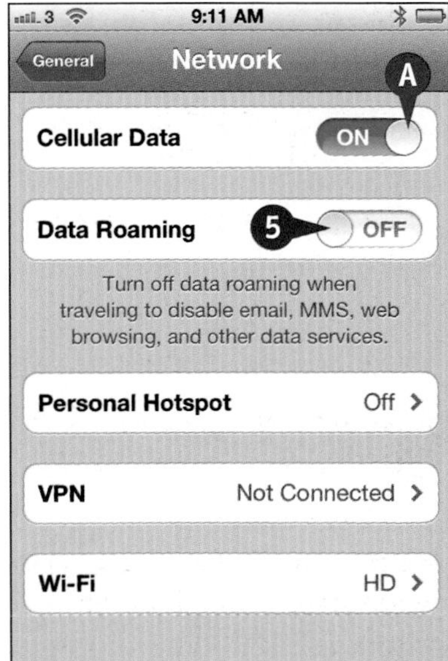

Connect Bluetooth Devices to Your iPhone

To extend your iPhone's functionality, you can connect devices to it that communicate using the wireless Bluetooth technology.

For example, you can connect a Bluetooth headset and microphone so that you can listen to music and make and take phone calls. Or you can connect a Bluetooth keyboard so that you can quickly type email messages, notes, or documents.

Connect Bluetooth Devices to Your iPhone

Set Up a Bluetooth Device

1. Press the Home button.

   The Home screen appears.

2. Tap **Settings**.

   The Settings screen appears.

3. Tap **General**.

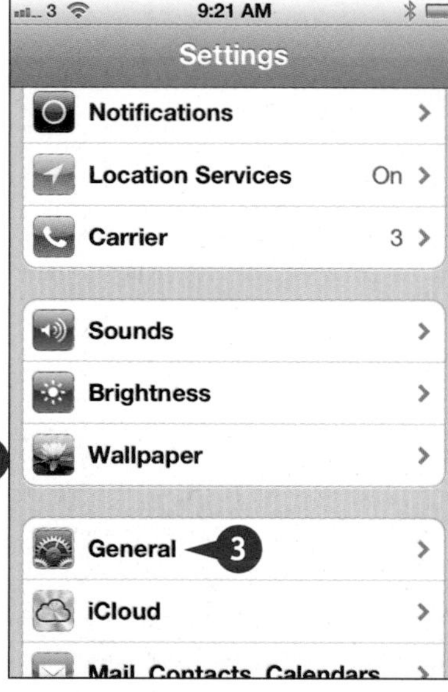

   The General screen appears.

4. Tap **Bluetooth**.

   The Bluetooth screen appears.

5. Tap the **Bluetooth** slider and move it to On.

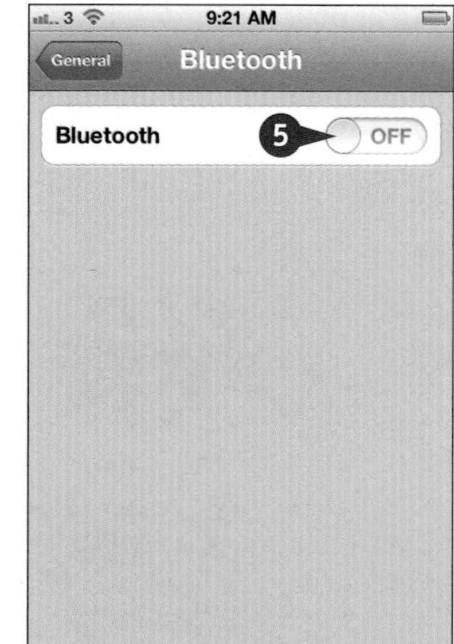

The Devices list appears, and the iPhone scans for Bluetooth devices.

6 Turn on the Bluetooth device and make it discoverable.

Note: Read the Bluetooth device's instructions to find out how to make the device discoverable via Bluetooth.

A The Bluetooth device appears in the Devices list, marked Not Paired.

7 Tap the device's button.

The iPhone pairs with the device, and then connects to it.

B The Devices list shows the device as Connected.

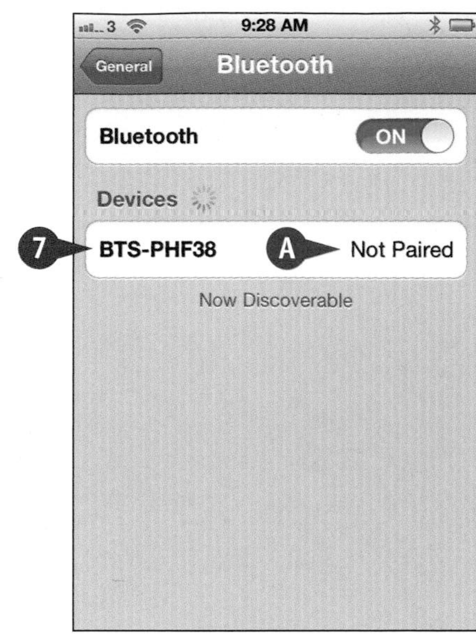

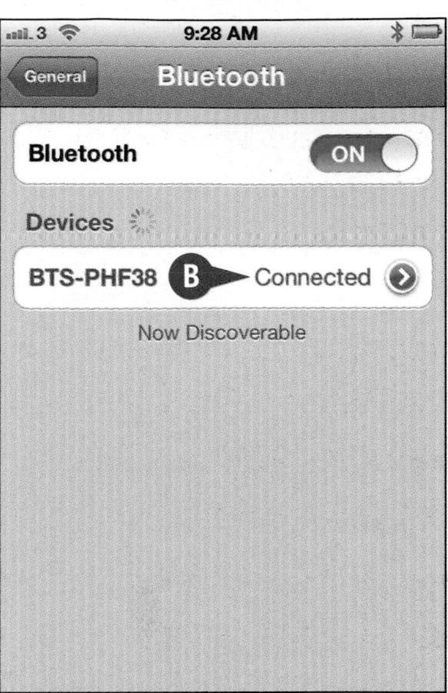

Choose the Device for Playing Audio or Taking a Call

1 When you start playing music or receive a phone call, your iPhone displays a dialog box for choosing which device to use. Touch the button for the device you want.

TIP

How do I stop using a Bluetooth device?

When you no longer need to use a particular Bluetooth device, tell your iPhone to forget it. Press the Home button, tap **Settings**, and then tap **General**. On the General screen, tap **Bluetooth**, and then tap the device's ⊙ button. On the device's screen, tap **Forget This Device**, and then tap **Forget Device** in the confirmation dialog box.

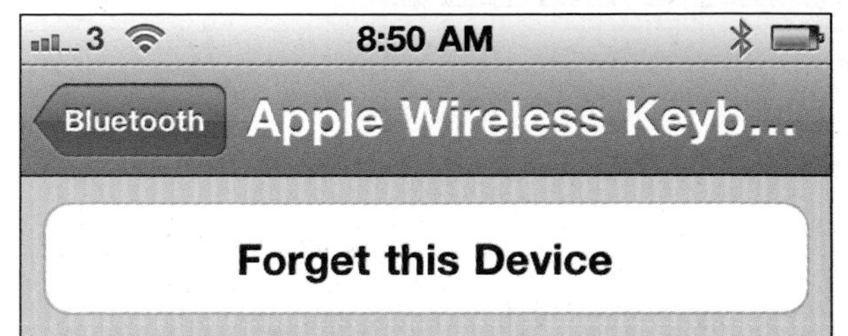

Share Your iPhone's Internet Access Using Personal Hotspot

Your iPhone can not only access the Internet itself from anywhere it has a suitable connection to the cell network, but it can also share that Internet access with your computer. This feature is called Personal Hotspot.

For you to use Personal Hotspot, your iPhone's carrier must permit you to use it. Most carriers charge an extra fee per month on top of the standard iPhone charge.

Share Your iPhone's Internet Access Using Personal Hotspot

Set Up Personal Hotspot

1. Press the Home button.

   The Home screen appears.

2. Tap **Settings**.

   The Settings screen appears.

3. Tap **Personal Hotspot**.

The Personal Hotspot screen appears.

4. Tap **Wi-Fi Password**.

   The Wi-Fi Password screen appears.

5. Tap ⊗ to clear the default password.

6. Type the password you want to use.

7. Tap **Done**.

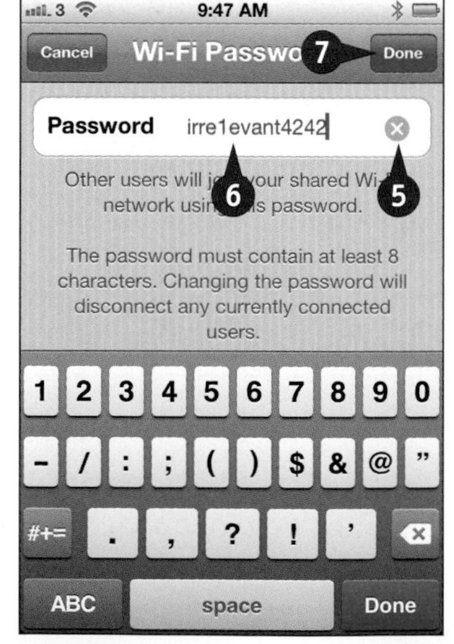

The Personal Hotspot screen appears again.

8 Tap the **Personal Hotspot** switch and move it to On.

The Personal Hotspot screen shows the message Now Discoverable and displays information for connecting computers and devices to the hotspot.

Note: When the Personal Hotspot is active — when a computer or device is using the connection — Personal Hotspot appears in a blue bar across the lock screen and the Home screen to remind you. The bar shows the number of connections.

You can now connect your PC or Mac to the iPhone's Internet connection.

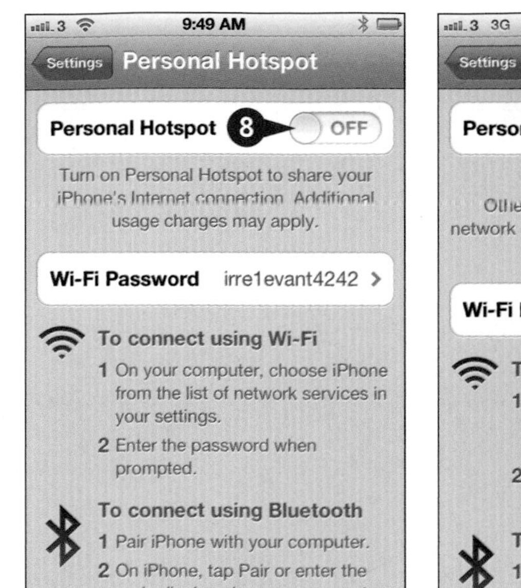

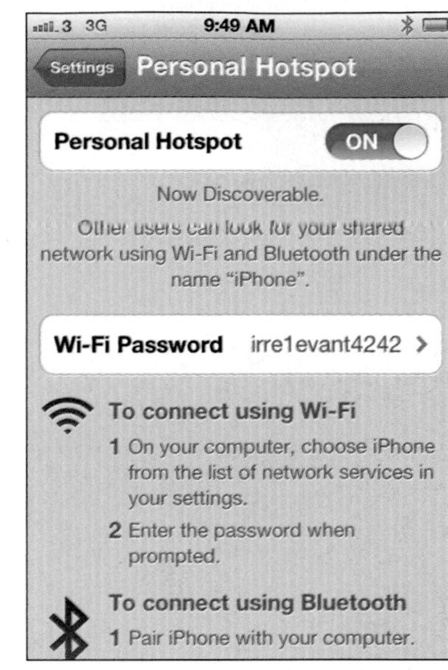

Connect a PC to the Personal Hotspot via USB

1 Turn on Personal Hotspot as described earlier.

2 Connect the iPhone to the PC via USB.

Windows detects the iPhone's Internet connection as a new network connection and installs it.

The Driver Software Installation dialog box opens.

3 Click **Close**.

The Set Network Location dialog box opens.

4 Click **Home network** or **Public network**, as appropriate.

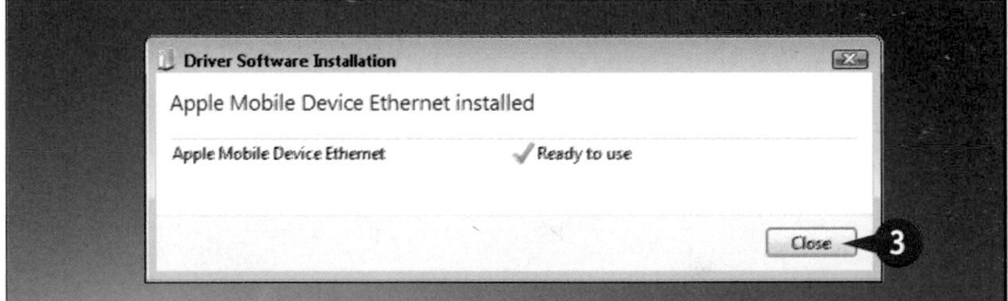

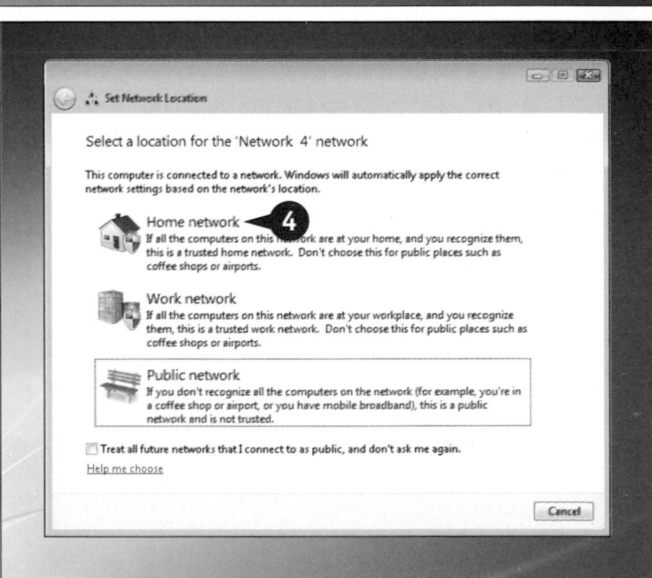

continued ►

Share Your iPhone's Internet Access Using Personal Hotspot (continued)

You can connect up to five computers or other devices, such as iPads or other tablet computers, to the Internet by using Personal Hotspot on your iPhone. Because the devices share the connection, the more devices you use, the slower the connection speed will appear to be on each device. Connecting more devices will also typically increase the amount of data transferred across the iPhone's Internet connection and so consume your data allowance faster.

Share Your iPhone's Internet Access Using Personal Hotspot (continued)

The Set Network Location dialog box updates its screen.

5 Click **Close**.

Your PC starts using the iPhone's Internet connection.

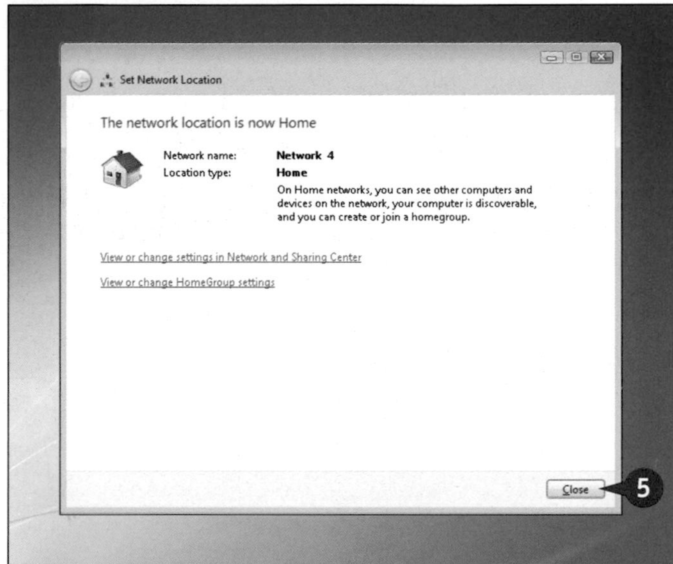

Connect a Mac via Personal Hotspot

1 Turn on Personal Hotspot as described earlier.

2 Connect the iPhone to the Mac via USB.

The A New Network Interface Has Been Detected dialog box opens.

3 Click **Network Preferences.**

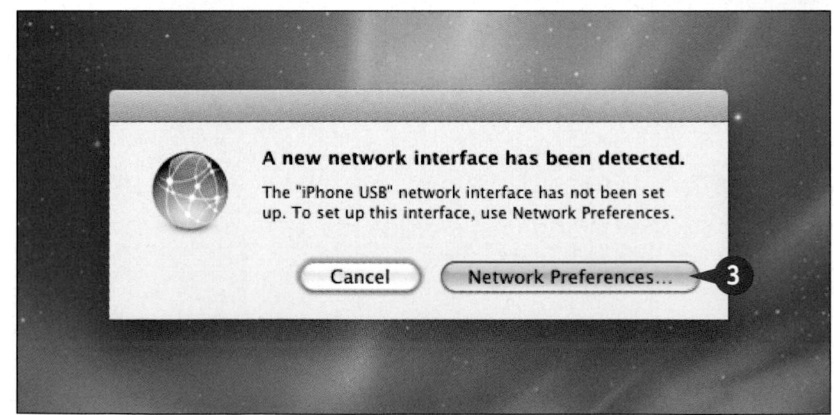

The Network preferences pane of System Preferences opens.

4 Click **iPhone USB**.

5 Click **Apply**.

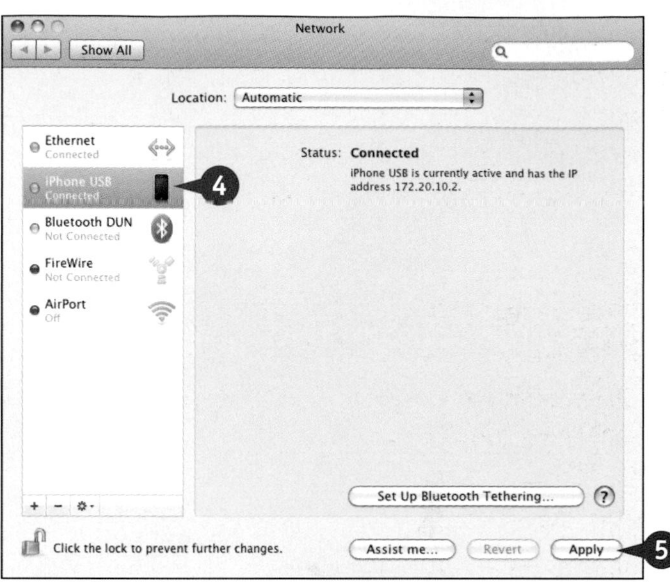

Stop Using Personal Hotspot

1 Display the Personal Hotspot screen by following steps **1** to **3** under the heading "Set Up Personal Hotspot" on the left page of the previous spread.

2 Tap the **Personal Hotspot** switch and move it to Off.

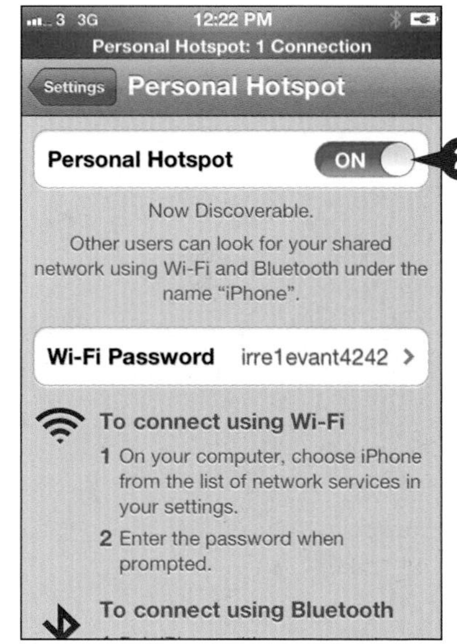

TIP

Can I use Personal Hotspot as my main Internet connection?

Yes. But make sure that your data plan provides enough data for your computer use as well as your iPhone use. If it does not, you may incur extra charges, and you will do better to use Personal Hotspot only when your main Internet connection is not available.

The Internet connection speeds you get from a connection to your iPhone's Personal Hotspot are usually slower than a broadband Internet connection such as a DSL or cable connection. But if your Internet use is light, you may find these speeds adequate.

Connect to Wi-Fi Networks

Your iPhone can connect to the Internet either via the cell phone network or via a Wi-Fi network. To conserve your data allowance, use a Wi-Fi network rather than the cell phone network whenever you can.

The first time you connect to a Wi-Fi network, you must provide the network's password. After that, the iPhone stores the password, so you can connect to the network without entering the password again.

Connect to Wi-Fi Networks

1. Press the Home button.

   The Home screen appears.

A. The Wi-Fi signal icon (📶) in the status bar and on the Wi-Fi Networks screen shows the strength of the Wi-Fi signal. The more bars that appear, the stronger the signal is.

2. Tap **Settings**.

   The Settings screen appears.

3. Tap **Wi-Fi**.

The Wi-Fi screen appears.

4. Tap the **Wi-Fi** switch and move it to On.

   The Choose a Network list appears. A lock icon (🔒) indicates the network has security such as a password.

5. Tap the network you want to connect to.

Note: If the network does not have a password, your iPhone connects to it without prompting you for a password.

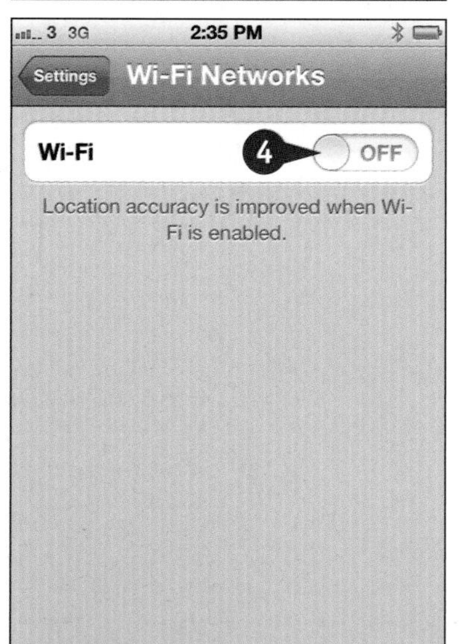

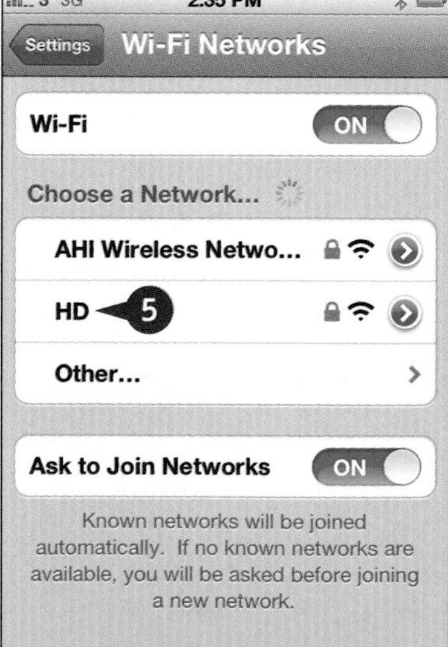

6 On the Enter Password screen, type the password.

7 Tap **Join**.

Your iPhone connects to the wireless network.

B The Wi-Fi Networks screen appears again, showing a check mark next to the network the iPhone has connected to.

Note: To stop your iPhone from connecting to a particular wireless network, tap ⊙ to the right of the network's name on the Wi-Fi Networks screen. On the network's screen, tap **Forget this Network**. In the dialog box that opens, tap **Forget**.

8 Tap **Settings**.

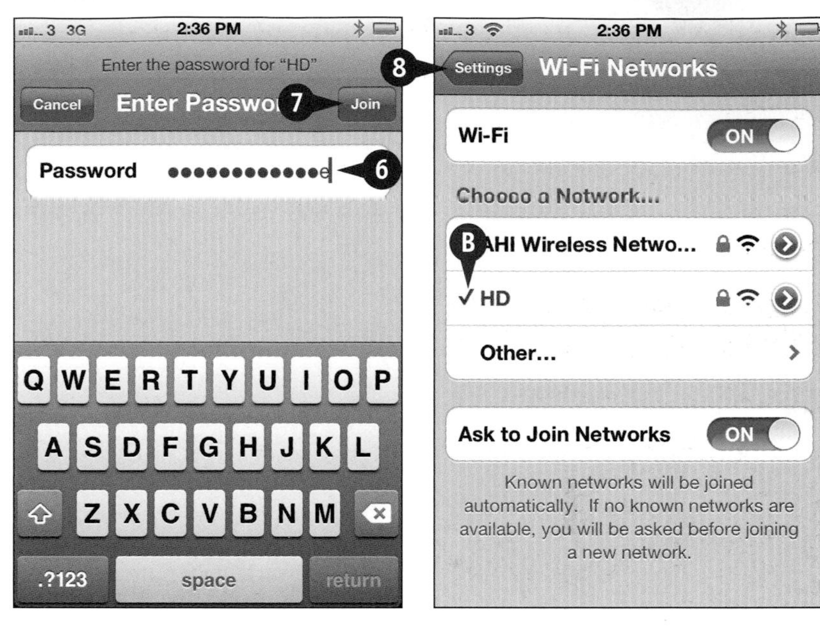

TIP

How do I connect to a network not listed on the Wi-Fi Networks screen?

If a wireless network is not broadcasting its network name, the network does not appear on the Wi-Fi Networks screen. Follow these steps:

1 From the Wi-Fi Networks screen, tap **Other**.

2 On the Other Network screen, type the network name.

3 Tap **Security**.

4 On the Security screen, tap the security type — for example, **WPA2**.

5 Tap **Other Network**.

6 Type the password in the Password box on the Other Network screen.

7 Tap **Join**.

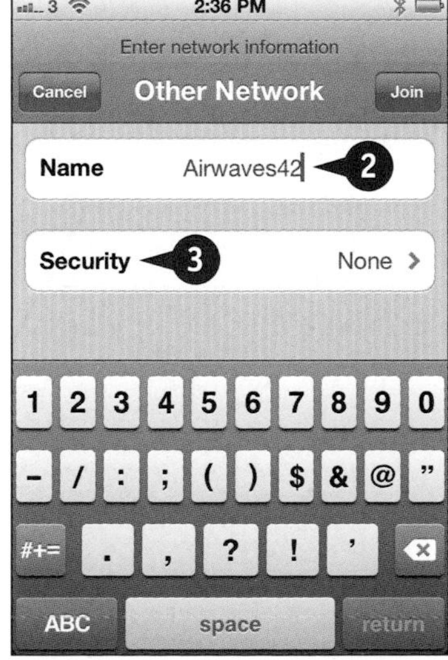

Log into Wi-Fi Hotspots

When you are in town or on the road, you can log in to Wi-Fi hotspots to enjoy fast Internet access without using your iPhone's data allowance.

You can find Wi-Fi hotspots at many locations, including coffee shops and restaurants, hotels, and airports. Some municipal areas, and even some parks and highway rest stops, also provide public Wi-Fi. Some Wi-Fi hotspots charge for access, whereas others are free to use.

Log into Wi-Fi Hotspots

1. Press the Home button.

   The Home screen appears.

2. Tap **Settings**.

   The Settings screen appears.

3. Tap **Wi-Fi**.

The Wi-Fi screen appears.

4. Tap the **Wi-Fi** switch and move it to On.

   The list of wireless networks appears.

5. Tap the Wi-Fi hotspot you want to join.

Note: If the iPhone prompts you to enter a username and password, enter those the hotspot operator has given you. Most Wi-Fi hotspots use a login page rather than a username and password.

A The iPhone joins the hotspot. The Wi-Fi Networks screen displays a check mark next to the hotspot.

6 If Safari opens and displays a login page, type the login information for the hotspot, and then tap the button for logging in.

After connecting to the hotspot, you can use the Internet. For example, you can browse the web using Safari or send and receive email using the Mail app.

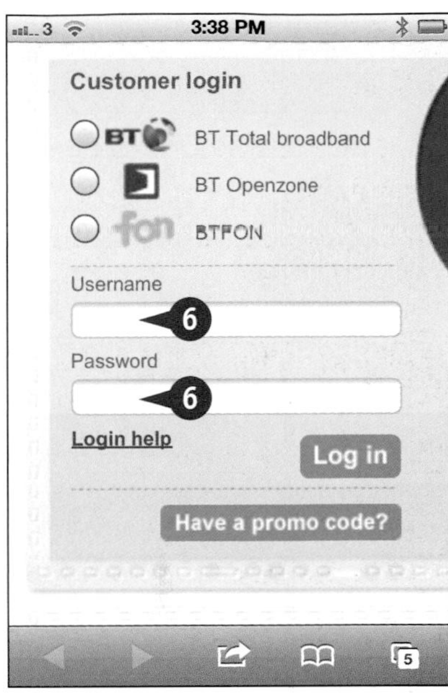

TIP

What precautions should I take when using Wi-Fi hotspots?

The main danger is that you may connect to a malevolent network.

To stay safe, connect only to hotspots provided by reputable establishments — for example, national hotel chains or restaurant chains — rather than hotspots run by unknown operators.

When you finish using a Wi-Fi hotspot that you do not plan to use again, tell the iPhone to forget the network using the technique described in the previous task.

Forgetting the network avoids this problem: After you have connected the iPhone to a wireless network, it will connect to another network that has the same name, security type, and password, even if that network is not the same network. This feature normally saves time, but it also enables an imposter to set up a fake hotspot that pretends to be a genuine hotspot you have previously used.

CHAPTER 7

Working with Apps

In this chapter, you first learn to customize the Home screen, putting the icons you need most right to hand and organizing them into folders. You then grasp how to use multitasking to keep multiple apps running at once, how to find the apps you need on Apple's App Store, and how to update and remove apps. You also learn to install apps provided by an administrator.

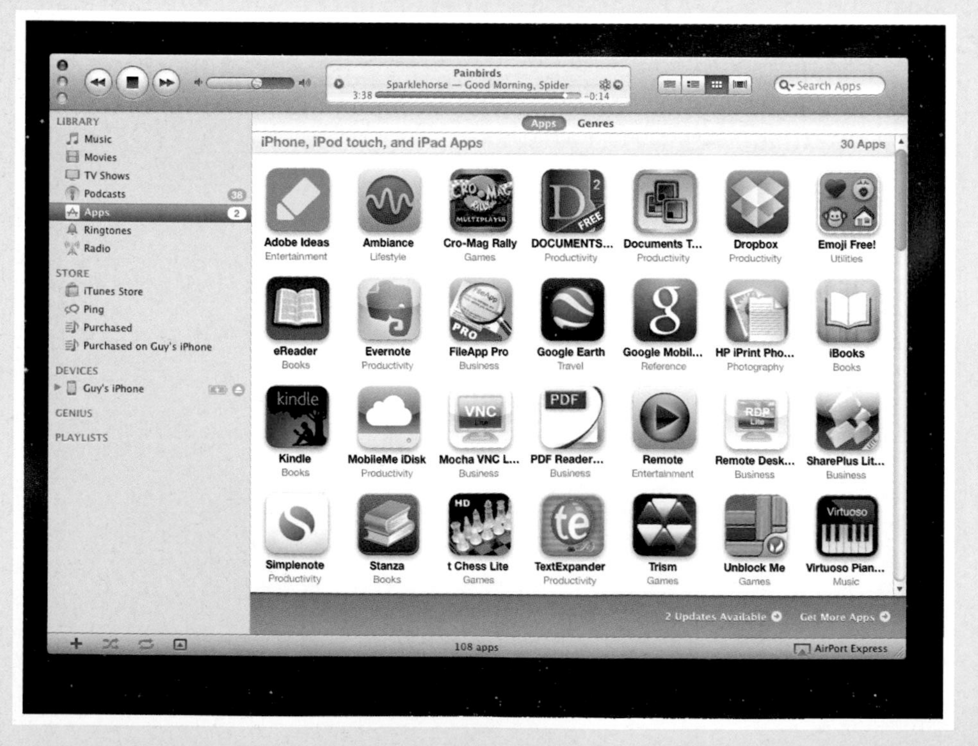

Customize the Home Screen

From the Home screen, you run the apps on the iPhone. You can customize the Home screen to put the apps you use most frequently within easy reach. When the first Home screen fills up with icons, the iPhone adds further Home screens automatically and puts on them apps you add. You can also create further Home screens as needed and move the app icons among them. You can customize the Home screen by working on the iPhone, as described here. If you synchronize your iPhone with a computer, you can use iTunes instead. This is an easier way to make extensive changes.

Customize the Home Screen

Unlock the Icons for Customization

1. Press the Home button.

   The Home screen appears.

2. Tap and drag left or right to display the Home screen you want to customize.

   Ⓐ You can also touch the dot for the Home screen you want to display.

3. Tap and hold the icon you want to move.

Note: You can tap and hold any icon until the apps start jiggling. Usually, it is easiest to tap and hold the icon you want to move, and then drag the icon.

The icons start to jiggle, indicating that you can move them.

Move an Icon within a Home Screen

1. After unlocking the icons, drag the icon to where you want it.

   The other icons move out of the way.

2. When the icon is in the right place, drop it.

   The icon stays in its new position.

Move an Icon to a Different Home Screen

1. After unlocking the icons, drag the icon to the left edge of the screen to display the previous Home screen or to the right edge to display the next Home screen.

   The previous Home screen or next Home screen appears.

2. Drag the icon to where you want it.

   The other icons move out of the way.

3. Drop the icon.

   The icon stays in its new position.

Stop Customizing the Home Screen

1. Press the Home button.

   The icons stop jiggling.

TIPS

How can I put the default apps back on the Home screen?
Press the Home button, tap **Settings**, and then tap **General**. Tap and drag up to scroll down to the bottom of the screen, and then tap **Reset**. On the Reset screen, tap **Reset Home Screen Layout**, and then tap **Reset Home Screen** (A) in the dialog box that opens. Press the Home button to return to the reset Home screen.

I have too many apps to navigate easily. Is there an easy fix?
Yes. You can create folders as discussed in the next task, and put the apps into the folders.

Organize Apps with Folders

To organize the Home screen, you can arrange the items into folders. The iPhone's default Home screen layout includes a folder named Utilities, but you can create as many other folders as you need.

You create a folder by dragging one icon onto another icon. Doing this creates a folder containing both items. You can then rename the folder.

Organize Apps with Folders

Create a Folder

1. Display the Home screen that contains the item you want to put into a folder.
2. Tap and hold the item until the icons start to jiggle.

Note: When creating a folder, you may find it easiest to first put both the items you will add to the folder on the same screen.

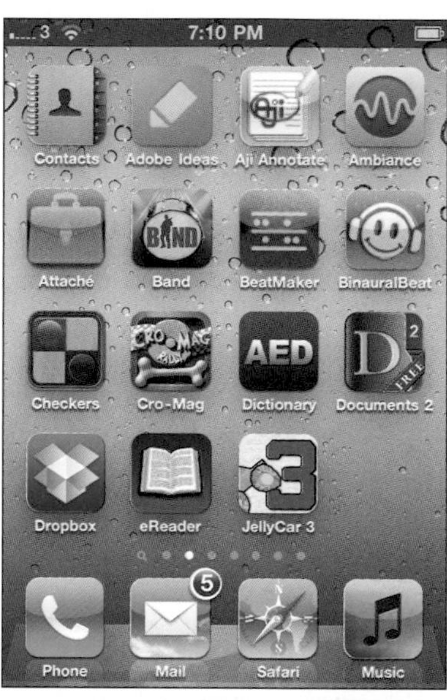

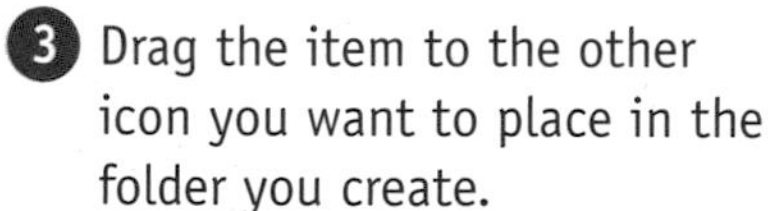

3. Drag the item to the other icon you want to place in the folder you create.

   The iPhone creates a folder, puts both icons in it, and assigns a default name.

4. Tap the × button in the folder name box.

   The keyboard appears.

5. Type the name for the folder.
6. Tap outside the folder.

   The iPhone applies the name to the folder.

Open an Item in a Folder

1. Display the Home screen that contains the folder.
2. Tap the folder's icon.

   The folder's contents appear, and the items outside the folder fade.
3. Tap the item you want to open.

   The item opens.

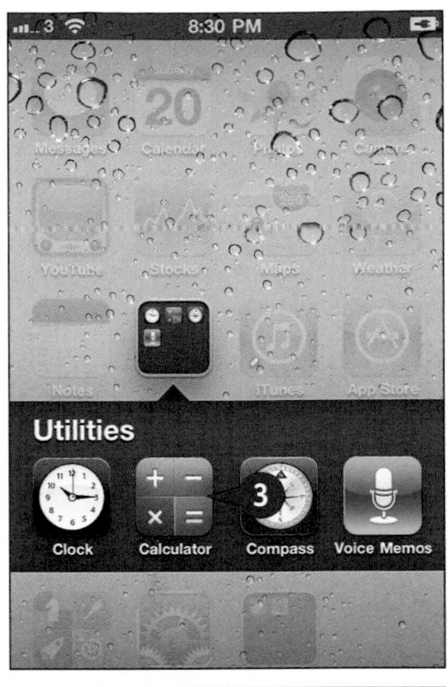

Add an Item to a Folder

1. Display the Home screen that contains the item.
2. Tap and hold the item until the icons start to jiggle.
3. Drag the icon on top of the folder and drop it there.

Note: If the folder is on a different Home screen from the icon, drag the icon to the left edge to display the previous Home screen or to the right edge to display the next Home screen.

The item goes into the folder.

4. Press the Home button to stop the icons jiggling.

TIP

How do I take an item out of a folder?

1. Tap the folder to display its contents.
2. Tap and hold the item until the icons start to jiggle.
3. Drag the item out of the folder. The folder closes and the Home screen appears.
4. Drag the item to where you want it, and then drop it.

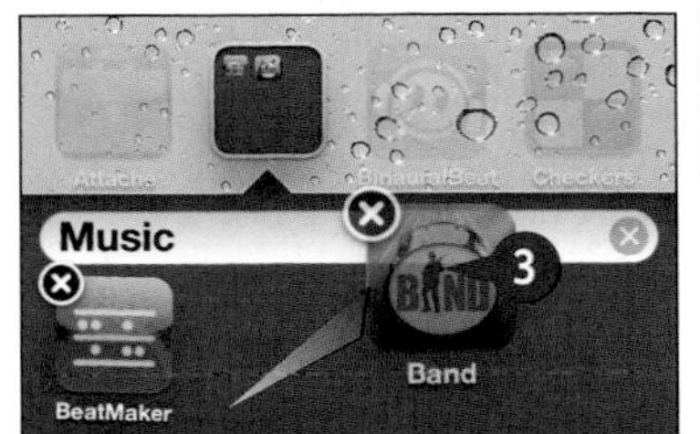

Keep Multiple Apps Running with Multitasking

When you press the Home button to return from an app to the Home screen, the iPhone normally pauses the app because you are no longer using it. But if the app uses one or more background services, such as playing audio or tracking your location with the GPS, the iPhone allows the app to keep running. When you need to be able to return quickly to what you were doing in an app, you can use the iPhone's multitasking feature to switch from one running app to another without displaying the Home screen.

Keep Multiple Apps Running with Multitasking

1. Press the Home button.

   The Home screen appears.

2. Tap the app you want to launch.

   The app's screen appears.

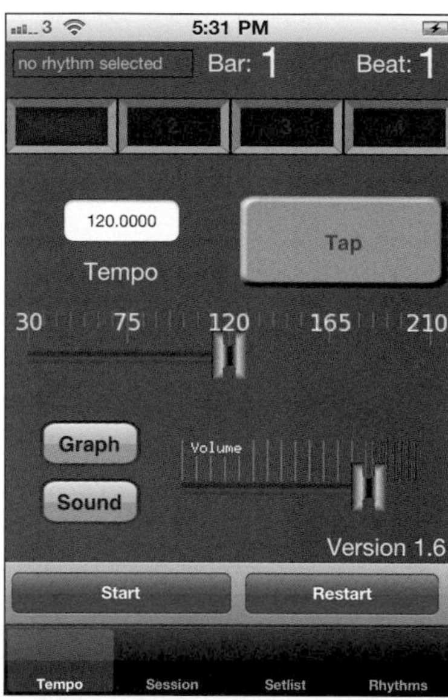

3. Start using the app as usual.
4. Press the Home button twice in quick succession.

   A. The multitasking bar appears.

5. Tap and drag left or right to scroll the multitasking bar until you see the app you want.

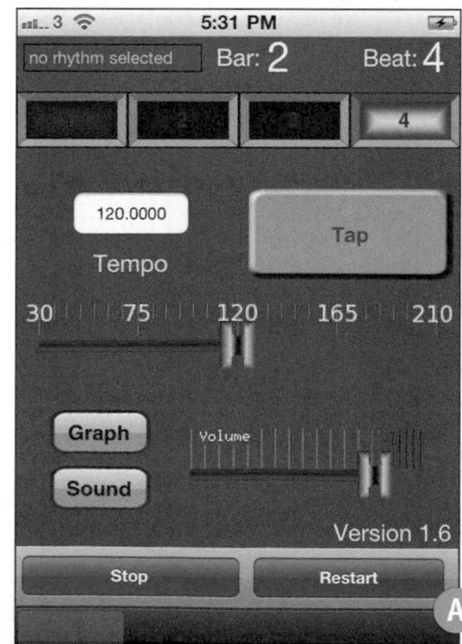

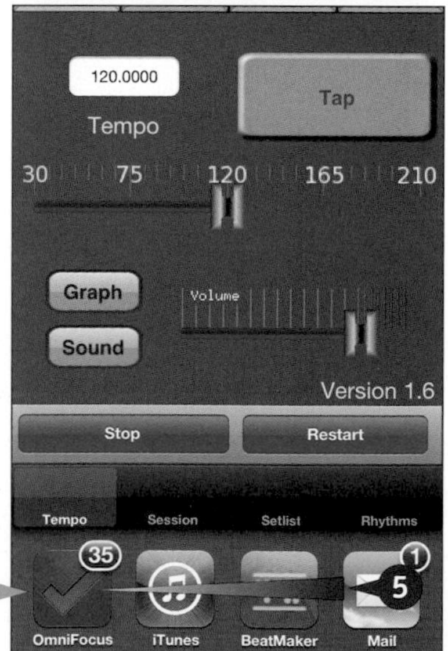

6 Tap the app in the multitasking bar.

The app appears.

7 When you are ready to switch back, press the Home button twice in quick succession.

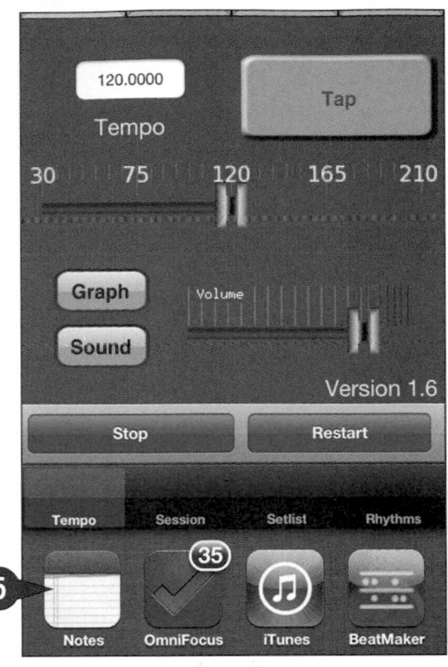

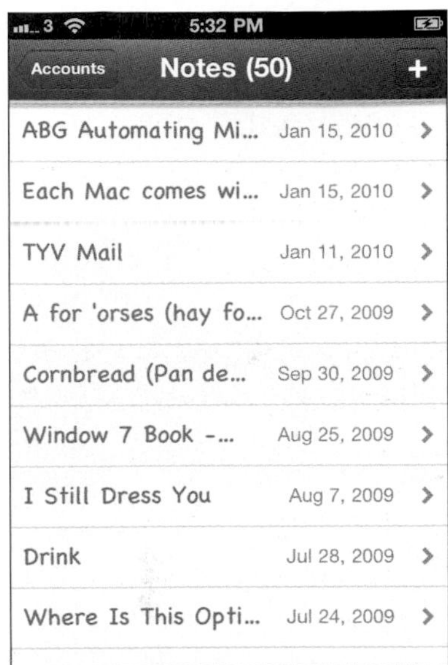

The multitasking bar appears.

8 Tap the app to which you want to return.

The app appears, ready to resume from where you stopped using it.

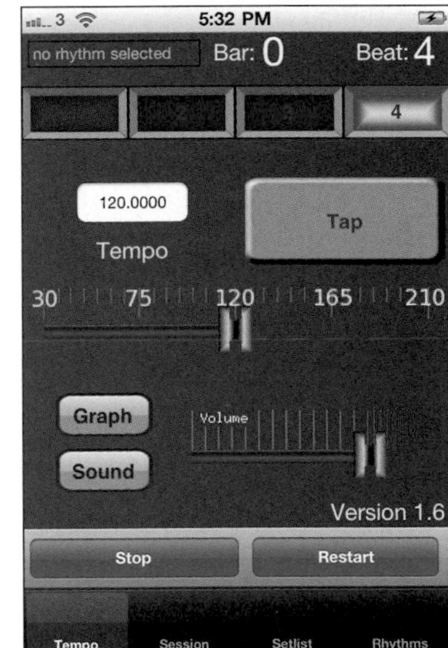

TIP

How do I stop an app that is not responding?
If an app stops responding, you can quickly close it from the multitasking bar. Press the Home button twice to open the multitasking bar. Tap and hold the app that has stopped responding (A). Tap the minus (–) button in the red badge on the app to close the app (B). Press the Home button to turn off the minus (–) buttons.

Find the Apps You Need on the App Store

The iPhone comes with essential apps, such as Safari for surfing the web, Mail for email, and Calendar for keeping your schedule. But to get the most out of your iPhone, you will likely need to add other apps.

To get apps, you use the App Store, which provides apps that Apple has approved as correctly programmed, suitable for purpose, and not containing malevolent code. Before you can download any apps, including free apps, you must create an App Store account.

Find the Apps You Need on the App Store

1. Press the Home button.

   The Home screen appears.

2. Tap **App Store**.

   The App Store screen appears.

3. Tap **Categories**.

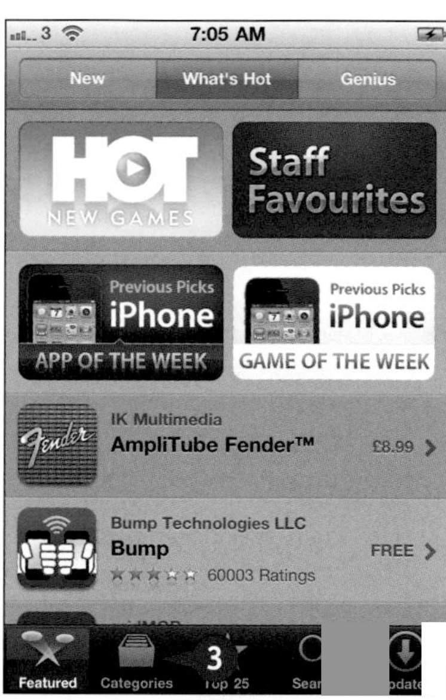

   The Categories screen appears.

4. Tap the category you want to see.

   The category screen appears.

5. Choose how to sort the apps by tapping **Top Paid**, **Top Free**, or **Release Date**. This example uses Top Free.

The screen shows the sort order you chose.

6. Tap the app you want to view.

   The app's screen appears.

Note: To understand what an app does and how well it does it, look at the app's rating, read the description, and read the user reviews.

7. Tap the price button or the **Free** button.

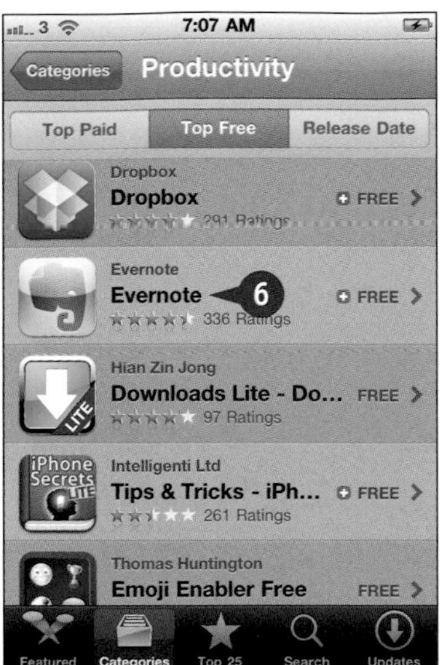

The price button or Free button changes to an Install button.

8. Tap **Install**.
9. If the iPhone prompts you to sign in, type your password and tap **OK**.

Note: If you have not created an App Store account already, the iPhone prompts you to create one now.

A. The iPhone downloads and installs the app.

10. Tap the app's icon on the Home screen to launch the app.

TIP

Why does the App Store not appear on the Home screen or when I search?

If the App Store does not appear on the Home screen, and if searching for it shows no result, the iPhone has restrictions applied that prevent you from installing apps. You can remove this restriction if you know the restrictions passcode. Press the Home button, tap **Settings**, and then tap **General**. Scroll down, and then tap **Restrictions**. Type the passcode on the Enter Passcode screen, and then tap the **Installing Apps** switch and move it to On.

Update and Remove Apps

To keep your iPhone's apps running well, you should install app updates when they become available. Most updates for paid apps are free, but you must pay to upgrade to a new version of the app. You can download and install updates either using iTunes or the iPhone.

When you no longer need an app, you can remove it from the iPhone.

Update and Remove Apps

Update an App

1. In iTunes, click **Apps**.

   The Apps list appears.

2. Click **Updates Available**.

   The Updates screen appears.

3. Click **Download All Free Updates**.

Note: If iTunes displays the Sign In to Download from the iTunes Store dialog box, type your password and click **Buy**.

4. In the Are You Sure You Want to Download All Free Updates? dialog box, click **Update All**.

A. If you do not want iTunes to confirm the download of free updates again, select the **Don't ask me about downloading free updates again** check box (☐ changes to ☑) before clicking **Update All**.

   iTunes downloads the updates.

5. Connect the iPhone if it is not already connected.

6. If the iPhone does not sync automatically, click **Sync** to start synchronization.

Remove an App from the iPhone

1. Press the Home button.

   The Home screen appears.

2. Display the Home screen that contains the app you want to delete.

3. Tap and hold the item until the icons start to jiggle.

4. Tap the × on the icon.

   The Delete dialog box appears.

5. Tap **Delete**.

   The iPhone deletes the app, and the app's icon disappears.

TIP

Can I update an app on the iPhone as well?

To update an app on the iPhone, press the Home button. The badge on the App Store icon (A) shows the number of updates available. Tap **App Store**, tap **Updates**, and then tap **Update All**. Type your password in the Apple ID Password dialog box, and then tap **OK**. The iPhone then downloads and installs the updates. The icons on the Home screen show the progress of the updates.

Install an App Provided by an Administrator

If you use an iPhone administered by a company or organization, an administrator may provide apps for you to install using iTunes. You will usually copy the app's file from a network drive, but you may also receive it attached to an email message.

To install the app, you add it to iTunes on your PC or Mac, and then sync the iPhone with iTunes.

Install an App Provided by an Administrator

Add the App to iTunes

1. Click **File**.

   The File menu opens.

2. Click **Add File to Library** in Windows or **Add to Library** on a Mac.

   The Add To Library dialog box opens.

Note: If you receive the app's file attached to an email message, save it to a folder, and then use the Add To Library dialog box to add it to iTunes. In Mail on a Mac, you can simply click an attached app's file to add it to iTunes.

3. Open the folder that contains the app's file.
4. Click the app's file.
5. Click **Open** in Windows or **Choose** on a Mac.

A. iTunes adds the app to the apps list.

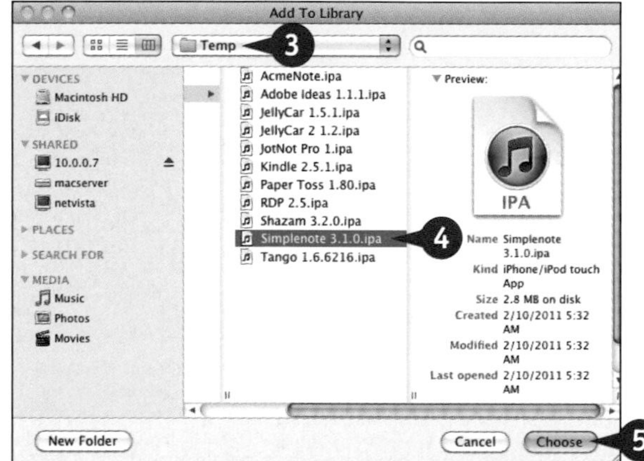

Sync the App to Your iPhone

1. Connect your iPhone to the PC or Mac via the USB cable.

   The iPhone appears in the Source list.

Note: You can also install an app provided by an administrator by syncing wirelessly.

2. Click the iPhone.

   The iPhone's control screens appear.

3. Click **Apps**.

The Apps screen appears.

4. Click **Sync Apps** (☐ changes to ☑).

5. Click the app's check box (☐ changes to ☑).

B. You can also click **Automatically sync new apps** (☐ changes to ☑) to make iTunes automatically sync all new apps.

6. Click **Apply**. If you have not made changes, this button is named **Sync**.

   iTunes installs the app on the iPhone.

TIP

Is there another way to add an app's file to iTunes?

You can quickly add an app's file to iTunes by dragging the app's file from a Windows Explorer window or a Finder window to the Library area at the top of the Source list on the left of the iTunes window. On a Mac, you can also add the app to iTunes by dragging the app's file to the iTunes icon on the Dock and dropping it there.

CHAPTER 8

Browsing the Web and Sending Email

Your iPhone is fully equipped to make the most of the Internet either via a Wi-Fi connection or cellular network. In this chapter, you learn to browse the web using the iPhone's Safari browser and to send email using the Mail app. Among other tasks, you learn to use bookmarks to mark websites for quick access and maintain a high level of security.

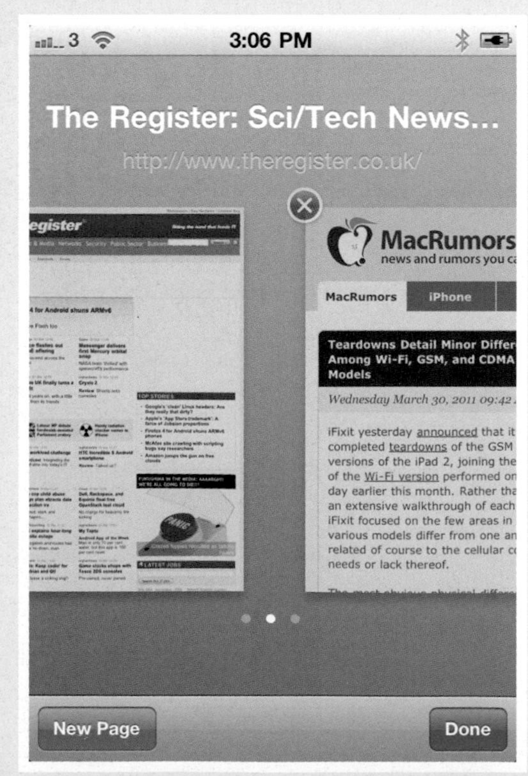

Browse the Web with Safari

Your iPhone comes equipped with the Safari app, which you use for browsing the web. You can quickly go to a web page by entering its address in the Address box or by following a link.

Although you can browse quickly by opening a single web page at a time, you may prefer to open multiple pages and switch back and forth among them. Safari makes this easy to do.

Browse the Web with Safari

Open Safari and Navigate to Web Pages

1. Press the Home button.

   The Home screen appears.

2. Tap **Safari**.

   Safari opens and loads the last web page that was shown.

3. Tap the Address box.

   The Address box expands, and the keyboard appears.

4. Type the address of the page you want to open.
5. Tap **Go**.

Note: You can also tap a search result that Safari displays below the Address box.

   Safari displays the page.

6. Tap a link on the page.

   Safari displays that page.

A. After going to a new page, tap ◀ to display the previous page. You can then tap ▶ to go forward again to the page you just went back from.

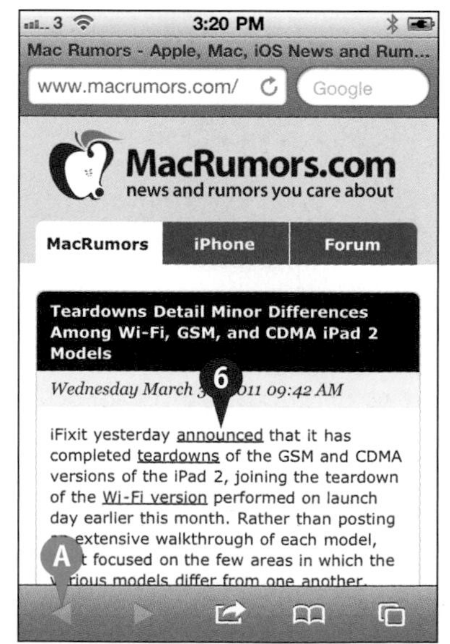

Open Multiple Pages and Navigate Among Them

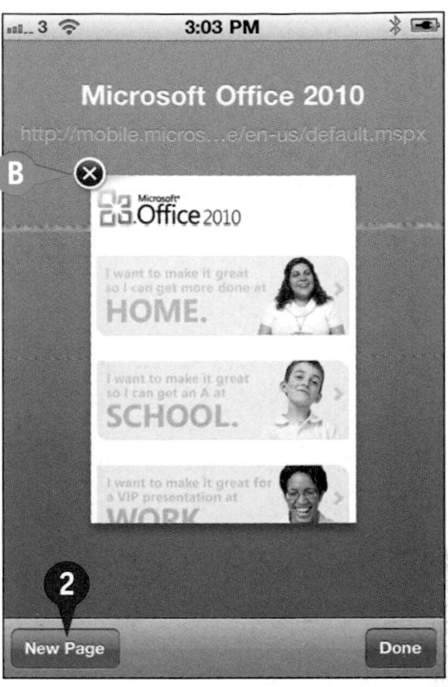

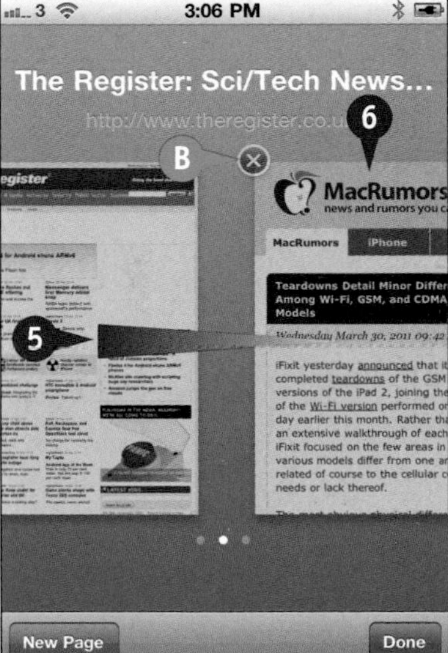

1. Tap **Pages** (▣).

   Safari shrinks the current page and displays a Close button (⊗).

2. Tap **New Page**.

   Safari opens a blank page and expands it to full screen.

3. Tap the Address box, and then go to the page you want.

Note: You can also go to a page by using a bookmark, as described in the next task.

   The page appears.

   The Pages button shows the number of pages open.

4. To switch to another page, tap **Pages** (▣).

   Safari shrinks the current page and displays a Close button (⊗).

5. Scroll left and right to the page you want.

6. Tap the page you want to see.

- B You can tap the **Close** button (⊗) to close a page.

TIP

How do I search for information?

Tap the Search box to display the Search screen, and then type your search terms (A). Safari searches as you type; you can type further to narrow down the results, and stop as soon as you see suitable results. Tap the result you want to see (B), and then tap a link on the results page that Safari opens.

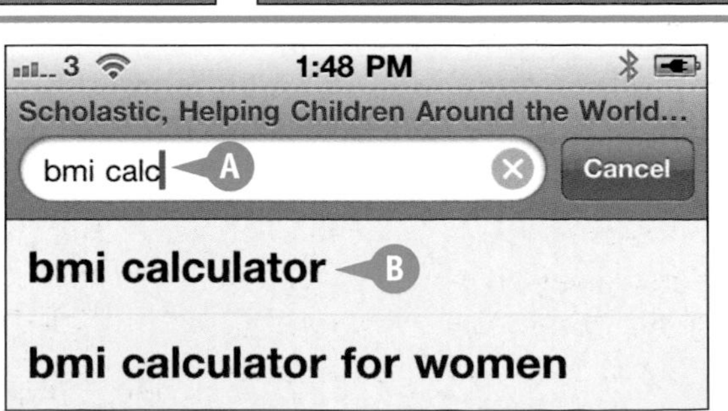

Access Websites Quickly with Your Bookmarks

Typing web addresses can be laborious, even with the help the iPhone's keyboard adds, so you will probably want to use bookmarks to access websites you value.

By syncing your existing bookmarks from your PC or Mac, as described in Chapter 2, you can instantly provide your iPhone with quick access to the web pages you want to visit most frequently. You can also create bookmarks on your iPhone, as discussed on the following pages.

Access Websites Quickly with Your Bookmarks

Open the Bookmarks Screen

1. Press the Home button.

   The Home screen appears.

2. Tap **Safari**.

   Safari opens.

3. Tap **Bookmarks** (📖).

   The Bookmarks screen appears.

Explore Your History

1. On the Bookmarks screen, tap **History**.

   A list of the web pages you have recently visited appears.

A. Tap a day to display the list of web pages you visited on that day.

2. Tap **Bookmarks** to return to the Bookmarks screen.

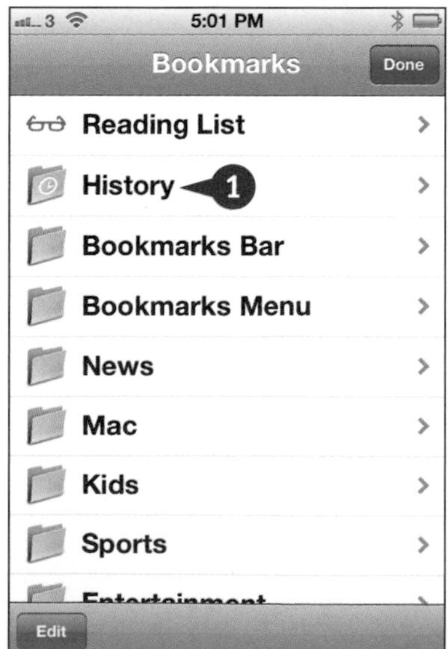

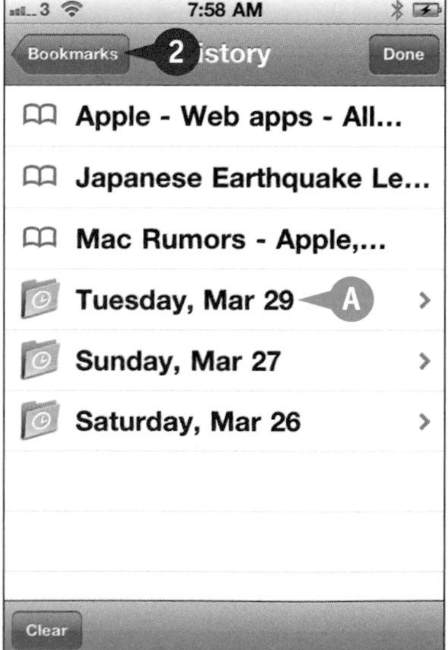

Explore a Bookmarks Category

1. On the Bookmarks screen, tap the bookmarks category you want to see. For example, tap **News**.

   The bookmarks category screen appears — for example, the News screen appears.

2. Tap **Bookmarks** to return to the Bookmarks screen.

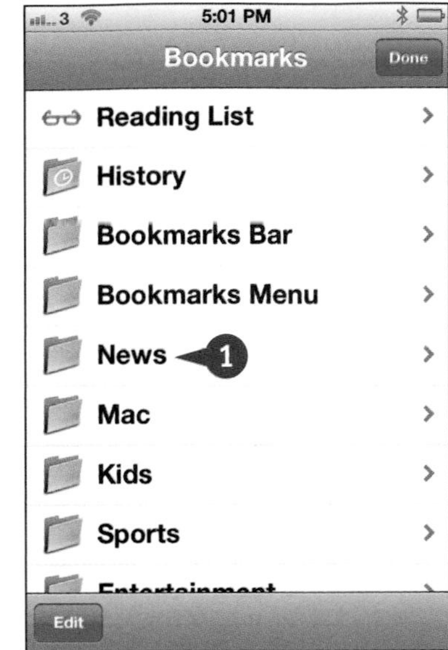

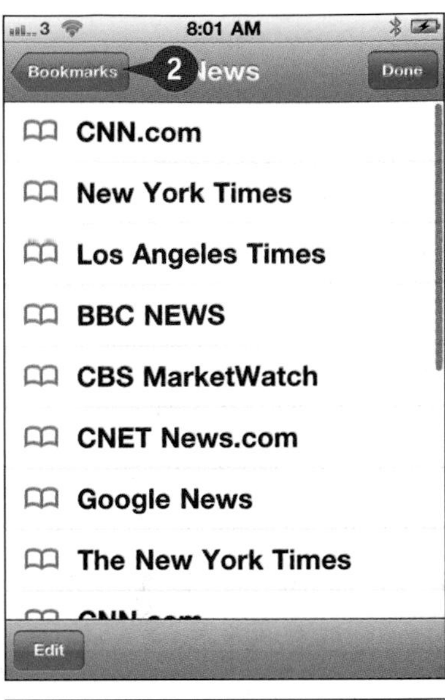

Open a Bookmarked Page

1. When you find the bookmark for the web page you want to open, tap the bookmark.

   The web page opens.

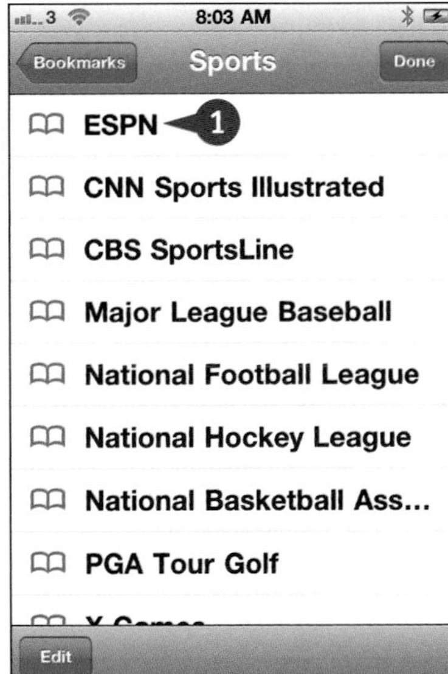

TIP

How can I quickly access a website?

Creating a bookmark within Safari is good for sites you access now and then, but if you access a site frequently, create an icon for it on your Home screen. Tap **Share** (icon), tap **Add to Home Screen** (A), type the name on the Add to Home screen, and then tap **Add**. You can then go straight to the page by tapping its icon on the Home screen.

Create Bookmarks and Share Web Pages

While browsing the web on your iPhone, you will likely find web pages you want to access again. To access such a web page easily, create a bookmark for it. If you have set your iPhone to sync bookmarks with your computer, the bookmark becomes available on your computer too when you sync. You can also add a web page to your Reading List so that you can access it again quickly.

To share a web page with other people, you can quickly send the page's address via email.

Create Bookmarks and Share Web Pages

Create a Bookmark on the iPhone

1. Press the Home button.

   The Home screen appears.

2. Tap **Safari**.

   Safari opens and displays the last web page you were viewing.

3. Navigate to the web page you want to bookmark.

4. Tap **Share** (![share icon]).

   The Share dialog box opens.

5. Tap **Add Bookmark**.

Note: To add the web page to your Reading List, tap **Add to Reading List** in the Share dialog box.

   The Add Bookmark screen appears.

6. Edit the suggested name, or type a new name.

7. Tap the Bookmarks button.

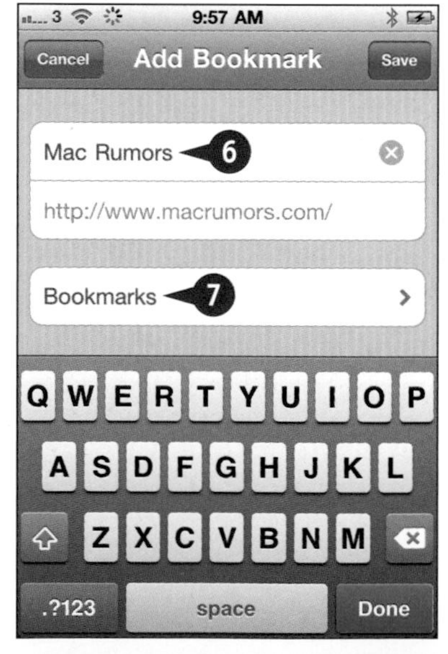

The Bookmarks screen appears.

8 Tap the folder you want to create the bookmark in.

The Add Bookmark screen appears again.

9 Tap **Save**.

Safari creates the bookmark.

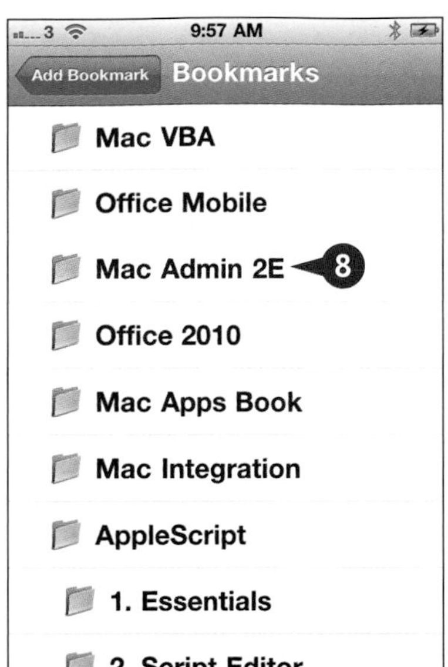

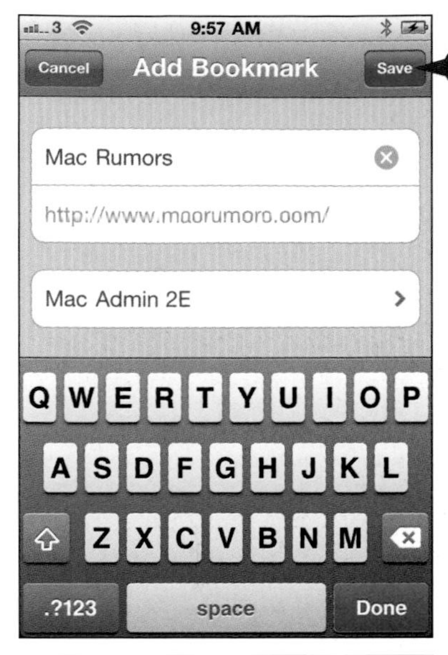

Share a Web Page's Address via Email

1 In Safari, navigate to the web page whose address you want to share.

2 Tap **Share** ( ).

The Share dialog box opens.

3 Tap **Mail Link to this Page**.

The iPhone starts a new message in the Mail app and adds the link to it.

4 Add the address by typing or by tapping ⊕ and choosing it from your Contacts list.

5 Edit the suggested subject line if necessary.

6 Type any explanatory text needed.

7 Tap **Send**.

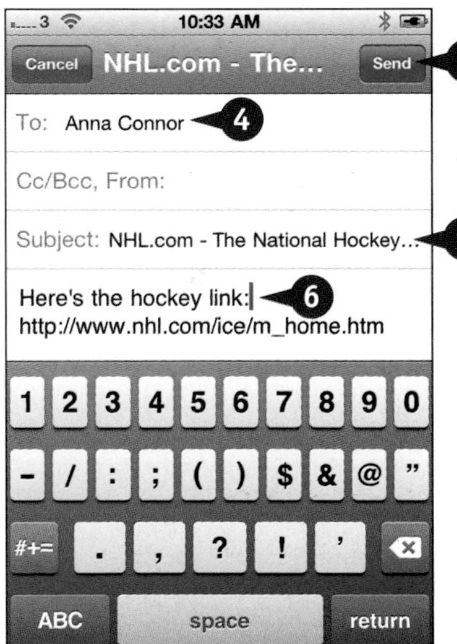

TIPS

Can I change a bookmark I have created?

Yes. Tap to display the Bookmarks screen, and then navigate to the bookmark you want to change. Tap **Edit** to display a button for opening a bookmark to change it and controls for deleting bookmarks and changing their order.

How do I access my Reading List?

Tap to display the Bookmarks screen, and then tap **Reading List** to display the Reading List screen. You can then tap the web page you want to view.

Configure Your Default Search Engine

To find information with Safari, you often need to search using a search engine. Safari's default search engine is Google, but you can change to another search engine. Your choices are Google, Yahoo!, and Bing.

Google, Yahoo!, and Bing compete directly with each other and return similar results to many searches. But if you experiment with the three search engines, you will gradually discover which one suits you best.

Configure Your Default Search Engine

1. Press the Home button.

   The Home screen appears.

2. Tap **Settings**.

   The Settings screen appears.

3. Tap and drag up to scroll down until the third box appears.

4. Tap **Safari**.

   The Safari screen appears.

5. Tap **Search Engine**.

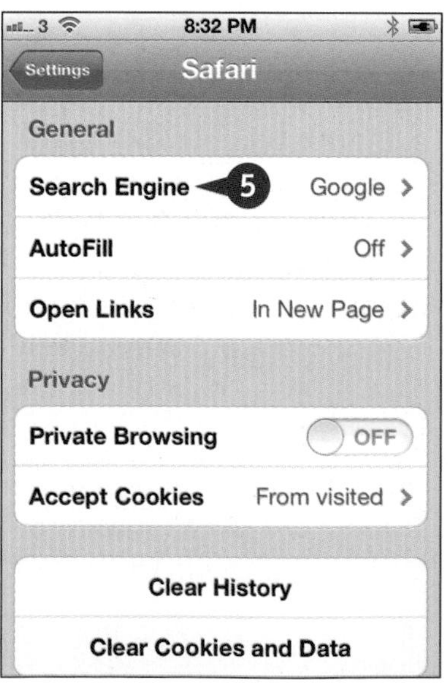

The Search Engine screen appears.

6. Tap the search engine you want — for example, **Yahoo!**.

   A check mark appears next to the search engine you tapped.

7. Tap **Safari**.

A. The Safari screen appears again, now showing the search engine you chose.

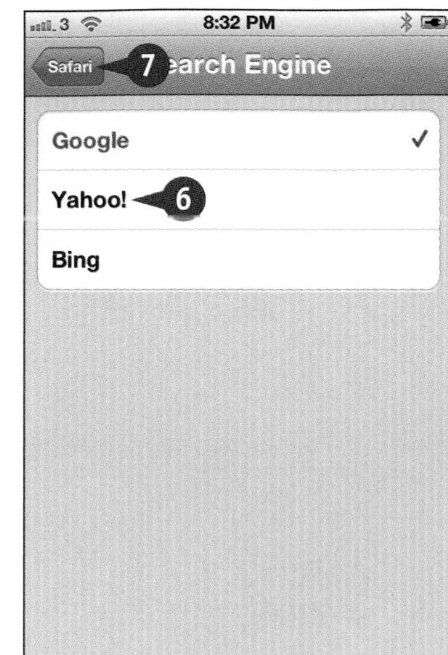

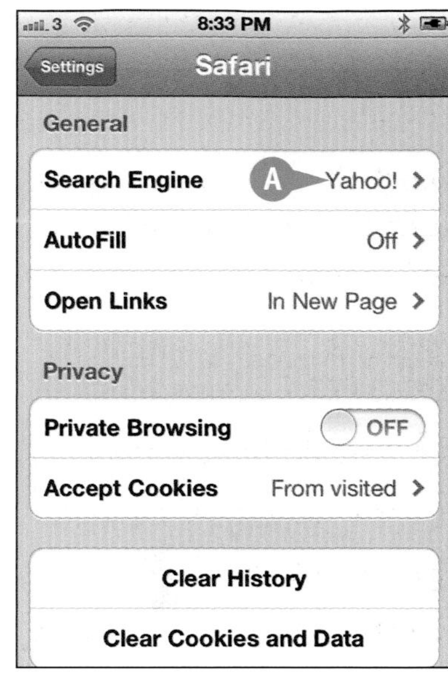

TIP

How can I search using a search engine other than Google, Yahoo!, or Bing?

You can search using any search engine you can find on the web. Open a web page to the search engine, and then perform the search using the tools on the page. At this writing, you cannot set any search engine other than Google, Yahoo!, or Bing as the iPhone's default search engine. Instead, either add the site to your Bookmarks bar or create a link on your Home screen to the site.

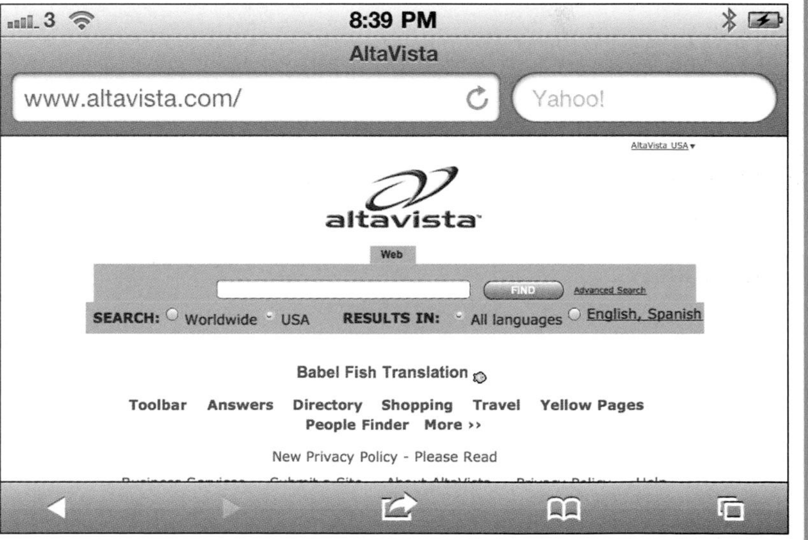

Fill in Forms Quickly with AutoFill

If you fill in forms using your iPhone, you can save time by enabling the AutoFill feature. AutoFill can automatically fill in standard form fields, such as name and address fields, using the information from a contact card you specify.

AutoFill can also automatically store other data you enter in fields, and can store usernames and passwords to enter them for you automatically. For security, you may prefer not to store your usernames and passwords with AutoFill.

Fill in Forms Quickly with AutoFill

1. Press the Home button.

   The Home screen appears.

2. Tap **Settings**.

   The Settings screen appears.

3. Tap and drag up to scroll down until the third box appears.

4. Tap **Safari**.

   The Safari screen appears.

5. Tap **AutoFill**.

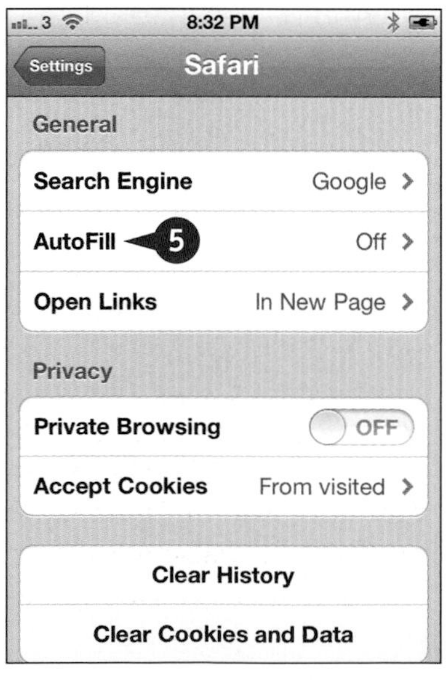

The AutoFill screen appears.

6. Tap the **Use Contact Info** switch and move it to On.
7. Tap **My Info**.

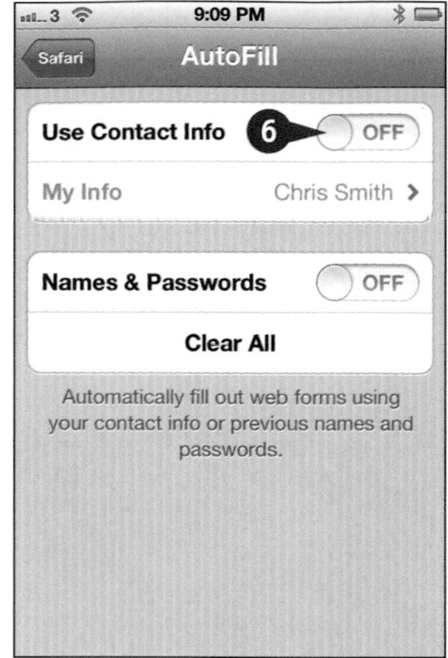

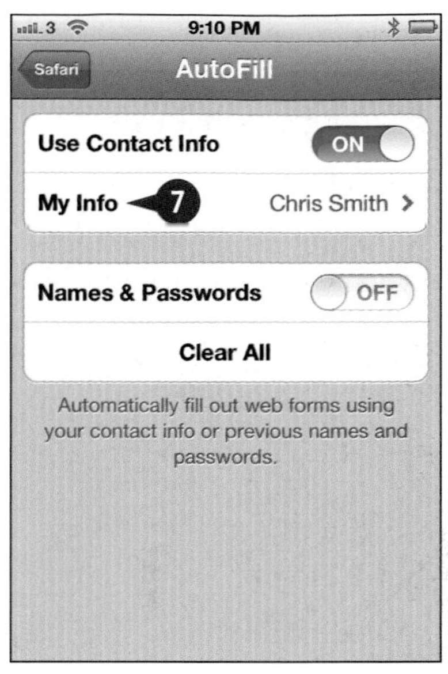

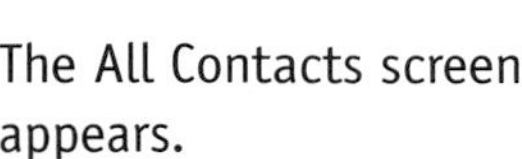

The All Contacts screen appears.

8. Tap the contact card that contains the information you want to use.

   The AutoFill screen appears again, with the name you chose in the My Info area.

9. Tap the **Names & Passwords** switch and move it to On.
10. Tap **Safari**.

    The Safari screen appears again.

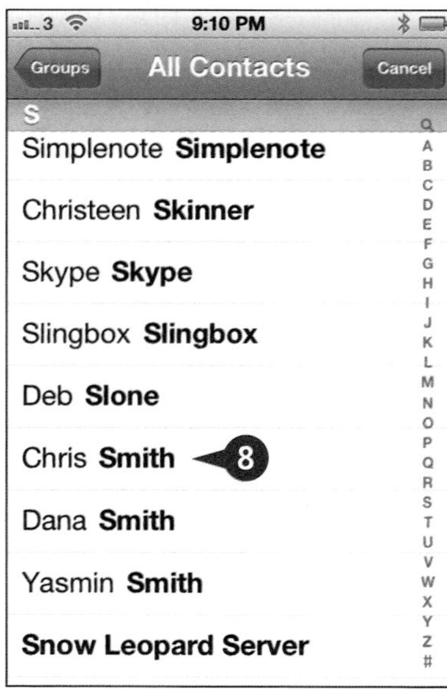

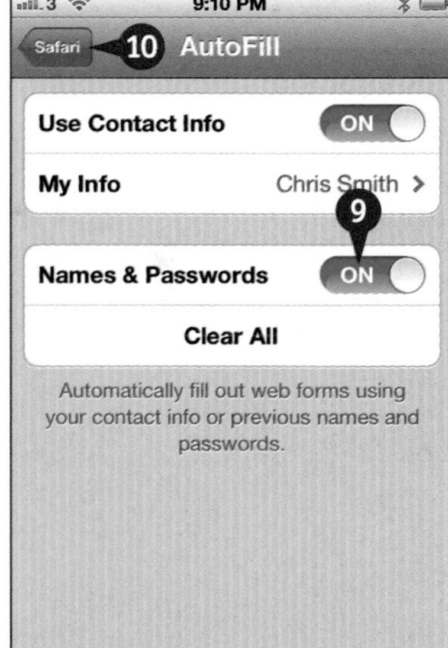

TIP

When should I clear my AutoFill information?
Clear your AutoFill information if you want to remove stored usernames and passwords from your iPhone, or if AutoFill has stored incorrect information that you have entered in forms. To clear your AutoFill information, tap **Clear All** (A) on the AutoFill screen, and then tap **Clear AutoFill Data** (B) in the confirmation dialog box that opens.

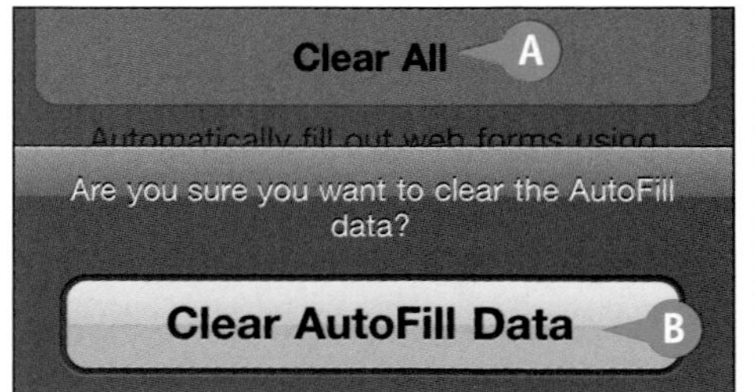

Tighten Up Safari's Security

Along with its many and varied sites that provide useful information or services, the web contains sites that try to infect computers with malevolent software, or *malware*, or lure visitors into providing sensitive personal or financial information. Although Apple has built the iPhone and Safari to be as secure as possible, it is wise to choose high-security settings. This task shows you how to turn on the Fraud Warning feature, block JavaScript and pop-ups, and choose which cookies to accept.

Tighten Up Safari's Security

1. Press the Home button.

   The Home screen appears.

2. Tap **Settings**.

   The Settings screen appears.

3. Tap and drag up to scroll down until the third box appears.

4. Tap **Safari**.

   The Safari screen appears.

5. Tap and drag up to scroll down to the bottom.

6. Tap the **Fraud Warning** switch and move it to On.

Note: The Fraud Warning warns you when you try to open a site on a blacklist of offending sites. This feature is not infallible, but it is helpful.

7. Tap the **JavaScript** switch and move it to Off.

Note: JavaScript is used to provide extra features on websites. Because JavaScript can be used to attack your iPhone, disabling JavaScript is the safest option. The disadvantage is that disabling JavaScript may remove some functionality of harmless sites.

8. Tap the **Block Pop-ups** switch and move it to On.

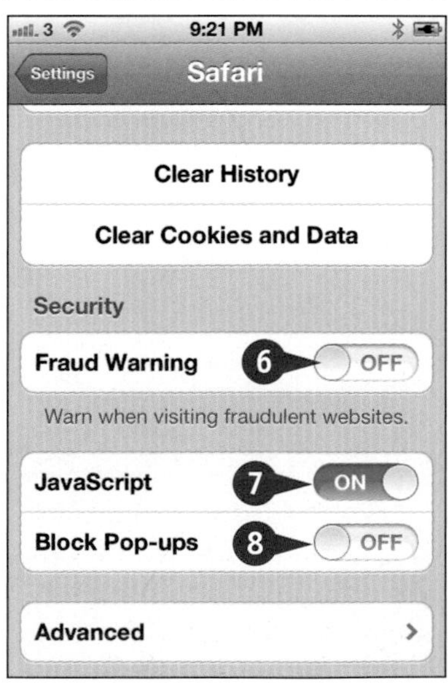

Note: A pop-up is an extra web page that opens automatically. Some pop-ups attempt to show information most visitors do not want to see.

9. Tap and drag down to scroll up a little way so that you can see the Privacy section.
10. Tap **Accept Cookies**.

    The Accept Cookies screen appears.
11. Tap **From visited**.
12. Tap **Safari**.

    The Safari screen appears again.
13. If you want to clear your browsing history, tap **Clear History**, and then tap **Clear History** in the dialog box that opens.
14. If you want to clear your cookies and cached data, tap **Clear Cookies and Data**, and then tap **Clear Cookies and Data** in the dialog box that opens.

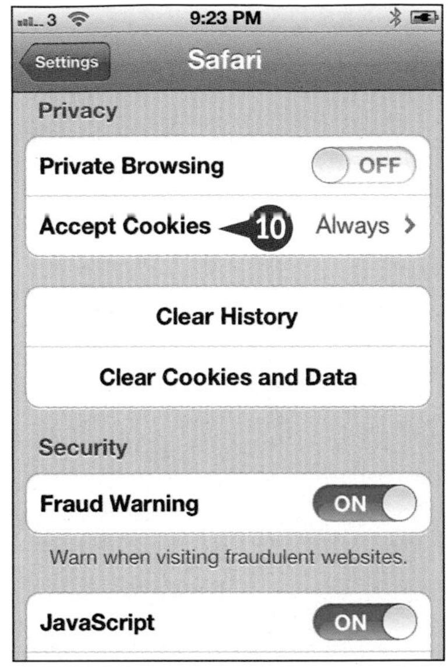

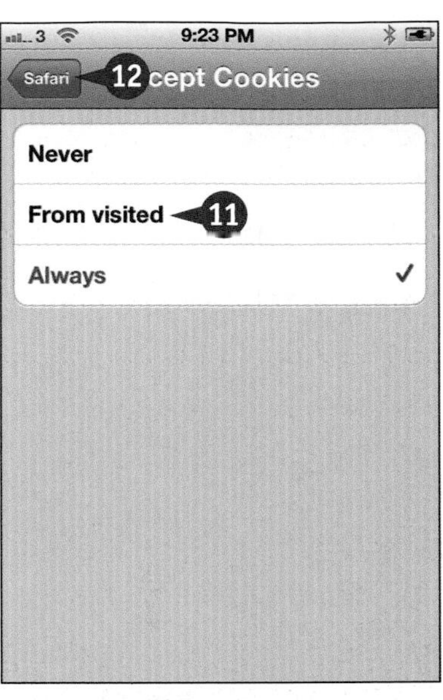

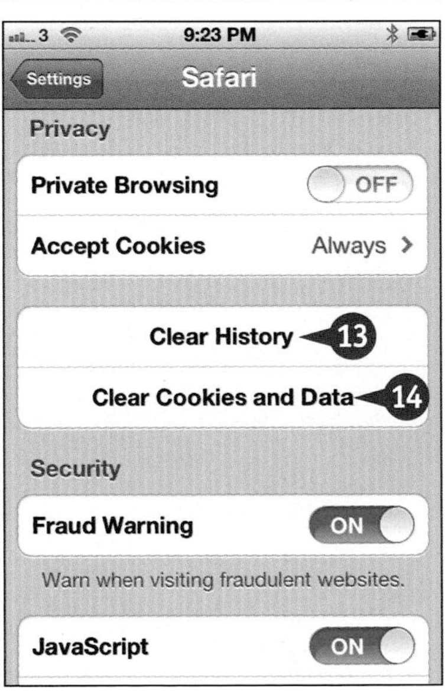

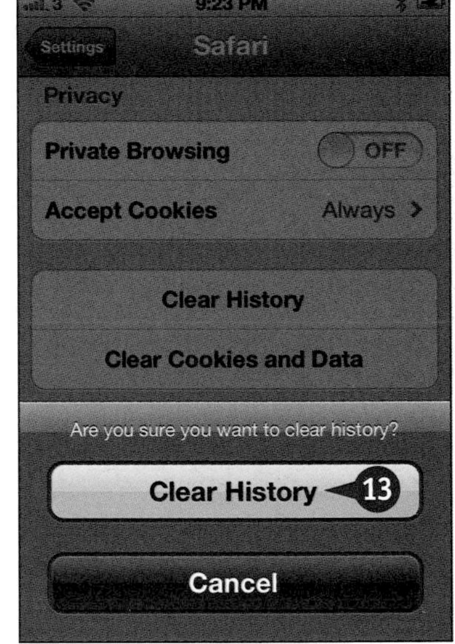

TIP

What are cookies and what threat do they pose?

A cookie is a small text file that a website places on a computer to identify it in future. This is helpful for many sites, such as shopping sites in which you add items to a shopping cart, but when used by malevolent sites, cookies can pose a threat to your privacy. You can set Safari to never accept cookies, but this prevents many legitimate websites from working properly. So accepting cookies only from sites you visit is normally the best compromise.

Read Your Email Messages

After you have set up Mail by synchronizing accounts from your computer, as described in Chapter 2, or by configuring accounts manually on the iPhone, as described in Chapter 4, you are ready to send and receive email messages using your iPhone.

This task shows you how to read your incoming email messages. You learn to reply to messages and write messages from scratch later in this chapter.

Read Your Email Messages

1. Press the Home button.

   The Home screen appears.

2. Tap **Mail**.

Note: The badge on the Mail icon shows how many unread messages Mail has found so far.

   The Mail screen appears.

Note: If Mail does not show the Mailboxes screen, tap the button in the upper-left corner until the Mailboxes screen appears.

3. Tap the inbox you want to see.

A. To see all your incoming messages together, tap **All Inboxes**. Depending on how you use email, you may find seeing all your messages at once helpful.

   The Inbox opens.

B. A blue dot to the left of a message indicates that you have not read the message yet.

4. Tap the message you want to open.

   The message opens.

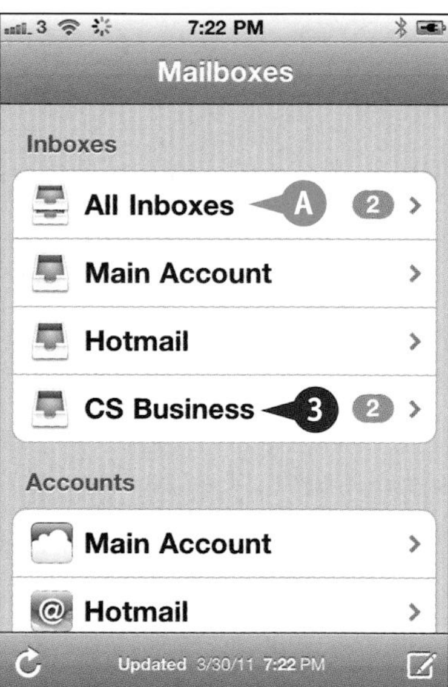

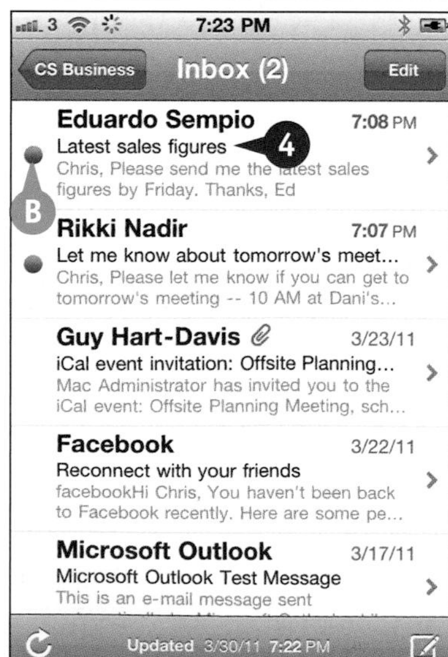

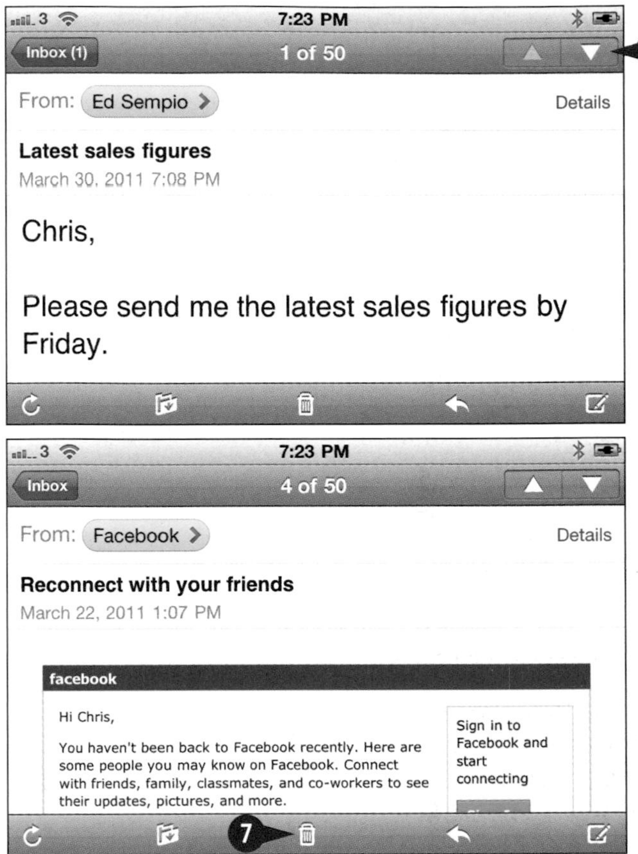

5 Turn the iPhone sideways if you want to view the message in landscape orientation.

In landscape orientation, you can see the message at a larger size, so it is easier to read.

6 Tap ▼.

The next message appears.

7 If you want to delete the message, tap 🗑.

Note: If you want to reply to the message, see the next task. If you want to file the message in a folder, see the task "Organize Your Messages in Mailbox Folders."

TIP

How do I view the contents of another mailbox?
From an open message, tap **Inbox** or **All Inboxes** to return to the inbox or the screen for all the inboxes. Tap **Mailboxes** to go back to the Mailboxes screen. You can then tap the mailbox you want to view.

Reply To or Forward an Email Message

After receiving an email message, you will often need to reply to it. You can choose between replying only to the sender of the message and replying to the sender and all the other recipients in the To field and the Cc field, if there are any. Recipients in the message's Bcc field, whose names you cannot see, do not receive your reply.

Other times, you may need to forward a message you have received to one or more other people. The Mail app makes both replying and forwarding messages as easy as possible.

Reply To or Forward an Email Message

Open the Message You Will Reply To or Forward

1. Press the Home button.

   The Home screen appears.

2. Tap **Mail**.

   The Mailboxes screen appears.

3. Tap the inbox you want to see.

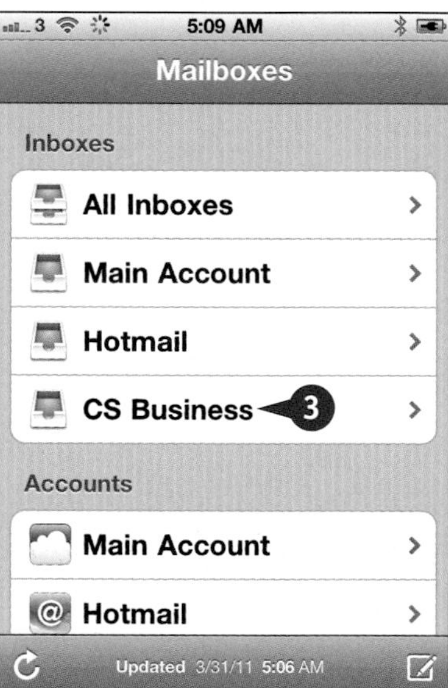

The Inbox opens.

4. Tap the message you want to open.

   The message opens.

5. Tap **Action** ().

   The Action dialog box opens.

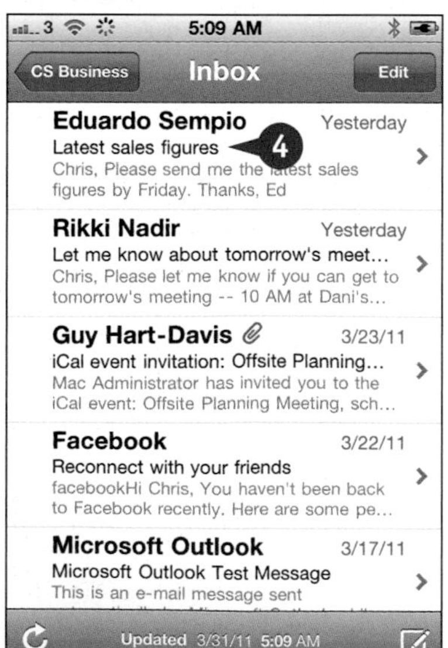

Reply to the Message

1. In the Action dialog box, tap **Reply**.

   A. To reply to all recipients, tap **Reply All**. Reply to all recipients only when you are sure that they need to receive your reply. Often, it is better to reply only to the sender.

   A screen containing the reply appears.

2. Type your reply to the message.
3. Tap **Send**.

   Mail sends the message.

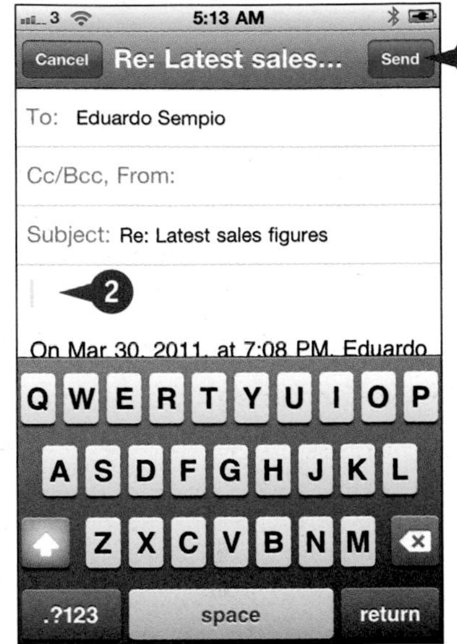

Forward the Message

1. In the Action dialog box, tap **Forward**.

   A screen containing the forwarded message appears.

2. Type the recipient's address.

   B. Alternatively, you can tap ⊕ and choose the recipient in your Contacts list.

3. Type a message if needed.
4. Tap **Send**.

   Mail sends the message.

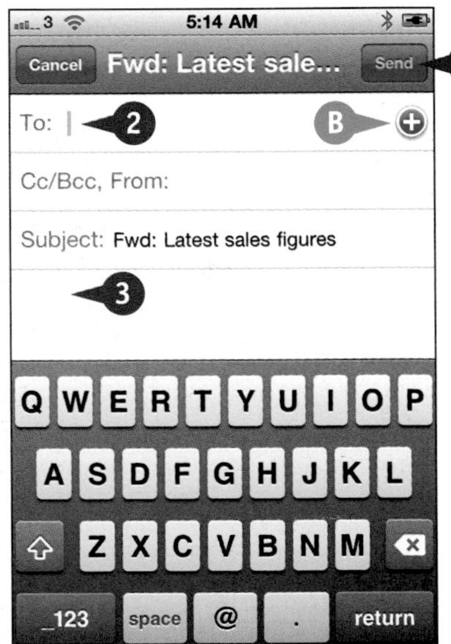

TIP

How can I tell whether a message is just to me or whether there are other recipients?

To see the list of recipients, tap **Details**. The list of recipients appears (A). Tap **Hide** (B) when you want to hide the list again.

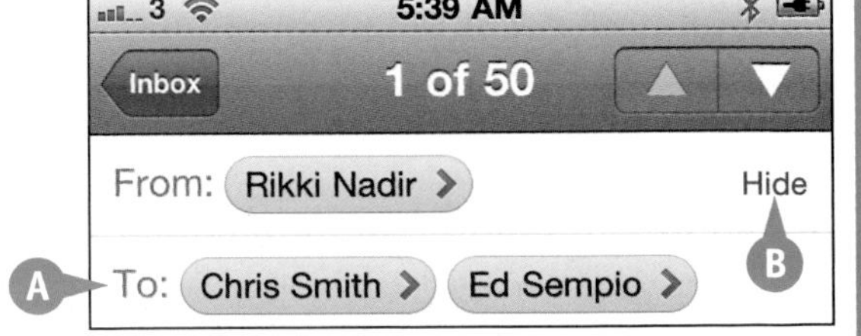

Organize Your Messages in Mailbox Folders

To keep your inbox or inboxes under control, you should organize your messages into mailbox folders.

You can quickly move a single message to a folder after reading it, or you can select multiple messages in your inbox and move them all to a folder in a single action.

Organize Your Messages in Mailbox Folders

Open Your Inbox

1. Press the Home button.

   The Home screen appears.

2. Tap **Mail**.

   The Mailboxes screen appears.

3. Tap the inbox you want to open.

   The Inbox opens.

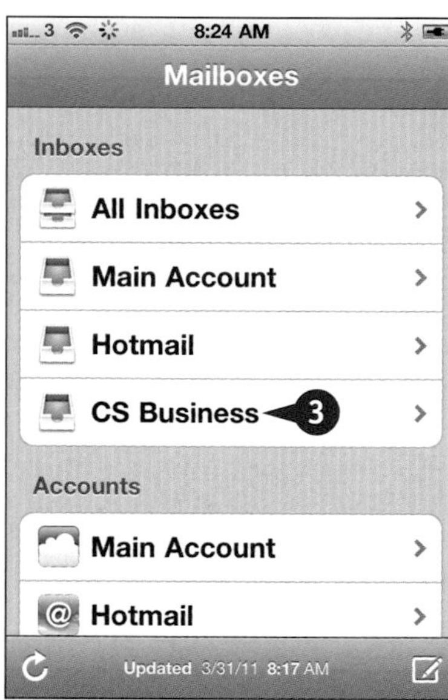

Move a Single Message to a Folder

1. Tap the message you want to read.

   The message opens.

2. Tap **Folders** (📁).

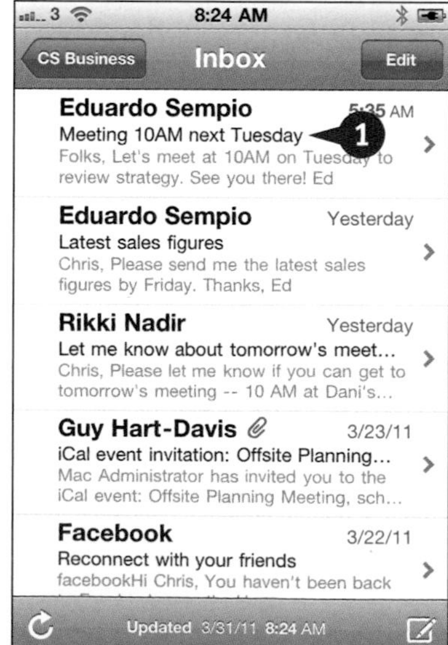

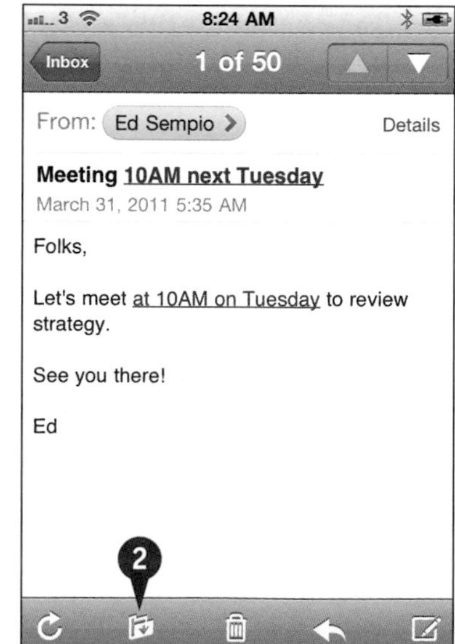

The Mailboxes screen appears.

3. Tap the mailbox to which you want to move the message.

   Mail moves the message.

   The next message in the inbox appears, so that you can read it and file it if necessary.

Move Multiple Messages to a Folder

1. In the inbox, tap **Edit**.

   An empty selection button appears to the left of each message, and the Delete button and Move button appear.

2. Tap the selection button (✔) next to each message you want to move.

3. Tap **Move**.

   The Mailboxes screen appears.

4. Tap the mailbox to which you want to move the messages.

   Mail moves the messages.

   Your inbox then appears again, so that you can work with other messages.

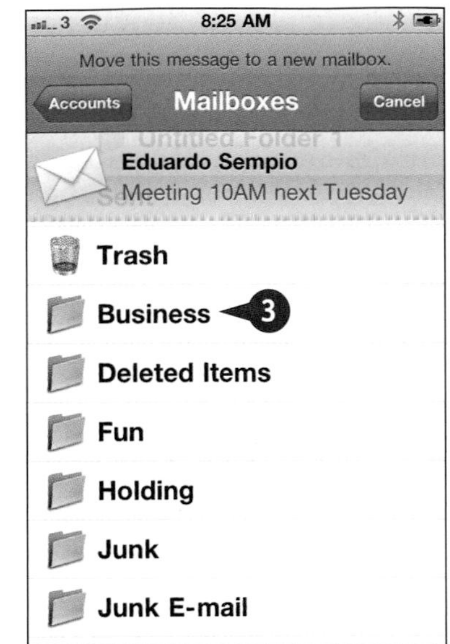

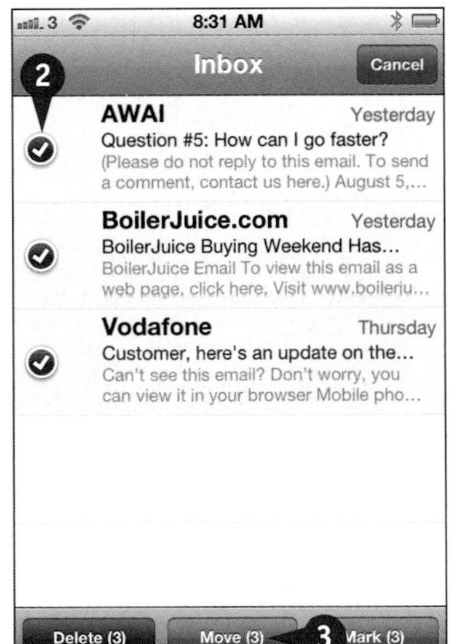

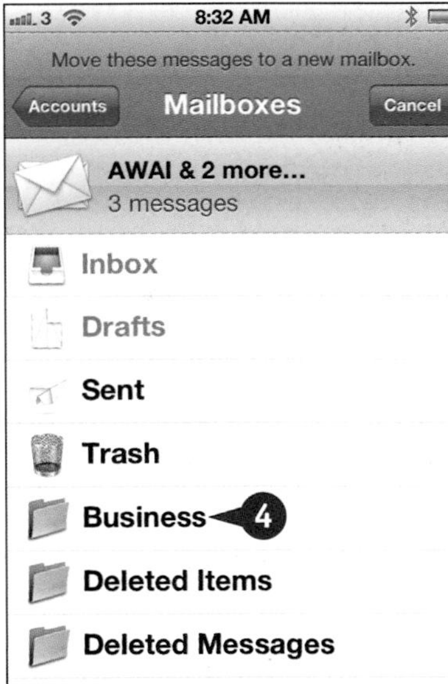

Can I move messages from an inbox in one account to a mailbox in another account?

Yes. In the inbox, tap **Edit**, and then tap the selection button (✔) for each message you want to affect. Tap **Move**, and then tap **Accounts**. On the Accounts screen, tap the account (A) that contains the mailbox to which you want to move the messages, and then tap the mailbox.

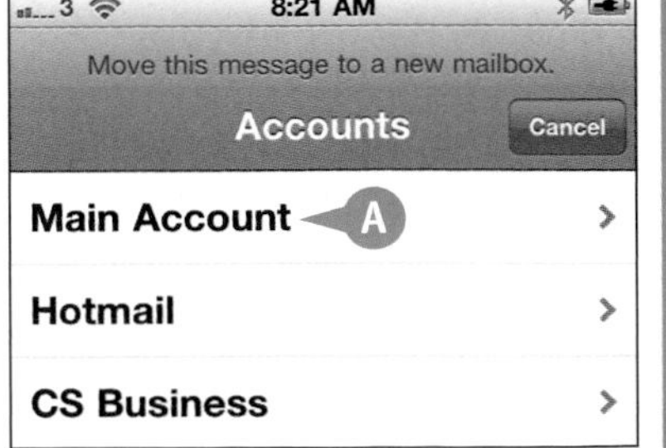

Write and Send Email Messages

Your iPhone is great for reading and replying to email messages you receive, but you will likely also need to write messages. When you do, you can use the data in the Contacts app to address your outgoing messages quickly and accurately. If the recipient's address is not one of your contacts, you can type the address manually.

You can attach one or more files to an email message to send those files to the recipient. This works well for small files, but many mail servers reject files larger than several megabytes in size.

Write and Send Email Messages

1. Press the Home button.

   The Home screen appears.

2. Tap **Mail**.

   The Mailboxes screen appears.

3. Tap **New Message** (✎).

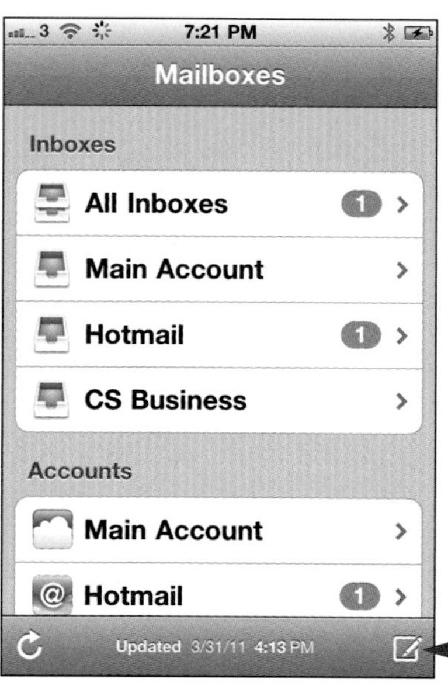

The New Message screen appears.

4. Tap ⊕.

   The All Contacts list appears.

Ⓐ If the person you are emailing is not a contact, type the address in the To area. You can also start typing here and then select a matching contact from the list the Mail app displays.

5. Tap the contact you want to send the message to.

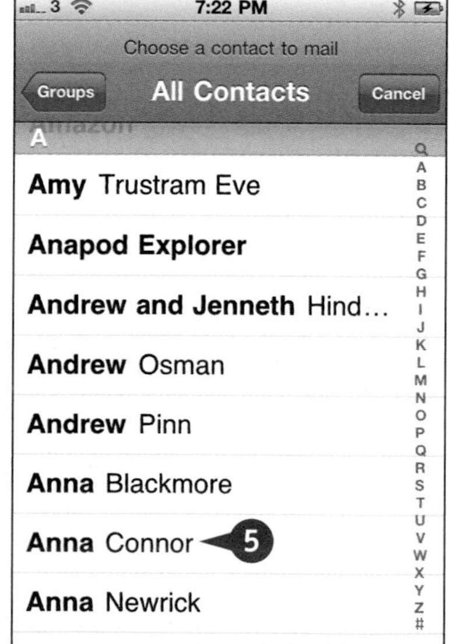

The contact's name appears as a button in the To area.

Note: You can add other contacts to the To area by repeating steps 4 and 5.

6. If you need to add a Cc or Bcc recipient, tap **Cc/Bcc, From.**

   The Cc, Bcc, and From fields expand.

7. Tap the Cc area or Bcc area, and then follow steps 4 and 5 above to add a recipient.

8. Tap **Subject**, and then type the message's subject.

B. To change the email account you are sending the message from, tap **From**, and then tap the account to use.

9. Tap below the Subject line, and then type the body of the message.

10. Tap **Send**.

    Mail sends the message.

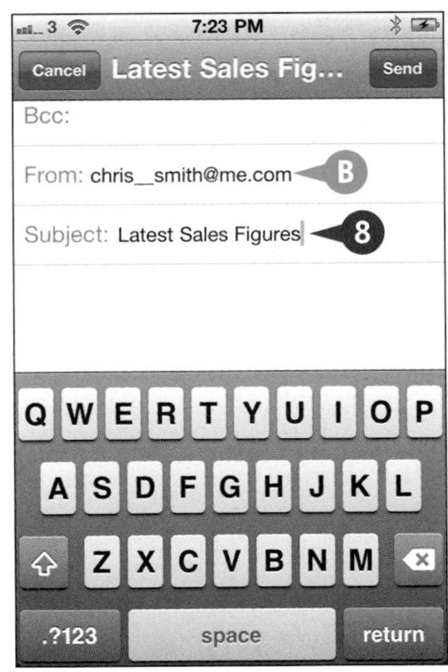

TIP

How do I attach a file to a message?

To attach a file to the message, start the message from the app that contains the file. For example, to send a photo, open the Photos app. Select the photo, tap **Share** (⎘), and then tap **Email Photo.** Mail starts a message with the photo attached. You then address the message and send it.

View Files Attached to Incoming Email Messages

Email is not just a great way to communicate, but you can use it to transfer files quickly and easily. When you receive an email message with a file attached to it, you can quickly view the file from the Mail app.

When you receive an email message that has a small file attached, the Mail app automatically downloads the whole file. If the attachment is a large file, the Mail app downloads part of it, and you must tap the attachment to download the rest of it. This behavior helps avoid filling the iPhone with large files you do not want and helps keep down the amount of data you transfer.

View Files Attached to Incoming Email Messages

1. Press the Home button.

   The Home screen appears.

2. Tap **Mail**.

   The Mailboxes screen appears.

3. Tap the inbox you want to open.

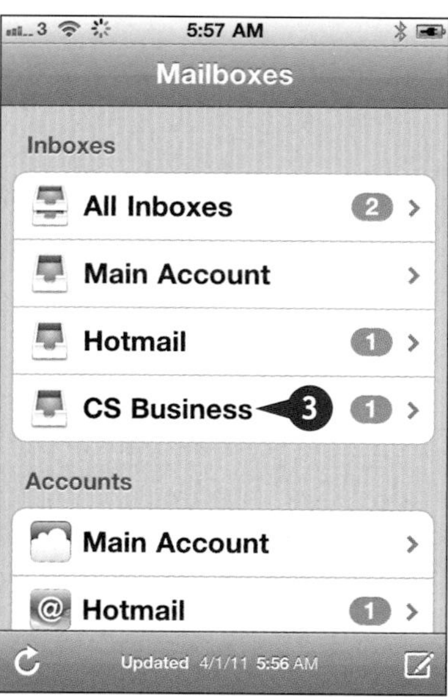

The Inbox opens.

- **A** A paperclip icon (📎) indicates that a message has one or more files attached.

4. Tap the message you want to open.

   The message opens.

5. If the attachment appears as an outline with a Download button (⬇), tap to download the attachment.

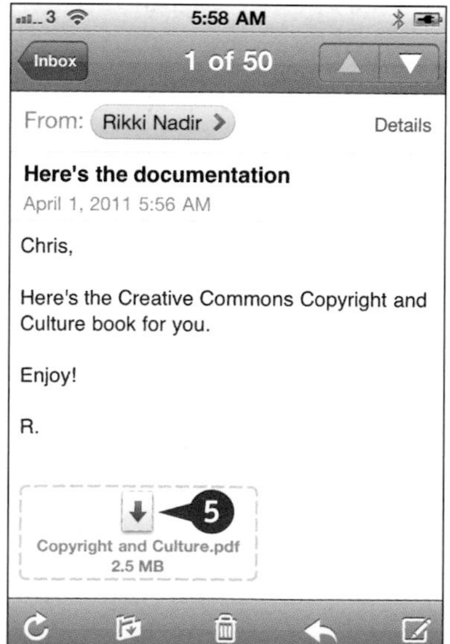

A button for the attachment appears.

6 Tap the attachment's button.

The attached file opens in the Viewer app.

Note: The Viewer app provides basic features for viewing widely used document types, such as PDF files, Microsoft Word documents, and Microsoft Excel workbooks.

7 Tap **Open Attachment** (icon).

A dialog box appears.

8 Tap **Open In**.

B The top button in the dialog box shows a suggested app for opening the file. Tap this button if you want to use this app.

A full list of compatible apps opens.

Note: The selection of apps depends on the apps you have installed on your iPhone.

9 Tap the app you want to use.

The file opens in the app you chose.

Note: After you open an attached file in an app, your iPhone stores a copy of the file in that app's storage. You can then open the file again directly from that app.

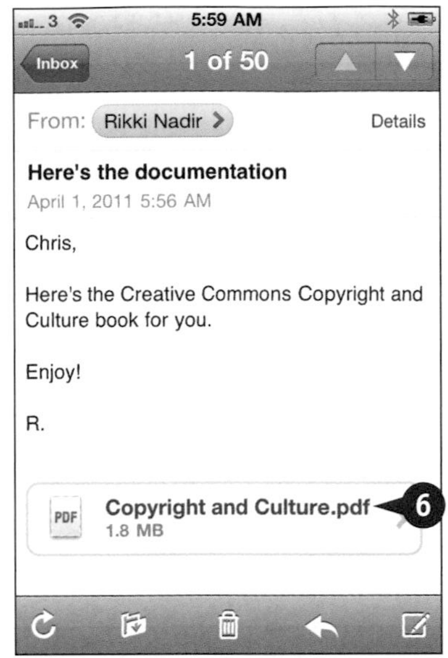

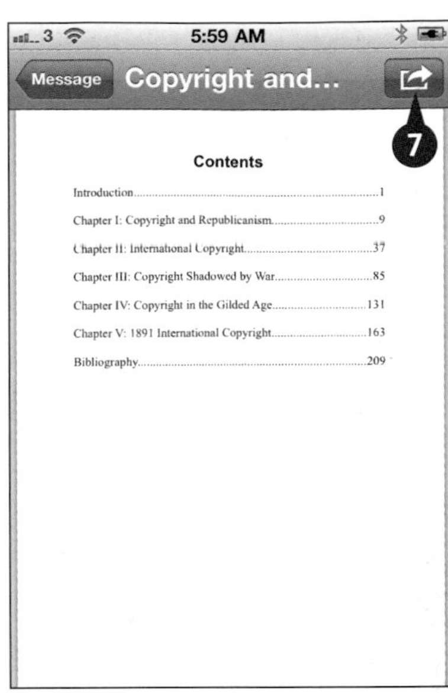

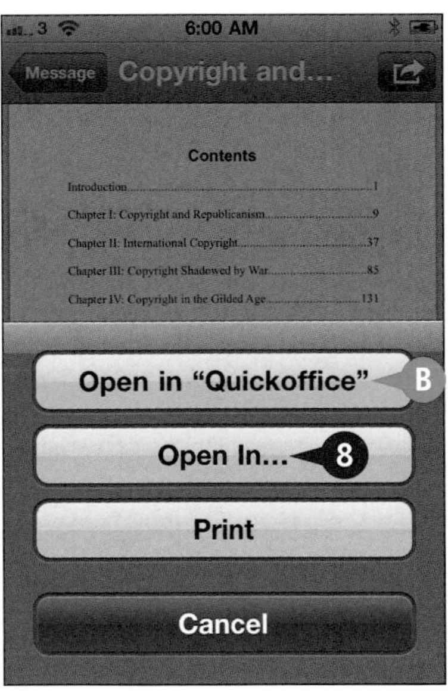

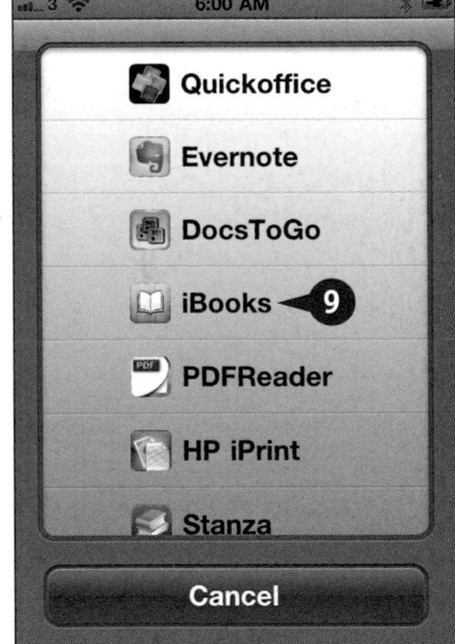

TIP

How can I delete an attached file from an email message?
You cannot directly delete an attached file from an email message on the iPhone at this writing. You can delete only the message along with its attached file. If you use an email app such as Apple Mail to manage the same email account, you can remove the attached file using that app. When you update your mailbox on your iPhone, the iPhone deletes the attached file but leaves the message.

Search for Email Messages

To find a particular email message, you can open the inbox for the account that contains it, and then browse for the message. But often you can locate a message more quickly by searching for it using a name or keyword that you know appears in the message's From field, To field, or Subject field.

You can search either in a single inbox or in all your inboxes at once. Searching all inboxes is useful when you are not sure which email account contains the message.

Search for Email Messages

1. Press the Home button.

   The Home screen appears.

2. Tap **Mail**.

   The Mailboxes screen appears.

3. Tap the inbox you want to open.

A. Tap **All Inboxes** if you want to search all your inboxes for the message.

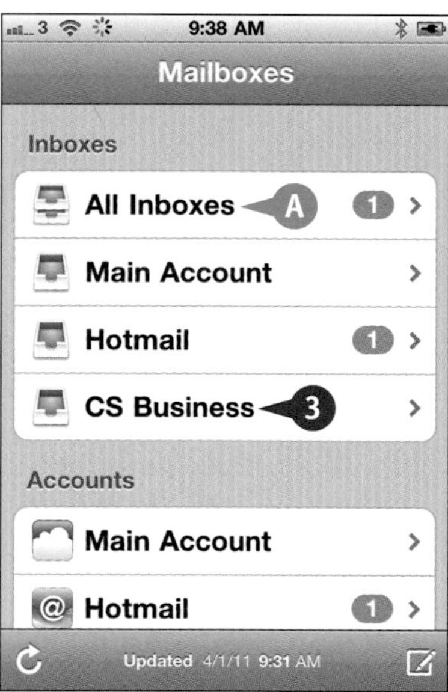

The Inbox opens.

4. Tap and drag down to scroll up to the top of the screen.

Note: You can also tap the bar at the top of the screen to scroll all the way up to the top.

The Search field appears.

5. Tap **Search**.

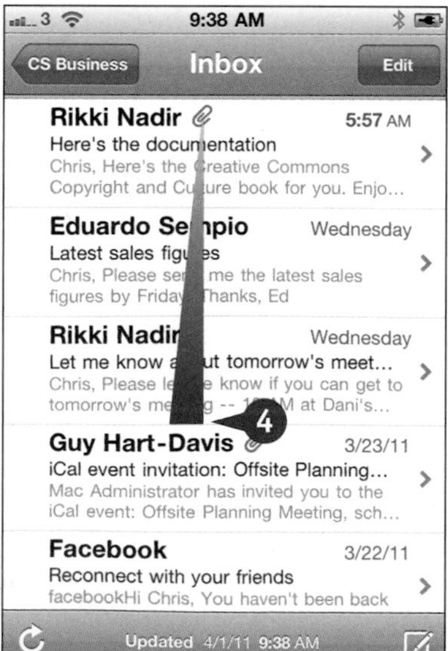

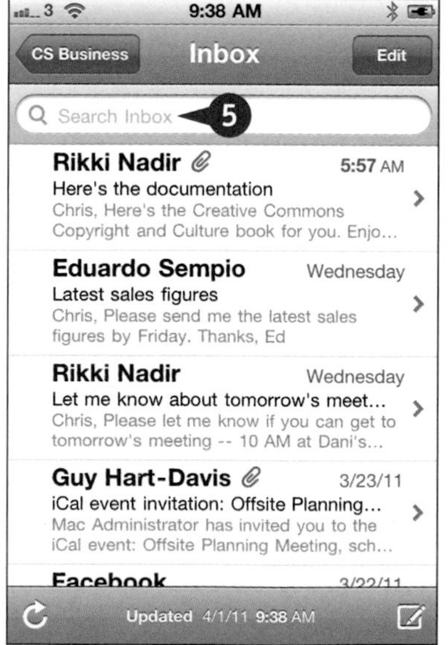

The Search screen appears.

6. Tap the message part you want to search in: From, To, Subject, or All. This example uses **Subject**.

7. Tap in the Search box and type your search term.

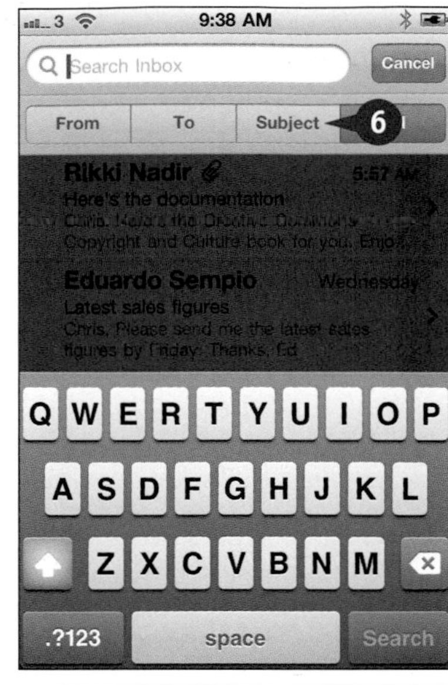

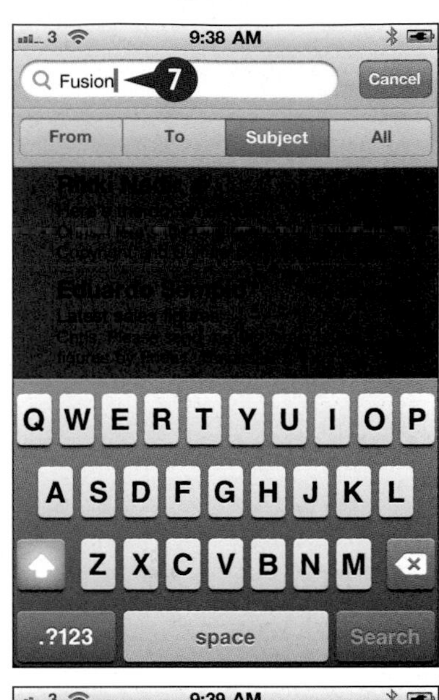

A list of search results appears.

8. Tap the message you want to open.

The message opens.

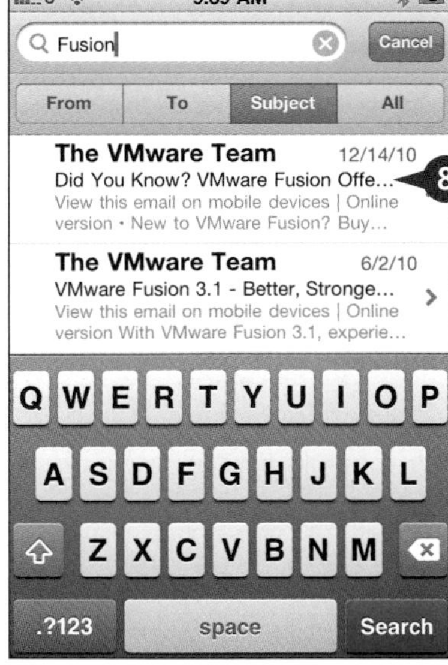

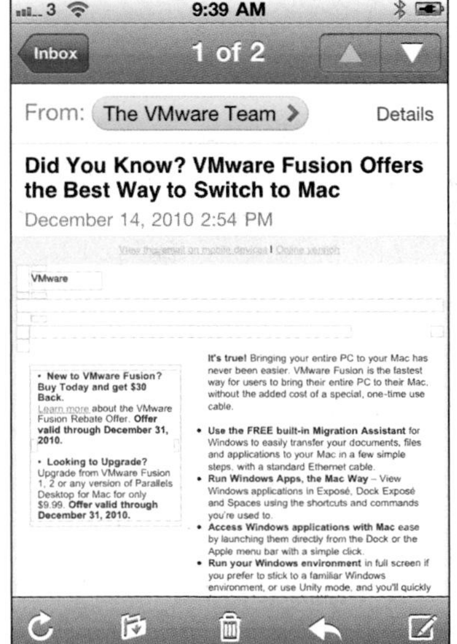

TIP

Is there another way to search for email messages?

Yes. You can use the iPhone's general search functionality to return email matches along with other search results. Press the Home button to display the Home screen, and then press again to display the Search screen. Type your search term (A), locate the Mail search results, and then tap the message (B) you want to see.

CHAPTER 9

Working with Contacts and Calendars

To stay organized, you can use your iPhone's Contacts app to manage your contacts and the Calendar app to track your time commitments.

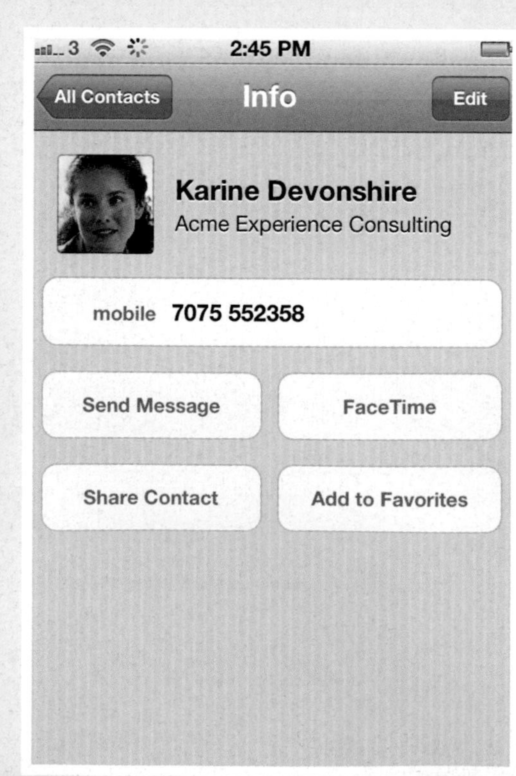

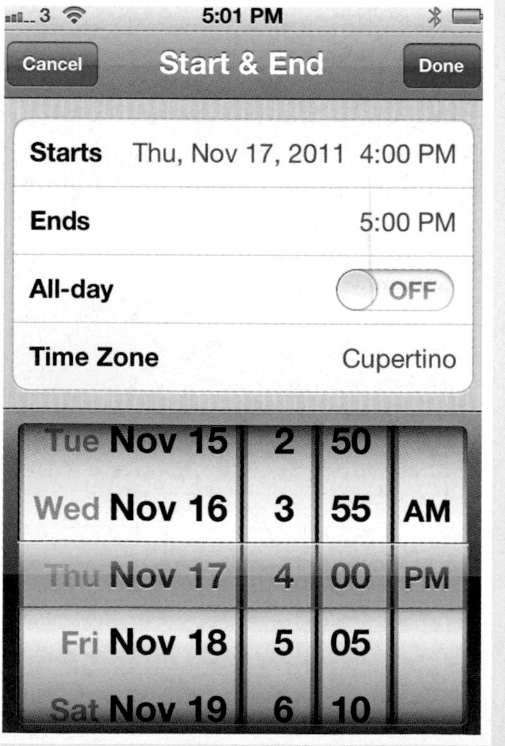

Browse or Search for Contacts

To see which contacts you have synced to your iPhone, or to find a particular contact, you can browse through the contacts.

You can either browse through your full list of contacts or choose a particular group to browse through. For example, you may want to browse through only your business contacts. You can also search for contacts to locate them.

Browse or Search for Contacts

Browse Your Contacts

1. Press the Home button.

   The Home screen appears.

2. Tap **Utilities**.

   The Utilities folder opens.

3. Tap **Contacts**.

   The Contacts screen appears.

A. To navigate the screen of contacts quickly, tap the letter on the right that you want to jump to. To navigate more slowly, scroll up or down.

4. Tap the contact whose information you want to view.

   The contact's screen appears.

Note: From the contact's screen, you can quickly phone the contact by tapping the phone number you want to use.

5. If necessary, tap and drag up to scroll down to display more information.

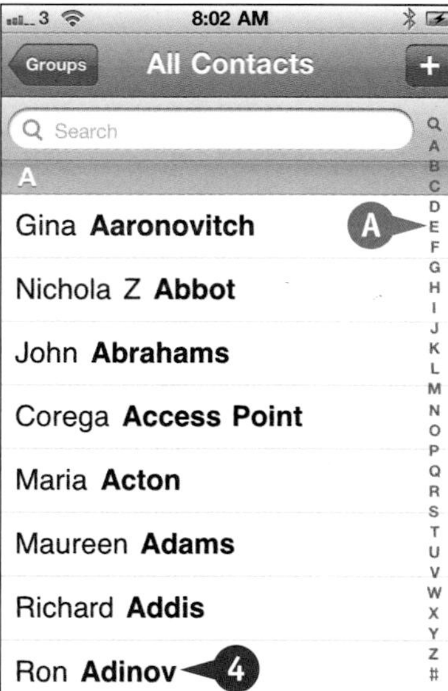

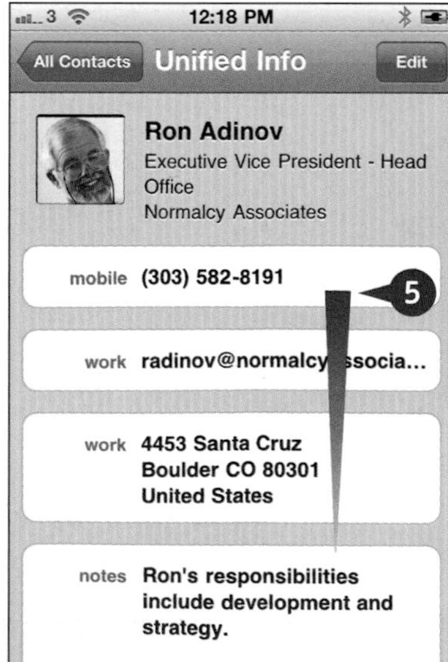

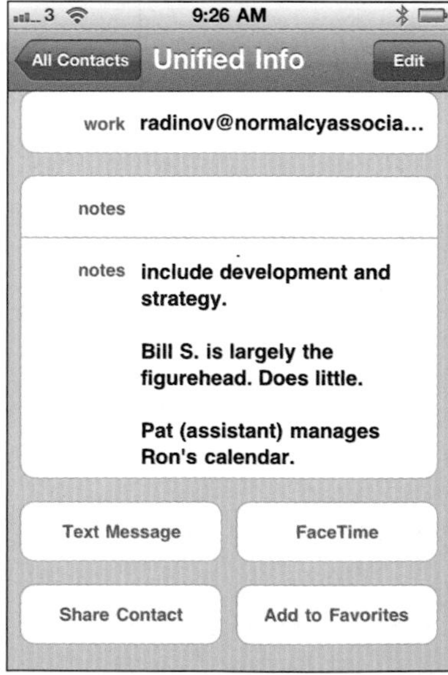

Browse a Group of Contacts

1. From the All Contacts list, tap **Groups**.

   The Groups screen appears.

2. Tap a group.

   The group's screen appears, showing only the contacts in the group.

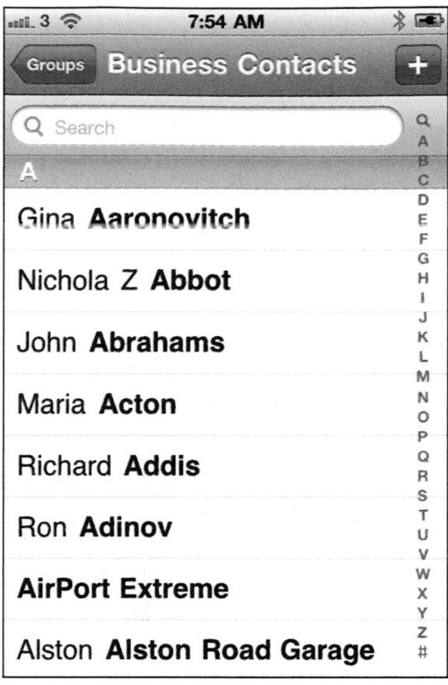

Search for Contacts

1. From the All Contacts list, tap **Search**.

   The Search screen appears.

2. Type the name you want to search for.

   A list of matches appears.

3. Tap the contact you want to view.

   The contact's information appears.

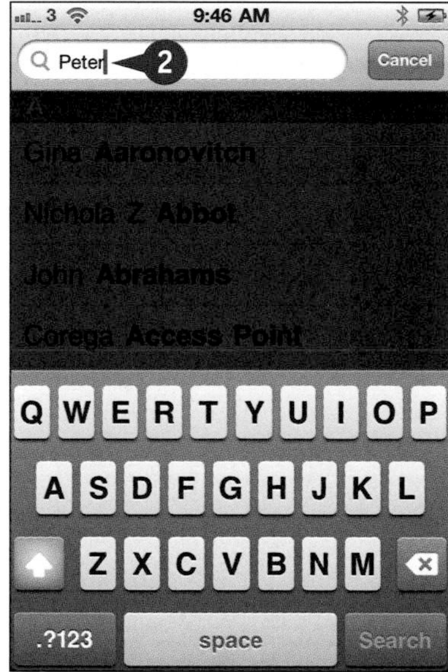

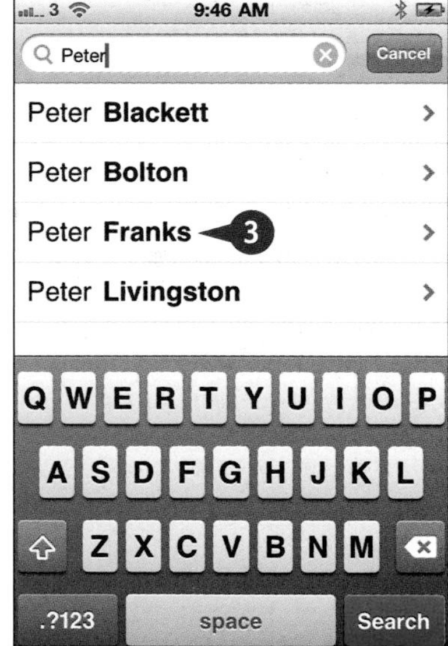

TIP

How do I make my iPhone sort my contacts by last names instead of first names?

Press the Home button. Tap **Settings** and then **Mail, Contacts, Calendars**. In the Contacts box, tap **Sort Order** (A). Tap **Last, First**.

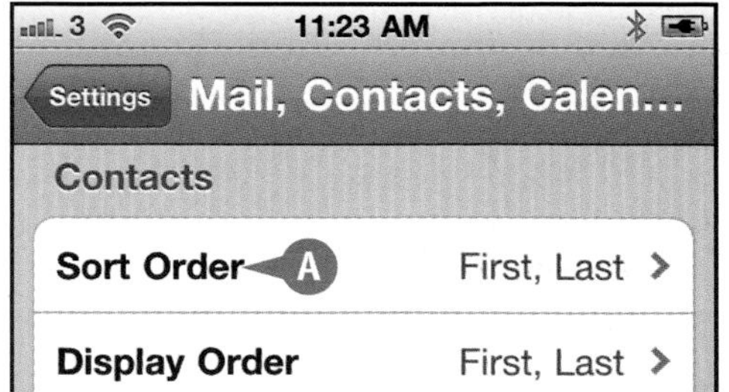

Create a New Contact

Normally, you put contacts on your iPhone by syncing them from existing records on your computer. But when necessary, you can create a new contact on your iPhone itself — for example, when you meet someone you want to remember.

You can then sync the contact record back to your computer, adding the new contact to your existing contacts.

Create a New Contact

1. Press the Home button.

   The Home screen appears.

2. Tap **Utilities**.

   The Utilities folder opens.

3. Tap **Contacts**.

   The Contacts screen appears.

Note: You can also access the Contacts app from within the Phone app. From the Home screen, tap **Phone**, and then tap the **Contacts** tab at the bottom.

4. Tap **Add** (+).

   The New Contact screen appears.

5. Tap **First**.

   The on-screen keyboard appears.

6. Type the first name.
7. Tap **Last**.
8. Type the last name.

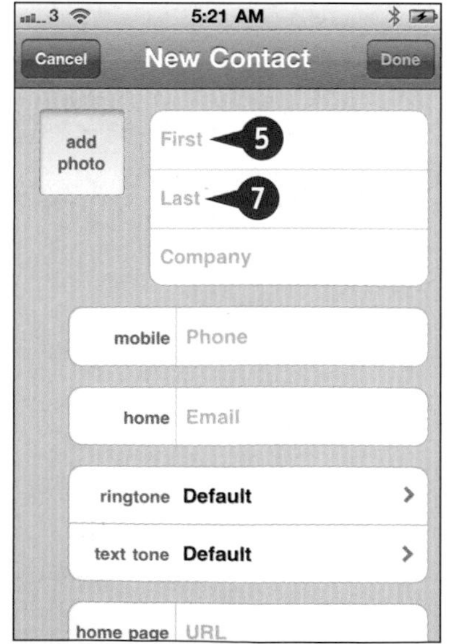

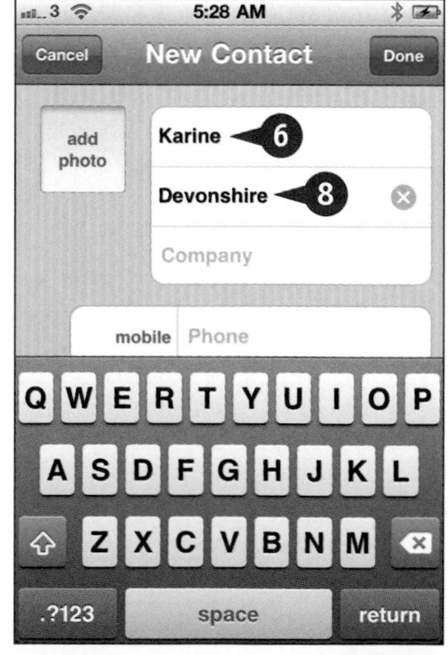

9. Add other information as needed by tapping each field and then typing the information.
10. To add a photo of the contact, tap **Add Photo.**

    The Photo dialog box opens.
11. Tap **Take Photo**.

    The Take Picture screen appears.
12. Compose the photo, and then tap **Take Picture** (📷).

    The Move and Scale screen appears.
13. Position the part of the photo you want to use in the middle.

Note: Pinch in with two fingers to zoom the photo out. Pinch out with two fingers to zoom the photo in.

14. Tap **Use Photo**.

    The photo appears in the contact record.
15. Tap **Done**.

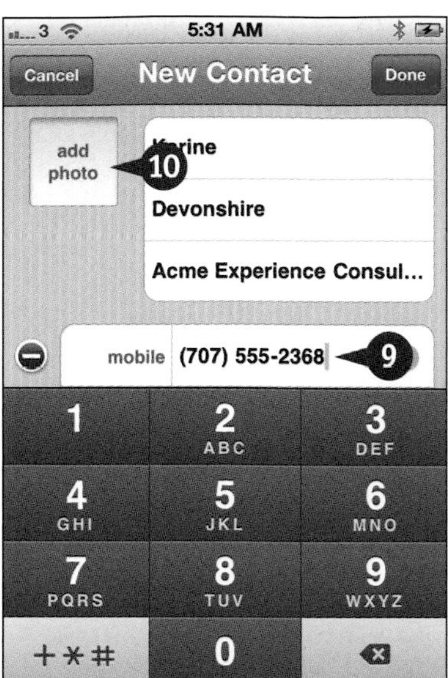

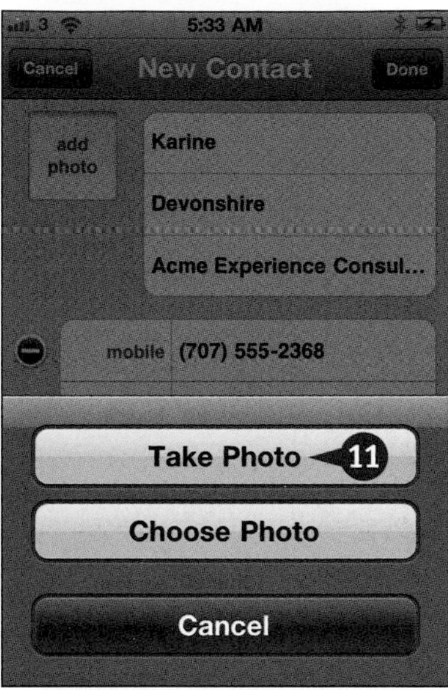

TIP

How do I assign my new contact an existing photo?

1. In the Photo dialog box, tap **Choose Photo**.
2. On the Photo Albums screen, tap the photo album.
3. Tap the photo.
4. On the Move and Scale screen, position the photo, and then tap **Choose**.

Share Contacts via Email and MMS

Often in business or your personal life, you will need to share your contacts with other people. Your iPhone makes it easy to share a contact record either via email or via Multimedia Messaging Service, MMS for short.

The iPhone shares the contact record as a virtual business card in the widely used vCard format. Most phones and personal-organizer software can easily import vCard files.

Share Contacts via Email and MMS

Open the Contact You Want to Share

1. Press the Home button.

   The Home screen appears.

2. Tap **Utilities**.

   The Utilities folder opens.

3. Tap **Contacts**.

   The Contacts screen appears.

Note: You can also access the Contacts app from within the Phone app. From the Home screen, tap **Phone**, and then tap the **Contacts** tab at the bottom.

4. Tap the contact you want to share.

   The Info screen for the contact appears.

5. Tap **Share Contact**.

   The Share Contact Using dialog box opens.

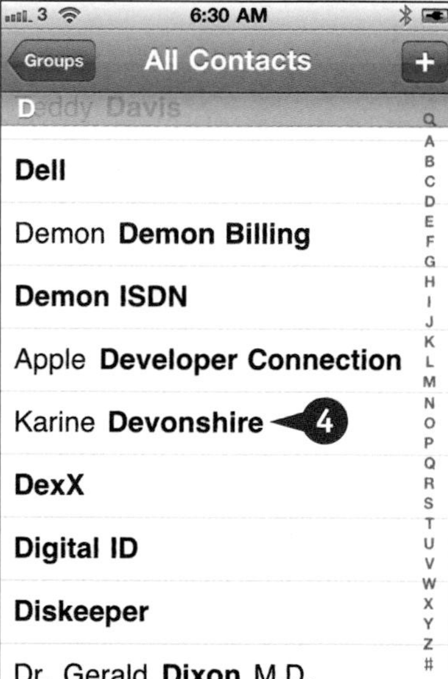

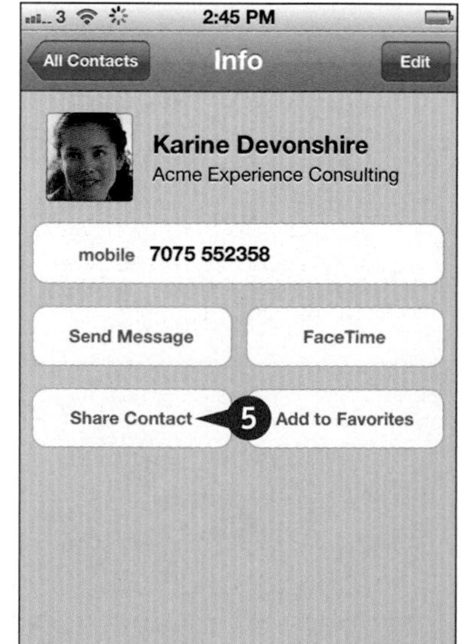

Share a Contact via Email

1. In the Share Contact Using dialog box, tap **Email**.

A. A new message titled Contact appears in the Mail app, with the contact record attached as a vCard file.

2. Address the message by typing the address or by tapping ⊕ and choosing a contact as the recipient.
3. Type a subject.
4. Type a message.
5. Tap **Send**, and Mail sends the message with the contact record attached.

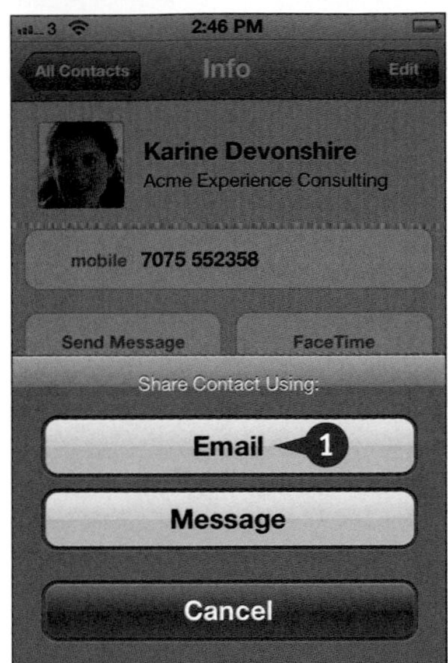

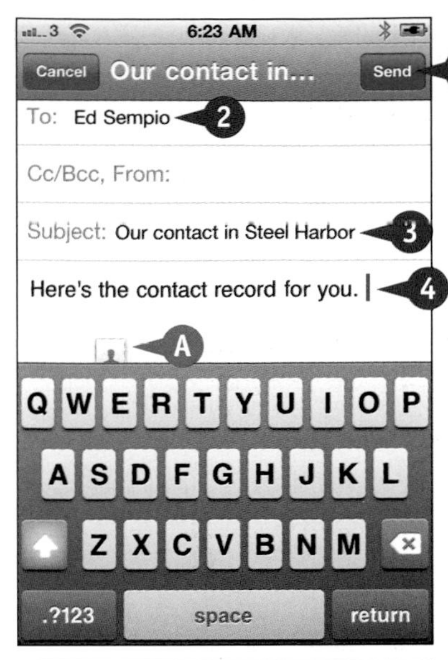

Share a Contact via MMS

1. In the Share Contact Using dialog box, tap **Message**.

B. The New MMS screen appears, with the contact record attached to the message.

2. Address the message by typing the name or number or by tapping ⊕ and choosing a contact as the recipient.
3. Type a message.
4. Tap **Send**, and the iPhone sends the message with the contact record attached.

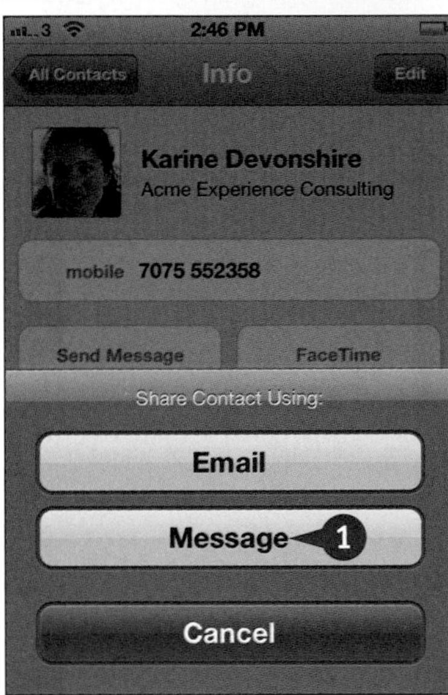

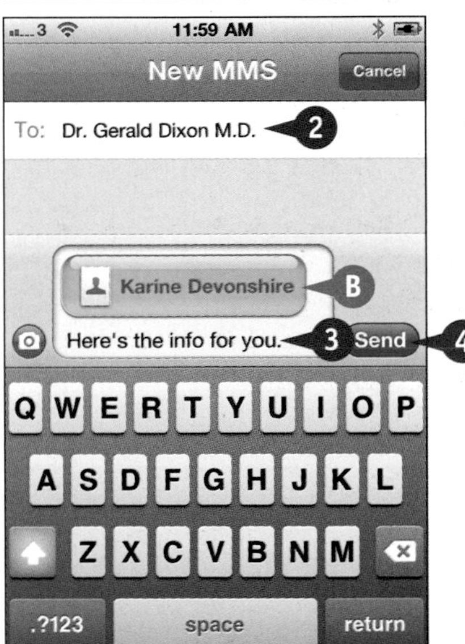

TIP

How do I add a vCard I receive in an email message to my contacts?

In the Mail app, tap the button for the vCard file. On the vCard screen that opens, scroll down to the bottom, and then tap **Create New Contact**. If the vCard contains extra information about an existing contact, tap **Add to Existing Contact**, and then tap the contact.

Browse Existing Events in Your Calendars

Your iPhone's Calendar app gives you a great way of managing your schedule and making sure you never miss an appointment.

After setting up your calendars to sync using iTunes or iCloud, as described in Chapter 2, you can take your calendars with you everywhere and consult them whenever you need to. You can view either all your calendars or only ones you choose.

Browse Existing Events in Your Calendars

Browse Existing Events in Your Calendars

1. Press the Home button.

   The Home screen appears.

2. Tap **Calendar**.

   The Calendar screen appears. Normally, you see the All Calendars screen.

3. Tap **Month** to see Month view, in which each day appears in a square.

Note: In Month view, a dot on a date indicates that one or more events occur on that day.

4. Tap the day you want to view.

   A The day's details appear below the list of days.

5. Tap **Day**.

   A timeline with events for the current day appears.

6. Tap **List**.

   A list of upcoming appointments appears.

7. Tap an appointment whose details you want to see.

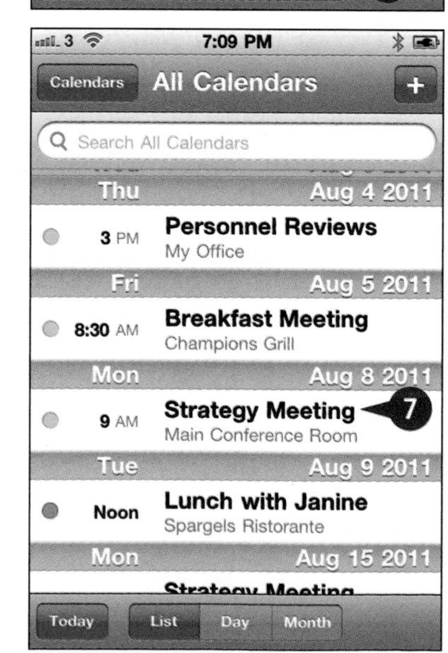

The Event Details screen appears, showing details of the event.

8 If you need to edit the event, tap **Edit**.

The Edit screen appears, and you can make changes to the event.

9 Tap **Done**.

Choose Which Calendars to Display

1 Tap **Calendars**.

The Calendars screen appears.

2 Tap to place a check mark next to a calendar you want to display, or tap to remove the check mark from a calendar you want to hide.

B Tap **Show All Calendars** to place a check mark next to each calendar. Tap **Hide All Calendars** to remove all check marks.

3 When you finish choosing calendars to display, tap **Done**.

The calendars you chose appear.

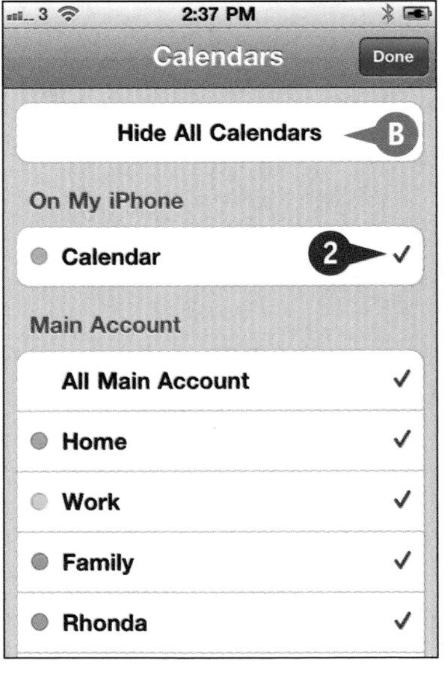

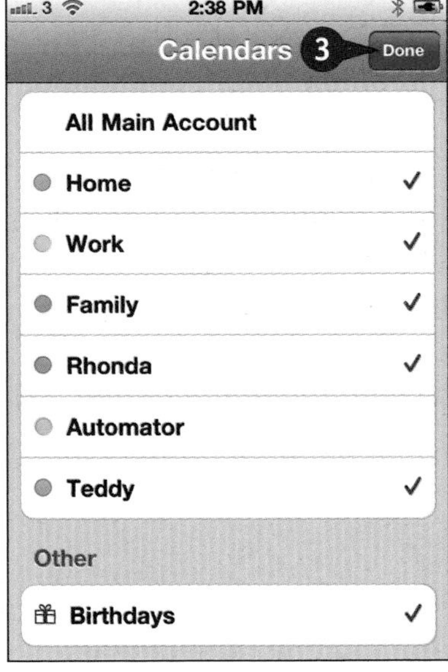

TIP

What is the Birthdays calendar?
The Birthdays calendar is a calendar that automatically displays birthdays of contacts whose data includes the birthday. To add the birthday to a contact, open the contact's record, tap **Edit**, and then tap **Add Field**. Tap **Birthday**, and then choose the date.

Create New Events in Your Calendars

Normally, you will probably create most new events in your calendars on your computer, and then sync them to your iPhone. But when you need to create a new event using the iPhone, you can easily do so.

You can create either a straightforward, one-shot appointment or an appointment that repeats on a schedule. And you can choose which calendar the appointment belongs to.

Create New Events in Your Calendars

1. Press the Home button.

   The Home screen appears.

2. Tap **Calendar**.

   The Calendar screen appears.

3. Tap **Month** to switch to Month view.

4. Tap the day on which you want to create the new event.

5. Tap **Add** (+).

The Add Event screen appears.

6. Tap **Title** and type the title of the event.

7. Tap **Location** and type the location of the event.

8. Tap **Starts, Ends**.

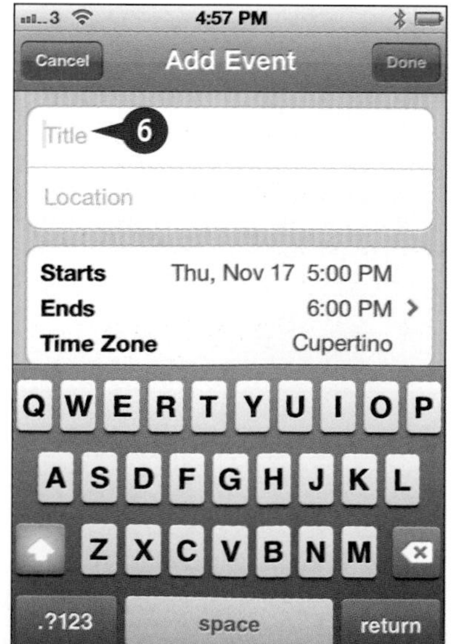

The Start & End screen appears.

9 Tap the date and time wheels to set the start time.

10 Tap **Ends**.

11 Tap the date and time wheels to set the end time.

A If this is an all-day appointment, tap the **All-day** switch and move it to On.

B If you need to change the time zone, tap **Time Zone**, type the city name, and then tap the time zone.

12 Tap **Done**.

13 On the Add Event screen, tap **Alert**.

14 On the Event Alert screen, tap the timing for the alert.

15 Tap **Done**.

16 Tap **Calendar**.

17 On the Calendar screen, tap the calendar for the event.

18 Tap **Done**.

19 On the Add Event screen, tap **Done**.

The event appears on your calendar.

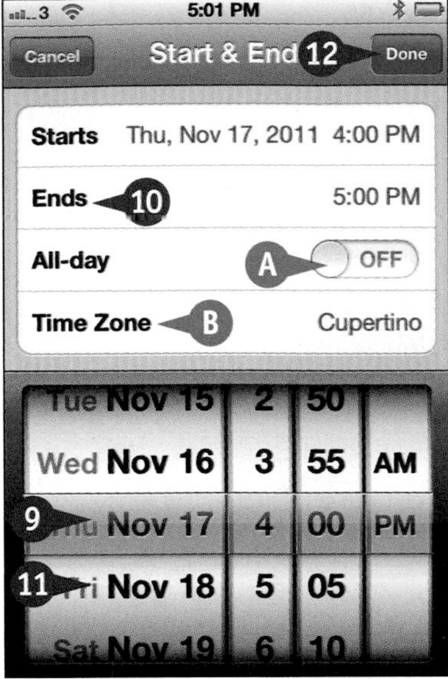

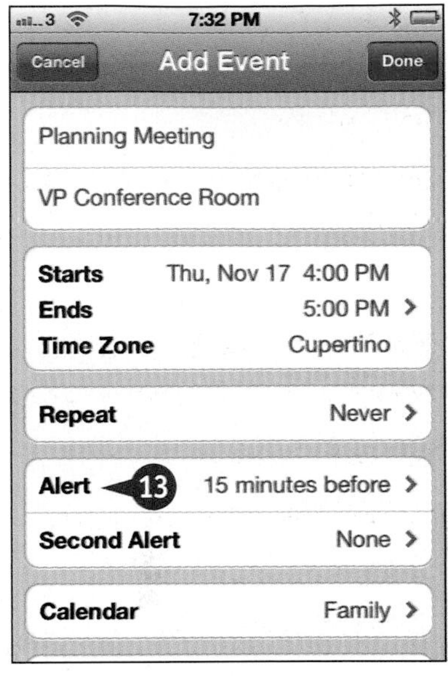

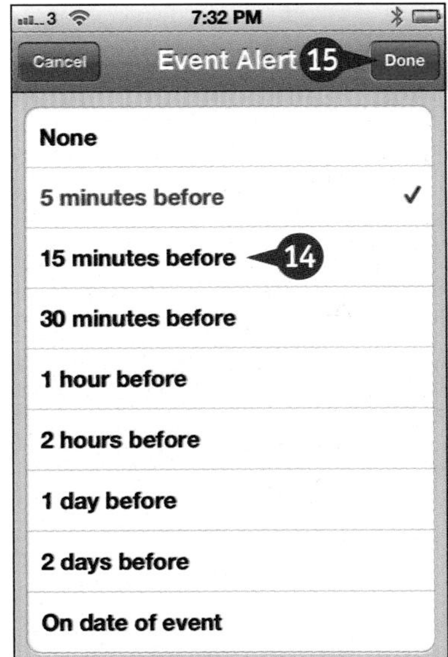

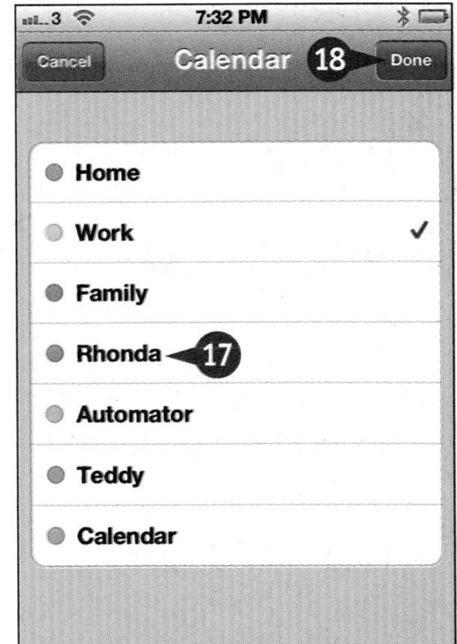

TIP

How do I set up an event that repeats every week?

On the Add Event screen, tap **Repeat**. On the Repeat Event screen, tap **Every Week** (A), placing a check mark next to it, and then tap **Done** (B).

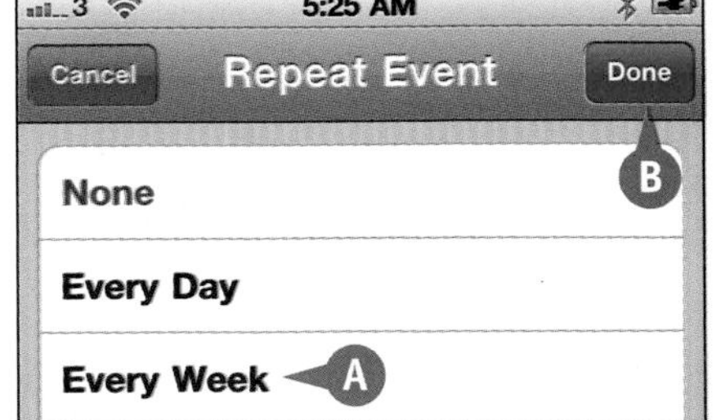

Work with Calendar Invitations

As well as events you create yourself, you may receive invitations to events that others create. When you receive an event invitation attached to an email message, you can choose whether to accept the invitation or decline it. If you accept the invitation, you can add the event automatically to your calendar.

Work with Calendar Invitations

1. In Mail, tap the message that contains the invitation.

   The message appears.

2. Tap the invitation.

   The Event Details screen appears.

3. Tap **Add To Calendar**.

Note: From within Calendar, you can check for outstanding invitations by tapping ▣.

The Choose Calendar screen appears.

4. Tap the calendar you want to add the event to.
5. Tap **Done**.

   The Event Details screen appears again.

6. Tap **Alert**.

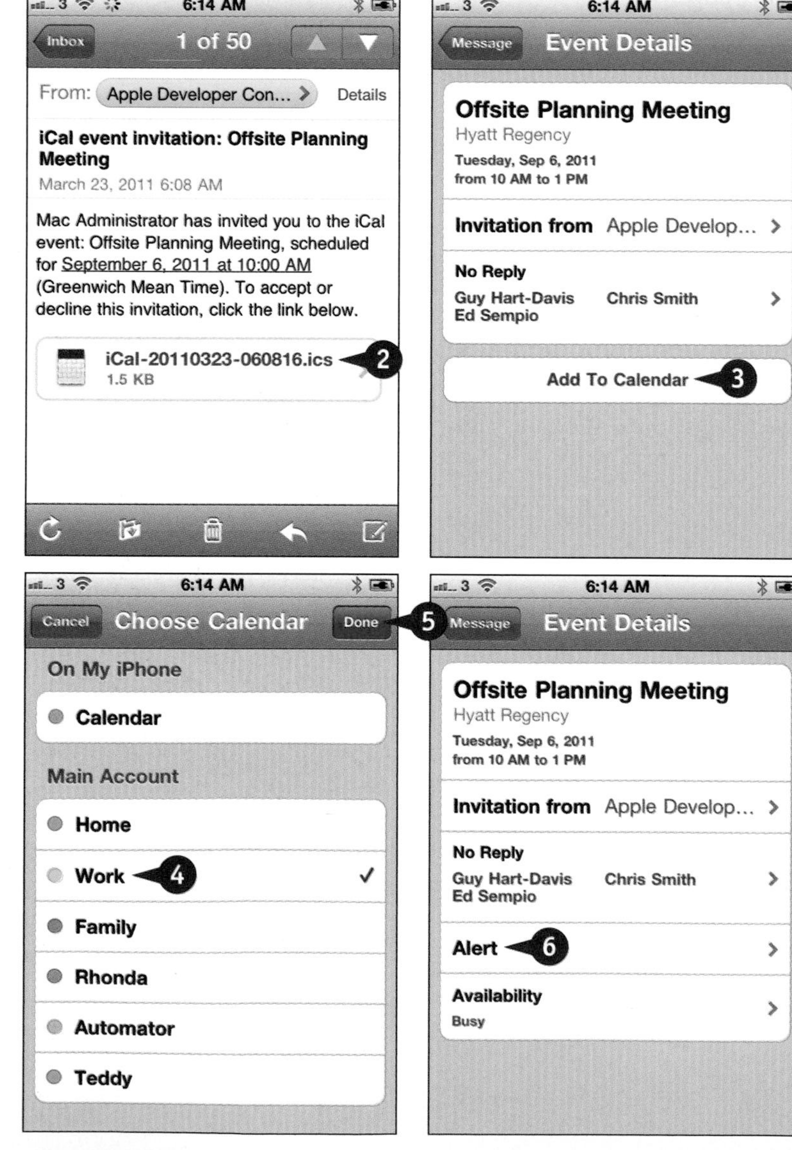

The Event Alert screen appears.

7 Tap the alert timing you want. For example, tap **15 minutes before**.

8 Tap the event name.

The Event Details screen appears again.

9 Tap **Availability**.

The Availability screen appears.

10 Tap **Busy** or **Free**, as appropriate.

11 Tap the event name.

The Event Details screen appears again.

12 Tap **Message**.

The message appears.

13 Press the Home button.

The Home screen appears.

14 Tap **Calendar**.

The Calendar screen appears.

A The appointment appears in your calendar.

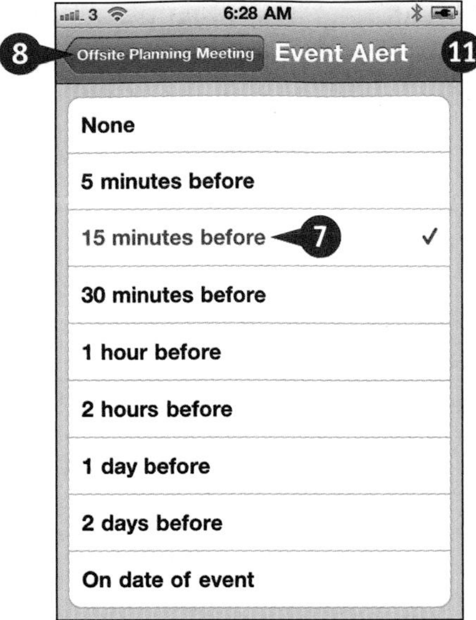

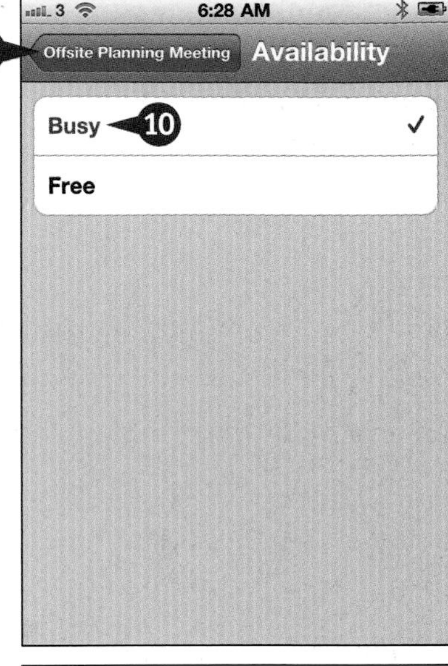

TIP

Why does an event appear at a different time than that shown in the invitation I accepted?

When you open the invitation, you see the event's time in the time zone in which it was created. If your iPhone is currently using a different time zone, the appointment appears in your calendar using that time zone's time, so the time appears to have changed.

Search for Calendar Events

If you have many events in your calendars, browsing for events may be a slow process. But you can find the events you need in moments by searching for them.

You can search using any information stored in the event — for example, the location, or the name of an invitee.

Search for Calendar Events

1. Press the Home button.

   The Home screen appears.

2. Tap **Calendar**.

   The Calendar screen appears.

3. Tap **List**.

The List screen appears.

A If you want to search only some calendars, tap **Calendars** to display the Calendars screen. Remove the check marks for the calendars you do not want to search, and then tap **Done**.

4. Tap **Search** (🔍).

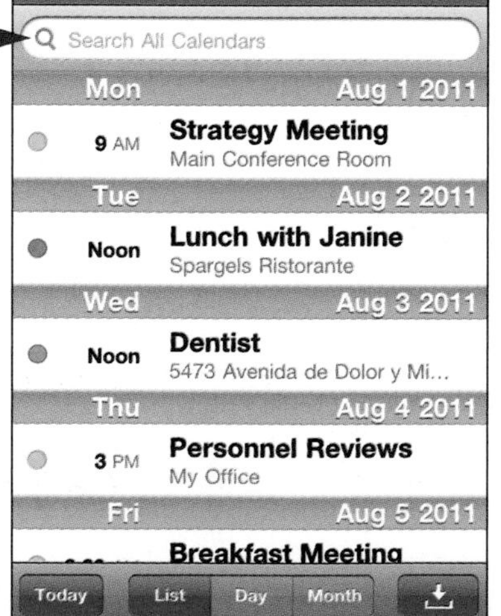

The Search screen appears.

5 Type your search term.

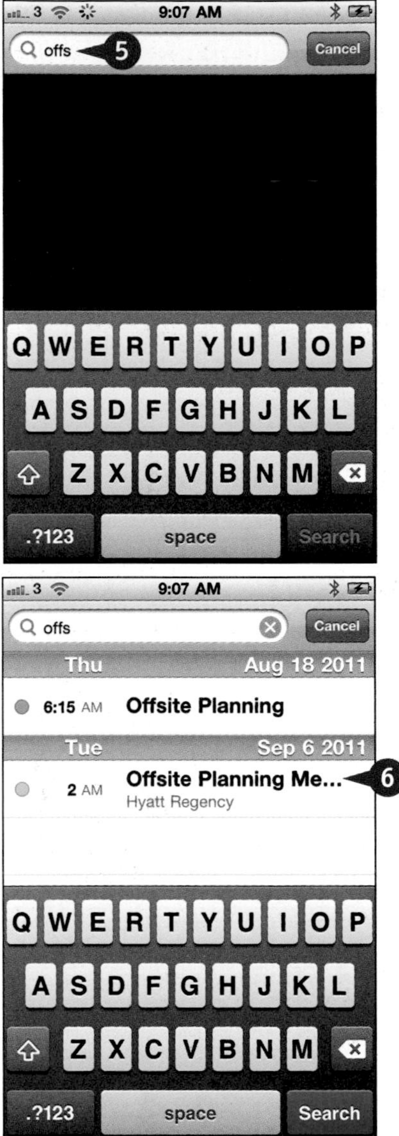

The Search screen displays events matching the search.

6 Tap the event you want to display.

Note: You can also find calendar events by searching using Spotlight, the iPhone's main search feature. Press the Home button to display the Home screen, and then scroll left to display the Spotlight screen. Type your search term. Spotlight finds all matching items, including Calendar items.

TIP

How do I edit an existing event?

Locate the event by browsing or by searching, as described in this task, and then tap the event to open it. Tap **Edit** to open the event for editing; make your changes, and then tap **Done.**

You cannot edit the details for an event you have added by accepting an invitation sent to you.

CHAPTER 10

Playing Music and Videos

As well as being a phone and a powerful handheld computer, your iPhone is also a full-scale music and video player. To play music, you use the Music app; to play videos, you use the Videos app. In this chapter, you learn to use the Music app to play back music, create playlists, and enjoy podcasts and iTunes U. You also learn how to play videos with the Videos app, view videos on websites, play YouTube videos, and shop on the iTunes Store.

Play Back Music Using the Music App

After loading music on your iPhone as described in Chapter 1, you can play it back using the Music app.

You can play music in several ways. You can play music by song or by album, as described in this task. You can play songs in exactly the order you want by creating a custom playlist, as described later in this chapter. You can also play by artist, by genre, or by composer.

Play Back Music Using the Music App

1. Press the Home button.

   The Home screen appears.

2. Tap **Music**.

   The Music screen appears.

3. Tap the button by which you want to sort. This example uses **Songs**.

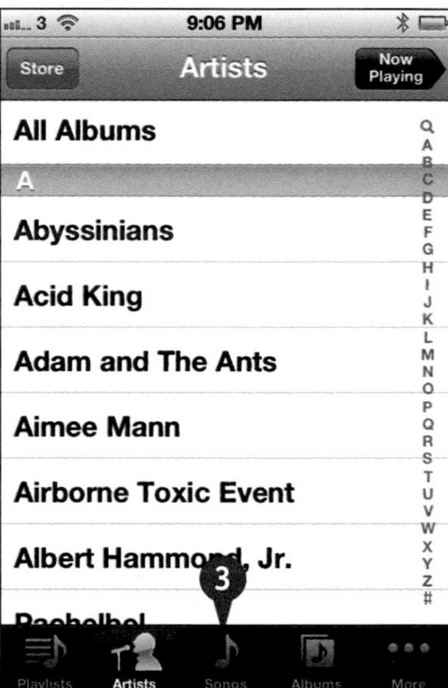

The list of songs appears.

A. To see the music listed by other categories, such as Composers or Genres, tap **More**, and then tap the category by which you want to sort.

4. Tap and drag up to scroll down if necessary.

5. Tap the song you want to play.

Note: Tap and hold for a moment to see the full information about the song — for example, if it does not fit in the listing.

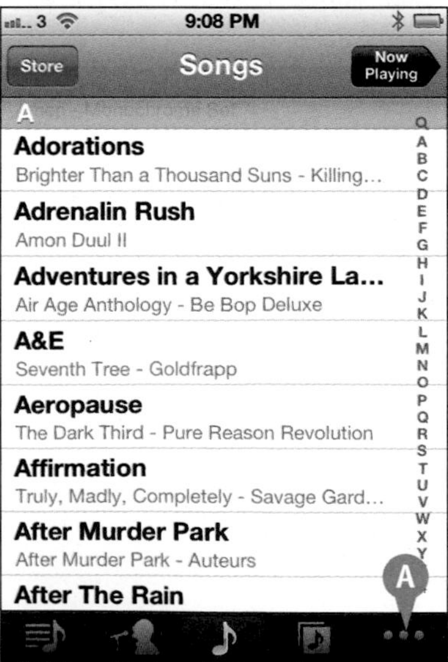

The song starts playing.

6. To rate the song or jump to another song, tap **Song List** (▤).

The song list appears.

7. Tap the appropriate star to rate the song.

8. Tap another song to play it, or tap **Song** to go back to the song.

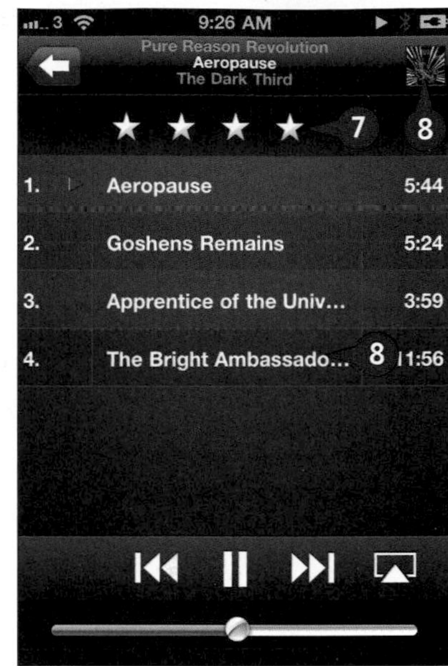

TIP

Is there a way to control the Music app's playback when I have switched to another app?

Yes. You can quickly control the Music app using the multitasking bar. Press the Home button twice in quick succession to display the multitasking bar, and then scroll left until you see the playback controls. Tap **Pause** (⏸) to pause the music, and tap **Play** (▶) to restart playback. Tap **Fast-Forward/Next** (⏭) to skip to the next track, or tap and hold to fast-forward. Tap **Rewind/Previous** (⏮) to go back to the beginning of the track; tap again to go to the previous track; or tap and hold to rewind. Tap **Music** (♫) to display the Music app.

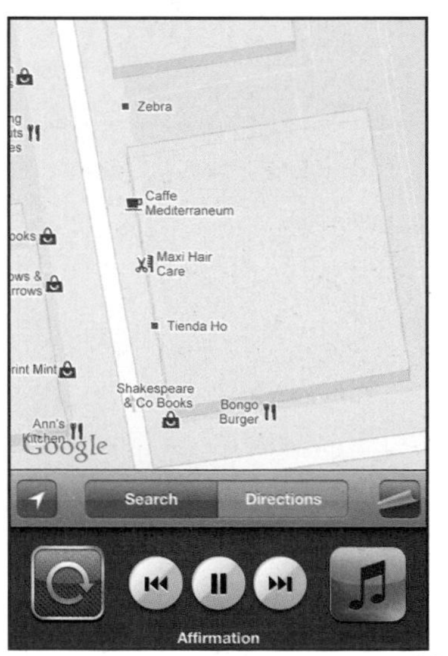

Play Back Videos Using the Videos App

To play videos — such as movies, TV shows, or music videos — you use the iPhone's Videos app. You can play back a video either on the iPhone's screen, which is handy when you are traveling, or on a TV to which you connect the iPhone, or to a TV connected to an AppleTV box. Using a TV is great when you need to share a movie or other video with family, friends, or colleagues.

Play Back Videos Using the Videos App

1. Press the Home button.

   The Home screen appears.

2. Tap **Videos**.

The Videos screen appears.

Note: Tap and drag up to scroll down to see more videos.

3. Tap the video you want to play.

Note: Your iPhone plays video in landscape orientation, so if you are holding the iPhone in its upright, portrait orientation, turn it on its side for viewing the video.

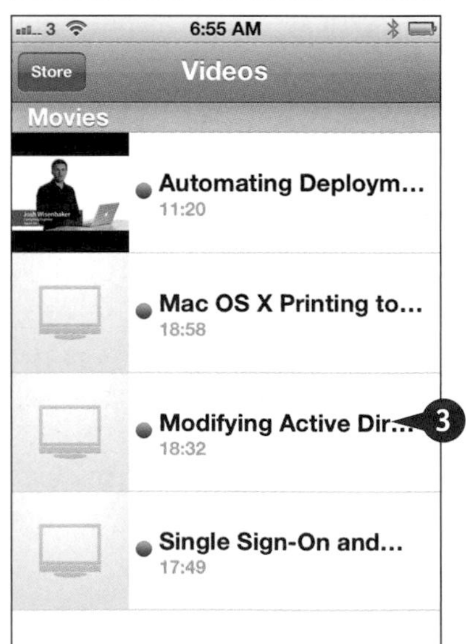

The video starts playing.

4 When you need to control playback, tap the screen.

The playback controls appear, and you can pause the video, move forward, or take other actions.

5 Tap **Done** when you want to stop playing the video.

TIP

How do I play back videos on my television from my iPhone?

First, check which connectors the television uses, and then get a suitable connector cable from the Apple Store (http://store.apple.com) or another supplier. For example, you may need the Apple Composite AV Cable or an equivalent.

Second, use the cable to connect the iPhone's dock connector port to the television.

Third, tap **Settings**, tap **General**, and then tap **TV Out** to display the TV Out screen. Tap the **Widescreen** switch and move it to On or Off, as needed. To change the TV output, tap **TV Signal**, and then tap **NTSC** or **PAL**, as needed.

Create a Playlist with the Music App

Instead of playing individual songs or playing a CD's songs from start to finish, you can create a playlist that contains only the songs you want in your preferred order. Playlists are a great way to enjoy music on your iPhone.

You can create either a standard playlist by putting the songs in order yourself, or use the Genius Playlist feature to have the Music app create the playlist for you. Before you can use the Genius Playlist feature, you must turn on Genius in iTunes and then sync your iPhone.

Create a Playlist with the Music App

1. Press the Home button.

   The Home screen appears.

2. Tap **Music**.

   The Music screen appears.

3. Tap **Playlists**.

   The Playlists screen appears.

   A. The Genius symbol (❋) indicates a Genius playlist.

4. Tap **Add Playlist**.

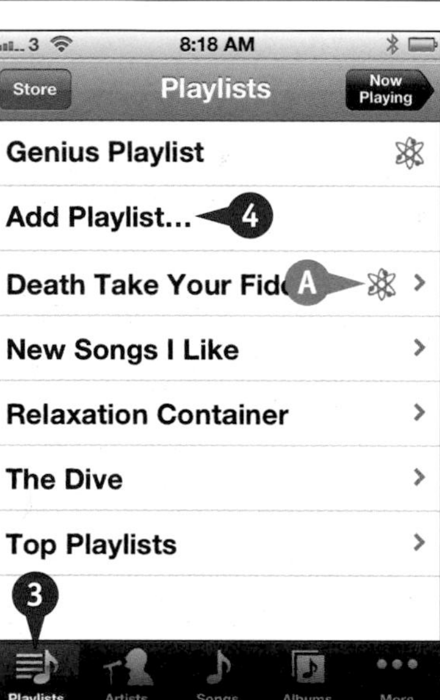

The New Playlist dialog box opens.

5. Type the name for the playlist.

6. Tap **Save**.

   The Songs screen appears.

7. Tap ⊕ for each song you want to add.

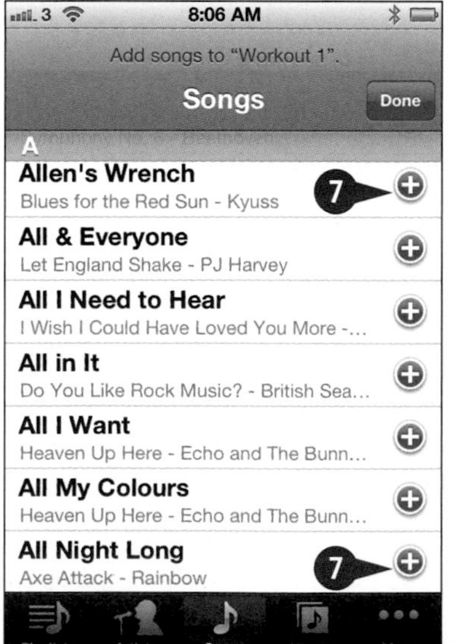

(B) The song button fades to gray to show you have added the song to the playlist.

(C) To browse by artists for songs to add, tap **Artists**. To browse by playlists, tap **Playlists**. To browse by albums, tap **Albums**.

8 Tap **Done**.

The playlist screen appears.

9 Tap **Edit**.

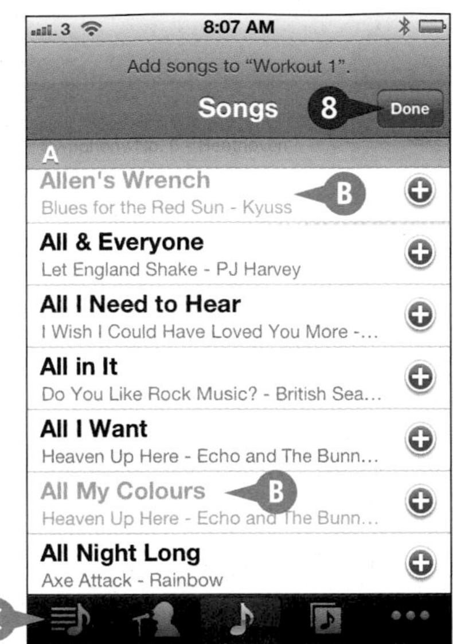

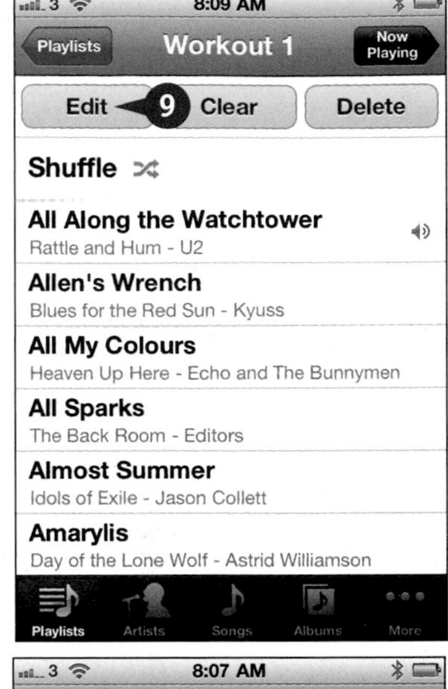

The screen for editing the playlist appears.

10 Tap ≡ and drag a song up or down to move it.

(D) To remove a song, tap ⊖. To add further songs, tap ⊞.

11 Tap **Done** at the top of the playlist-editing screen.

12 Tap a song to start the playlist playing.

(E) Tap **Shuffle** if you want to play the playlist's songs in random order.

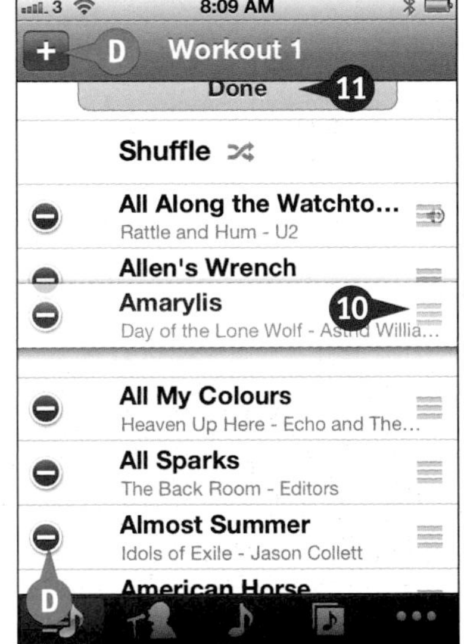

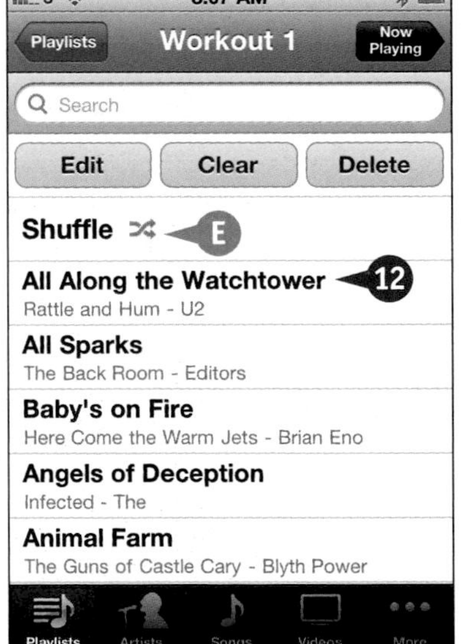

How do I create a Genius playlist on my iPhone?

Press the Home button. Tap **Music**, tap **Playlists**, and then tap **Genius Playlist**. Tap the song to base the playlist on (A). The Music app creates the playlist and sets it playing.

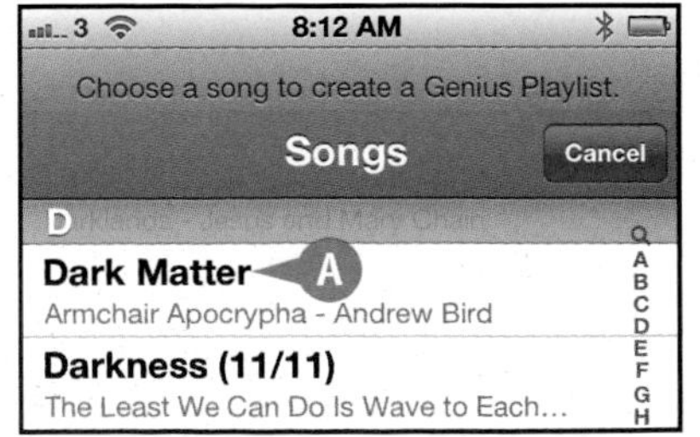

Customize the Music App's Interface

The Music app comes set up so that you can easily browse by playlists, artists, songs, or albums. If you want to browse by other categories, such as by composers or by genres, you can customize the Music app's interface to put these items at the tip of your finger.

Customize the Music App's Interface

1. Press the Home button.

   The Home screen appears.

2. Tap **Music**.

   The Music screen appears.

3. Tap **More**.

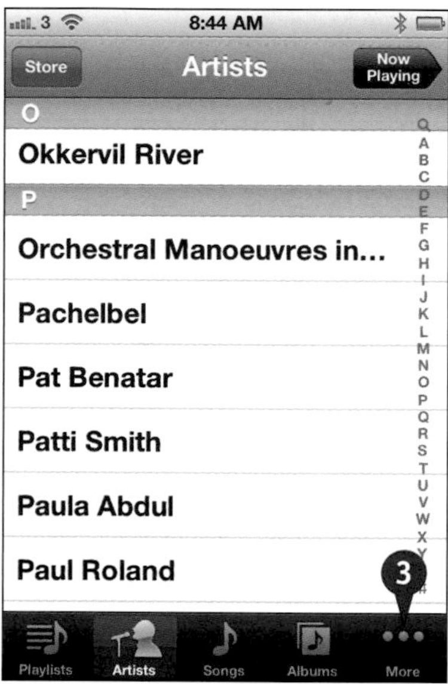

The More screen appears.

4. Tap **Edit**.

   The Configure screen appears.

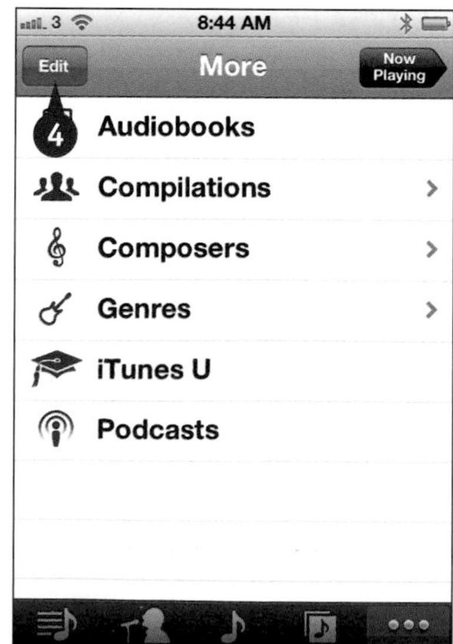

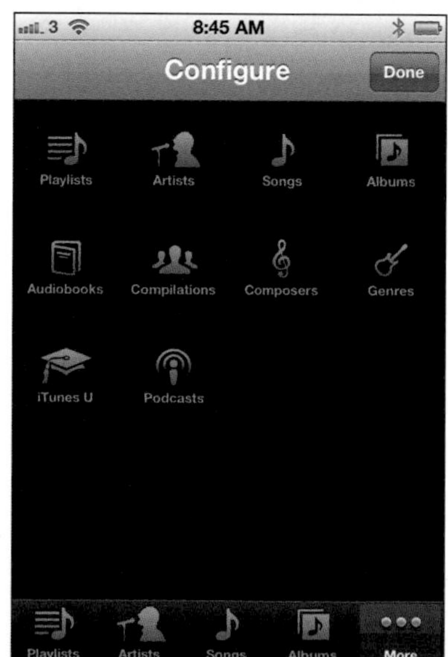

5 Tap a button and drag it to replace a button on the button bar. For example, tap **Genres** and drag it on top of **Albums**.

The button you dropped replaces the button you dropped it on.

6 Change other buttons as needed.

Note: You can change the position of the buttons on the button bar by tapping a button and dragging it left or right to where you want it.

7 Tap **Done**.

You can then use your customized version of the Music screen.

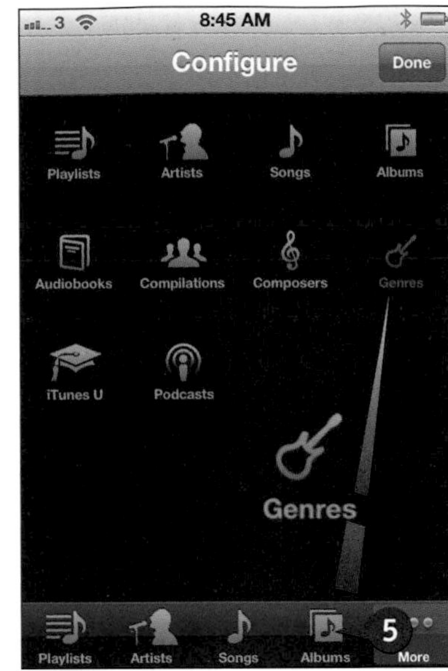

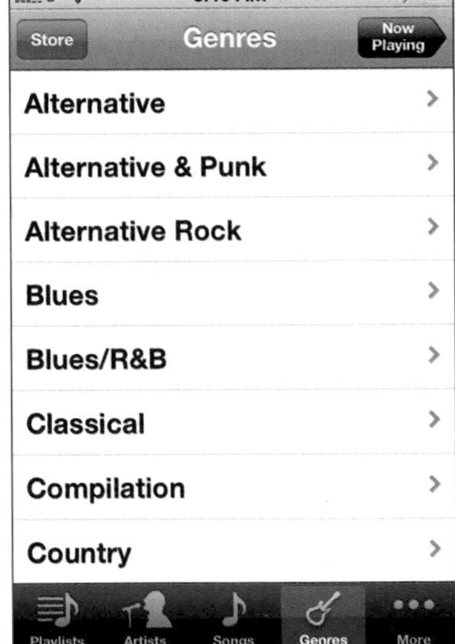

TIP

How do I reset the Music screen to its default settings?

The straightforward way to reset the Music app's screen to its default settings is to display the Configure screen as described in this task, and drag the icons into their default order: Playlists, Artists, Songs, Albums, and More.

You can also return the Music app's screen to its default configuration from the Reset screen in Settings, but this is a wide-ranging change that you will normally not want to make.

Use Podcasts and iTunes U

Besides listening to music and watching videos, you can use the iPhone to watch or listen to *podcasts*, which are video or audio programs released via the Internet.

You can find podcasts covering many different topics on the iTunes Store. Through the iTunes Store you can also access iTunes U, podcasts containing free educational content.

Use Podcasts and iTunes U

Open the iTunes App

1. Press the Home button.

   The Home screen appears.

2. Tap **iTunes**.

   The iTunes screen appears.

3. Tap **More**.

   The More screen appears.

Find and Download a Podcast

1. On the More screen, tap **Podcasts**.

   The Podcasts screen appears.

2. Tap the tab you want to view.

   The screen you chose appears.

3. Tap the topic you want.

4. Tap the podcast you want to learn about.

   The podcast's screen appears.

5. To get an episode, tap its **Free** button.

   The Free button changes to a Download button.

6. Tap the **Download** button.

   The iTunes app downloads the podcast.

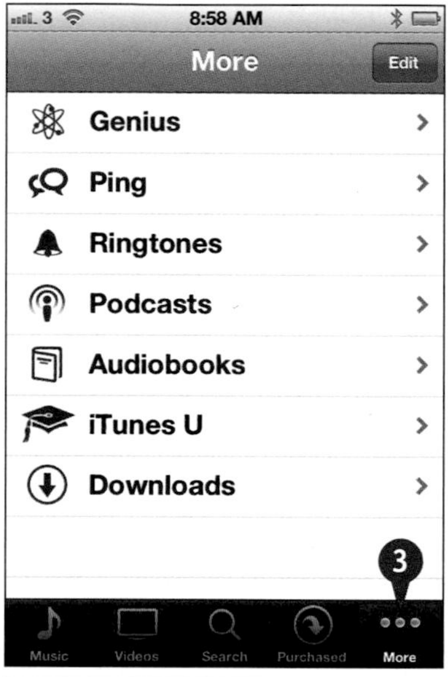

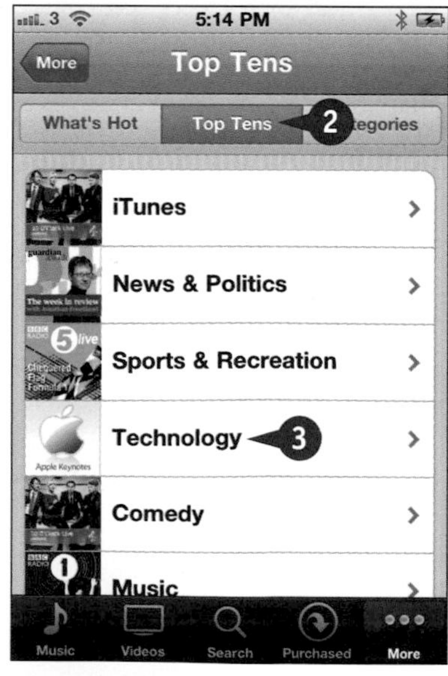

Find and Download iTunes U Content

1. From the More screen, tap **iTunes U**.

   The iTunes U screen appears.

2. Tap the tab you want to view — What's Hot, Top Tens, or Categories. This example uses **What's Hot**.

   The screen you chose appears.

3. Tap the iTunes U course you want to view.

   The category screen appears.

   The course's screen appears.

4. To get a lecture, tap its **Free** button.

   The Free button changes to a Download button.

5. Tap the **Download** button.

   The iTunes app downloads the lecture.

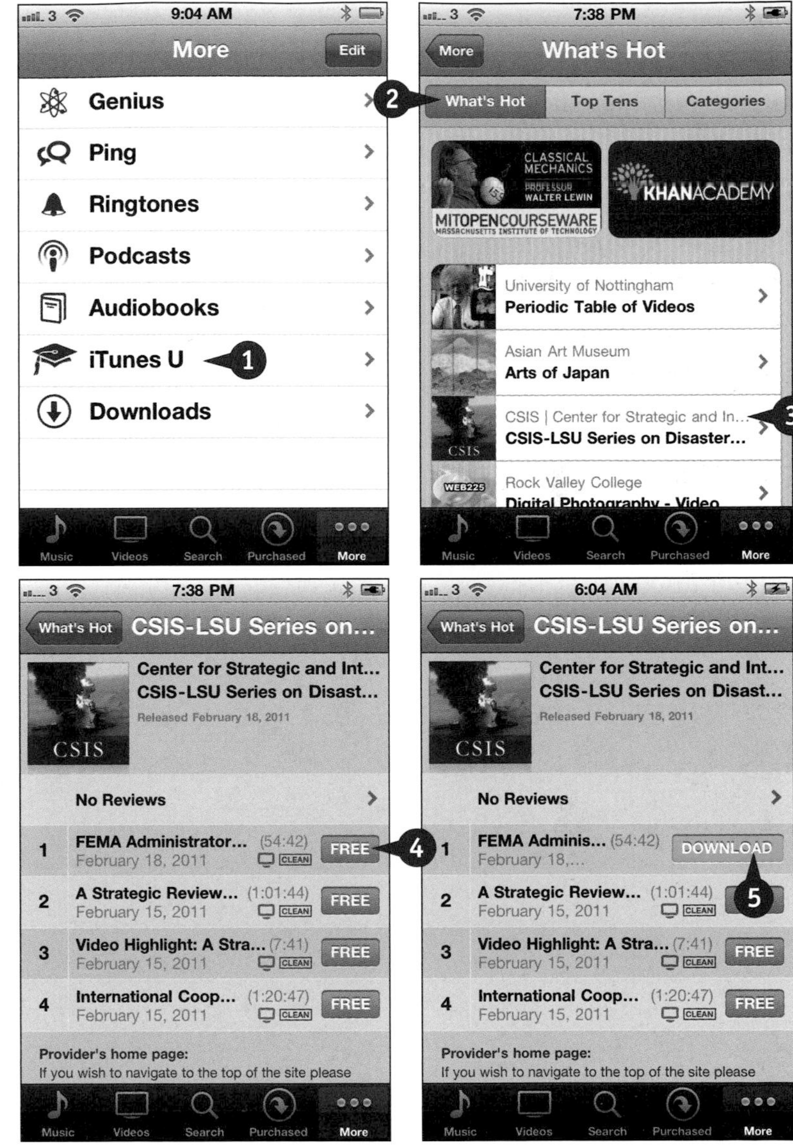

TIP

How do I play the podcasts and iTunes U content I have downloaded?

Press the Home button to display the Home screen, and then tap **Music** to launch the Music app. Tap **More** on the button bar at the bottom to display the More screen. You can then tap **Podcasts** to display the Podcasts screen or tap **iTunes U** to display the iTunes U screen. Tap the podcast you want to play.

View Videos on Websites

Some websites include videos that you can watch using the Safari web browser. You view these sites directly in Safari, which automatically displays controls for controlling playback.

Other websites include links to videos stored on the YouTube video-sharing site. When you open one of these links, your iPhone automatically opens the video in the YouTube app.

View Videos on Websites

1. Press the Home button.

   The Home screen appears.

2. Tap **Safari**.

   The Safari screen appears.

3. Go to the website and locate the page that contains the video you want to view.

Note: Your iPhone plays video in landscape orientation, so if you are holding the iPhone in its upright, portrait orientation, turn it on its side for viewing the video.

Note: See Chapter 8 for instructions on how to browse the web with Safari.

4. Tap the video's **Play** button (▶) to start the video playing.

5. Tap outside the controls to hide the controls.

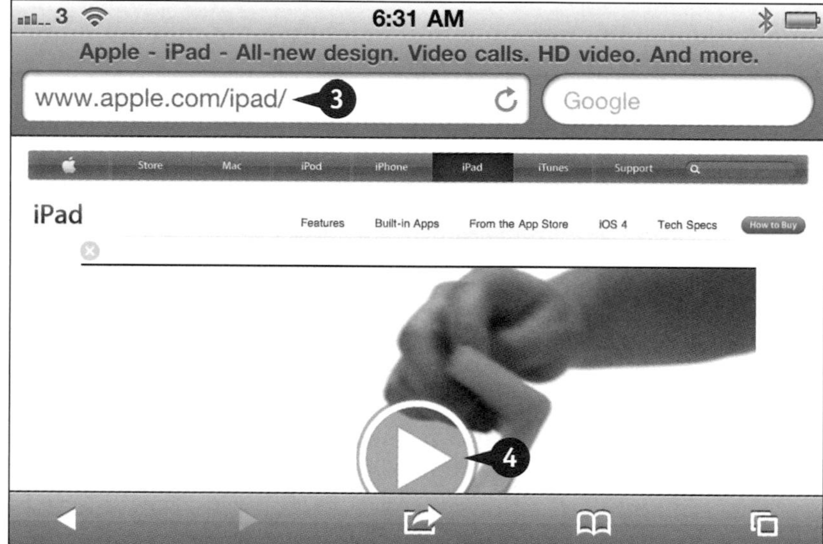

The controls disappear.

6 Tap to display the controls again.

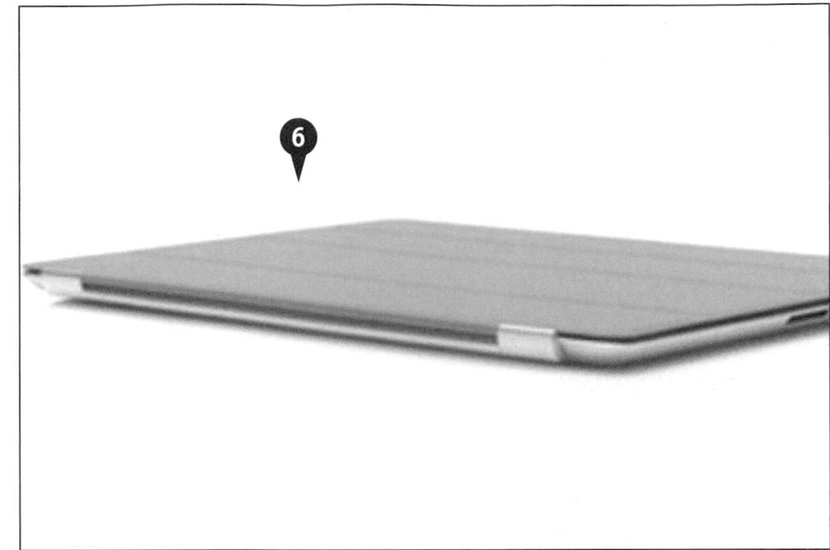

The controls reappear.

7 Tap **Done** when you have finished viewing.

The web page reappears.

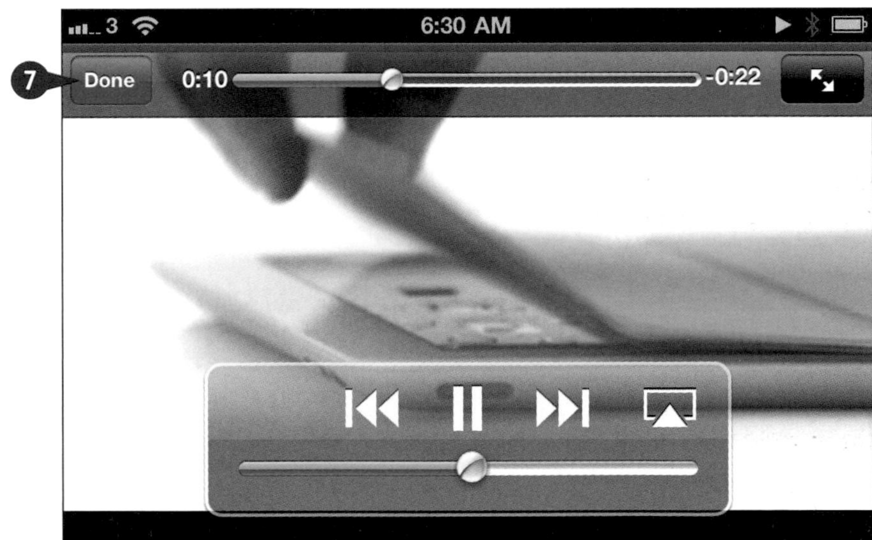

TIPS

How can I work around a YouTube error that occurs when I try to play a video in Safari?
When you try to play a video in Safari that is linked to YouTube, your iPhone automatically switches to the YouTube app for playing the video. If an error occurs with this process, open the YouTube app manually, and then search for the video, as described later in this chapter.

Why can Safari not play some video content on websites?
Many websites use a technology called Flash to display videos and other animated content on their pages. Safari does not support Flash, so it cannot play back these videos.

Shop for Music and Video at the iTunes Store

To find music and videos for your iPhone, you can shop at Apple's iTunes Store by using the iTunes app.

When you buy music or videos from the iTunes Store using the iTunes app, the iPhone downloads the files, so you can play them immediately. When you sync your iPhone with your computer, iTunes copies the music or videos you have bought to your computer. If you use your iPhone without a computer, you can sync the files to iCloud so that you can use them on your other devices — for example, on an iPad.

Shop for Music and Video at the iTunes Store

1. Press the Home button.

   The Home screen appears.

2. Tap **iTunes**.

   The iTunes screen appears.

3. Tap **Music** or **Videos** on the button bar to display the type of content you want. This example uses **Music**.

   The screen you chose appears.

4. Tap the tab at the top for the category you want — New Releases, Top Tens, or Genres. This example uses **Genres**.

   The screen you chose appears.

Note: When browsing videos, the tabs are Films, TV Programs, and Music Videos.

5. Tap the genre you want to display.

   The genre's screen appears.

6. Tap the album you want to display.

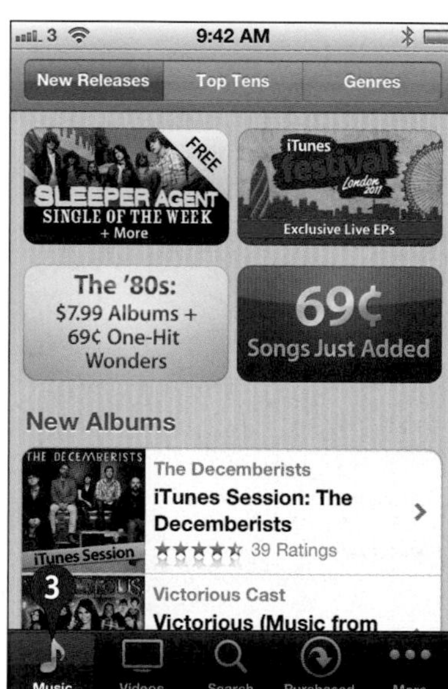

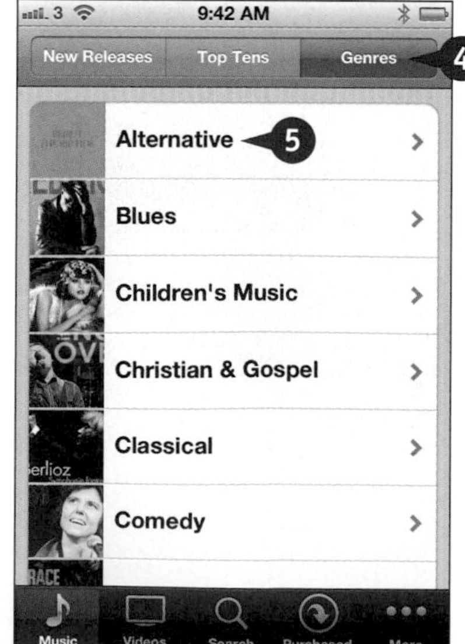

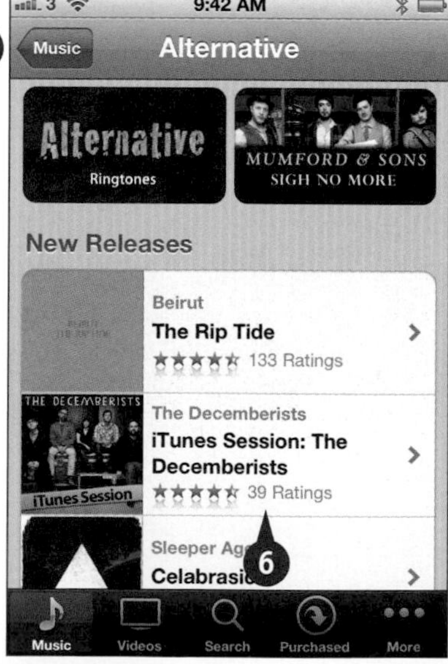

The album's screen appears.

7. Tap a song title to play a preview.

A. Tap **Stop** (■) to stop the preview playing.

8. To buy a song, tap the price button.

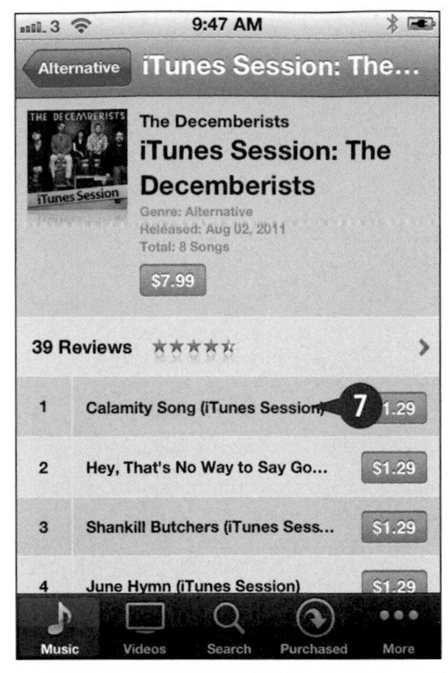

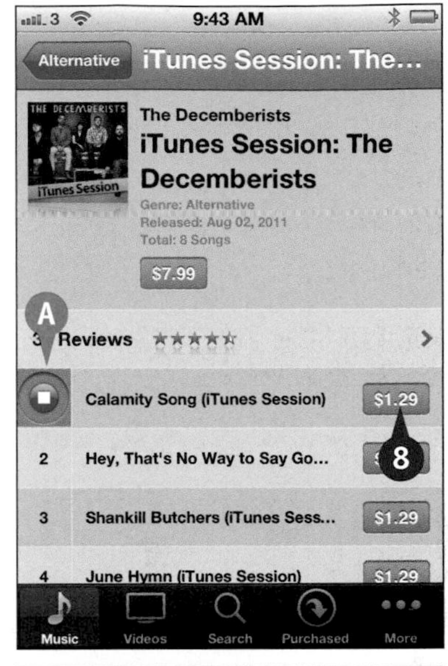

The Buy Song button replaces the price button.

9. Tap **Buy Song**.

The Apple ID Password dialog box opens.

10. Type your password.

11. Tap **OK**.

iTunes downloads the song, and you can play it using the Music app.

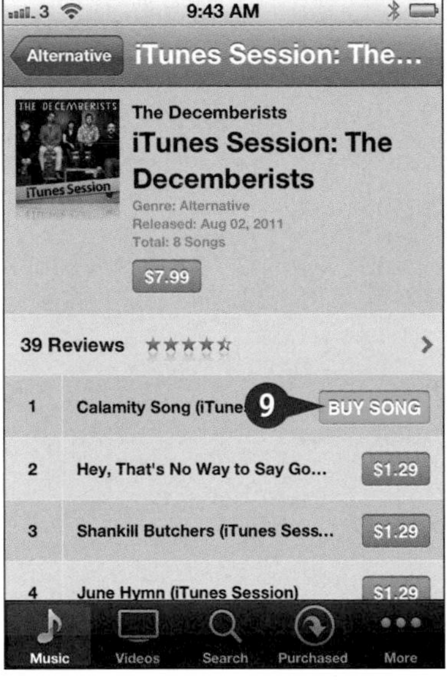

TIP

How can I find the music I want at the iTunes Store?

You can easily search for music within the iTunes app. Tap **Search** on the button bar at the bottom of the screen, and then type a search term (A). iTunes shows matching results as you type. Tap the result you want to view.

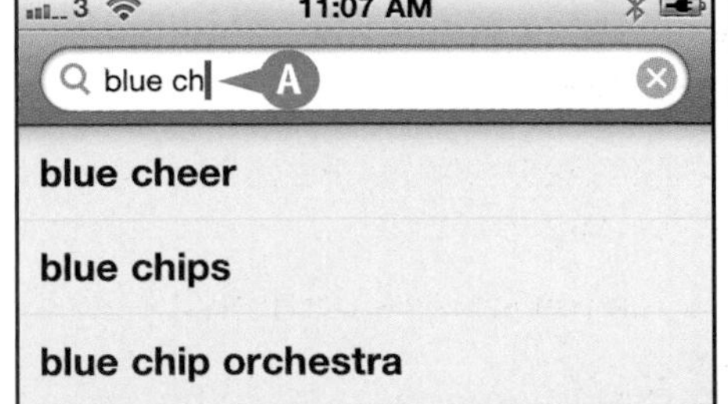

Play YouTube Videos

YouTube is the biggest video site on the Internet at this writing, with millions of videos covering almost every subject imaginable. Your iPhone includes a YouTube app that makes it easy to watch YouTube videos at the best size for your iPhone's screen.

You can find videos by browsing through lists or categories or by searching using keywords. If you create an account, you can assign ratings to other people's videos and upload your own video content.

Play YouTube Videos

Open the YouTube App and Browse Videos

1. Press the Home button.

   The Home screen appears.

2. Tap **YouTube**.

   The YouTube app opens and the Featured screen appears.

A. If the Featured screen does not appear, tap **Featured** to display it.

3. Tap and drag up to scroll down if you want to see more Featured videos.
4. Tap **Most Viewed**.

   The Most Viewed screen appears.

5. Tap **Today**, **This Week**, or **All** to choose the time frame.
6. Tap and drag up to scroll down if you want to see more Most Viewed videos.

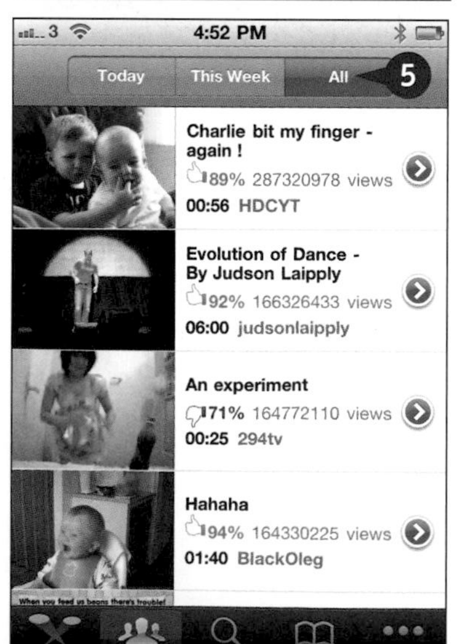

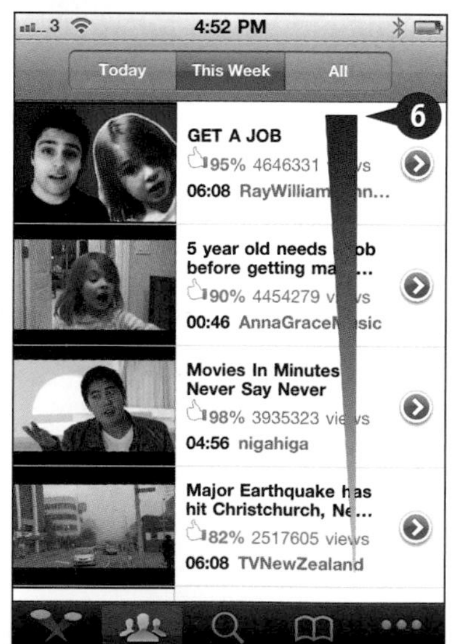

Search for a Video

1. Tap **Search**.

   The Search screen appears.

2. Type your search term.
3. Tap **Search**.

   A list of matching results appears.

Play a Video

1. Tap the video you want to play.

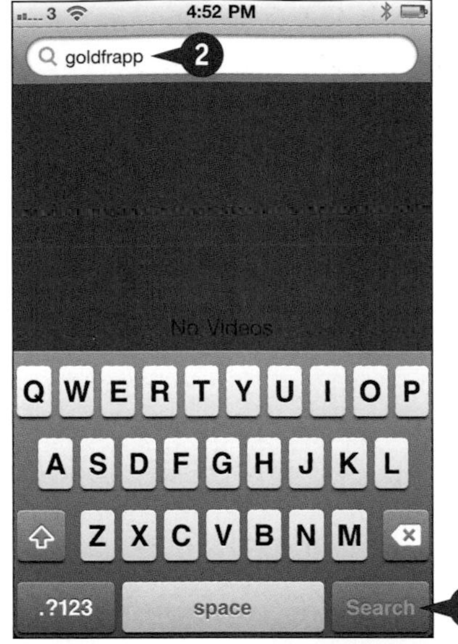

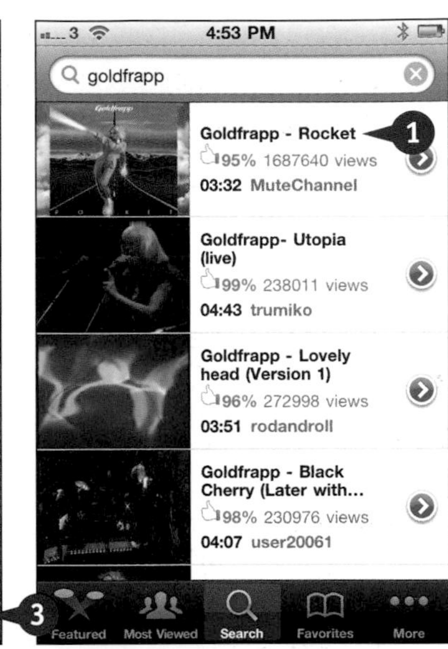

2. Tap **Play** (▷).

   The video starts playing, and the playback controls disappear.

Note: Tap anywhere to display the playback controls again.

3. Tap **Done**.

   The More Info screen appears.

TIP

How do I assign a rating to a video?

1. On the More Info screen, tap **Rate, Comment or Flag**.
2. In the dialog box that opens, tap **Rate or Comment**.
3. On the Comment screen, tap **Like** or **Dislike**.
4. Tap **Send**.

CHAPTER 11

Working with Photos and Books

In this chapter, you learn to use your iPhone's Photos app to view photos. You also learn to use the iBooks app to read ebooks.

Browse Your Photos Using Events, Faces, and Places

You can use the Photos app to browse the photos you have taken with your iPhone's camera, photos you have synced using iTunes or via your Photo Stream on iCloud, and photos you receive in email messages or download from web pages.

The most straightforward way to browse is by albums, but you can also browse by events, faces, and places. An *event* is a named collection of photos associated with a particular date or happening; a *face* is a person's face you teach iPhoto to recognize; and a *place* is a geographical location.

Browse Your Photos Using Events, Faces, and Places

Open the Photos App and Browse by Albums

1. Press the Home button.

   The Home screen appears.

2. Tap **Photos**.

   The Photos app opens.

3. Tap **Albums**.

   The Albums screen appears.

4. Tap the album you want to view.

   The Photo Library screen appears.

Note: The Camera Roll album contains the photos you have taken using the iPhone's camera.

5. Tap and drag up to scroll down through the photos.

6. Tap the photo you want to view.

   The photo appears.

Note: Swipe your finger to the left to display the next photo, or swipe to the right to display the previous photo.

7. Tap **Photo Library** to return to the Photo Library.

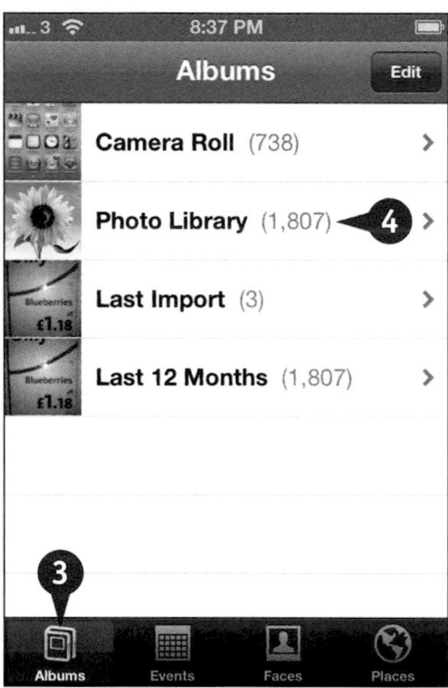

Browse by Events

1. In the Photos app, tap **Events**.

   The list of events appears.

2. Tap the event you want to view.

   The photos in the event appear.

3. Tap the photo you want to see.

   The photo appears.

Note: Swipe your finger to the left to display the next photo, or swipe to the right to display the previous photo.

4. Tap the event name when you want to return to the event.

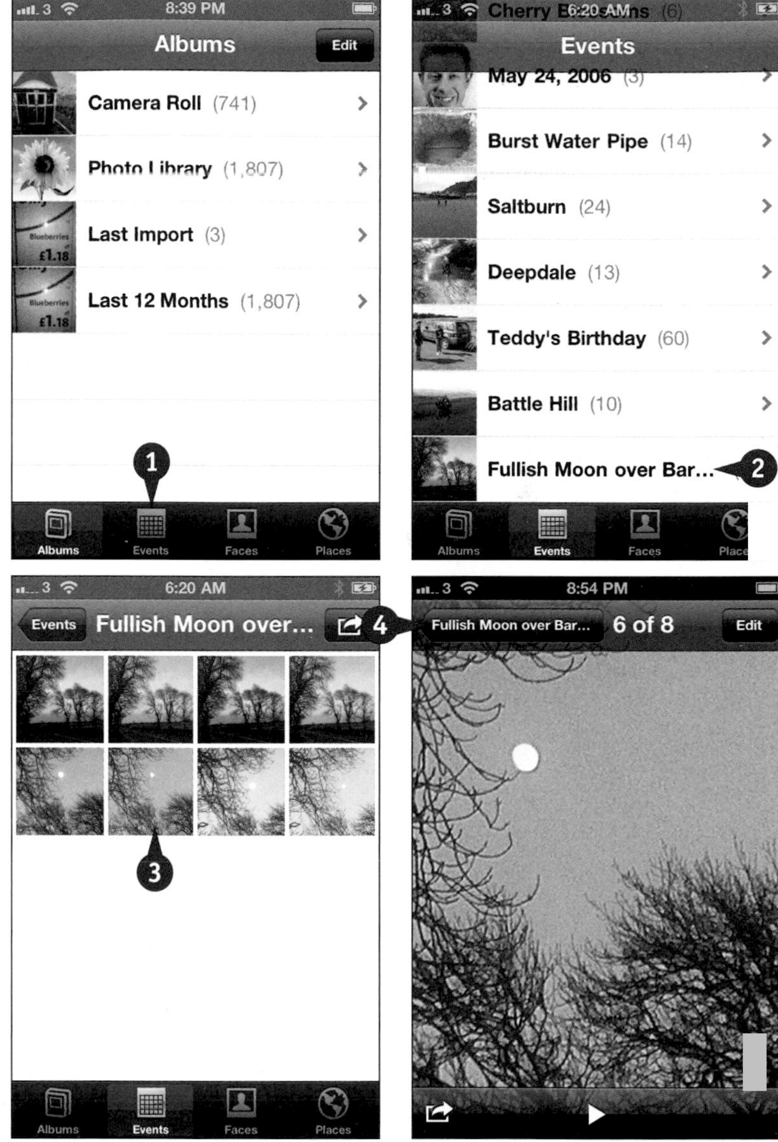

TIP

How can I move through a long list of photos more quickly?
You can move through the photos more quickly by using momentum scrolling. Tap and flick up with your finger to set the photos scrolling. As the momentum drops, you can tap and flick up again to scroll further. Tap and drag your finger in the opposite direction to stop the scrolling.

continued ►

If you allow the Camera app to access location information on your iPhone, the Camera app automatically tags each photo with the GPS information for where you took it. You can then sort your photos by using the Places feature.

Being able to identify photos by location can be great for finding the photos you want. But it means that anybody you share the photos with knows exactly when and where you took them.

Browse Your Photos Using Events, Faces, and Places (continued)

Browse by Faces

1. In the Photos app, tap **Faces**.

   The list of faces appears.

2. Tap the face you want to view.

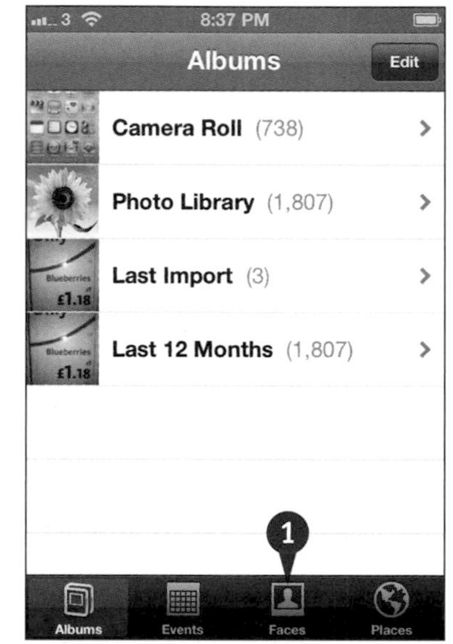

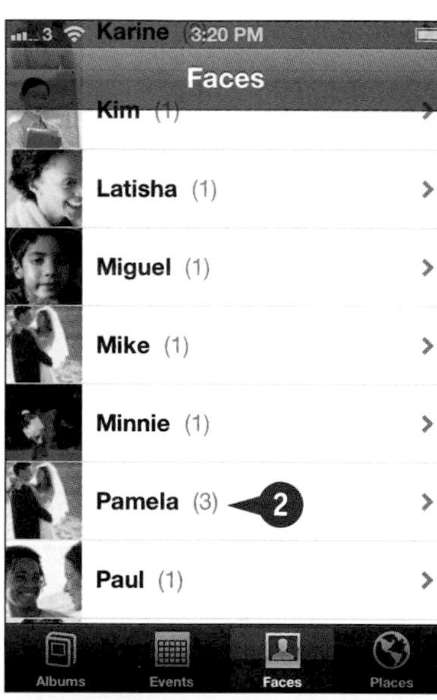

   The list of photos for the face appears.

3. Tap the photo you want to view.

   The photo appears.

Note: Swipe your finger to the left to display the next photo, or swipe to the right to display the previous photo.

4. Tap the face's name button to return to the thumbnails of that individual's face.

5. Tap the **Faces** button to return to the Photo Library.

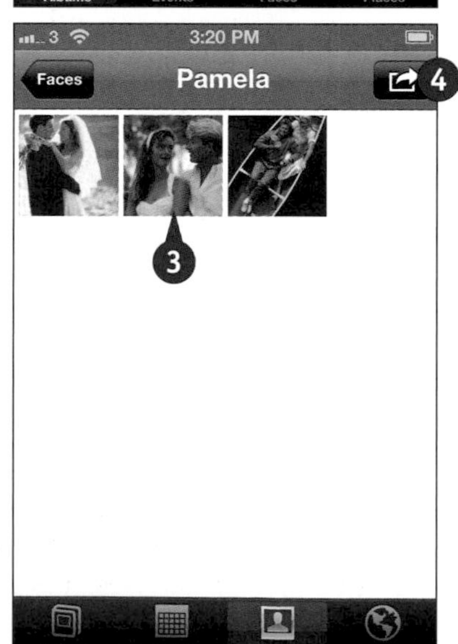

Browse by Places

1. In the Photos app, tap **Places**.

   The Places map appears.

2. Pinch out to zoom in on what you want to view.

Note: You can also zoom in by increments by double-tapping the target area of the screen.

3. Tap the pinhead for the place you want to view.

   The number of photos for the place appears.

4. Tap ⊙.

   The photos in the place appear.

5. Tap the photo you want to view.

   The photo appears.

Note: Swipe your finger to the left to display the next photo, or swipe to the right to display the previous photo.

6. Tap **Photos** to return to the Photo Library.

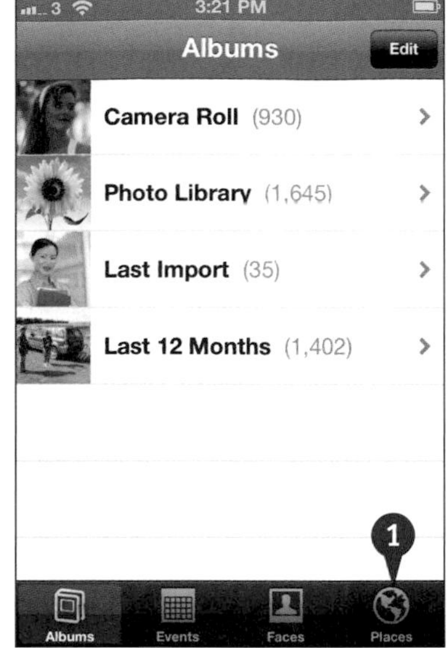

TIP

Why does the Photos button bar not show a Faces button?

The Faces button appears on the button bar in the Photos app only when you have synced photos with marked faces using iTunes. You must also have started using the Faces feature in iPhoto; if you have not, none of your photos will have marked faces. The iPhone does not recognize Face information or Place information you assign in an image-editing application in Windows.

Share Photos via Email and Messaging

From your iPhone's Photos app, you can quickly share a photo either by sending it as an attachment to an email message or by inserting it in a Multimedia Messaging Service, or MMS, message.

Share Photos via Email and Messaging

Select the Photo and Open the Share Dialog Box

1. Browse to the photo you want to share — see the preceding task.
2. Tap **Share** (📤).

   The Share dialog box opens. You can now share the photo as described in the following sections.

Share the Photo via Email

1. In the Share dialog box, tap **Email Photo**.

   Your iPhone creates a new email message in the Mail app with the photo attached to the message.
2. Tap in the To box and address the email message.
3. Tap in the Subject line and type the subject for the email message.
4. Tap in the body area, and then type any text needed.
5. Tap **Send**.
6. If the Photos Size dialog box opens, tap the button for the size of photo you want to send.

   Mail sends the message.

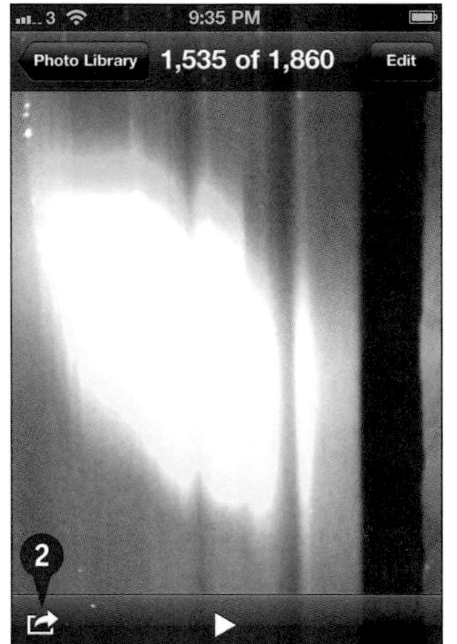

Share the Photo via Messaging

1. In the Share dialog box, tap **Message**.

   Your iPhone creates a new message in the Messages app with the photo attached to the message.

2. Tap in the To box and address the MMS message.
3. Tap in the body area, and then type any text needed.
4. Tap **Send**.

   The Messages app sends the message.

TIPS

How do I send multiple photos at once via email?

From a screen that shows multiple photos, such as the Photo Library screen, tap **Share** (). The Select Photos screen appears. Tap each photo you want to send (A), placing a check mark, up to a maximum of five photos. Then tap **Share** (B), and then tap **Email** in the dialog box that opens.

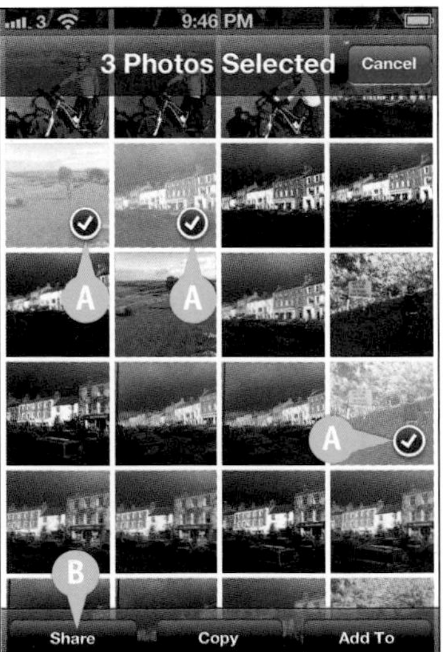

What is the best size to use when sending photos via email?

This depends on what the recipient will do with the photo. If the recipient needs to edit the photo, choose **Actual Size.** If the recipient will merely view the photo on-screen, choose **Large** or **Medium**. The **Small** size works for contact card images, but its picture quality is too low for most other uses.

Play Slideshows of Your Photos

Your iPhone can not only display your photos but also play them as a slideshow. The slideshow feature is limited to using existing groups of photos — you cannot create a slideshow group on the iPhone — but you can shuffle the photos into a different order if you want. To make the most of your slideshows, you first choose the slide timing in the Photos screen in Settings. You can also choose to repeat the slideshow or run the photos in random order. Then, when you start the slideshow, you can choose which transition to use and add music if you want.

Play Slideshows of Your Photos

1. Press the Home button.
2. On the Home screen, tap **Settings**.
3. On the Settings screen, tap **Photos**.

A. Tap the **Photo Stream** switch and move it to On if you want to synchronize your new photos to all your Apple devices via iCloud.

4. To make the slideshow repeat, tap the **Repeat** switch and move it to On.
5. To play the photos in random order, tap the **Shuffle** switch and move it to On.
6. Tap **Play Each Slide For**.
7. Tap the appropriate button.
8. Tap **Photos**.
9. Press the Home button.
10. On the Home screen, tap **Photos**.
11. On the Photos screen, locate the photos for the slideshow. For example, tap **Events**, and then tap the event.
12. When the photos appear, tap the photo at which you want to start the slideshow.

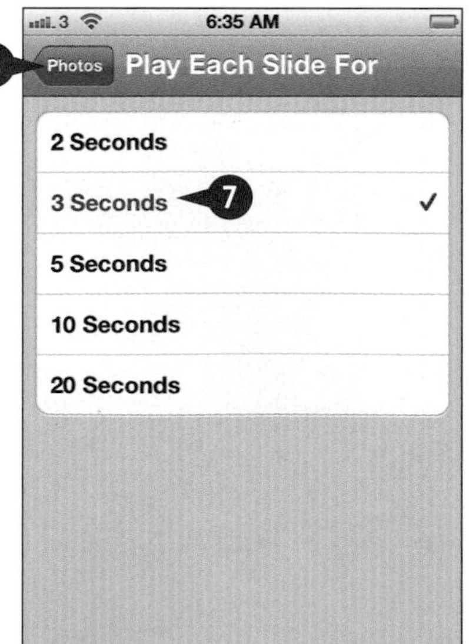

The photo appears.

13 Tap **Start Slideshow** (▶).

The Slideshow Options screen appears.

14 Tap **Transitions**.

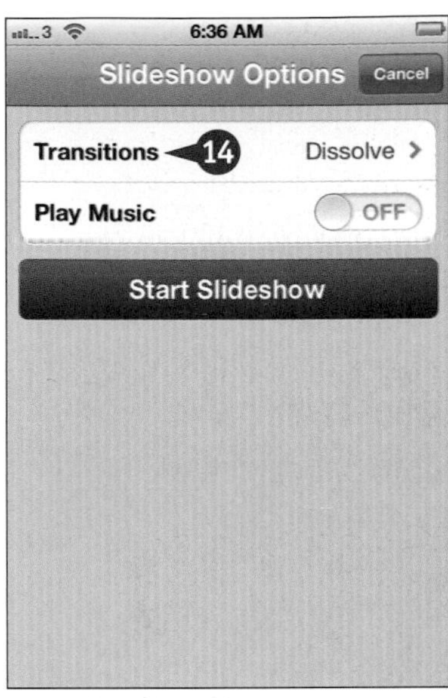

The Transitions screen appears.

15 Tap the transition you want.

16 Tap **Slideshow Options**.

The Slideshow Options screen appears.

17 If you want to play music during the slideshow, tap the **Play Music** switch and move it to On.

The Music button appears.

18 Tap **Music**.

The Music screen appears.

19 Tap the song, album, or playlist you want to play.

The Slideshow Options screen appears again.

20 Tap **Play Slideshow**.

The slideshow starts.

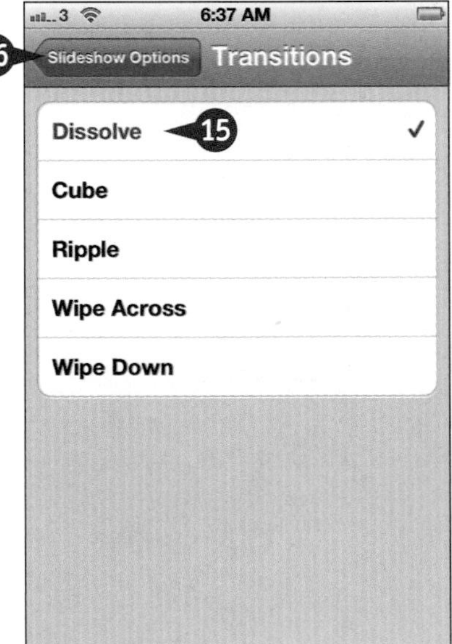

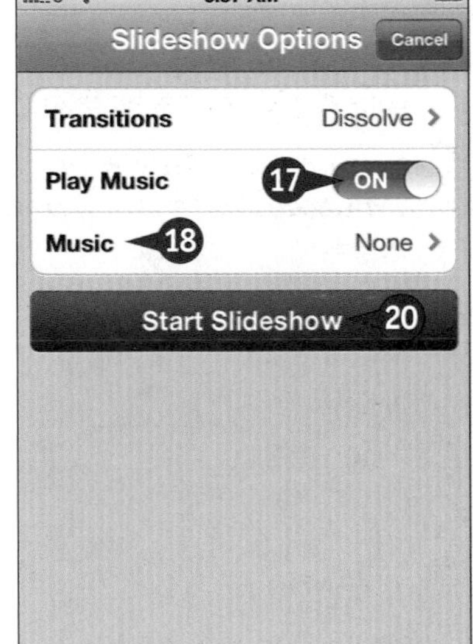

TIP

How can I play a custom slideshow on the iPhone?

You cannot create a custom slideshow on the iPhone at this writing, so you need to set up the custom slideshow beforehand. In iPhoto on a Mac, create an album or an event that contains the photos you want to show; in Windows, place the photos in a folder or create an album in an image-editing application. Use iTunes to sync the photos to your iPhone. You can then open the group of photos and set it playing as a slideshow.

Play Photos from the iPhone on a TV

When you want to share your photos with other people, you can connect your iPhone to a TV, and then display the photos on the TV screen. This is a great way to share the pictures at a size that a group of people can comfortably view.

To connect your iPhone to a TV, you must get a cable with suitable connectors for the TV, such as the Apple Composite AV Cable or the Apple Component AV Cable. To play content, you must also set the iPhone to provide the right type of video output for the TV.

Play Photos from the iPhone on a TV

Connect the iPhone to the TV

First connect the dock connector on the TV cable to the iPhone.

Note: To find the right kind of cable, check which type of input your TV uses.

Then connect the other end of the TV cable to the TV's port or ports.

Choose Video Output Settings

1. Press the Home button.

   The Home screen appears.

2. Tap **Settings**.

   The Settings screen appears.

3. Tap and drag up to scroll down until the third box appears.
4. Tap **General**.

   The General screen appears.

5. Tap **TV Out**.

Note: The TV Out item appears only when you have connected the iPhone to a TV.

The TV Out screen appears.

6 Tap the **Widescreen** switch and move it to On or Off, as needed for the TV.

7 Tap **TV Signal**.

The TV Signal screen appears.

8 Tap **NTSC** or **PAL**, as needed for the TV. See the tip for advice on which to choose.

9 Tap **TV Out**.

10 Press the Home button.

The home screen appears.

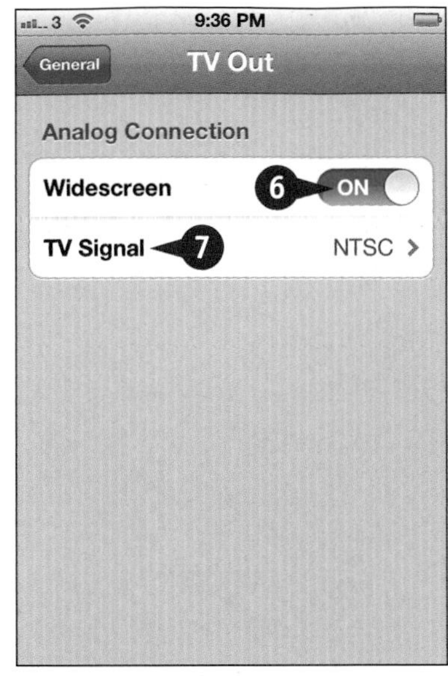

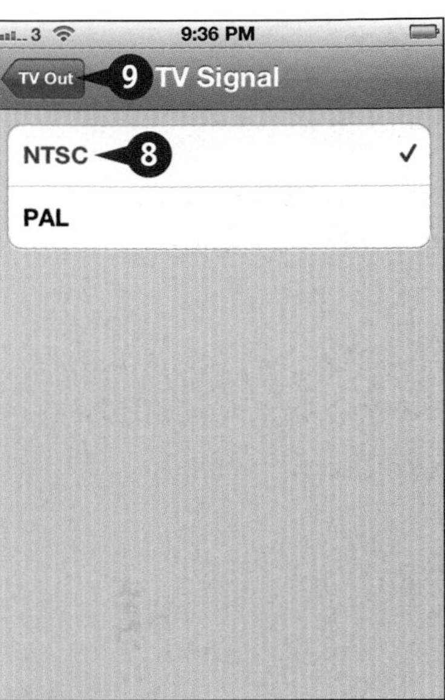

Play Photos on the TV

1 Press the Home button.

The home screen appears.

2 Tap **Photos**.

The Photos screen appears.

3 Locate the photos for the slideshow. For example, tap **Events**, and then tap the event.

The photos appear.

4 Tap the photo you want to display first.

The photo appears on the TV. You can then display further photos by swiping a finger to the left or right.

TIP

Should I choose NTSC or PAL on the TV Signal screen?

Normally, you need to choose the setting for the geographical area in which you are using the TV or from which the TV came. Most TV sets in North America use the NTSC format. Most TV sets in Europe use the PAL format. If in doubt, consult your TV's documentation.

Read Digital Books with iBooks

To enjoy electronic books, or *ebooks*, on your iPhone, download the free iBooks app from the App Store. Using iBooks, you can read ebooks that you load on the iPhone from your computer, download free or paid-for ebooks from online stores, or read PDF files you transfer from your computer.

If you have already loaded some ebooks, you can read them as described in this task. If iBooks contains no books, see the next task, "Browse and Buy Digital Books with iBooks," for instructions on finding and downloading ebooks.

Read Digital Books with iBooks

1. Press the Home button.

   The Home screen appears.

2. Navigate to the Home screen that contains the iBooks icon. For example, tap and drag left to scroll to the right one or more times.

3. Tap **iBooks**.

   The Books screen appears.

A. If the Books button does not appear in the upper-middle area of the iBooks screen, tap the button that appears there. On the Collections screen that appears, tap **Books** to display the Books screen.

4. Tap the book you want to open.

   The book opens.

Note: When you open a book, iBooks displays your current page. When you open a book for the first time, iBooks displays the book's cover or first page.

5. Tap anywhere on the screen to hide the reading controls.

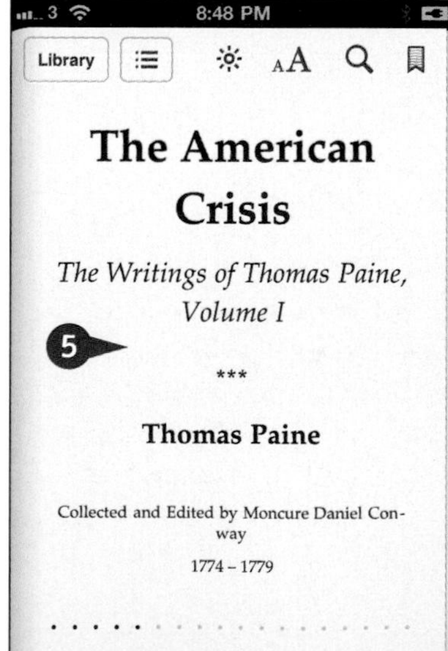

The reading controls disappear.

Note: To display the reading controls again, tap anywhere on the screen.

6 Tap the right side of the page to display the next page.

Note: To display the previous page, tap the left side of the page. Alternatively, tap the left side of the page and drag to the right.

7 To look at the next page without fully revealing it, tap the right side and drag to the left. You can then either drag further to turn the page or release the page and let it fall closed.

8 To jump to another part of the book, tap **Table of Contents** (≡).

9 When the table of contents appears, tap the part of the book you want to display.

10 To search in the book, tap **Search** (🔍).

11 On the Search screen, type the search term.

12 Tap the match you want to display.

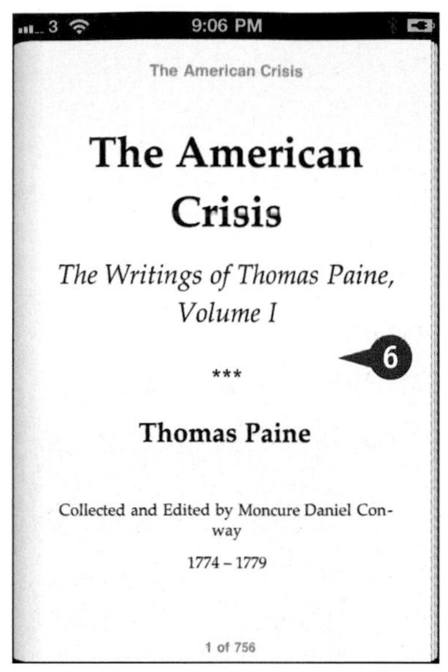

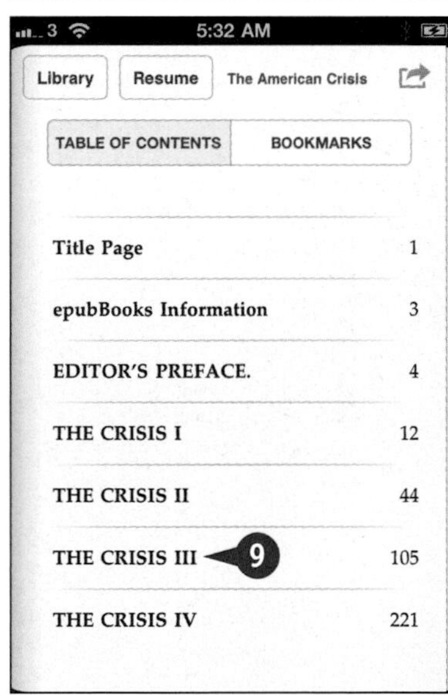

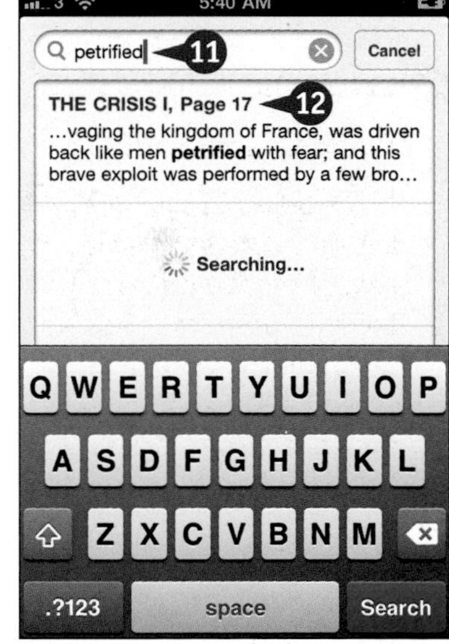

How do I change the font iBooks uses?

Tap the screen to display the controls, and then tap **Font Settings** (ᴀA). In the Font Settings dialog box, tap **Small** (A) or **Large** (B) to change the font size. Tap **Fonts** (C) to display the font list, and then tap the font you want to use. Finally, tap outside the Font Settings dialog box to close it.

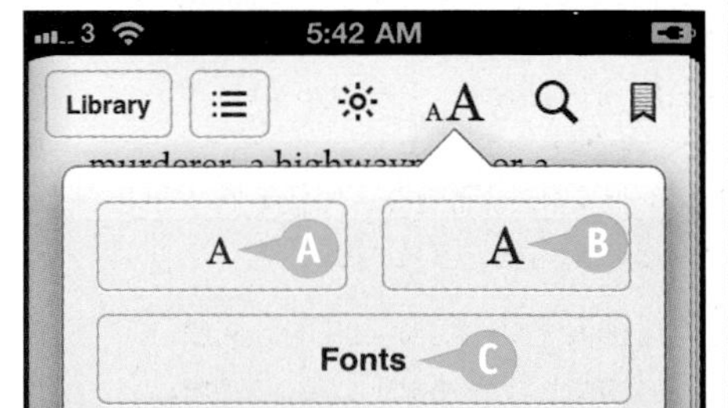

Browse and Buy Digital Books with iBooks

The iBooks app connects directly to online bookstores, which you can browse to find ebooks. Some ebooks are free; others you have to pay for, but many have samples that you can download to help you decide whether to buy the book.

After you download an ebook, it appears on your iBooks bookshelf. You can then open it and read it as described in the preceding task, "Read Digital Books with iBooks."

Browse and Buy Digital Books with iBooks

1. Open iBooks as described in the preceding task.
2. Tap **Store**.

   The Store screen appears.
3. Tap **Featured**.

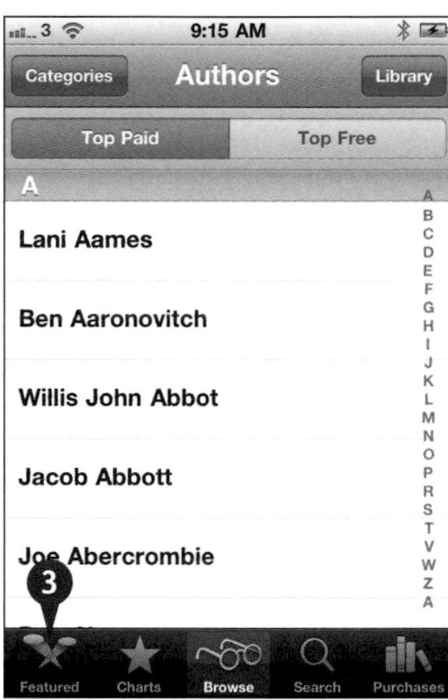

   The Books screen appears, showing a list of featured books.
4. Tap **Categories**.

   The Categories screen appears.
5. Tap the category you want to view. For example, tap **Health, Mind & Body**.

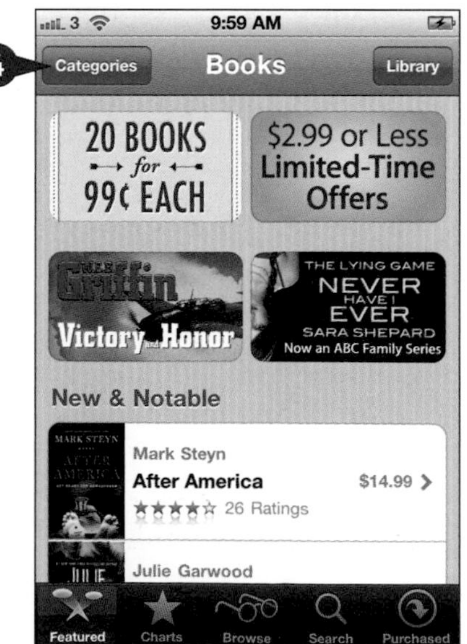

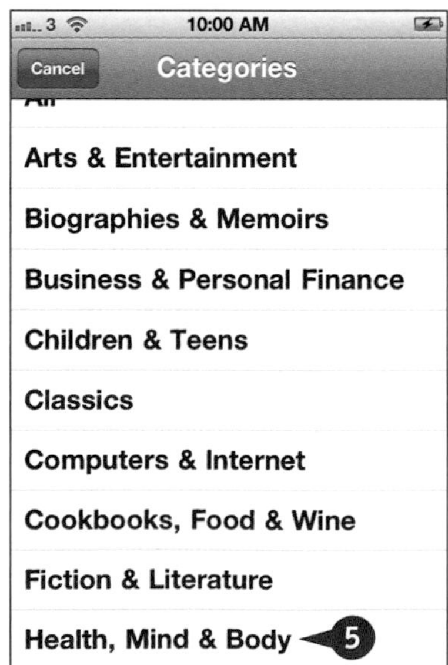

The screen appears for the category you chose.

6. Tap **Charts**.

   The Top Charts screen appears.

A. From the Top Charts screen, you can tap **Categories** to display the Categories screen, and then tap the category whose chart you want to see.

7. Tap the book whose information you want to view.

   The book's screen appears.

8. Tap **Get Sample** to get a sample of the book, or tap the price button to buy the book.

   The sample or book appears on your iBooks bookshelf.

9. Tap the sample or book to open it.

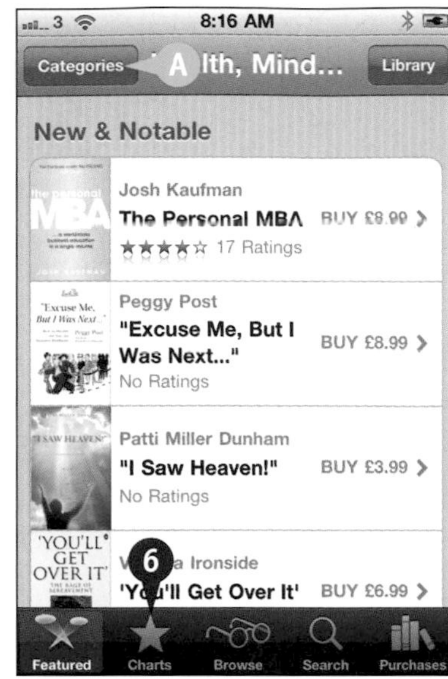

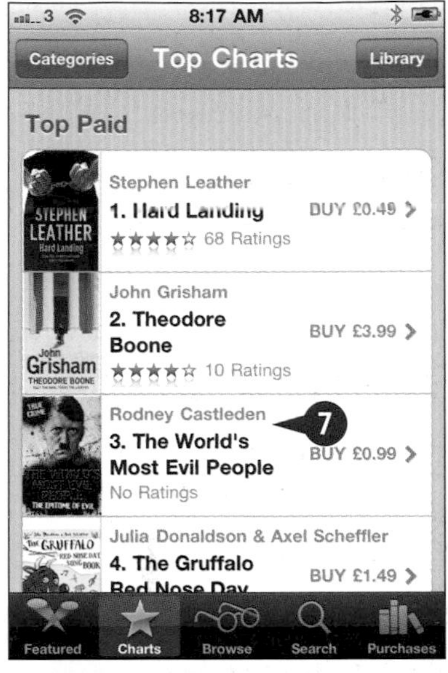

Where can I find free ebooks to read in iBooks?

Open iBooks as described in the previous task. Tap **Browse** in the button bar at the bottom of the iBooks screen, and then tap **Top Free** (A) to display an alphabetical list of authors by whom free books are available.

Other sources of free ebooks include Project Gutenberg (www.gutenberg.org) and the Baen Free Library (www.baen.com/library).

Add PDF Files to iBooks and Read Them

These days, many books, reports, and other documents are available as Portable Document Format files, or PDF files. You can load PDF files on your iPhone and read them using iBooks. This is a great way to take your required reading with you so that you can catch up on it anywhere.

Add PDF Files to iBooks and Read Them

Add PDFs to iBooks Using iTunes

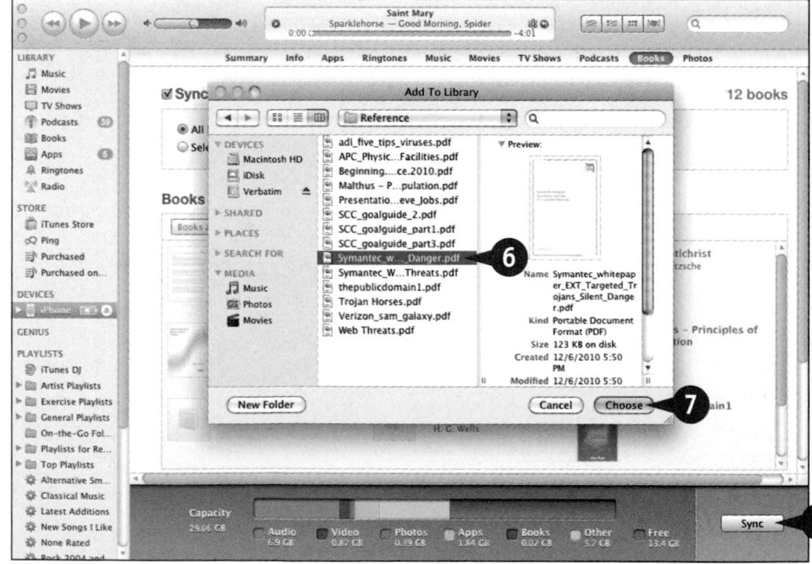

1. Connect your iPhone to your computer via the USB cable.

   The iPhone appears in the Devices list in iTunes.

2. Click your iPhone in the Devices list.

   The iPhone's control screens appear.

3. Click **Books**.

   The Books screen appears.

4. Click the **File** menu.

   The File menu opens.

5. Click **Add to Library**.

   The Add To Library dialog box opens.

6. Click the PDF file or select the PDF files you want to add.

7. Click **Open** in Windows or **Choose** on a Mac.

   iTunes adds the PDF file or files to the Books list.

8. Click **Sync**.

   iTunes syncs the PDF files to the iPhone.

9. Disconnect the iPhone from the USB cable.

Read a PDF File Using iBooks

1. Press the Home button.

   The Home screen appears.

2. Navigate to the Home screen that contains the iBooks icon. For example, tap and drag left to scroll to the right one or more times.

3. Tap **iBooks**.

   The Books screen appears.

4. Tap **Books**.

   The Collections screen appears.

5. Tap **PDFs**.

   The PDFs screen appears.

6. Tap the PDF file you want to open.

   The PDF file appears. You can then read the PDF file using the techniques described earlier in this chapter.

Note: If you open a PDF file while browsing the web in Safari, you can open the file in iBooks. To do so, tap the screen, and then tap **Open in iBooks** on the command bar that pops up.

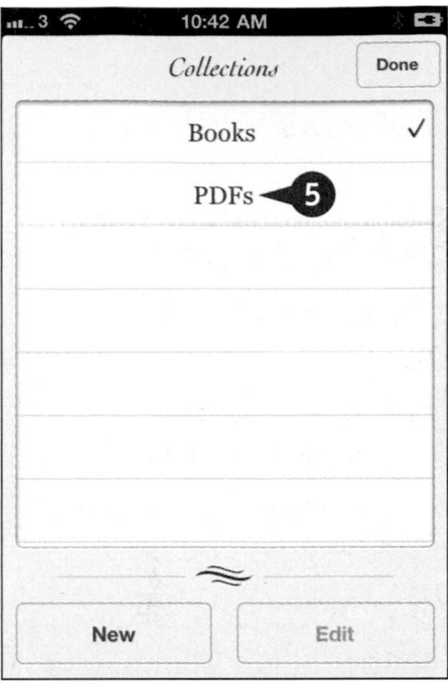

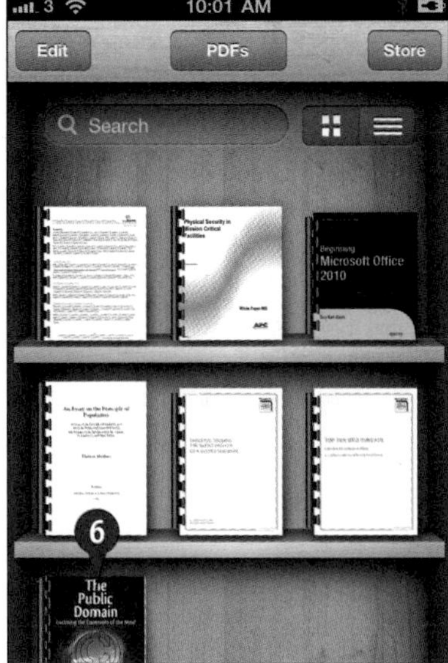

TIP

How do I change the font size on the PDF file?

You cannot change the font size on the PDF file. This is because PDF is a graphical format — essentially a picture — rather than a text format. To make the PDF file more readable on the iPhone, rotate the iPhone to a landscape orientation, so that the screen is wider than it is tall. Then pinch outward to zoom the text to a larger size.

CHAPTER 12

Using the Bundled Apps

Your iPhone comes with an impressive suite of bundled apps that enables you to make the most of its features right out of the box. This chapter shows you how to use the Maps app, the Stocks app, the Calculator app, the Clock app, and the Voice Memos map. And if you get a sensor to slip into your sneakers, you can work out with the Nike + iPod feature.

Find Your Location with Maps' GPS and Compass

Your iPhone's Maps app can pinpoint your location by using the Global Positioning System, or GPS, or wireless networks. You can view your location on a road map, a satellite picture, or a hybrid that shows street annotations on the satellite picture. You can easily switch among map types to find the most useful one for your current needs. To help you get your bearings, the Tracking feature in the Maps app can show you which direction you are facing.

Find Your Location with Maps' GPS and Compass

Find Your Location

1. Press the Home button.

   The Home screen appears.

2. Tap **Maps**.

   The Maps screen appears.

A. A blue dot shows your current location. The expanding circle around the blue dot shows that Maps is determining your location.

Note: It may take a minute for Maps to work out your location accurately. While Maps determines the location, the blue dot moves, even though the iPhone remains stationary.

3. Tap and pinch in with two fingers.

Note: You can tap and pinch out with two fingers to zoom in.

   The map zooms out, showing a larger area.

4. Tap **Map Options** (▨).

   The screen of map options appears.

5. Tap **Satellite**.

   The Satellite view appears.

6. Tap **Map Options** (▨).

   The screen of options appears.

7. Tap **Hybrid**.

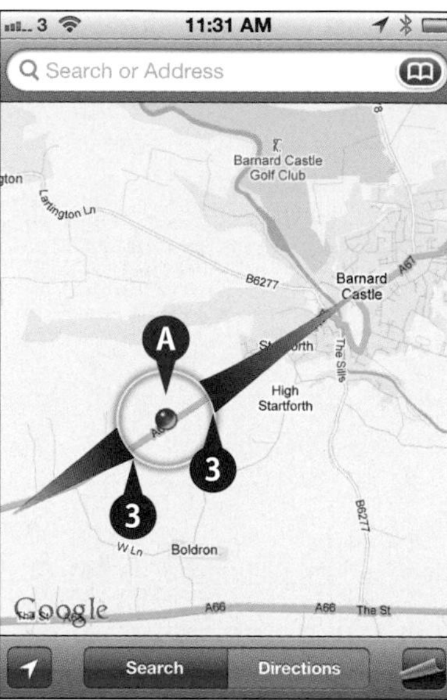

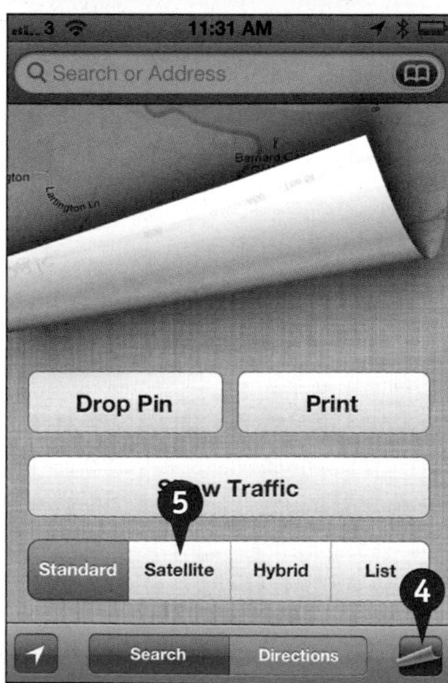

The satellite map appears with road names and place names overlaid on it.

8 Tap **Location** (◢).

The map turns to show the direction the iPhone is facing, so that you can orient yourself.

Get Your Bearings with the Compass App

1 Press the Home button.

The Home screen appears.

2 Tap **Utilities**.

The Utilities folder opens.

3 Tap **Compass**.

The Compass screen appears and shows your bearing.

Note: Unlike a physical compass, the iPhone's compass works with the iPhone held in any orientation. You do not need to hold the iPhone flat to get an accurate bearing.

4 Tap **Location** (◢) if you want to display the Maps app and show your location.

Does the Compass app use True North or Magnetic North?
The Compass app can show either True North or Magnetic North. To switch, tap **Info** (◢). On the screen that appears, tap **True North** (A) or **Magnetic North**, as needed, placing a check mark next to it. Tap **Done**.

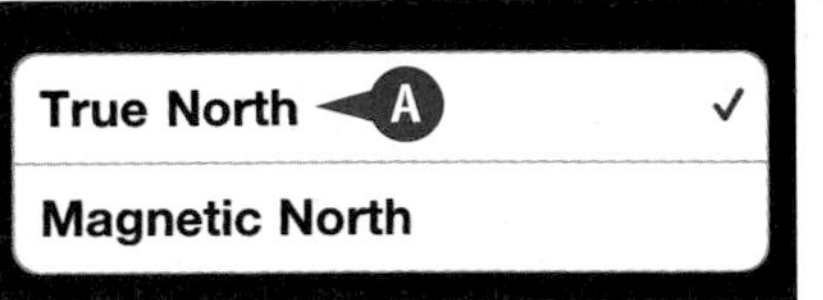

Find Directions with the Maps App

Your iPhone's Maps app can give you directions to where you want to go. Maps can also show you current traffic congestion to help you identify the most viable route for a journey.

Maps displays driving directions by default, but you can also display public transit directions and walking directions.

Find Directions with the Maps App

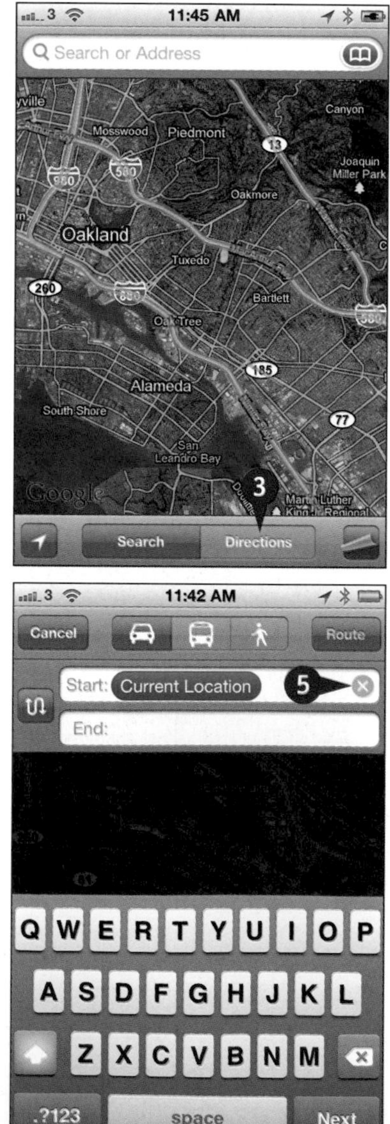

1. Press the Home button.
2. On the Home screen, tap **Maps**.
3. On the Maps screen, tap **Directions**.
4. On the Directions screen, tap **Start**.

   The Current Location text changes to a blue button.
5. Tap ⊗ to delete the Current Location button.

Note: If you want the directions to start from your current location, leave Current Location in the Start box. Skip to step **7**.

6. Type the start location for the directions.

Note: If the starting location or ending location is an address in the Contacts app, tap **Contacts** (📖) and then tap the contact.

7. Type the end location.

A. Tap **Switch Places** (⇅) to switch the start location and end location.

8. Tap **Route**.

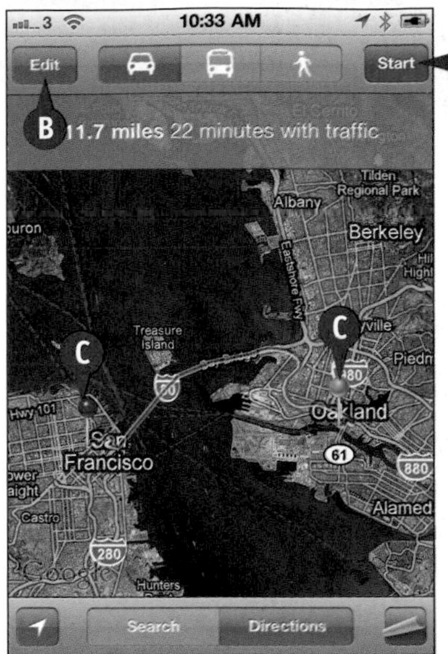

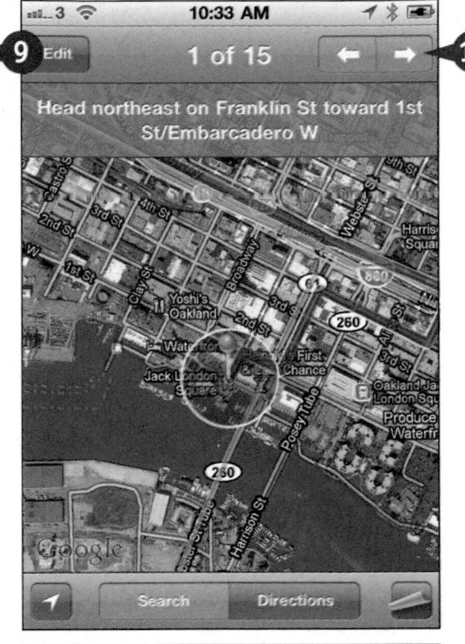

B To change the route, tap **Edit**.

C A screen showing the driving directions appears. The green pin marks the start, and the red pin marks the end.

9 Tap **Start**.

The first screen of directions appears.

10 Tap **Next** (➡).

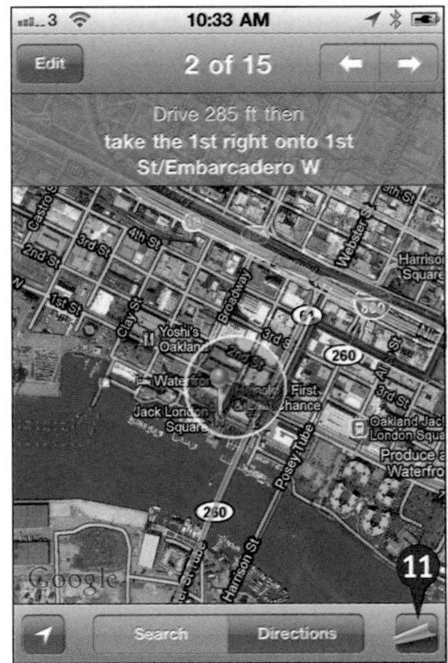

The next screen of directions appears.

11 Tap **Map Options** (▨).

The screen of options appears.

12 Tap **Show Traffic**.

D The directions screen appears again, showing any traffic congestion flashing red.

TIP

How do I get directions for public transit or walking?

Tap 🚌 to display the details of available public transport. Tap 🚶 to display the distance and time for walking the route.

It is a good idea to double-check public transit directions against the latest published schedules, because Google's information is sometimes out of date.

Be aware that walking directions may be inaccurate. Before walking the route, check that it does not send you across pedestrian-free bridges or through rail tunnels.

Explore with Street View

Maps is not only great for finding out where you are and for getting directions to places, but it can also show you the view at ground level by using Street View.

Street View displays images from Google's vast database of city streets and rural areas. You can pan around the area at which you enter Street View, enabling you to get a good idea of what a place looks like. Bear in mind that the place may have changed since the Street View photos were taken.

Explore with Street View

1. Press the Home button.

   The Home screen appears.

2. Tap **Maps**.

   The Maps screen appears.

3. Display the area of interest in the middle of the screen. For example, tap and drag the map, or search for the location you want.

4. Tap **Map Options** (▪).

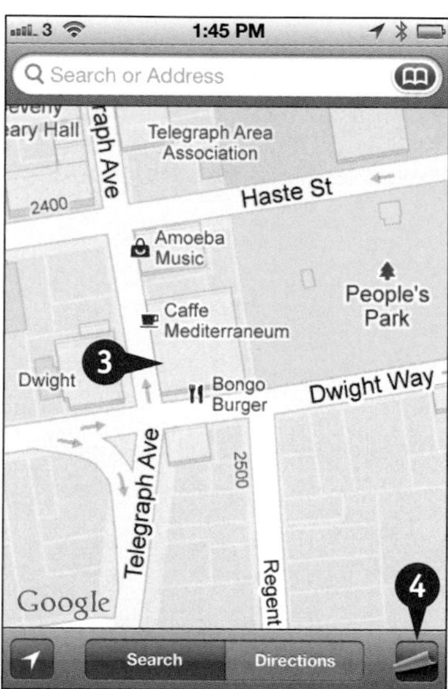

The screen of options appears.

5. Tap **Drop Pin**.

   The Maps app drops a pin in the middle of the screen.

6. Tap and hold the pin, and then drag it to exactly where you want it.

7. Tap **Street View** (◙).

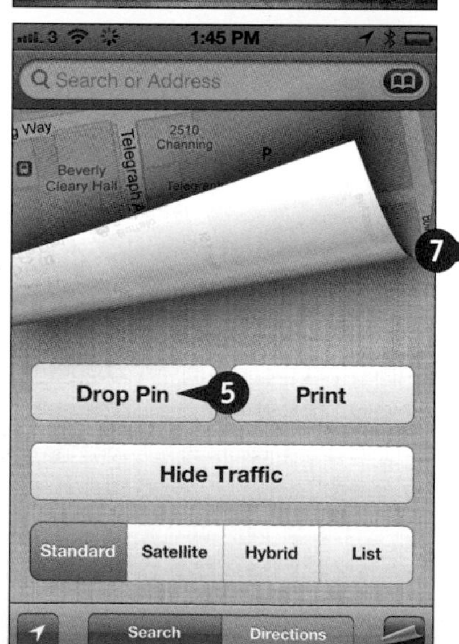

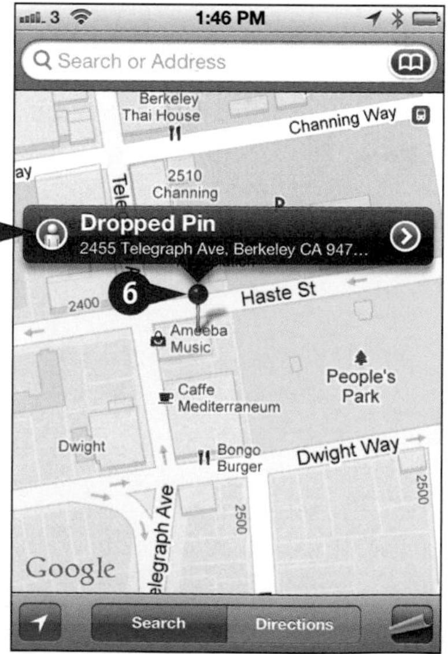

The Maps app displays Street View in landscape orientation, so you need to hold your iPhone in landscape orientation to use Street View effectively.

A The circle in the lower right corner shows the pin's location on a map. The highlighted segment indicates the direction in which you are looking.

8 Tap and drag left to pan clockwise, or tap and drag right to pan counterclockwise.

The next section of the view appears.

9 To leave Street View, tap anywhere on-screen.

The control bar appears across the top of the screen.

10 Tap **Done**.

The Maps app displays the map and pin again.

TIP

How do I move along the street in Street View?
Tap a white arrow (A) on the street to move along the street in that direction.

Use Maps' Bookmarks and Contacts

When you need to be able to return to a location easily in the Maps app, you can place a bookmark at the location.

Similarly, you can add a location to your contacts, so that you can access it either from the Contacts app or from the Maps app. You can either create a new contact or add the location to an existing contact.

You can also return quickly to locations you have visited recently but not created a bookmark or contact for.

Use Maps' Bookmarks and Contacts

1. Press the Home button.

   The Home screen appears.

2. Tap **Maps**.

   The Maps screen appears.

3. Find the place you want to bookmark. For example, tap and drag the map, or search for the location you want.

4. Tap and hold the place you want to bookmark.

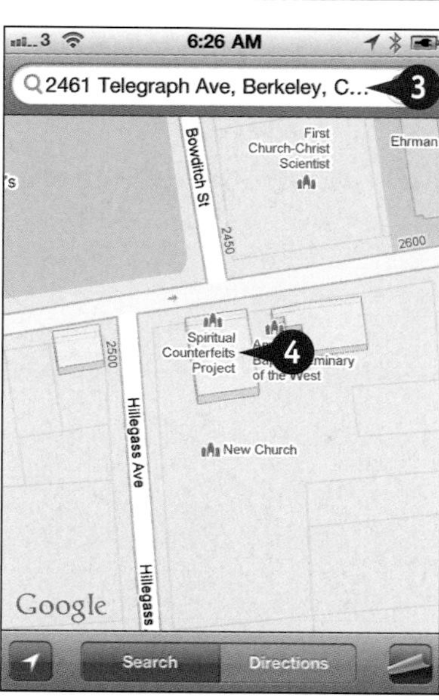

The Maps app drops a pin on the place.

5. Tap ⊙.

   The Info screen appears.

6. Tap **Add to Bookmarks**.

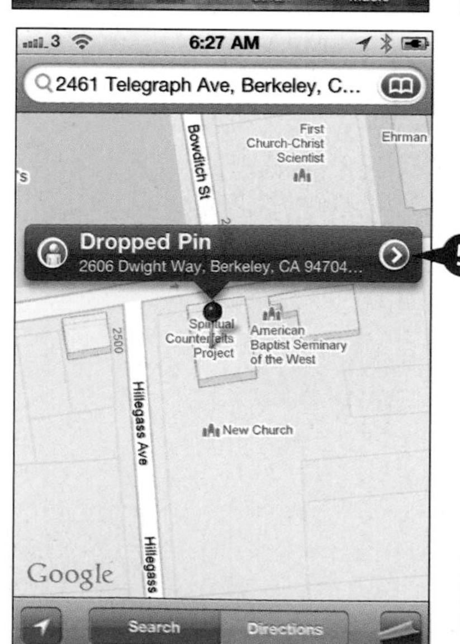

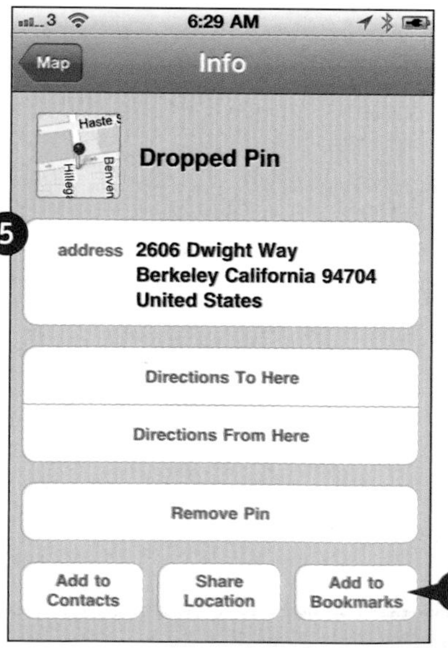

The Add Bookmark screen appears.

7. Type the name for the bookmark.
8. Tap **Save**.

A. The name appears on the Info screen.

9. Tap **Add to Contacts**.

The Contact dialog box opens.

10. To create a new contact, tap **Create New Contact**.

The New Contact screen appears.

B. To add the location to an existing contact, tap **Add to Existing Contact**, and then tap the contact on the All Contacts list.

11. Type the details for the contact.
12. Tap **Done**.

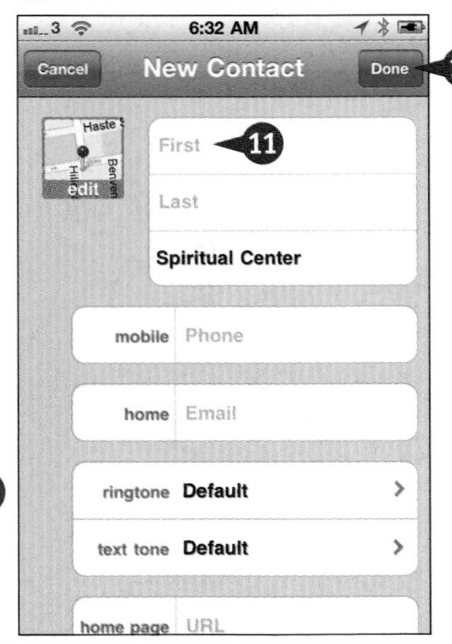

TIP

How do I go to a location I have bookmarked or created a contact for?

In the Maps app, tap **Bookmarks** ( ). On the Bookmarks screen, tap **Bookmarks** or **Contacts**, and then tap the location.

You can also go back to a recent location by tapping **Recents**, and then tapping the location.

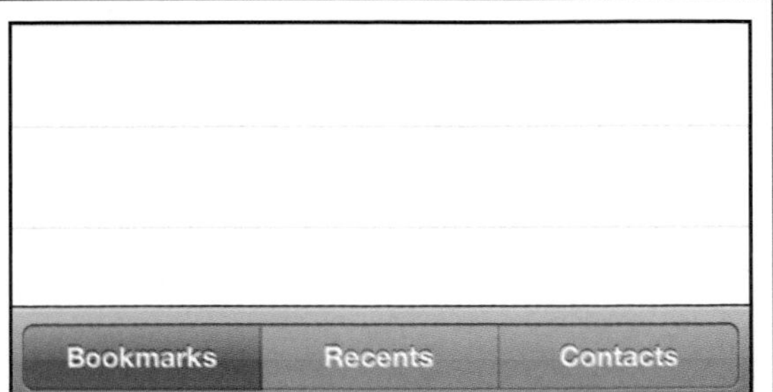

Share a Location via Email and Instant Messaging

Often, you will find it useful to share a location with other people. The Maps app enables you to share a location in moments via either email or instant messaging.

You can share your current location, a location you have bookmarked or created a contact for, or a location on which you drop a pin.

Share a Location via Email and Instant Messaging

Find the Location and Open the Share Location Using Dialog Box

1. Press the Home button.

   The Home screen appears.

2. Tap **Maps**.

   The Maps screen appears.

3. Find the location you want to bookmark.

4. If the location does not already have a bookmark or contact, tap and hold it to drop a pin on it.

5. Tap ⊙.

   The Info screen appears.

A. If you have just dropped a pin, you may want to name it rather than leaving the default name, Dropped Pin. Tap **Add to Bookmarks**, type the name, and then tap **Done**.

6. Tap **Share Location**.

   The Share Location Using dialog box opens.

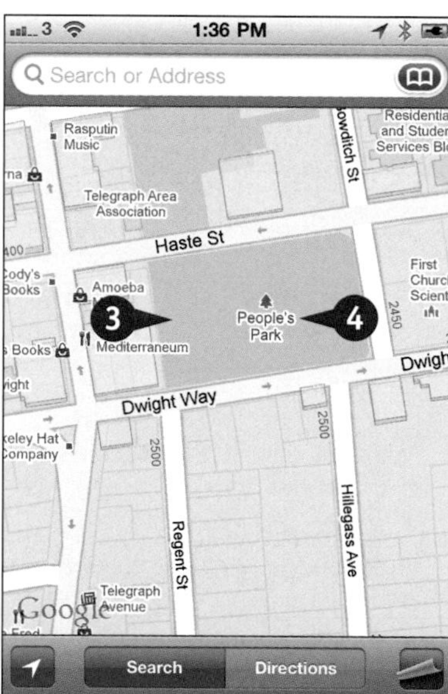

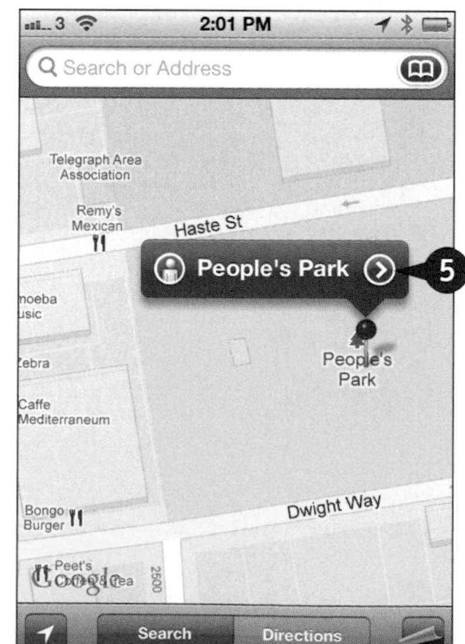

Share the Location via Email

1. In the Share Location Using dialog box, tap **Email**.

   Your iPhone creates a new email message in the Mail app with the location's link inserted in the message.

2. Tap in the To box and address the email message.
3. Tap in the Subject line and type the subject for the email message.
4. Optionally, tap in the body area, and then type any text needed.
5. Tap **Send**.

Share the Location via Instant Messaging

1. In the Share Location Using dialog box, tap **Message**.

   Your iPhone creates a new message in the Messages app with the location attached to the message.

2. Tap in the To box and address the message.
3. Optionally, tap in the body area, and then type any text needed.
4. Tap **Send**.

Can I send a location from the Contacts app?

Yes. If you have created a contact for the location, you can share the contact from the Contacts app. Tap the contact's entry to display the Info screen, and then tap **Share Contact**. In the Share Contact Using dialog box, tap **Email** or **Message**, as needed. You can then complete the message and send it.

Track Stock Prices with the Stocks App

If you own or follow stocks, you can use the iPhone's Stocks app to track stock prices so that you can take immediate action as needed.

The Stocks app displays a default selection of stock information at first, including the Dow Jones Industrial Average, the NASDAQ Composite, the Standard & Poor 500, and Apple, Google, and Yahoo! stocks. You can customize the Stocks app to display only those stocks that interest you.

Track Stock Prices with the Stocks App

Open the Stocks App

1. Press the Home button.

   The Home screen appears.

2. Tap **Stocks**.

   The Stocks screen appears, showing a default selection of stocks.

Choose the Stocks You Want to Track

1. Tap **Info** (ⓘ).

   The Stocks configuration screen appears.

2. Tap **+**.

   The Search screen appears.

3. Type the company's name or stock ID.

4. Either tap **Search** or simply wait for the Stocks app to search.

   A list of matching company names and stock symbols appears.

5. Tap the item you want to add.

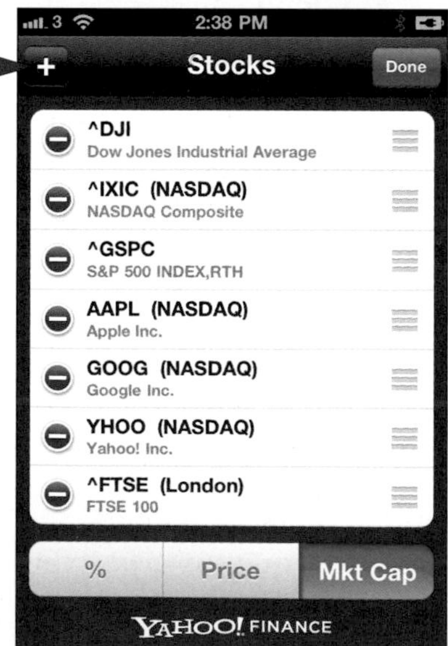

The stock listing appears.

6 To remove a stock listing, tap ⊖.

7 Tap the **Delete** button.

The stock listing disappears.

8 To change the order, tap ≡ and drag up or down.

9 Tap **%**, **Price**, or **Mkt Cap** to control which statistic the Stocks app displays first.

10 Tap **Done**.

View Information for a Stock

1 On the Stocks screen, tap the stock for which you want to see information at the bottom of the screen.

2 Tap the first dot to see the summary information, the second dot to see the stock chart, or the third dot to see stock-related headlines.

Note: You can also scroll the lower part of the screen to switch among the summary information, the stock chart, and the headlines.

3 Tap to switch among percentage changes, price changes, and market capitalization.

TIPS

What does the Y! button do?
Tap **Yahoo!** (Y!) to display the Yahoo! Finance page for the selected stock listing in Safari.

How can I read the stock chart more easily?
Turn the iPhone to landscape orientation to see the stock chart on its own and at a larger size.

Use the Calculator App

Your iPhone includes a full-featured Calendar app that is great for performing calculations wherever you need them.

The Calculator app starts in portrait orientation with regular features, but you can reveal a full scientific calculator by turning the iPhone to landscape orientation.

Use the Calculator App

1. Press the Home button.

   The Home screen appears.

2. Tap **Utilities**.

   The Utilities folder opens.

3. Tap **Calculator**.

The Calculator app opens, showing regular features for a pocket calculator.

4. Tap the calculator buttons to perform calculations.

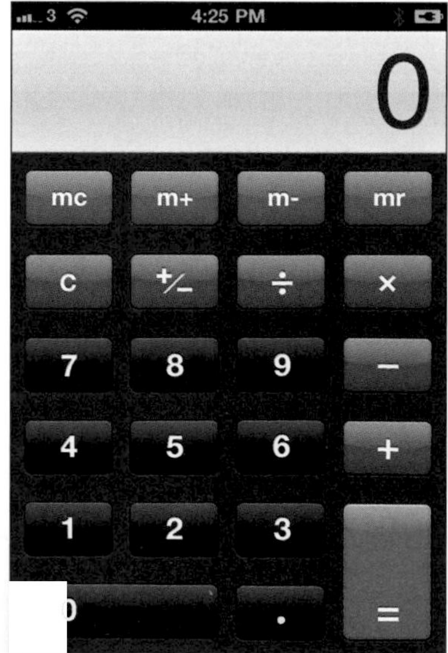

5 Turn the iPhone to landscape orientation to reveal the full range of scientific features.

6 Perform calculations by tapping the calculator buttons.

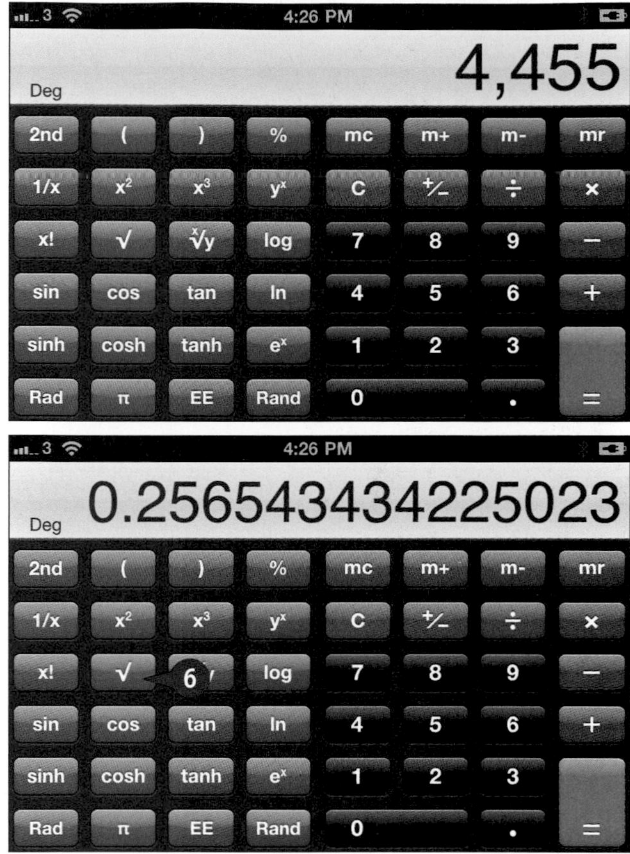

TIP

How do I use the memory in the Calculator app?

Tap **mc** to clear whatever is in the memory. Tap **m+** to add the currently displayed value to the memory. Tap **m–** to subtract the currently displayed value from the memory. Tap **mr** to return the memory's current value so that you can use it in a calculation.

Set Up the Clock App with Multiple Time Zones

When you travel, or when you work with people in different time zones, you may need to track the time in different time zones. You can set up your iPhone's Clock app with the different time zones you need so that you can instantly see the local time in each time zone you need to track.

Set Up the Clock App with Multiple Time Zones

1. Press the Home button.

   The Home screen appears.

2. Tap **Clock**.

The Clock app appears.

Note: When you open the Clock app, it displays the last screen you used in the app.

3. Tap **World Clock.**

   The World Clock screen appears.

4. Tap ⊞.

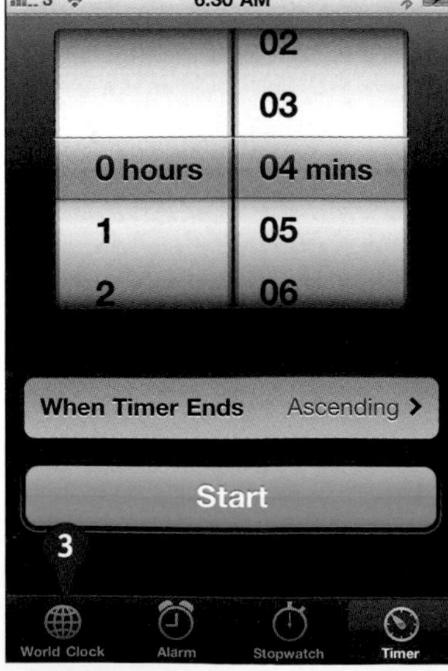

The Search screen appears.

5. Type the city or time zone you want to find.

A list of matches appears.

6. Tap the time zone you want to add.

The World Clock shows the clock you added.

7. Tap **Edit**.

The World Clock screen opens for editing.

8. Tap ≡ next to a clock and drag it up or down the list as needed.

Note: To delete a clock, tap ⊖ next to it, and then tap **Delete**.

9. Tap **Done**.

The clocks appear in your chosen order.

You can now easily see what time it is in each of the time zones you are tracking.

TIPS

Why do some clocks have black faces and others white faces?
A black clock face indicates that it is currently between 6pm and 6am in that time zone. A white clock face indicates that it is between 6am and 6pm.

How do I set the time on my iPhone's main clock?
Normally, your iPhone sets the time automatically, but you can set the time manually if you want. From the Home screen, tap **Settings**, and then tap **General**. Tap **Date & Time**, and then use the controls on the Date & Time screen.

Set Alarms

As well as showing the time in multiple locations, the Clock app includes full Alarm features. You can set as many alarms as you need, and create different schedules for the alarms — for example, you can set an alarm to wake you each weekday but not at the weekend.

Set Alarms

1. Press the Home button.

   The Home screen appears.

2. Tap **Clock**.

   The Clock screen appears.

3. Tap **Alarm**.

   The Alarm screen appears.

4. Tap **+**.

   The Add Alarm screen appears.

5. Tap the time controls to set the alarm time.

6. To set a repeating alarm, tap **Repeat**.

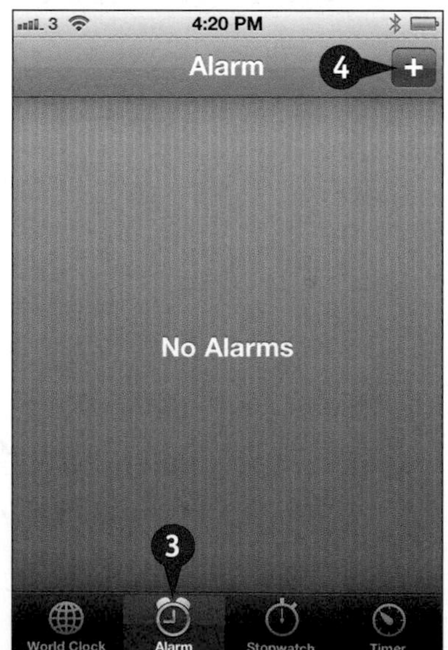

The Repeat screen appears.

7 Tap to place a check mark next to each day you want the alarm to sound.

8 Tap **Back**.

The Add Alarm screen appears again.

9 Tap **Sound**.

The Sound screen appears.

10 Tap a sound to preview it.

A check mark appears next to the sound.

11 When you have chosen the alarm sound, tap **Back**.

The Add Alarm screen appears again.

12 Tap **Label**.

The Label screen appears.

13 Type the name for the alarm.

14 Tap **Done**.

The Add Alarm screen appears again.

15 Tap the **Snooze** switch and move it to On or Off, as needed.

16 Tap **Save**.

The Alarm screen appears.

17 Move the alarm's switch to On or Off, as needed.

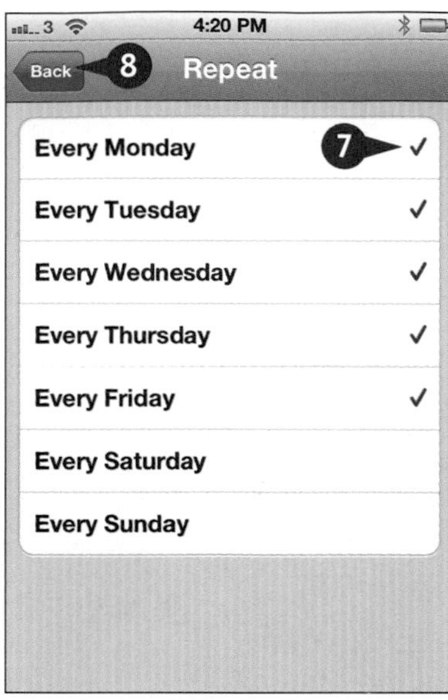

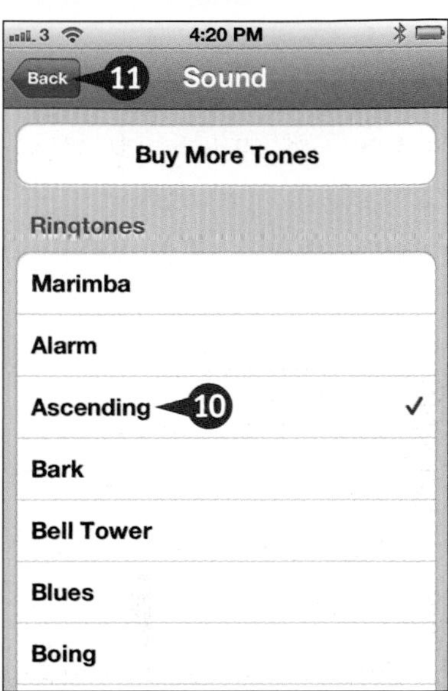

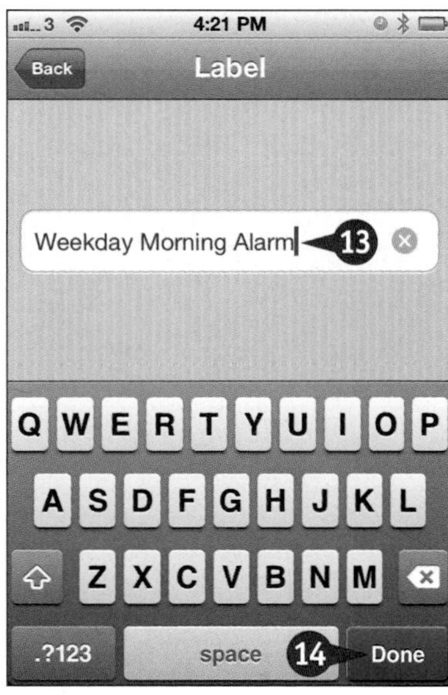

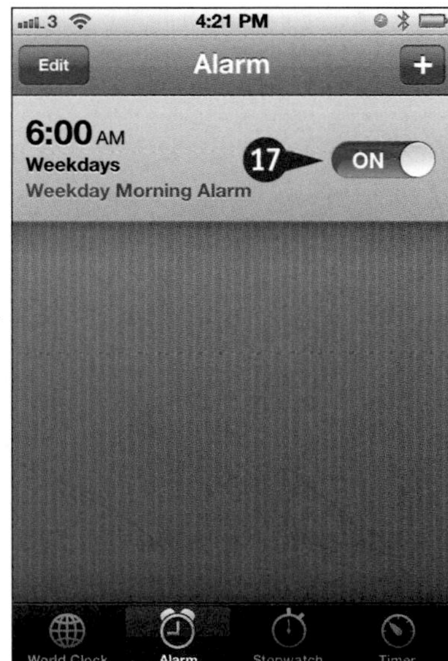

TIP

Is there an easy way to tell whether an alarm is set?
Yes. The alarm icon ( ) appears in the status bar when an alarm is set.

Use the Stopwatch and Timer

Your iPhone's Clock app includes a Stopwatch feature and a Timer feature. Stopwatch provides a handy way of timing events such as races. Timer enables you to count down from a set time and sound an alarm when the time elapses.

Use the Stopwatch and Timer

Open the Clock App

1. Press the Home button.

   The Home screen appears.

2. Tap **Clock**.

   The Clock screen appears.

Use the Stopwatch

1. Tap **Stopwatch**.

   The Stopwatch screen appears.

2. Tap **Start**.

   The stopwatch starts running.

3. Tap **Lap** to mark a lap time.

A. The lap time appears in the list.

B. The top readout shows the time since the last lap mark.

4. Tap **Stop**.

5. Tap **Reset** when you need to reset the stopwatch.

Use the Timer

1. Tap **Timer**.

   The Timer screen appears.

2. Tap the time controls to set the number of hours and minutes.

3. Tap **When Timer Ends**.

   The When Timer Ends screen appears.

4. Tap a sound to preview it.

   A check mark appears next to the sound.

5. When you have chosen the alarm sound, tap **Set**.

   The Timer screen reappears.

6. Tap **Start**.

   The Timer starts running.

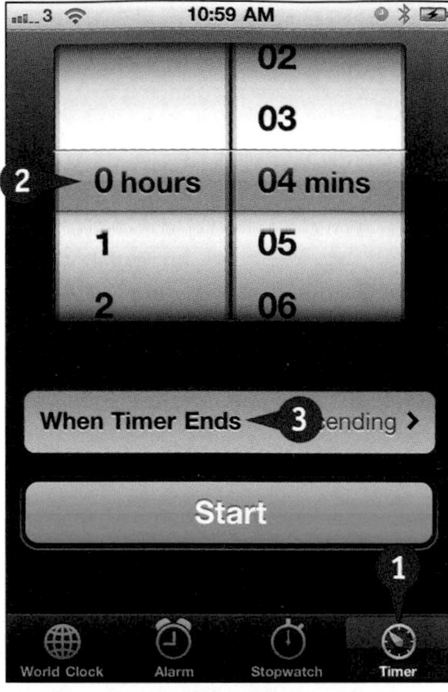

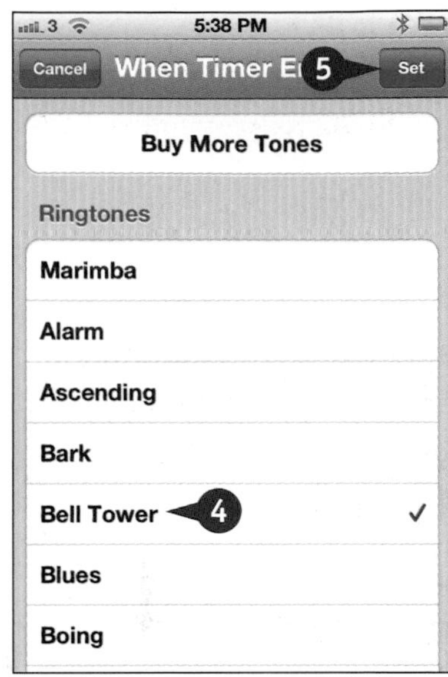

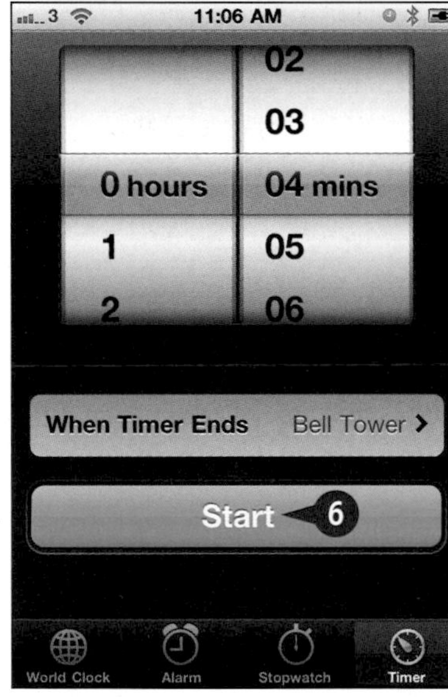

TIP

How can I make the iPhone play music for a while as I go to sleep?
To play music and shut it off automatically after a set time, set the Timer feature to the interval you want. Tap **When Timer Ends**, scroll down to the bottom of the screen, and tap **Sleep iPod**. Then tap **Set**.

Record Voice Memos

Equipped as it is with a microphone and plenty of storage space, your iPhone is a great tool for recording voice memos. Using the Voice Memos app, you can record any audio from quick notes to lecture notes or concerts — assuming that you have permission to record them.

After recording a voice memo, you can listen to it and quickly trim it down to only the part that you want to keep.

Record Voice Memos

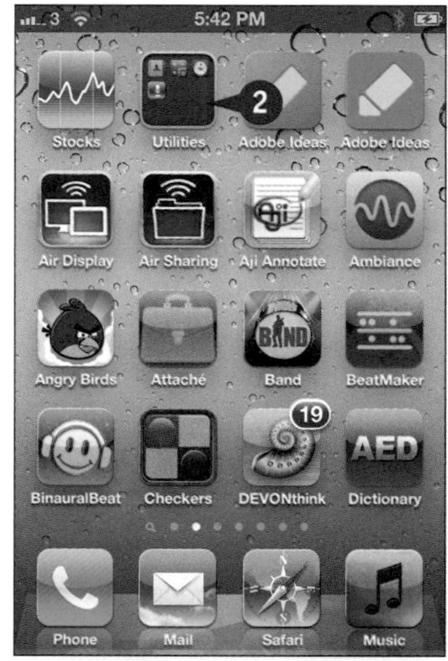

1. Press the Home button.

   The Home screen appears.

2. Tap **Utilities**.

   The Utilities folder opens.

3. Tap **Voice Memos**.

   The Voice Memos recording screen appears.

4. Prepare your sound source, and then tap **Record** (◉).

   Recording begins.

Note: If you need to pause recording, tap ◉. Tap ◉ when you are ready to resume recording.

5. Tap **Stop** (◉).

   Recording ends.

6. Tap **Voice Memos** (◉).

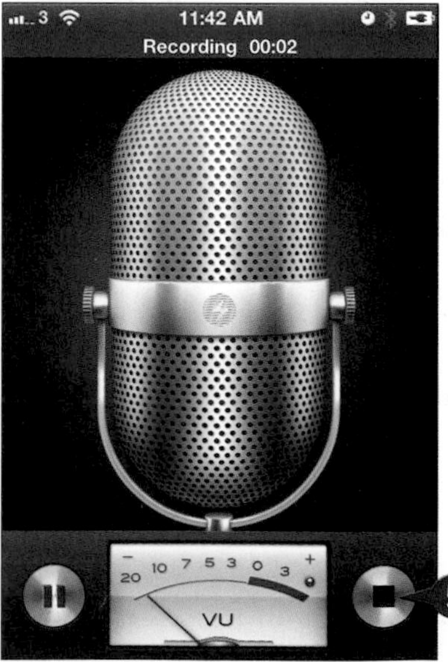

The Voice Memos screen appears.

The memo you just recorded starts playing automatically.

7 Tap **Pause** (⏸) if you want to stop the voice memo playing.

8 Tap ⊙.

The Info screen for the voice memo appears.

9 If you need to shorten the voice memo, tap **Trim Memo**.

The trim controls appear.

10 Tap the left trim handle and drag it to the right, as needed.

11 Tap the right trim handle and drag it to the left, as needed.

12 Tap **Trim Voice Memo**.

The Voice Memos app trims the memo and displays the Info screen.

13 Tap **Voice Memos**.

The Voice Memos screen appears.

14 Tap **Done**.

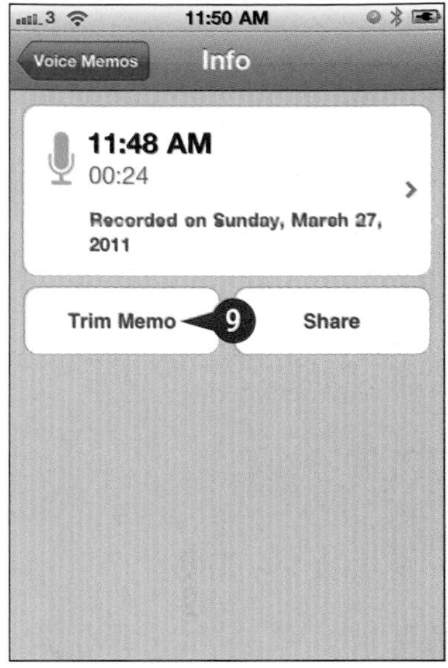

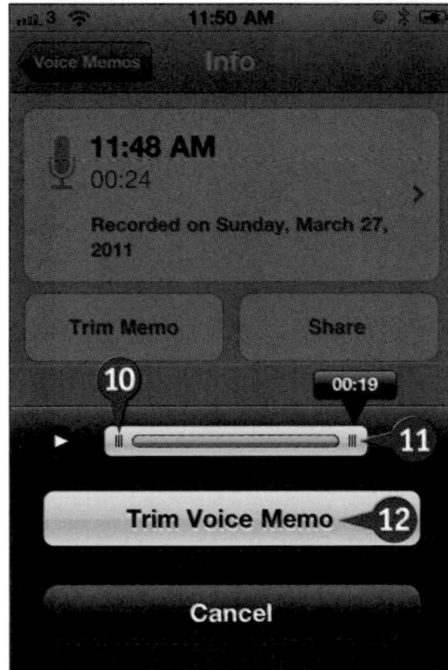

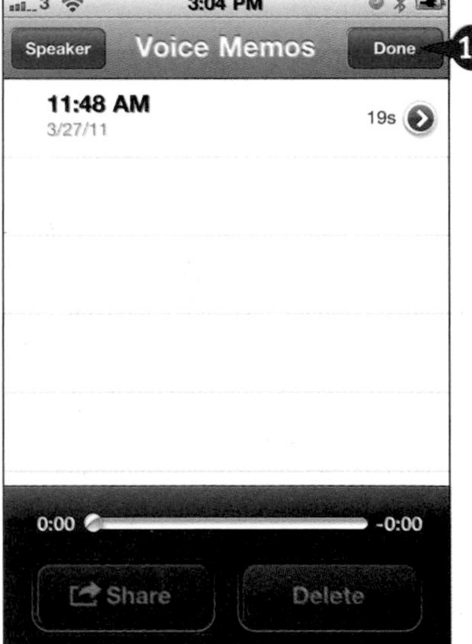

TIP

How can I sort my voice memos into different categories?
From the Info screen for a voice memo, tap the big button that shows the memo's date and time. On the Label screen, tap the label you want — for example, **Idea**. You can create a custom label by tapping **Custom** and typing the name on the Custom screen.

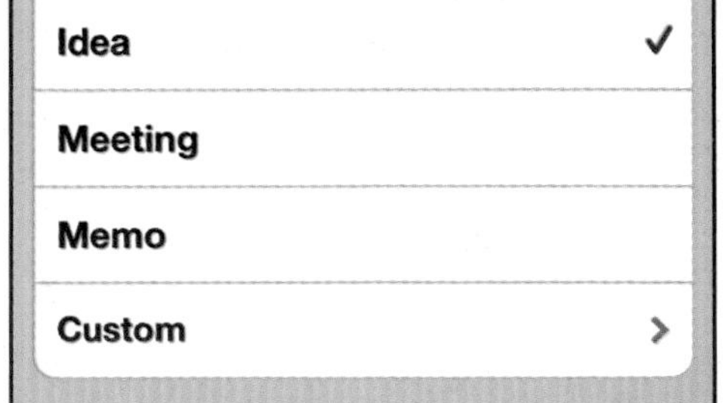

Look Up Forecasts in Weather

Along with much other useful information, your iPhone can put the weather forecasts in the palm of your hand. By using the Weather app, you can quickly learn the current conditions and forecast for as many cities as you need. The Weather app comes set to show the weather in Cupertino, the city where Apple's headquarters is located, but you can choose whichever cities you want. You can then move quickly from city to city as needed.

Look Up Forecasts in Weather

Open the Weather App and Add Your Cities

1. Press the Home button.

   The Home screen appears.

2. Tap **Weather**.

   The Weather app opens and displays the weather for either your current location or for Cupertino.

3. Tap **Info** (ⓘ).

   The Weather screen appears.

Note: The Local Weather switch on the Weather screen controls whether your iPhone automatically gets local weather conditions as well as weather for the cities you have chosen. The iPhone uses GPS or Wi-Fi location information to determine where it is. Move the switch to Off if you do not want to get local weather.

4. Tap +.

   The Search screen appears.

5. Type the city you want to add.

6. Either tap **Search** or simply wait while the Weather app returns results.

7. Tap the result you want to add.

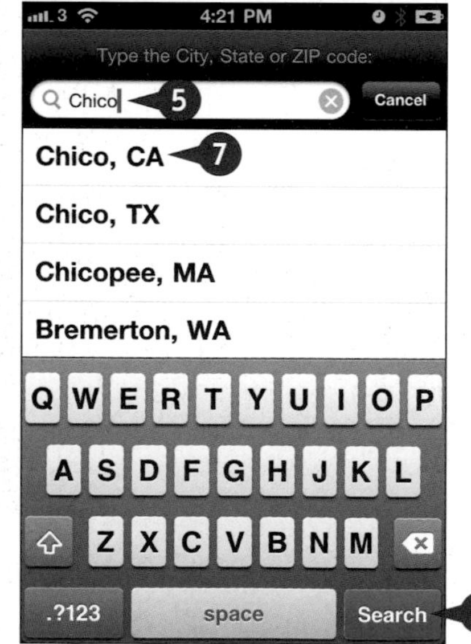

The Weather screen appears, showing the city you added.

Note: You can now add other cities as needed.

8. Tap ≡ and drag a city up or down as needed.
9. To delete a city, tap ⊖, and then tap **Delete**.
10. Tap **Done**.

The Weather app displays the screen for the first city in the list.

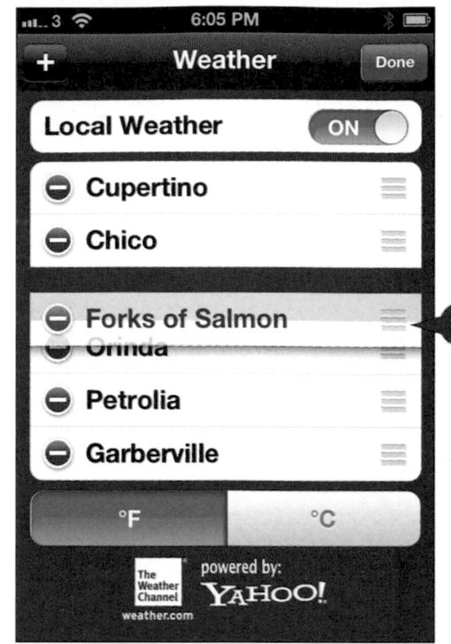

Navigate from City to City

1. Tap and drag to the left.

   The next screen appears.

2. Tap a dot to the left or right of the current dot.

   The next screen in that direction appears.

TIPS

How do I change from Centigrade to Fahrenheit?
Tap **Info** (ⓘ) to display the Weather screen, and then tap **°F** or **°C**, as needed.

What does the Y! button in the Weather app do?
Tap **Yahoo!** (Y!) button to display the Yahoo! Weather page for the current city in Safari.

Work Out with Nike + iPod

Your iPhone can help you with most everyday tasks — and it can keep track of your running workouts as well. By using the Nike + iPod app, you can use your iPhone to track the pace and duration of your workouts, and to calculate the number of calories you have burned.

To use the Nike + iPod app, you must add a Nike + iPod sensor to your sneakers and enable the app, as described on the first spread of this task. You can then work out with the app as described on the second spread of this task.

Work Out with Nike + iPod

Set Up Nike + iPod

1. Insert the Nike + iPod sensor flat side up in the socket in your left Nike sneaker.
2. On the iPhone, press the Home button.

   The Home screen appears.
3. Tap **Settings**.

   The Settings screen appears.
4. Tap and drag up to scroll down.

   The lower part of the screen appears.
5. Tap **Nike + iPod**.

   The Nike + iPod screen appears.
6. Tap the **Nike + iPod** switch and move it to On.

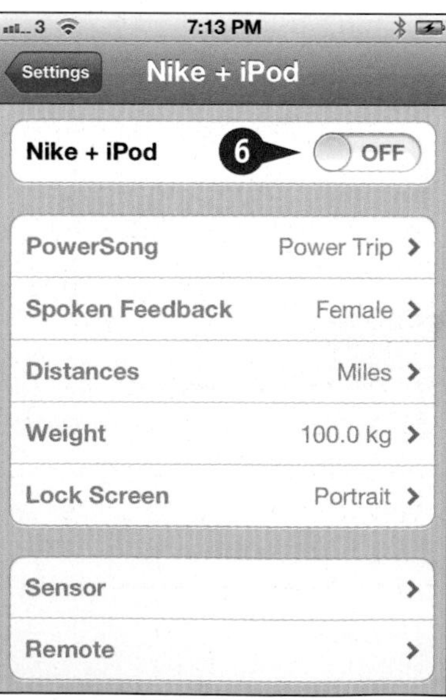

The other controls become enabled.

7 Tap **PowerSong**.

The Select a PowerSong screen appears.

8 Tap the song you want to make your PowerSong — the song to play when you need a boost.

The Nike + iPod screen appears again.

9 Tap **Weight**.

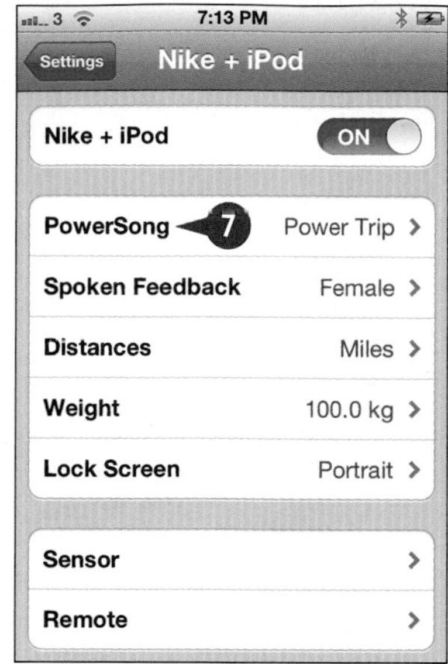

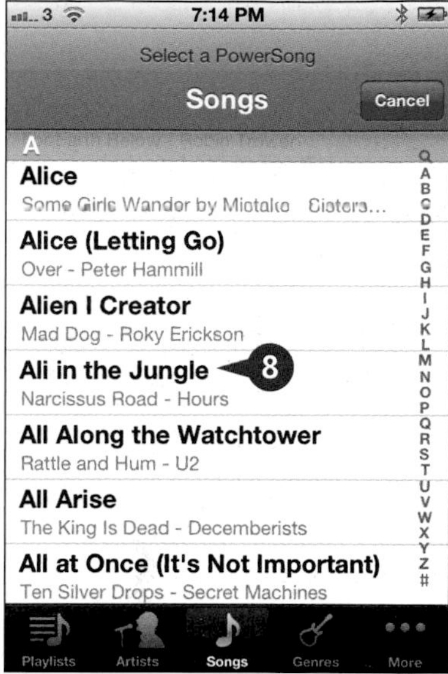

The Weight screen appears.

10 Tap the dials to set your weight in pounds or kilograms.

11 Tap **Nike + iPod**.

The Nike + iPod screen appears again.

12 Press the Home button.

A The Home screen appears, with the Nike + iPod icon now added to it.

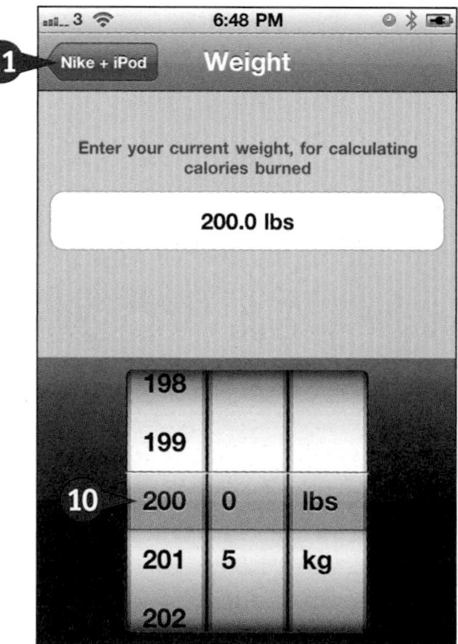

TIP

Must I buy Nike shoes to use the Nike + iPod feature?

No. Instead of using Nike shoes with a compartment for the Nike + iPod sensor, you can buy a pouch designed to hold the sensor snugly. You attach the pouch to the laces of your left sneaker, and the Nike + iPod feature then works as normal.

continued ►

After you have installed the sensor in your sneaker and chosen Nike + iPod settings on your iPhone, you are ready to track your running workouts with the Nike + iPod hardware and software.

The Nike + iPod hardware and software enable you to perform various types of workouts, including open-ended workouts in which you choose the start and end points, time-duration workouts, distance-based workouts, and calorie-target workouts. This task gets you started with the Nike + iPod app, leaving you to explore further on your own.

Work Out with Nike + iPod (continued)

Perform Your First Workout with Nike + iPod

1. Press the Home button.

   The Home screen appears.

2. Tap **Nike + iPod**.

   The Nike + iPod app's first screen appears.

3. Tap **Basic**.

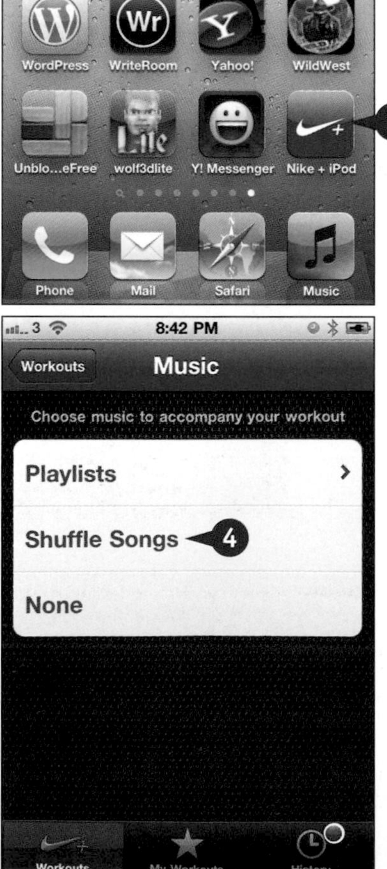

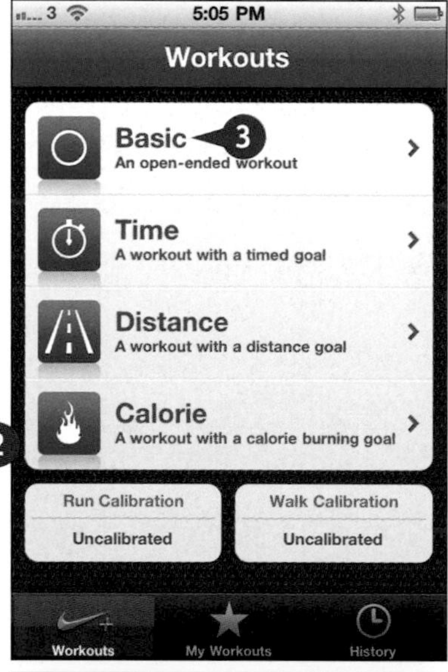

   The Music screen appears.

4. Choose the music to accompany your workout. For this example, tap **Shuffle Songs**.

   The setup screen for the workout appears.

The Sensor screen appears.

5. Walk, jog, or stamp around to activate the Nike + iPod sensor in or on your shoe.

   The starting screen for the workout appears.

6. Tap **Start** (▶).

   The workout starts.

7. Run.

   The Nike + iPod app tracks your progress, but you will likely be looking where you are going instead of at the iPhone.

8. When you finish your workout, tap **End Workout**.

   The workout's statistics appear.

9. If you want to calibrate the Nike + iPhone hardware and software, tap **Calibrate**.

Note: The Calibration screen enables you to tell Nike + iPod the actual distance you have run. By correcting the distance Nike + iPod has recorded, you can calibrate the app to track your average stride length more accurately.

10. Tap **Done**.

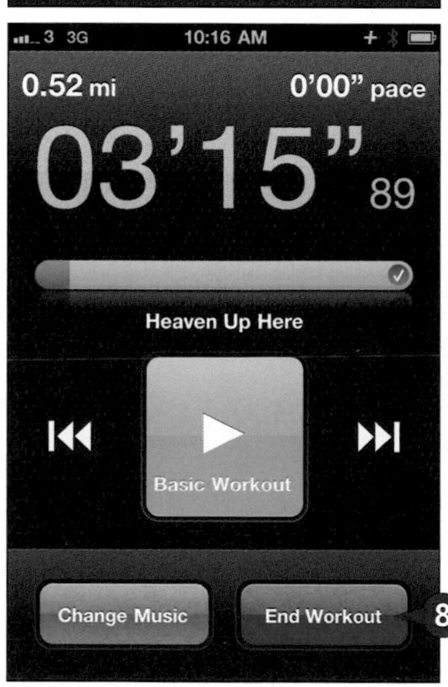

TIP

What other features does the Nike + iPod app offer?

The Nike + iPod app offers many features that this task does not have space to cover. You can create custom workouts by tapping **My Workouts** and then working on the My Workouts screen. You can examine your workout history by tapping **History**. And you can upload your workout statistics to the Nike + iPod online service so that you can share them with others.

CHAPTER 13

Taking Photos and Videos

In this chapter, you begin by using the Camera app to take both still photos, using the flash and the high dynamic range feature when needed, and videos. You then learn to edit videos using the Trim feature, share your photos and videos with others, and create movies complete with titles and soundtracks by using Apple's iMovie app.

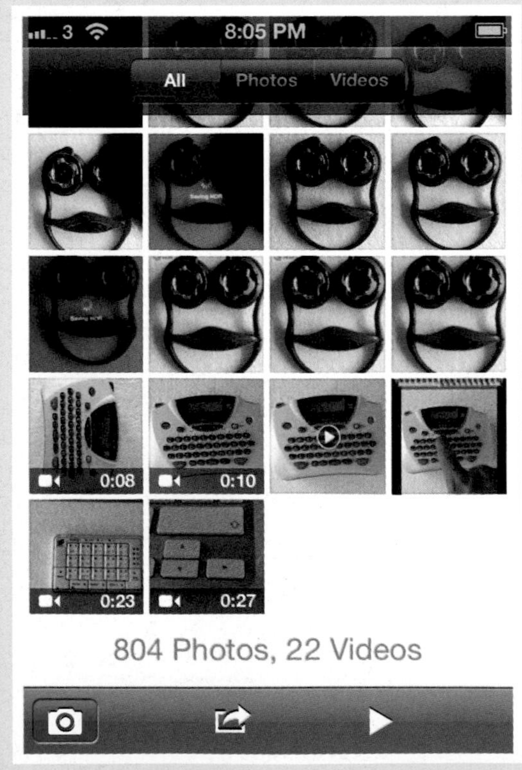

Take Photos with the Camera App

Your iPhone includes a high-resolution camera in its back for taking both still photos and videos, plus a lower-resolution camera in the front, for taking photos and videos of yourself.

To take photos using the camera, you use the Camera app. This app includes a digital zoom feature for zooming in and out, plus a flash that you can set to On, Off, or Auto.

Take Photos with the Camera App

Open the Camera App

1. Press the Home button.

   The Home screen appears.

2. Tap **Camera**.

   The Camera app opens. At first, the app shows a dark screen with shutter panels, which then open to display what is positioned in front of the lens.

Compose the Photo and Zoom If Necessary

1. Aim the iPhone so that your subject appears in the middle of the photo area. If you need to focus on an item that is not in the center of the frame, tap the object to move the focus rectangle to it.

Note: If you need to take tightly composed photos, get a tripod that fits the iPhone. You can find various models on eBay and photography sites.

2. If you need to zoom in or out, tap the screen anywhere there is no icon.

   The zoom slider appears.

3. Tap + to zoom in or – to zoom out. Tap as many times as needed.

A. You can also zoom by tapping and dragging the zoom slider.

Choose Whether and How to Use the Flash

1. Tap the Flash button.

   The Flash settings appear.

2. Tap **On** to use the flash, **Auto** to use the flash if there is not enough light without it, or **Off** to turn the flash off.

Take the Photo and View It

1. Tap **Take Photo** (📷).

   The Camera app takes the photo and displays a thumbnail.

2. Tap the thumbnail.

   The photo appears.

B From the photo screen, you can navigate as discussed in Chapter 11. For example, swipe your finger to the left to display the next photo, or swipe to the right to display the previous photo. Tap 🗑 to delete the photo.

3. Tap **Camera** (📷) when you want to go back to the Camera app.

TIP

How do I switch to the front-facing camera?
Tap **Switch Cameras** (📷) to switch from the rear-facing camera to the front-facing camera. The image the front-facing camera is seeing appears on screen, and you can take pictures as described in this task. Tap **Switch Cameras** (📷) again when you want to switch back to the rear-facing camera.

Take HDR Photos and Use the Grid

The Camera app includes a feature called *high dynamic range*, or HDR. HDR takes three photos in immediate succession with slightly different exposure settings, and then combines them into a single photo that has a better color balance and intensity than a single photo.

To take an HDR photo with your iPhone, you turn on the HDR feature in the Camera app, and then take the photo as normal. The Camera app also has a Grid feature that you can turn on to help you compose your pictures.

Take HDR Photos and Use the Grid

Open the Camera App

1. Press the Home button.

   The Home screen appears.

2. Tap **Camera**.

   The Camera app opens. At first, the app shows a dark screen with shutter panels, which then open to display what is positioned in front of the lens.

Turn On the HDR Feature

1. Tap **Options**.

Ⓐ The Options pop-up panel appears.

Note: You cannot use the HDR feature together with flash. So when you turn HDR on, your iPhone automatically turns the flash off, and vice versa.

2. Tap the **Grid** switch and move it to On if you want to display the Grid.

3. Tap the **HDR** switch and move it to On to make the Camera app use HDR.

Note: The Grid is helpful both for making sure your subject is centered and for checking that you are holding the iPhone so that uprights run vertically and horizontal items run horizontally.

4. Tap **Done**.

   The Options pop-up panel closes.

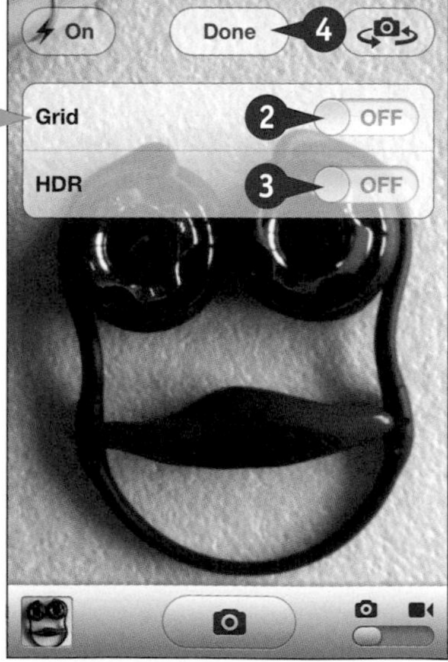

Take the HDR Photo and View It

1. Tap **Take Photo** (📷).

   The Camera app takes the photo, displaying Saving HDR and a wait symbol as it does so.

   When the Camera app finishes taking the photo, it displays a thumbnail.

2. Tap the thumbnail.

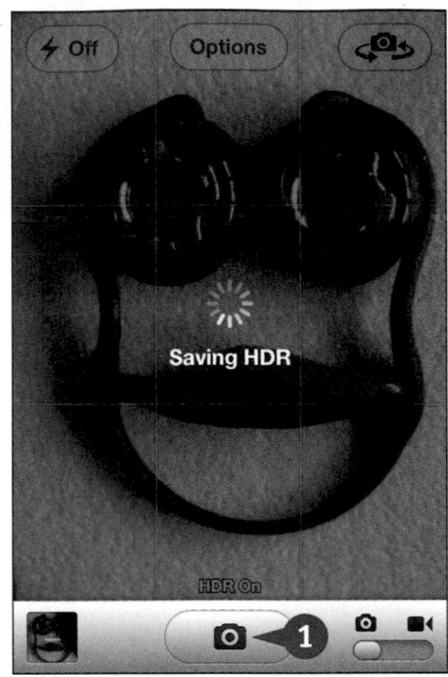

   The second version of the photo appears.

Note: Swipe your finger left to display the first version of the photo.

3. Tap **Camera** (📷) when you want to return to the Camera app.

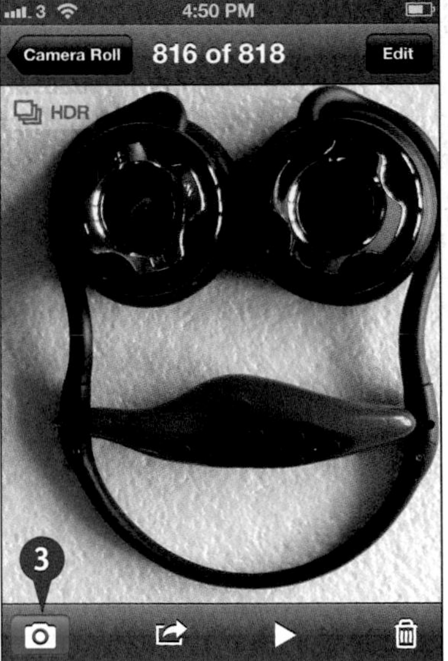

Note: HDR combines three differently-exposed photos into a single picture. It also saves the normal version of the photo — a version with a single exposure. If you do not want to save the normal version, turn off saving the normal version as described in the tip.

TIP

How do I control whether the Camera app keeps the normal version of the HDR photo?

1. Press the Home button.
2. Tap **Settings**.
3. Tap and drag up to scroll down to the third box.
4. Tap **Photos**.
5. Tap the **Keep Normal Photo** slider and move it to On or Off, as needed.

Capture Video

As well as capturing still photos, your iPhone's camera can capture high-quality, full-motion video. To capture video, you use the Camera app. You launch the Camera app as usual, and then switch it to Video mode. After taking the video, you can view it on the iPhone's screen.

Capture Video

1. Press the Home button.

   The Home screen appears.

2. Tap **Camera**.

   The Camera screen appears, showing the image the lens is seeing.

3. Tap the **Camera** switch and move it to Video.

   The video image and video controls appear.

Note: If the still camera is zoomed out all the way when you switch to the video camera, the picture appears to zoom in. This is because the video camera uses a focal length longer than the wide-angle setting of the still camera.

4. Aim the camera at your subject.

5. Tap **Record** (●).

A. If you need to use the flash for the video, tap the flash button, and then tap **Auto** or **On**. When you are shooting video, the flash is effective only at short range.

B The camera starts recording, the Record button glows brighter red, and the time readout shows the time that has elapsed.

6 To finish recording, tap **Record** (●).

The Camera app stops recording and displays a thumbnail of the video's first frame.

7 Tap the thumbnail.

The video appears.

8 Tap **Play** (▶).

The video starts playing.

9 Tap anywhere on the screen to display the video controls.

Note: If you want to trim the video, follow the procedure described in the next task before tapping **Done**.

10 When you finish viewing the video, tap **Camera** (📷).

The Camera app appears again.

TIP

What does the bar of miniature pictures at the top of the video-playback screen do?
The navigation bar gives you a quick way of moving forward and backward through the movie. Tap the vertical playhead bar, and then drag to the right or to the left until the movie reaches the part you want. You can use the navigation bar either when the movie is playing or when it is paused.

Edit with the Trim Feature

When you capture video, you normally shoot more footage than you want to keep. You then edit the video down to keep only the footage you need.

The Camera app includes a straightforward Trim feature that you can use to trim the beginning and end of a video clip to where you want them. For greater precision in editing, or to make a movie out of multiple clips, you can use the iMovie app, as described later in this chapter.

Edit with the Trim Feature

1. Press the Home button.

   The Home screen appears.

2. Tap **Camera**.

   The Camera screen appears, showing the image the lens is seeing.

3. Tap the **Camera** switch and move it to Video.

4. Tap the thumbnail.

   The photos and videos in the Camera Roll appear.

Note: If the latest photo appears, tap **Camera Roll** to display the Camera Roll photos and videos.

5. Tap **Videos**.

   The videos appear.

6. Tap the thumbnail for the video you want to trim.

   The video opens.

7. Tap the left handle and drag it to the right.

   The trim handles and the bottom of the navigation bar turn yellow to indicate that they are active.

8. Stop dragging when the frame appears where you want to trim the clip.

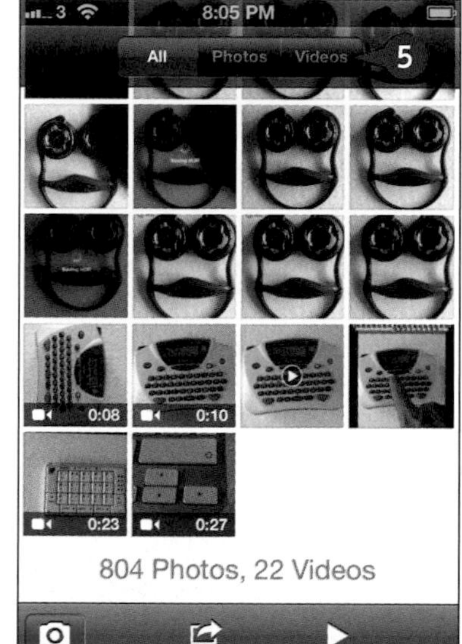

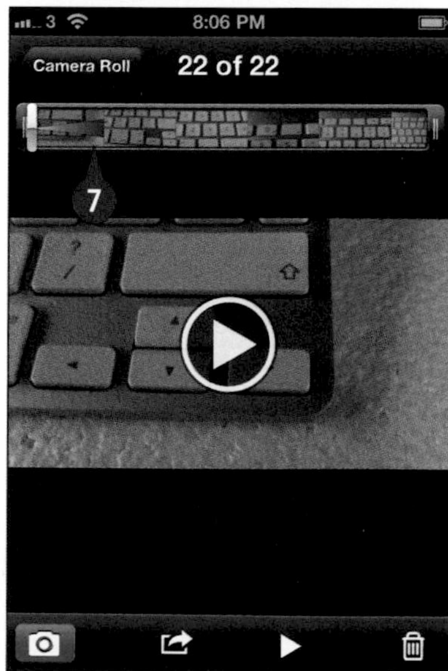

9 Tap the right handle and drag it to the left until the frame to which you want to trim the end appears.

10 Tap **Trim.**

The Trim dialog box appears.

11 Tap **Trim Original** if you want to trim the original clip. Tap **Save as New Clip** to create a new clip from the trimmed content, leaving the original clip unchanged.

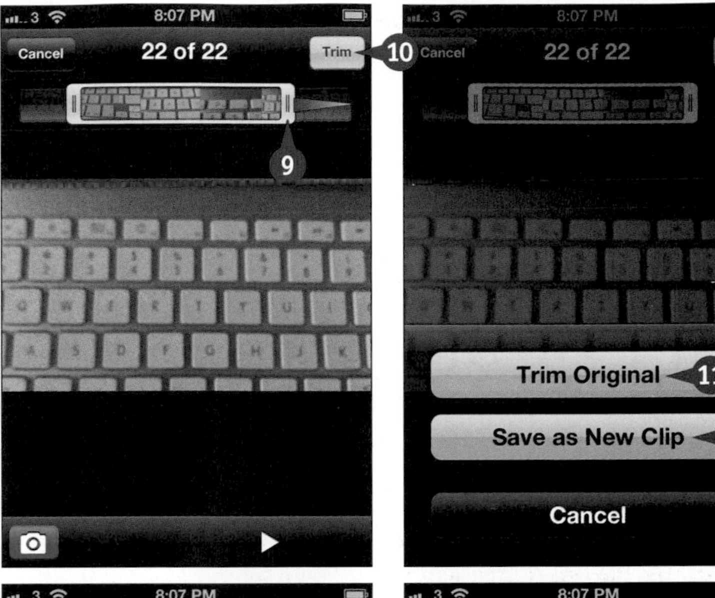

A The Trimming Video progress indicator appears while the Camera app trims the video.

12 Click **Camera** (📷).

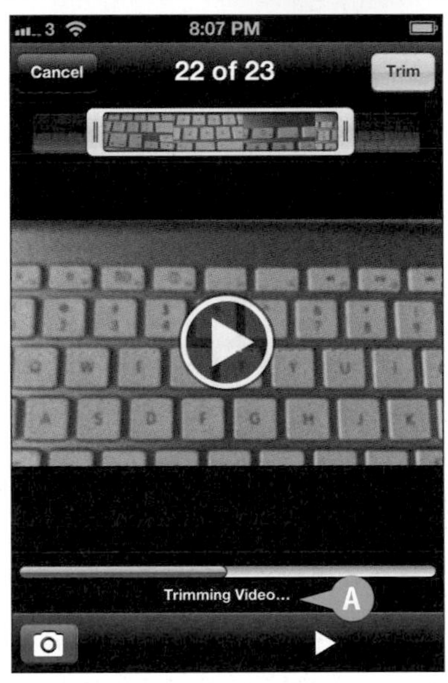

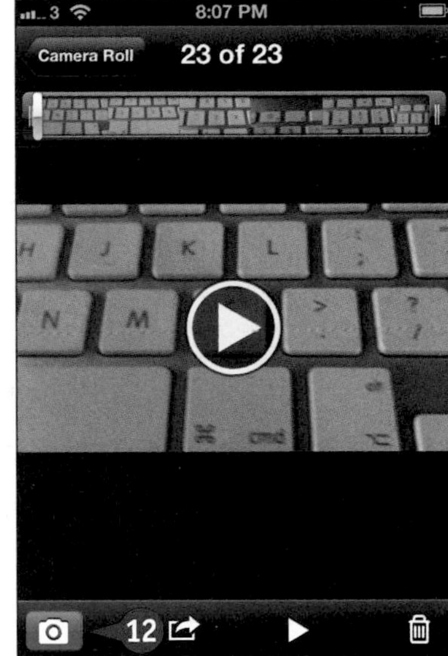

TIP

Is there an easier way of trimming my videos?

If you need to trim your videos on your iPhone, try turning the iPhone to landscape orientation. This makes the navigation bar longer and the trimming handles easier to use.

If you have a Mac, you can trim your videos more precisely, and make many other changes, by importing the clips into iMovie on the Mac, and then working with them there.

Share Your Photos and Videos

After taking photos and videos with your iPhone's camera, or after loading photos and videos on the iPhone using iTunes, you can share them with other people.

Chapter 11 explains how to share photos via email and MMS. This task explains how to tweet photos to your Twitter account, assign photos to contacts, use photos as wallpaper, or print photos.

Share Your Photos and Videos

Select the Photo or Video to Share

1. Press the Home button.
2. On the Home screen, tap **Photos**.
3. On the Photos screen, tap the photo or video you want to share.
4. Tap **Share** (![share icon]) to open the Share dialog box for photos or the Share dialog box for videos.

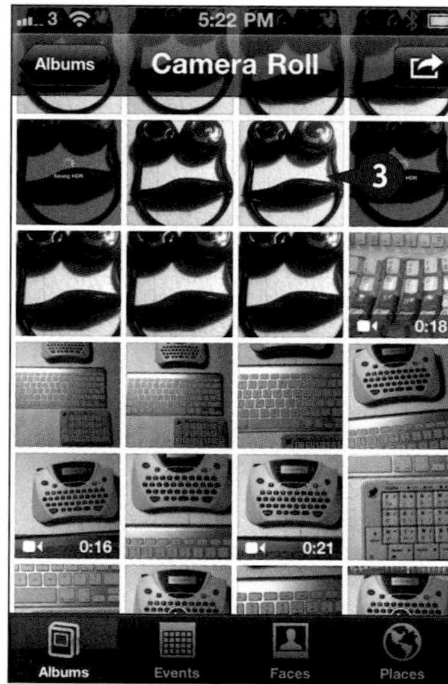

Share a Photo on Twitter

1. In the Share dialog box, tap **Tweet**.
2. Type the text of the tweet.
3. Tap **Add Location** if you want to add your location to the tweet.
4. Click **Send**.

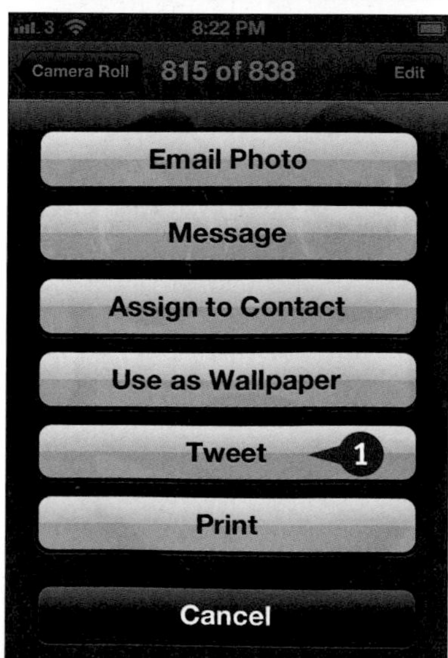

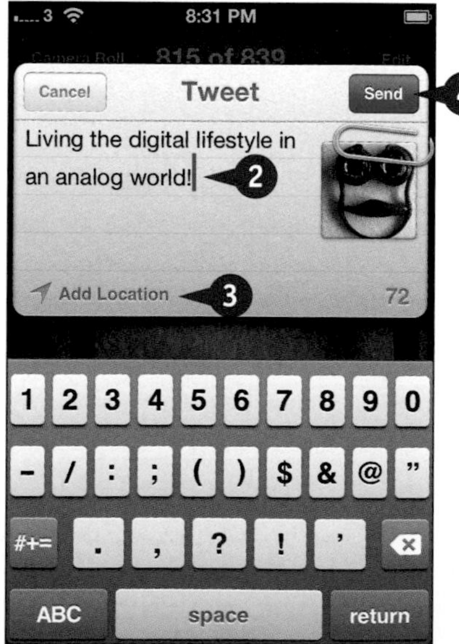

Assign a Photo to a Contact

1. In the Share dialog box, tap **Assign to Contact**.

   The list of contacts appears.

2. Tap the contact you want to assign the photo to.

   The Move and Scale screen appears.

3. Move the photo so that the face appears centrally.

4. If necessary, pinch in to shrink the photo or pinch out to enlarge it.

5. Tap **Set Photo**.

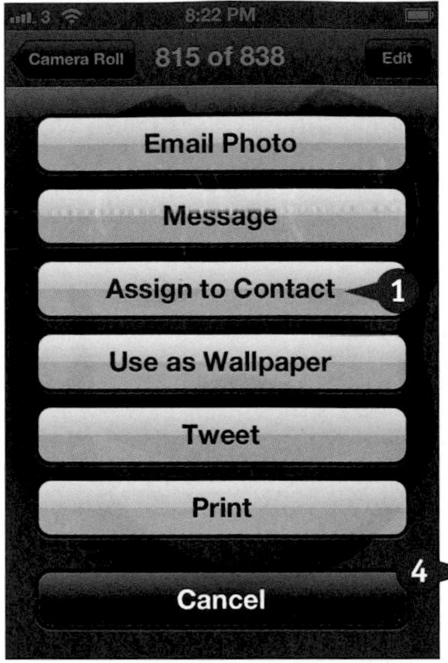

Set a Photo as Wallpaper

1. In the Share dialog box, tap **Use as Wallpaper**.

   The Move and Scale screen appears.

2. Move the photo to display the part you want.

3. If necessary, pinch in to shrink the photo or pinch out to enlarge it.

4. Tap **Set**.

   The Set Wallpaper dialog box appears.

5. Tap **Set Lock Screen**, **Set Home Screen**, or **Set Both**, as needed.

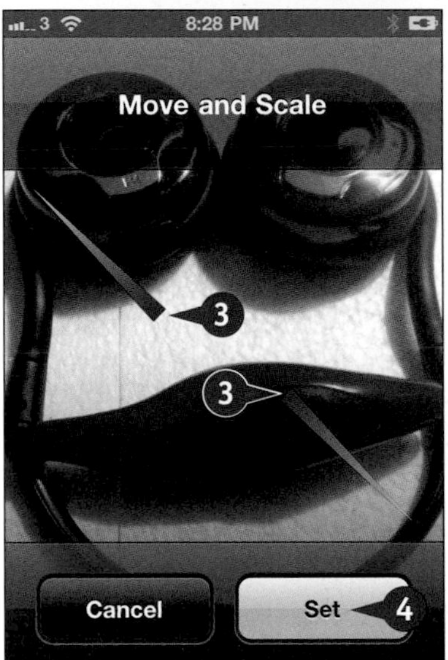

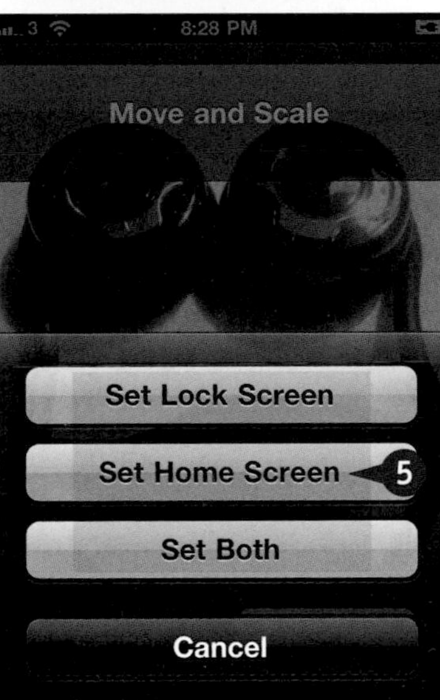

TIP

How do I print a photo?

Display the photo you want to print, and then tap **Share** () to display the Share dialog box. Tap **Print** to display the Printer Options screen. If the Printer readout does not show the correct printer, tap **Select Printer**, and then tap the printer. Tap **Print** to print the photo.

Create Movies Using Apple's iMovie App

By installing Apple's iMovie app on your iPhone, you can add the ability to create movies on the iPhone itself. This task shows you how to create a movie project, trim movie clips to length and add them, add titles and a soundtrack, and change the project's theme.

Before you can follow these instructions, you will need to buy iMovie from the iTunes Store and install it as described in Chapter 7.

Create Movies Using Apple's iMovie App

Launch iMovie and Start a Movie Project

1. Press the Home button.

   The Home screen appears.

2. Navigate to the Home screen that contains the iMovie icon.

3. Tap **iMovie**.

   The iMovie screen appears.

4. Tap +.

   iMovie creates a new project.

Add Video Clips to Your Movie

1. Tap **Insert Media** (▣).

   The Video screen appears.

   A. You can also record video from the iPhone's camera directly into iMovie by tapping ■◀.

2. Tap the video clip you want to add.

   A selection border appears around the clip, and yellow cropping handles appear before and after it.

Note: If the clip is the right length, you do not need to crop it.

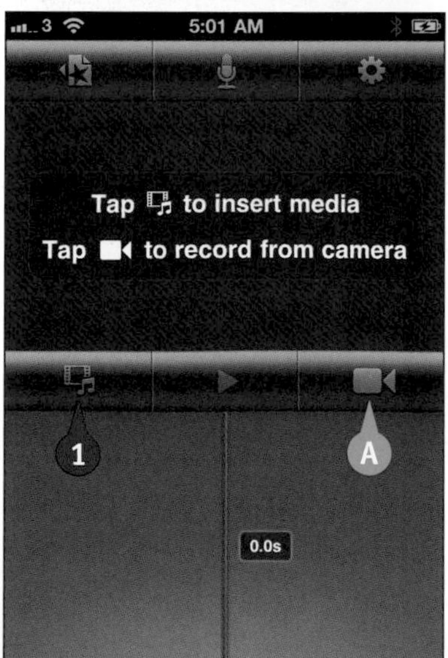

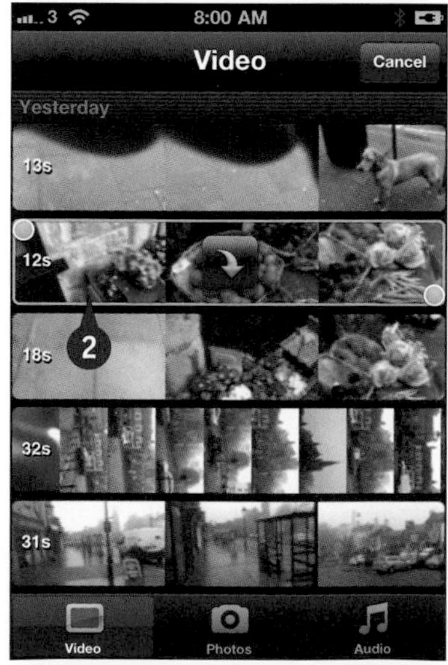

3 Tap the left cropping handle and drag right to where you want the clip to start.

4 Tap the right cropping handle and drag left to where you want the clip to end.

5 Tap **Insert** (■).

B iMovie adds the video clip to the movie timeline.

C To view the clip, tap **Play** (■). iMovie rewinds to the beginning of the movie and plays it back. To view part of the movie, drag the timeline left or right so the playhead's red line appears where you want to start. Then tap **Play** (■).

You can now add further clips as needed.

Add a Title

1 Tap in the timeline and scroll left until the first clip appears.

2 Double-tap the first clip.

3 In the Clip Settings dialog box, tap **Title Style**.

4 In the Title Style dialog box, tap a title type.

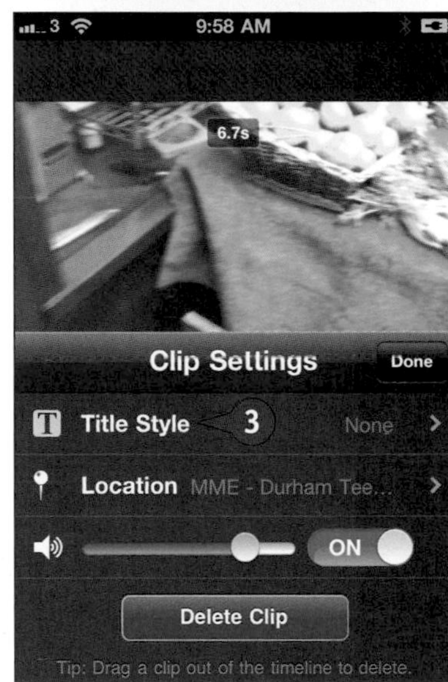

TIP

How do I remove a video clip from my movie?
Tap the clip in the timeline and drag it up to the top of the screen. The clip vanishes in a puff of smoke. If you find this move difficult, double-tap the clip to display the Clip Settings dialog box, and then tap **Delete Clip**.

continued ►

Despite the constraints of your iPhone's screen size, iMovie gives you surprisingly full features for composing and editing movies. For example, you can add a soundtrack of canned music or effects, pick the perfect playlist from the Music app, or record narration or other audio.

When you have finished creating your movie, you can share it directly from iMovie to online sites such as YouTube or Facebook.

Create Movies Using Apple's iMovie App (continued)

The opening title appears in the upper part of the screen.

5. Tap the Title Text Here placeholder.

   The on-screen keyboard appears.

6. Type the title text.
7. Tap **Done**.

Note: Use the Ending title style to add a title to the end of your movie. Use the Middle title style to add a title to a clip in the middle.

Add a Soundtrack to the Movie

1. Tap on the movie-building screen.

   The Video screen appears.

2. Tap **Audio**.

   The Audio screen appears.

3. Tap the music category you want. This example uses **Theme Music**.

   The screen for the music you chose appears.

4. Tap the music item to use.

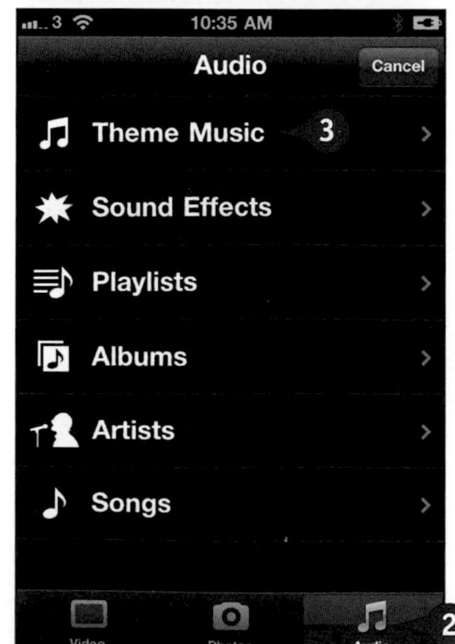

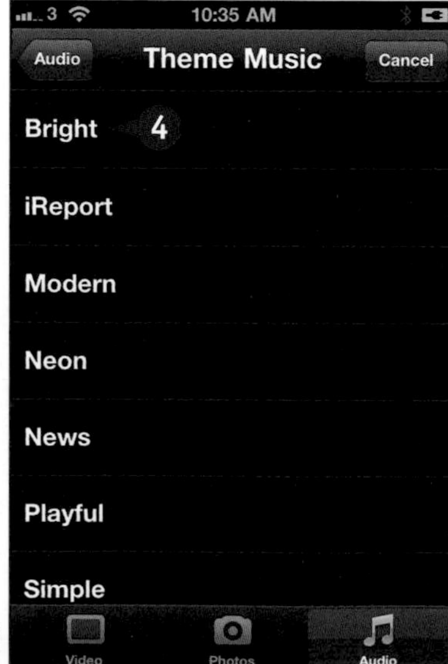

Ⓐ iMovie adds the music as a green bar.

5 Double-tap the first clip.

The Clip Settings dialog box opens.

6 To turn the clip's audio off, tap the **Audio** switch and move it to Off.

Ⓑ To mix the audio, tap and drag the volume slider in the Clip Settings dialog box.

7 Tap **Done**.

You can now repeat this procedure for the other clips in the movie.

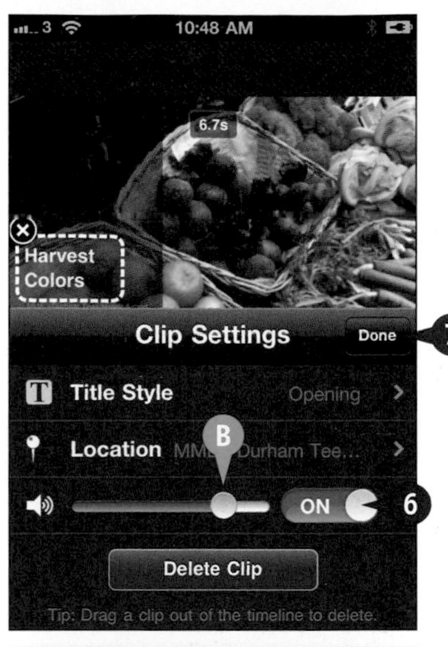

Change the Movie's Theme

1 Tap **Settings** (⚙).

The Project Settings dialog box opens.

2 In the theme bar, tap the theme you want to apply.

3 Tap **Done**.

Note: In the Project Settings dialog box, you can also turn the theme music on or off, choose whether to loop the background music, and make the movie fade in from black or fade out to black.

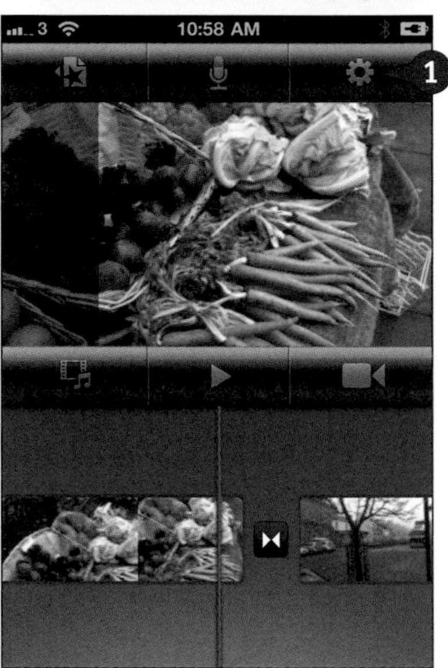

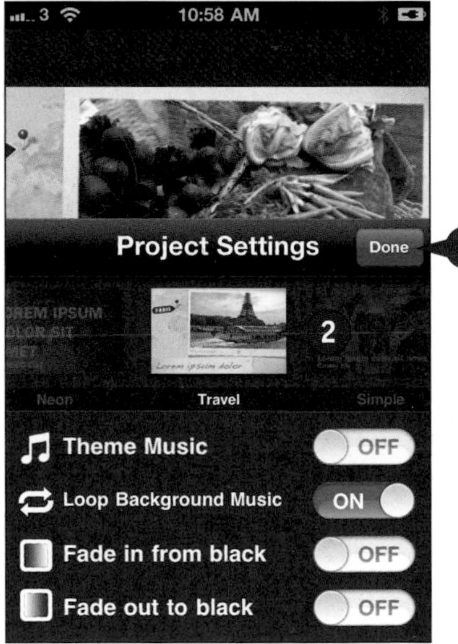

TIPS

Where can I learn more information about what iMovie can do and how to use it?
You can learn more information about iMovie by tapping the **Help** icon (?) on the iMovie Home screen. You can also find information online by searching for "iMovie iPhone."

How do I share a movie on YouTube?
Tap **Share** (↗) on the iMovie project screen, and then tap **YouTube** in the Share Movie To box on the screen that appears.

CHAPTER 14

Using Advanced Features

Your iPhone includes advanced features that enable you to control it using your voice or have the iPhone announce the names of screen items to you. You can configure the iPhone quickly by installing configuration profiles, connect to a work network across the Internet, or connect to Exchange Server. You may also want to use other accessibility features and prevent ads from tracking your location.

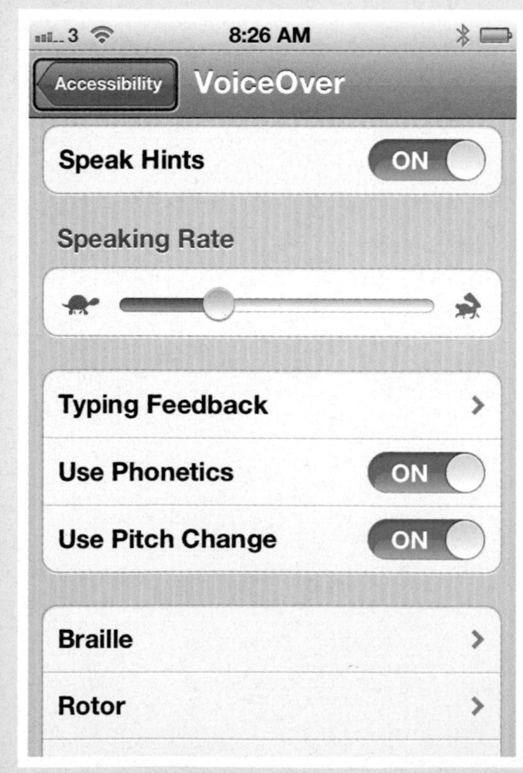

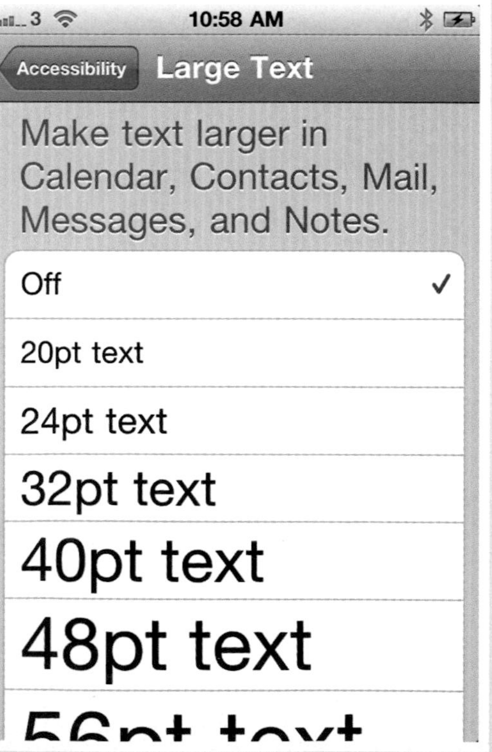

Control Your iPhone with Your Voice

Often, speaking is easier than using your iPhone's touch screen — especially when you are out and about or on the move. The iPhone's powerful Siri feature enables you to take essential actions by using your voice to tell your iPhone what you want.

You can use Siri either with the iPhone's built-in microphone or with the microphone on the headset. Unless you are in a quiet environment, or you hold your iPhone close to your face, the headset microphone gives much better results than the built-in microphone. Search on "Teach Yourself VISUALLY iPhone 4S" at www.wiley.com/go/visual for further information on using Siri.

Open Siri

From the Home screen or any app, press the Home button or the headset clicker button for several seconds. The Siri screen appears. A tone indicates that Siri is ready to take your commands.

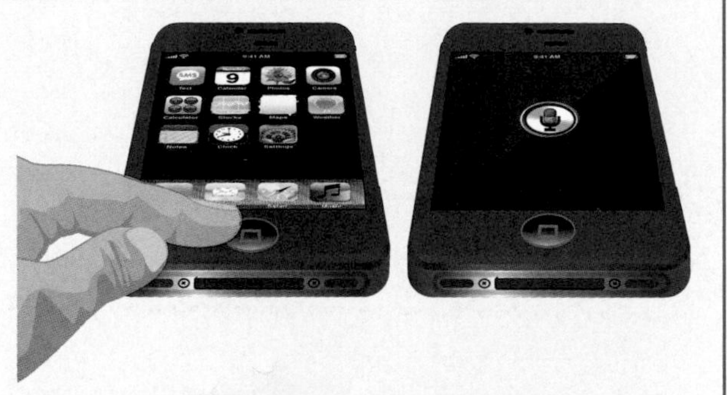

Send an Email Message

Say "Email" and the contact's name, followed by the message. Siri creates an email message to the contact and enters the text. Review the message, and then tap **Send** to send it.

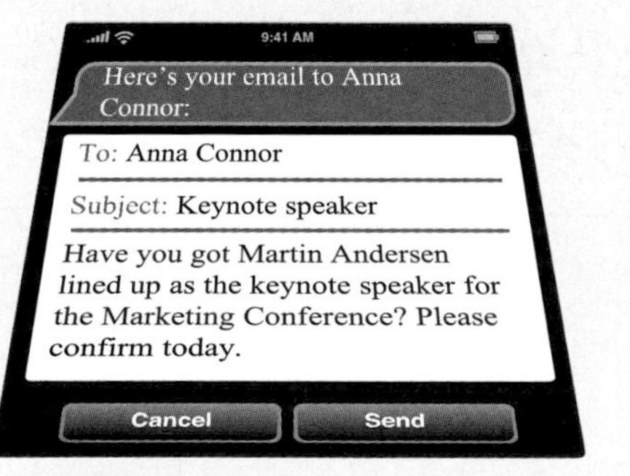

Send a Text Message

Say "Tell" and the contact's name. When Siri responds, say the message you want to send. For example, say "Tell Chris Smith" and then "I'm stuck in traffic but I'll be there in an hour." Siri creates a text message to the contact, enters the text, and sends the message.

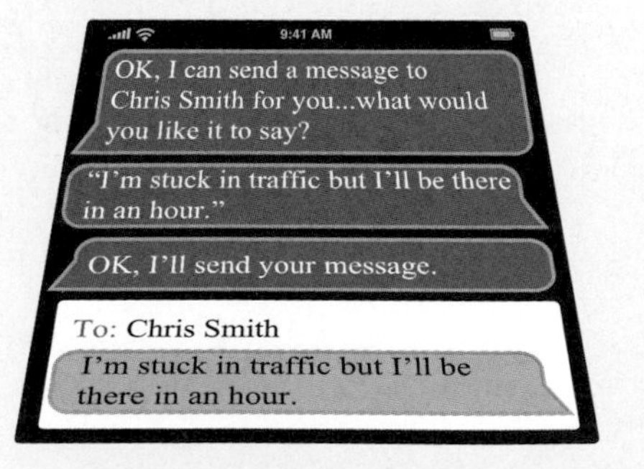

Set a Reminder for Yourself

Say "Remind me" and the details of what you want Siri to remind you of. For example, say "Remind me to take my iPad to Acme Industries tomorrow morning." Siri listens to what you say and creates a reminder. Check what Siri has written, and then tap **Confirm** if it is correct.

Set an Alarm

Say "Set an alarm for 5 a.m." and check the alarm that Siri displays.

Set Up a Meeting

Say "Meet with" and the contact's name, followed by brief details of the appointment. For example, say "Meet with Don Williamson for lunch at noon on Friday." Siri listens, schedules a meeting with the contact, and adds it to your calendar.

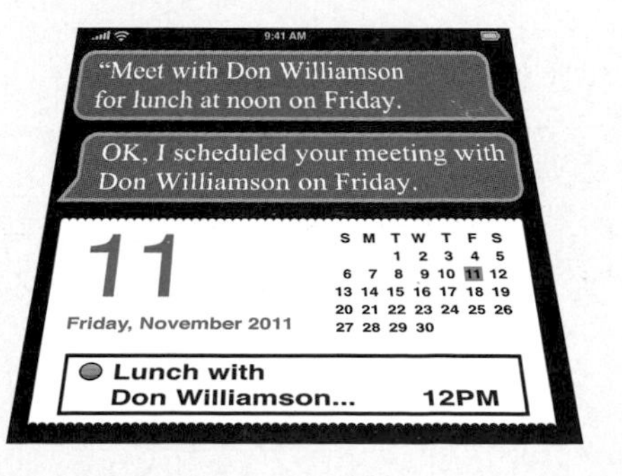

Install Configuration Profiles on the iPhone

As described earlier in this book, you can configure your iPhone by choosing settings in the Settings app. But you can also configure the iPhone by installing one or more configuration profiles provided by an administrator. The most common way of providing a configuration profile is via email.

Usually, you will need to install configuration profiles only when your iPhone is managed by an administrator rather than by yourself. For example, a configuration profile can contain the settings needed for your iPhone to connect to a corporate network or a campus network.

Install Configuration Profiles on the iPhone

1. Press the Home button.

   The Home screen appears.

2. Tap **Mail**.

   The Mailboxes screen appears.

3. Tap the mailbox that contains the message with the configuration profile.

A. You can tap **All Inboxes** to display all your inboxes.

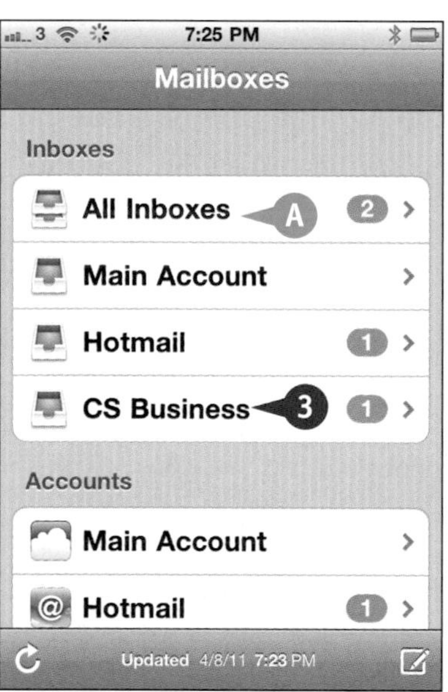

The mailbox opens.

4. Tap the message that contains the configuration profile.

   The message opens.

5. Tap the button for the configuration profile.

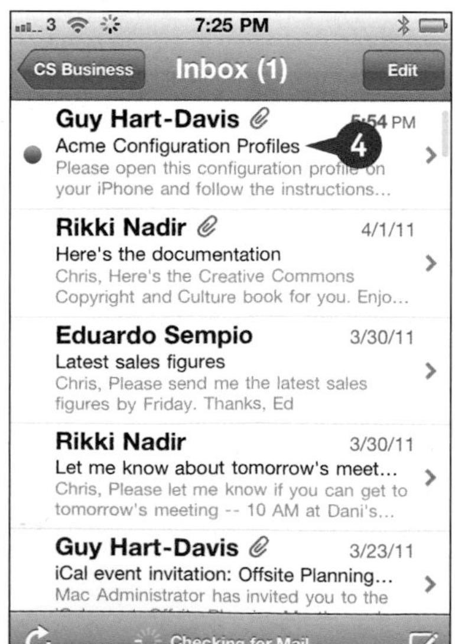

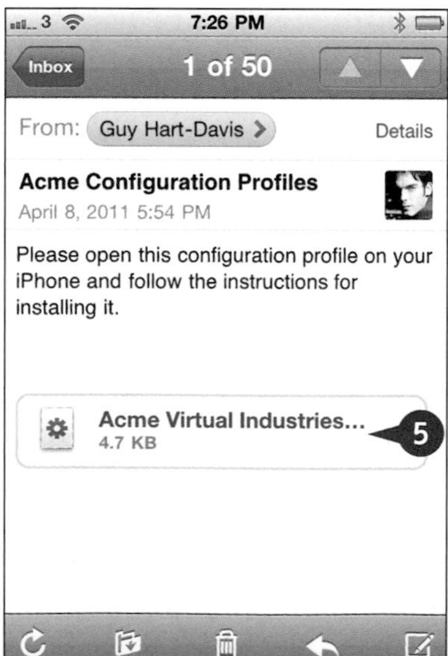

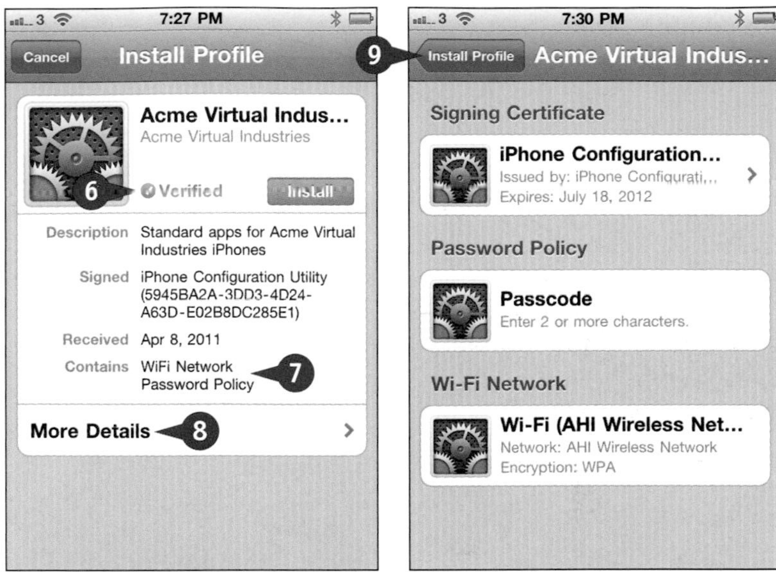

6 On the Install Profile screen, look for the Verified badge.

Note: Never install a configuration profile that does not have the Verified badge. The configuration profile may not be from the source claimed and may damage your iPhone, compromise your data, or both.

7 Review the configuration profile.

8 Tap **More Details** for more information.

Note: You can tap an item on the Details screen to see further details.

9 Tap **Install Profile**.

10 On the Install Profile screen, tap **Install** to open the Install Profile dialog box.

11 Tap **Install Now**.

Your iPhone installs the configuration profile.

Note: If the configuration profile requires you to set information, the appropriate screens appear. For example, if the configuration profile requires you to create a passcode, the Set Passcode screen appears.

12 On the Profile Installed screen, tap **Done**.

TIP

Is there a way of installing a configuration profile other than using email?

Yes. An administrator can place a configuration profile on a web page. You download the configuration profile using Safari, and then install it using installation screens similar to those shown in this task. By sending a text message to your iPhone, an administrator can easily direct you to a web page that contains a configuration profile specific to your iPhone rather than a general profile for iPhones.

Connect to a Work Network via VPN

If you use your iPhone for work, you may need to connect it to your work network. By using the settings, username, and password that the network's administrator provides, you can connect via virtual private networking, or VPN, across the Internet.

VPN uses encryption to create a secure connection across the Internet. By using VPN, you can connect securely from anywhere you have an Internet connection.

Connect to a Work Network via VPN

Set Up the VPN Connection on the iPhone

1. Press the Home button.

   The Home screen appears.

2. Tap **Settings**.

   The Settings screen appears.

3. Tap and drag up to scroll down until the third box appears.

4. Tap **General**.

   The General screen appears.

5. Tap **Network**.

   The Network screen appears.

6. Tap **VPN**.

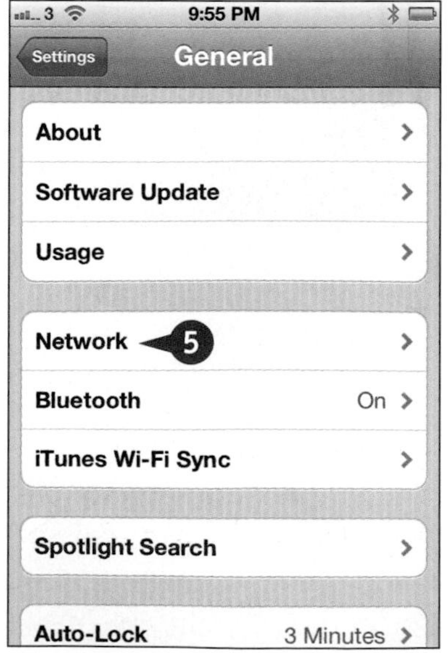

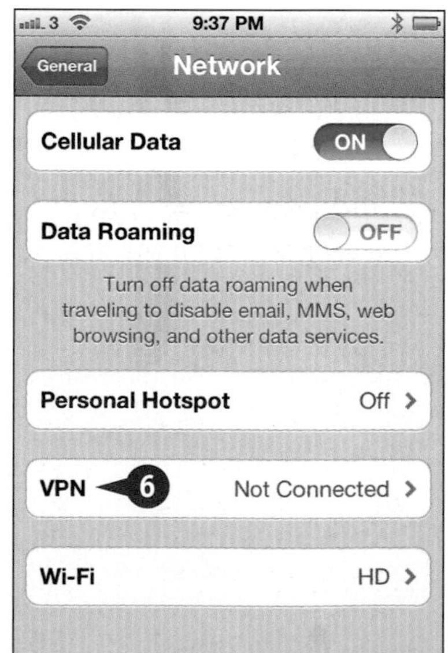

7 On the VPN screen, tap **Add VPN Configuration**.

Note: If your iPhone already has a VPN you want to use, tap it, and then go to step **1** of the next section.

8 On the Add Configuration screen, tap the tab for the VPN type: **L2TP**, **PPTP**, or **IPSec**.

9 Fill in the details of the VPN.

10 Tap **Save**.

The VPN configuration appears on the VPN screen.

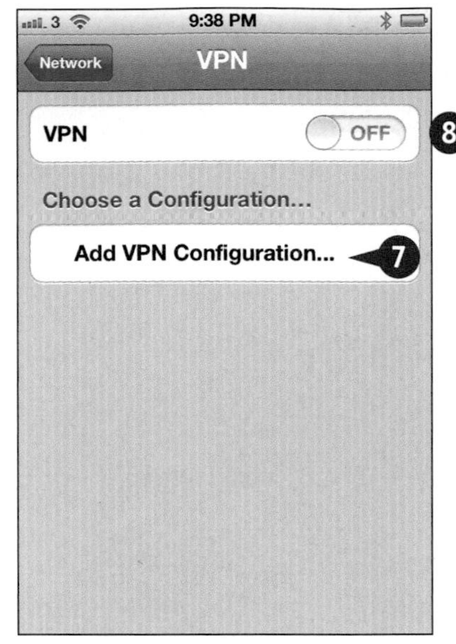

Connect to the VPN

1 On the VPN screen, tap the **VPN** switch and move it to On.

The iPhone connects to the VPN.

A The Status readout shows Connected and the duration, and the VPN indicator appears in the status bar.

2 Work across the network connection as if you were connected directly to the network.

3 When you are ready to disconnect from the VPN, tap the **VPN** switch on the VPN screen and move it to Off.

TIP

Is there an easier way to set up a VPN connection?
Yes. An administrator can provide the VPN details in a configuration profile, as discussed earlier in this chapter. When you install the configuration profile, your iPhone adds the VPN automatically. You can then connect to the VPN.

Connect Your iPhone to Exchange Server

If your company or organization uses Microsoft Exchange Server, you can set up your iPhone to connect to Exchange for email, contacts, and calendaring.

Before setting your Exchange account, ask an administrator for the details you need. These are your email address, your password, the server name, and the domain name.

Connect Your iPhone to Exchange Server

1. Press the Home button.

   The Home screen appears.

2. Tap **Settings**.

   The Settings screen appears.

Note: If you have not yet set up an email account on the iPhone, you can also open the Add Account screen by tapping **Mail** on the iPhone's Home screen.

3. Tap and drag up to scroll down until the third group of buttons appears.

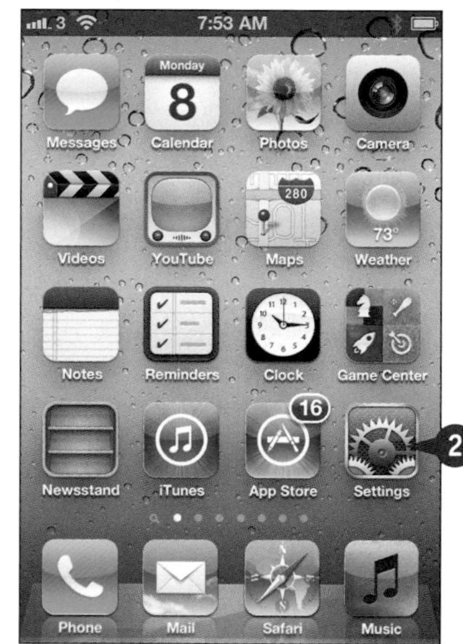

4. Tap **Mail, Contacts, Calendars.**

   The Mail, Contacts, Calendars screen appears.

5. Tap **Add Account.**

6 On the Add Account screen, tap **Microsoft Exchange**.

7 On the Exchange screen, type your email address.

8 Type in the domain if it is required.

9 Type your username.

10 Type your password.

11 Type a descriptive name for the account in the Description field.

12 Tap **Next**.

The Exchange screen adds the Server field.

13 Type the server's address.

14 Tap **Next**.

15 On the Exchange Account screen, tap the **Mail** switch and move it to On.

16 Tap the **Contacts** switch and move it to On.

17 Tap the **Calendars** switch and move it to On.

18 Tap **Save**.

The Exchange account appears on the Mail, Contacts, Calendars screen.

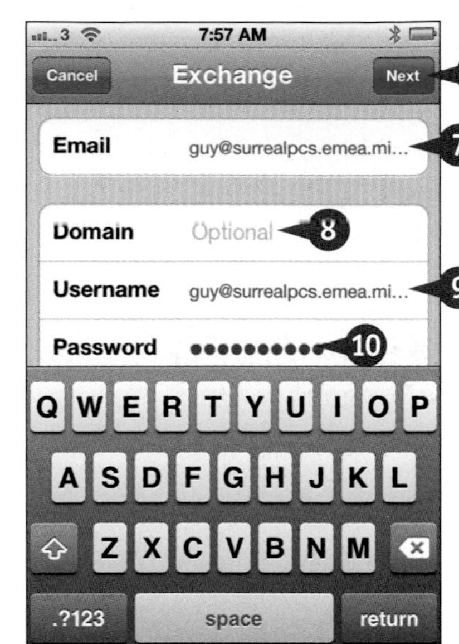

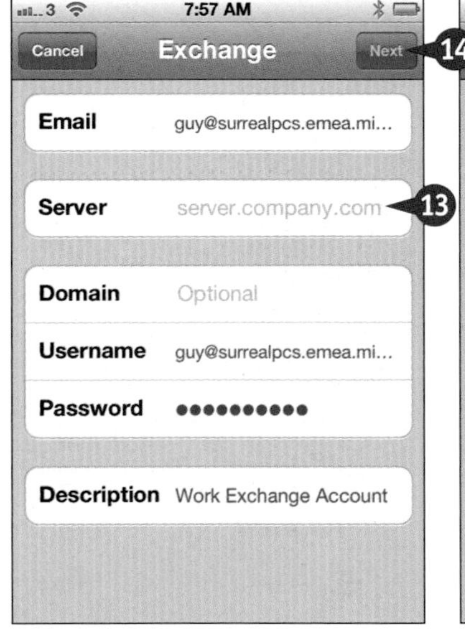

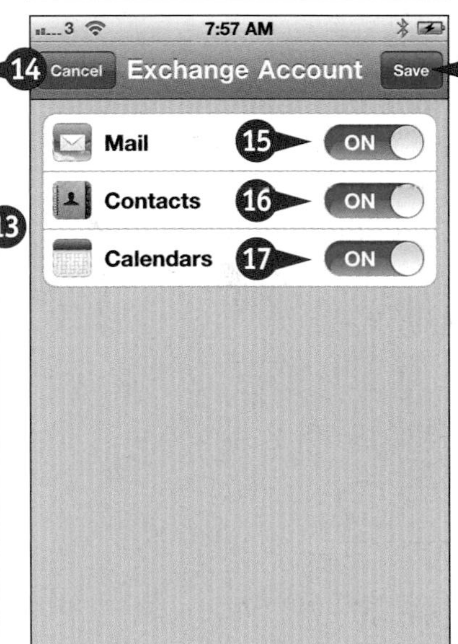

TIPS

Is there an alternative way to set up an Exchange account?

Yes. An administrator can provide the Exchange details in a configuration profile, as discussed earlier in this chapter. If you have another email account on your iPhone, the administrator can send you the profile. Otherwise, you may need to download the profile from a web page.

How do I know whether to enter a domain name when setting up my Exchange account?

You need to ask an administrator because some Exchange implementations require you to enter a domain, whereas others do not.

Use VoiceOver to Identify Items On-Screen

If you have trouble identifying the iPhone's controls on-screen, you can use the VoiceOver feature to read them to you. VoiceOver changes your iPhone's standard finger gestures so that you tap to select the item whose name you want it to speak, double-tap to activate an item, and flick three fingers to scroll.

VoiceOver can make your iPhone easier to use. Your iPhone also includes other accessibility features, which you can learn about in the next task.

Use VoiceOver to Identify Items On-Screen

1. Press the Home button.

   The Home screen appears.

2. Tap **Settings**.

   The Settings screen appears.

3. Tap and drag up to scroll down until the third box of settings appears.

   The bottom of the screen appears.

4. Tap **General**.

The General screen appears.

5. Tap and drag up to scroll all the way down.

   The bottom of the screen appears.

6. Tap **Accessibility**.

   The Accessibility screen appears.

7. Tap **VoiceOver**.

Note: You cannot use VoiceOver and Zoom at the same time. If Zoom is on when you try to switch VoiceOver on, your iPhone prompts you to choose which of the two to use.

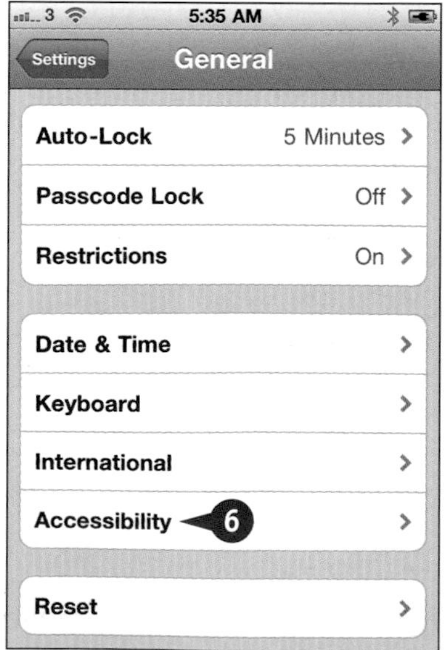

8 Tap the **VoiceOver** switch and move it to On.

9 Tap **VoiceOver Practice**.

A selection border appears around the button, and VoiceOver speaks its name.

10 Double-tap **VoiceOver Practice**.

11 Practice tapping, double-tapping, triple-tapping, and swiping. VoiceOver identifies each gesture and displays an explanation.

12 Tap **Done** to select the button, and then double-tap **Done**.

13 Swipe up with three fingers.

The screen scrolls down.

14 Move the **Speak Hints** switch to On if you want VoiceOver to speak hints about using VoiceOver.

15 Tap **Speaking Rate** to select it, and then swipe up or down to adjust the rate.

16 Tap **Typing Feedback** to select it, and then double-tap.

17 Tap the feedback type you want: **Nothing**, **Characters**, **Words**, or **Characters and Words**.

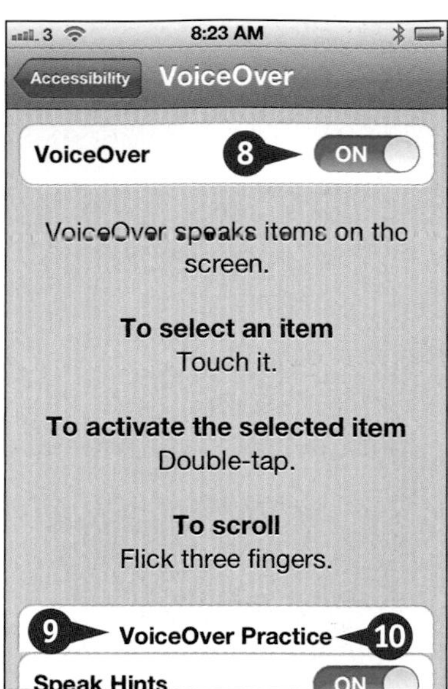

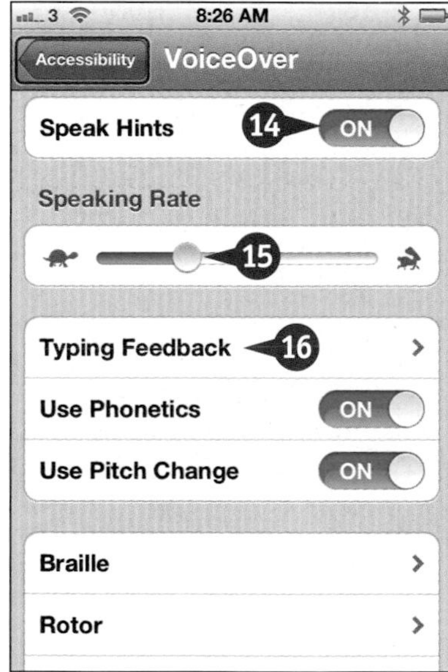

TIP

Is there an easy way to turn VoiceOver on and off?

Yes. You can set your iPhone to toggle VoiceOver on or off when you press the Home button three times in rapid sequence. From the Accessibility screen, tap **Triple-click Home** to display the Home screen. Tap **Toggle VoiceOver** (A), placing a check mark next to it, and then tap **Accessibility** (B).

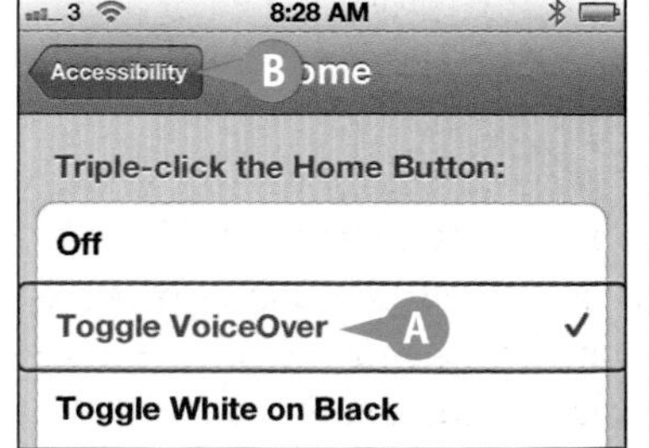

Use Other Accessibility Features

VoiceOver can be helpful, but you will probably also want to explore the other accessibility features that your iPhone offers. These include zooming in the screen, displaying text at a larger size, changing the screen to reverse video, playing audio in mono, and speaking automatic corrections made while you type.

Use Other Accessibility Features

1. Press the Home button.

   The Home screen appears.

2. Tap **Settings**.

   The Settings screen appears.

3. Tap and drag up to scroll down until the third box of settings appears.

   The bottom of the screen appears.

4. Tap **General**.

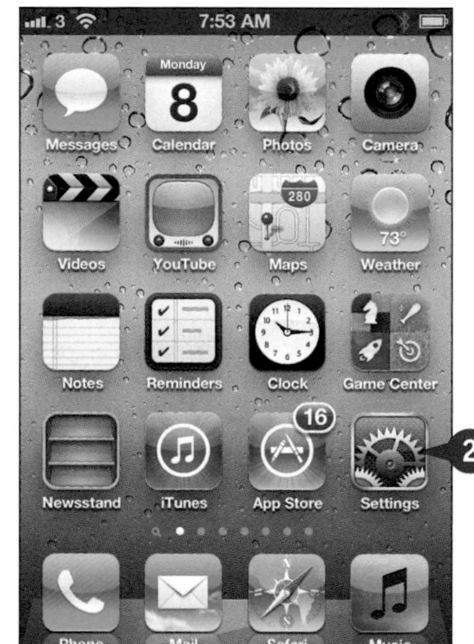

The General screen appears.

5. Tap and drag up to scroll all the way down.

   The bottom of the screen appears.

6. Tap **Accessibility**.

   The Accessibility screen appears.

7. Tap **Zoom**.

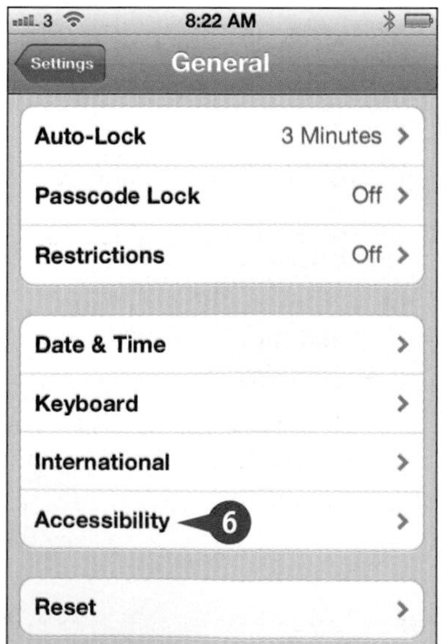

8 On the Zoom screen, tap the **Zoom** switch and move it to On.

9 Double-tap the screen with three fingers.

The screen zooms in.

10 Double-tap again with three fingers.

The screen zooms out again.

11 Tap **Accessibility**.

12 On the Accessibility screen, tap **Large Text**.

13 On the Large Text screen, tap the text size you want.

14 Tap **Accessibility**.

15 On the Accessibility screen, tap the **White on Black** switch and move it to On.

The screen changes to reverse video.

Note: Tap the **Mono Audio** switch and move it to On if you want to use mono audio.

16 Tap the **Speak Auto-text** switch and move it to On if you want your iPhone to speak text corrections.

17 Tap **General**.

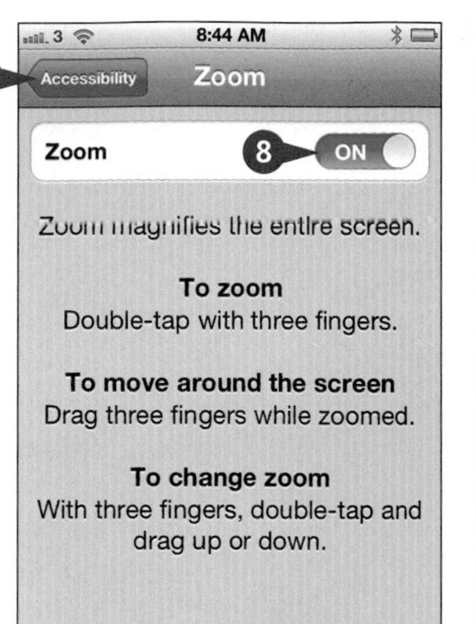

TIP

Is there an easy way to turn the Zoom feature on and off?

Yes. You can set your iPhone to toggle Zoom on or off when you press the Home button three times in rapid sequence. From the Accessibility screen, tap **Triple-click Home** to display the Home screen. Tap **Toggle Zoom** (A), placing a check mark next to it, and then tap **Accessibility** (B). You can also use the Home triple-press to toggle the White on Black feature.

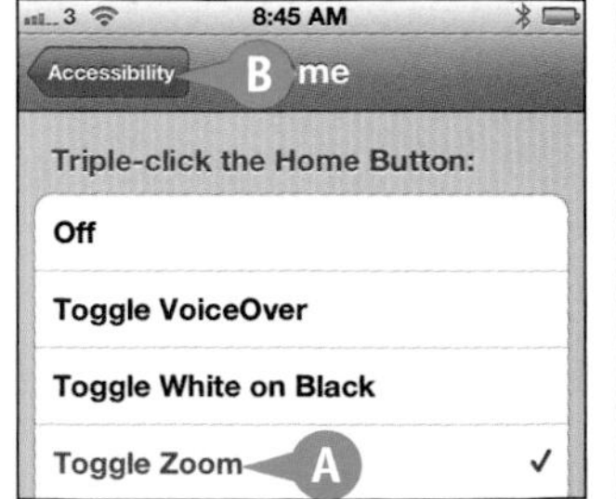

Opt Out of iAd Location Services

Your iPhone includes a feature called iAd, which enables apps to display advertisements to you. These apps help developers to release free or low-cost apps by displaying advertisements to generate revenue.

To help app developers reach their target markets, iAd can access information collected by your iPhone about what you buy online or what you download. If you do not want your iPhone to provide this personal and potentially sensitive data, you can opt out of iAd location services.

Opt Out of iAd Location Services

1. Press the Home button.

   The Home screen appears.

2. Tap **Settings**.

   The Settings screen appears.

3. Tap **Location Services**.

   The Location Services screen appears.

4. Tap and drag up to scroll down to the bottom of the screen.

5. Tap **System Services**.

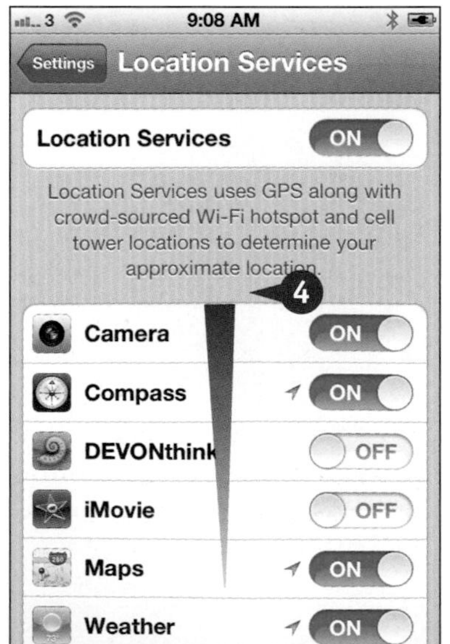

The System Services screen appears.

6 Tap the **Location-Based iAds** switch and move it to Off.

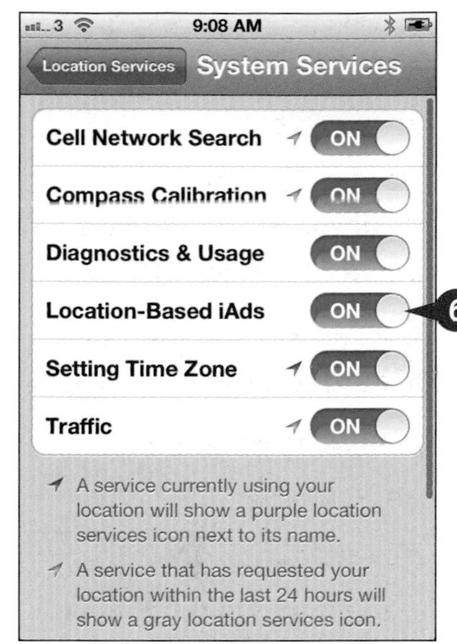

7 Tap **Location Services.**

The Location Services screen appears.

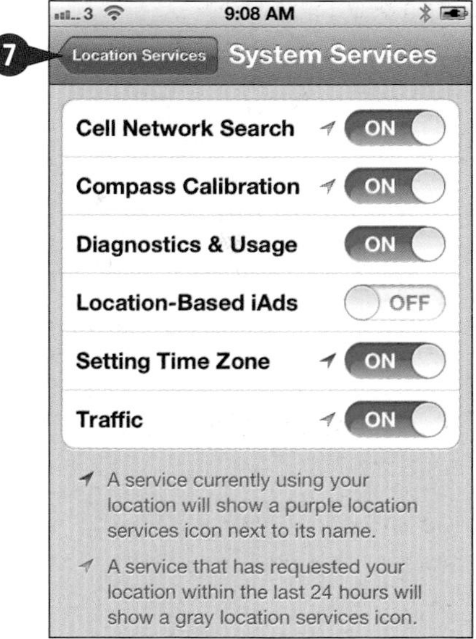

TIPS

Does this procedure disable iAd completely?
No. Even after you turn off location-based iAds as described in this task, iAd continues to run, and you see the same number of apps. But iAd is unable to collect the data it would normally use to personalize the ads that the apps display to you.

Does following this procedure work for the iPad and iPod touch as well?
Yes, but you must follow this procedure on each device that you want to prevent from collecting data with iAd. Turning off data collection on one device has no effect on your other devices.

CHAPTER 15

Troubleshooting Your iPhone

To keep your iPhone running well and to enjoy the latest features that Apple adds, you should update its software when a new version becomes available. You will also want to back up your iPhone's data and settings, reduce the iPhone's power consumption to extend runtime on the battery, reset your iPhone's settings, and troubleshoot connection and sync problems. And if you lose your iPhone, you can locate it using the Find My iPhone feature.

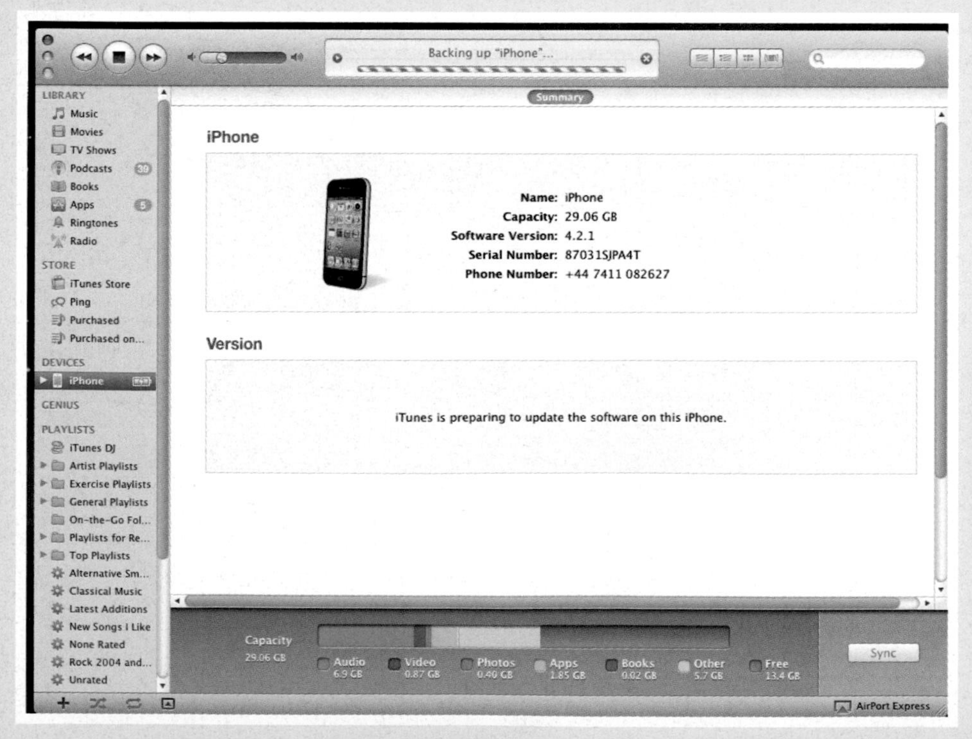

Update Your iPhone's Software

Apple periodically releases new versions of the iPhone's software to fix problems, improve performance, and add new features. To keep your iPhone running fast and smoothly, and to add the latest features that Apple provides, you should update the iPhone's software when a new version becomes available.

iTunes and your iPhone notify you automatically when a new version of the iPhone's software is available. You can also check manually for new versions of the software.

Update Your iPhone's Software

1. Connect your iPhone to your computer via the USB cable.

   The iPhone appears in the Devices list in iTunes.

   A dialog box appears telling you that a new software version is available.

2. Click **Update**.

iTunes downloads the new software, extracts it, and begins to install it.

The Summary screen shows the progress of the installation.

A. If iTunes does not display the iPhone's control screens, click the iPhone in the Devices list to make the control screens appear.

When the installation is complete, iTunes displays a dialog box telling you that the iPhone will restart in 15 seconds.

3 Click **OK** or wait for the countdown to complete.

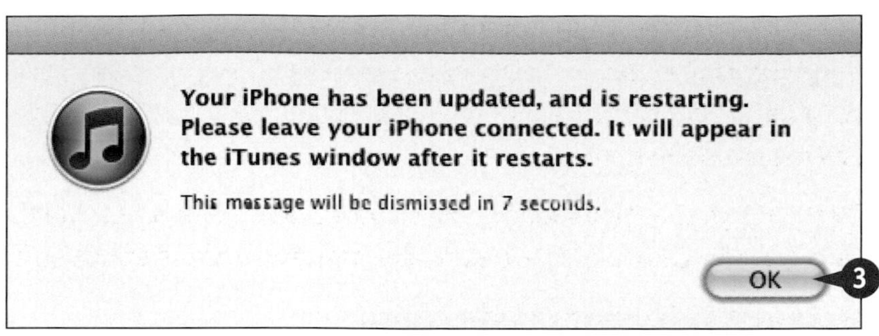

The iPhone restarts, and then reappears in the Devices list in iTunes.

4 Click your iPhone in the Devices list.

The iPhone's control screens appear.

5 Verify the version number in the Software Version readout in the iPhone box.

6 Disconnect your iPhone from the USB cable. You can now start using the iPhone as usual.

TIPS

How do I make iTunes check for a new version of my iPhone's software?

Connect your iPhone to your computer via the USB cable so that the iPhone appears in the Devices list in iTunes. When the Summary screen appears, click **Check for Update** in the Version box.

Can I update my iPhone's software without using a computer?

Yes. You can update your iPhone "over the air" by using a wireless network. Press the Home button, tap **Settings**, tap **General**, and then tap **Software Update** to check for new software. You can also update over the air using 3G, but because iPhone software updates may involve transferring hundreds of megabytes of data, it is better to use a wireless network.

Extend Your iPhone's Runtime on the Battery

To keep your iPhone running all day long, you need to charge the battery fully by plugging the iPhone into a USB socket or into the iPhone Power Adapter or another power source. You can extend your iPhone's runtime by reducing the demands on the battery in several ways. You can dim your iPhone's screen so that it consumes less power. You can set your iPhone to go to sleep quickly. You can turn off Wi-Fi and Bluetooth when you do not need them, and you can turn off the power-hungry GPS feature.

Extend Your iPhone's Runtime on the Battery

Dim the iPhone's Screen

1. Press the Home button.
2. On the Home screen, tap **Settings**.
3. On the Settings screen, tap **Brightness**.
4. On the Brightness screen, tap the **Brightness** slider and drag it to the left to dim the screen.

A. Move the **Auto-Brightness** switch to On if you want the iPhone to adjust the brightness automatically.

5. Tap **Settings**.

Turn Off Wi-Fi and Bluetooth

1. On the Settings screen, tap **Wi-Fi**.
2. On the Wi-Fi Networks screen, tap the **Wi-Fi** switch and move it to Off.
3. Tap **Settings**.
4. On the Settings screen, tap **General**.
5. On the General screen, tap **Bluetooth**.

The Bluetooth screen appears.

6 Tap the **Bluetooth** switch and move it to Off.

7 Tap **General**.

The General screen appears.

8 Tap **Settings**.

The Settings screen appears.

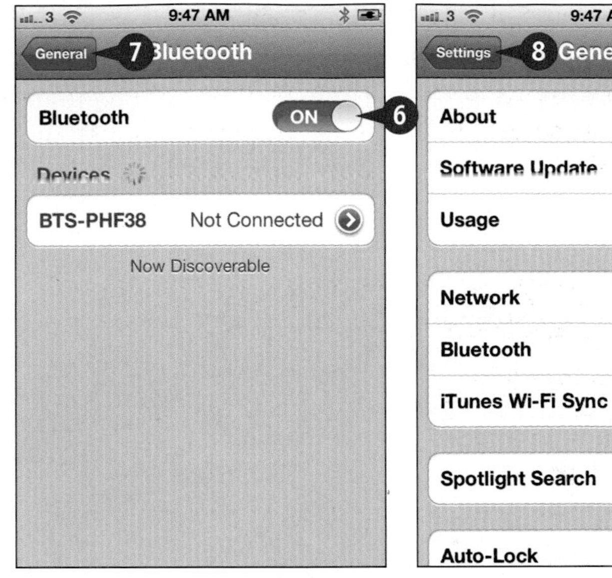

Turn Off the GPS Feature

1 On the Settings screen, tap **Location Services**.

The Location Services screen appears.

2 Tap the **Location Services** switch and move it to Off.

3 Tap **Settings**.

The Settings screen appears.

TIP

How can I make my iPhone put itself to sleep quickly?
You can set a short time for the Auto-Lock setting. To do so, press the Home button. Tap **Settings**, tap **General**, and then tap **Auto-Lock**. Tap a short interval — for example, **1 Minute** (A).

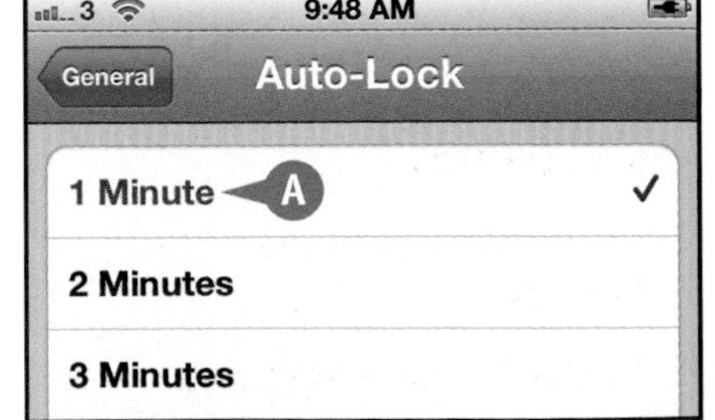

Back Up and Restore Your iPhone's Data and Settings with Your Computer

When you sync your iPhone with your computer, iTunes automatically creates a backup of the iPhone's data and settings. If your iPhone suffers a software or hardware failure, you can restore the data and settings to your iPhone. You can also sync your data and settings to a new iPhone, an iPad, or an iPod touch.

iTunes backs up the data that is unique on the iPhone, such as the iPhone's settings and notes you have created on the iPhone, but does not back up music files, video files, or photos that you have synced to the iPhone from your computer. For these types of files, which are still available on your computer, iTunes keeps a list of the files you have synced but does not keep extra copies of them.

Back Up and Restore Your iPhone's Data and Settings with Your Computer

1. Connect your iPhone to your computer via the USB cable.

   The iPhone appears in the Devices list in iTunes.

2. Click your iPhone in the Devices list.

   The iPhone's control screens appear.

3. Click **Summary**.

   The Summary screen comes to the front.

4. Click **Restore**.

   iTunes prompts you to back up the settings on the iPhone.

5. Click **Back Up**.

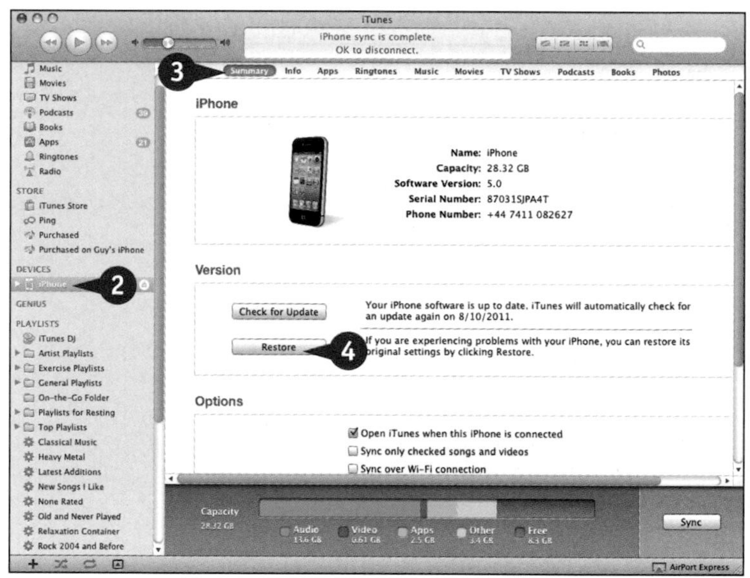

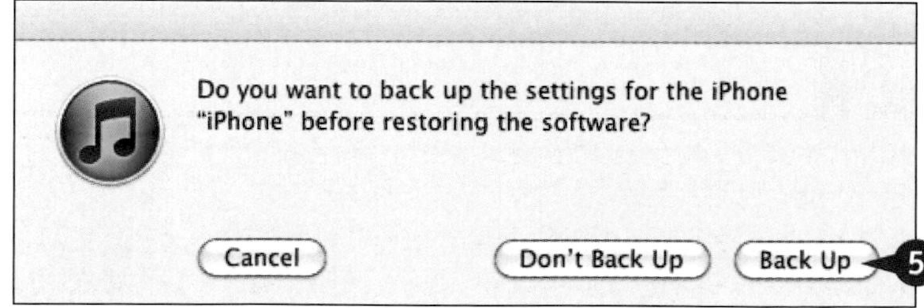

iTunes confirms that you want to restore the iPhone to its factory settings.

6 Click **Restore**.

iTunes backs up the iPhone's data, restores the software on the iPhone, and returns the iPhone to its factory settings.

Note: Do not disconnect the iPhone during the restore process. Doing so can leave the iPhone in an unusable state.

iTunes displays the Set Up Your iPhone screen.

7 Click **Restore from the backup of** (○ changes to ◉).

8 Click the pop-up menu and choose your iPhone by name.

9 Click **Continue**.

iTunes restores the data and settings to your iPhone.

Your iPhone restarts, appears in the Devices list in iTunes, and then syncs.

10 Disconnect the iPhone.

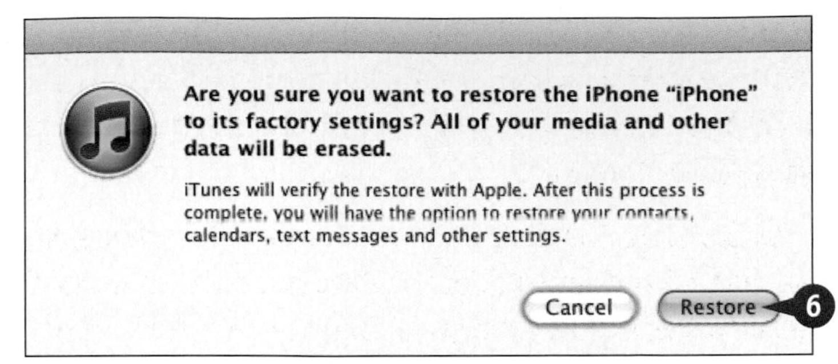

TIP

How can I protect confidential information in my iPhone's backups?

On the Summary screen in iTunes, click **Encrypt iPhone backup** (☐ changes to ☑). In the Set Password dialog box, type the password (A), and then click **Set Password** (B). iTunes then encrypts your backups using strong encryption.

Back Up and Restore Your iPhone's Data and Settings with iCloud

When you sync your iPhone with iCloud, you create a backup of the iPhone's data and settings in your storage area on iCloud. If your iPhone suffers a software or hardware failure, you can restore the data and settings to your iPhone. At this writing, a standard free iCloud account gives you 5 GB of data storage. This is enough to store your iPhone's settings and your most important data and files. You can buy more storage if necessary, but even if you do, you must set your iPhone to back up exactly those items you want to keep in iCloud. The iTunes Store lets you download again all the apps, media files, and games you have bought, so you do not need to back these files up.

Back Up and Restore Your iPhone's Data and Settings with iCloud

Choose Which Items to Back Up to iCloud

1. Press the Home button.

   The Home screen appears.

2. Tap **Settings**.

   The Settings screen appears.

3. Tap and drag up to scroll down until the third box appears.

4. Tap **iCloud**.

   The iCloud screen appears, showing the name of the iCloud account you have set up.

5. Choose the data you want to synchronize with iCloud by moving the Mail, Contacts, Calendars, Reminders, Bookmarks, and Notes switches to On or Off as needed.

6. If you need to buy more storage, tap your account name.

   The Account screen appears, showing your storage amount in the Storage Plan area.

7. Tap the Storage Plan button.

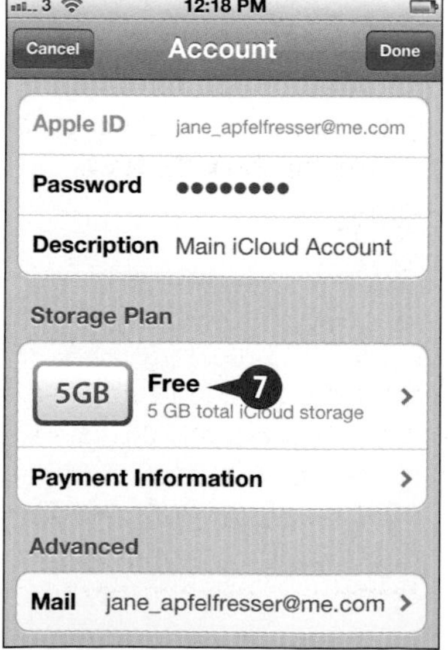

8 Tap the storage plan you want, tap **Buy**, and follow through the payment process.

9 Tap **Photo Stream**.

10 Tap the **Photo Stream** switch and move it to On or Off, as needed.

11 Tap the name of your iCloud account.

12 On the Account screen, tap **Documents & Data**.

13 Tap the **Documents & Data** switch and move it to On or Off, as needed.

14 Tap the **Use Cellular** switch and move it to On or Off, as needed.

15 Tap the name of your iCloud account.

16 Tap the **Find My iPhone** switch and move it to On or Off, as needed.

17 Tap **Storage & Backup**.

18 Tap the **iCloud Backup** switch and move it to On.

19 If you want to back up your iPhone now, tap **Back Up Now**.

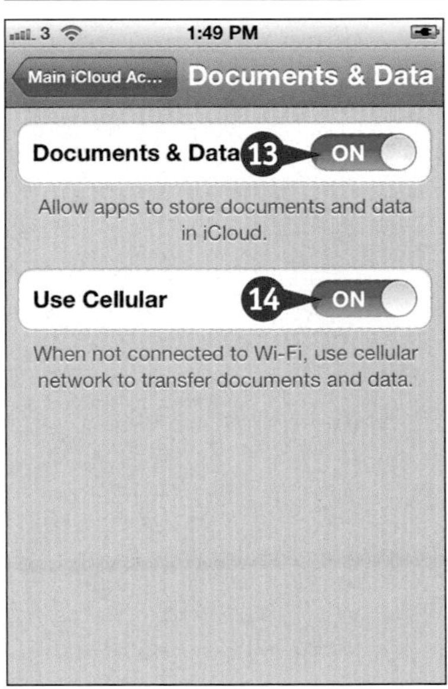

TIP

How do I restore my iPhone from its iCloud backup?

First, reset the iPhone to factory settings. Press the Home button, tap **Settings**, tap **General**, tap **Reset**, and tap **Erase All Content and Settings**. Tap **Erase iPhone** in the confirmation dialog box. When the iPhone restarts and displays its setup screens, choose your language and country. On the Set Up iPhone screen, tap **Restore from iCloud Backup**, and then tap **Next**. On the Apple ID screen, enter your Apple ID, and then tap **Next**. On the Choose Backup screen, tap the backup you want to use — normally, the most recent backup — and then tap **Restore**.

Reset Your Network, Dictionary, and Home Screen Settings

After experimenting with changes to your iPhone's settings, you may want to restore the iPhone to the default settings to undo the changes you have made. For example, you may want to restore your Home screen to its default settings to undo customizations.

From the Reset screen, you can quickly reset your network settings, your keyboard dictionary, your Home screen layout, or your location warnings. You can also reset all settings, as discussed in this task.

Reset Your Network, Dictionary, and Home Screen Settings

1. Press the Home button.

   The Home screen appears.

2. Tap **Settings**.

   The Settings screen appears.

3. Tap and drag up to scroll down until the third box appears.

4. Tap **General**.

   The General screen appears.

5. Scroll down all the way to the bottom.

The lower part of the General screen appears.

6 Tap **Reset**.

The Reset screen appears.

7 Tap **Reset Network Settings**, **Reset Keyboard Dictionary**, or **Reset Home Screen Layout**, as needed.

Note: Resetting the network settings deletes all network information you have entered, such as passwords for wireless networks. Resetting the keyboard dictionary deletes the custom words you have added to it. Resetting the Home screen layout puts the Home screen icons back in their default places.

A confirmation dialog box opens, showing a brief explanation of what the command will reset.

8 Tap the **Reset** button in the dialog box.

The iPhone resets the item you chose.

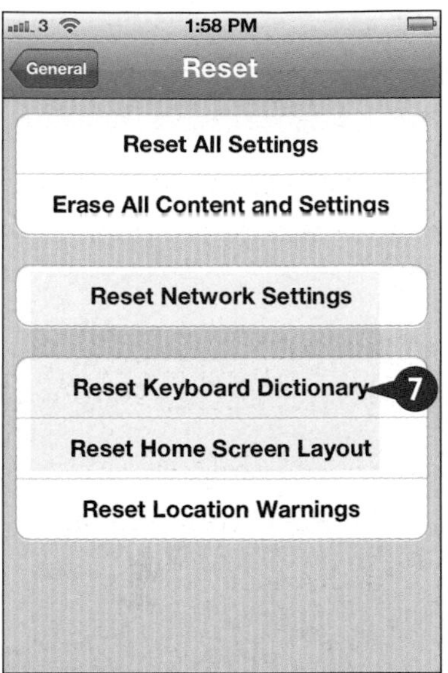

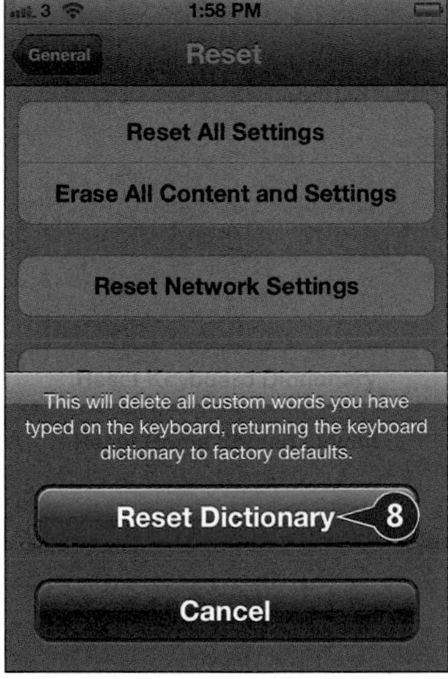

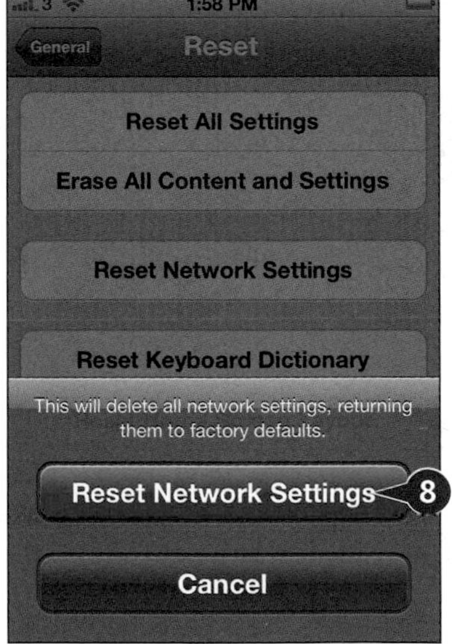

TIP

What does the Reset Location Warnings button on the Reset screen do?
When an app first requests location information, your iPhone asks your permission. For example, when you first take a photo using the Camera app, the Camera app requests your location so that it can store it in the photo. After you tap **OK** (A) for such a request, your iPhone does not ask you again for the same app. Resetting the location warnings makes each app request permission again.

Restore Your iPhone to Factory Settings

If your iPhone starts malfunctioning and you cannot get iTunes to recognize it, you may need to restore the iPhone to factory settings. This is an operation you perform on the iPhone itself when severe problems occur with its settings, to get the iPhone into a state where it can communicate with iTunes again.

If iTunes can recognize the iPhone, use iTunes to restore the iPhone instead of resetting the iPhone as described here.

Restore Your iPhone to Factory Settings

1. Press the Home button.

   The Home screen appears.

2. Tap **Settings**.

   The Settings screen appears.

3. Scroll down until the third box appears.

Note: If your iPhone is not responding to the Home button or your taps, press and hold the Sleep/Wake button and the Home button for about 15 seconds to reset the iPhone.

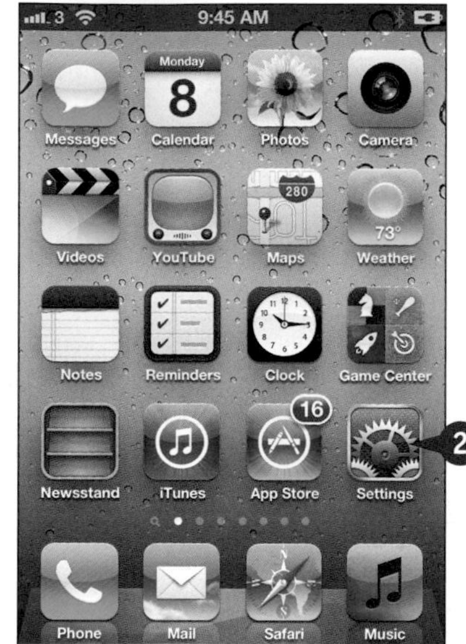

4. Tap **General**.

   The General screen appears.

5. Scroll down all the way to the bottom.

The lower part of the General screen appears.

6 Tap **Reset**.

The Reset screen appears.

7 Tap **Reset All Settings**.

Note: If you have applied a restrictions passcode to the iPhone, you must enter the passcode after tapping Reset All Settings.

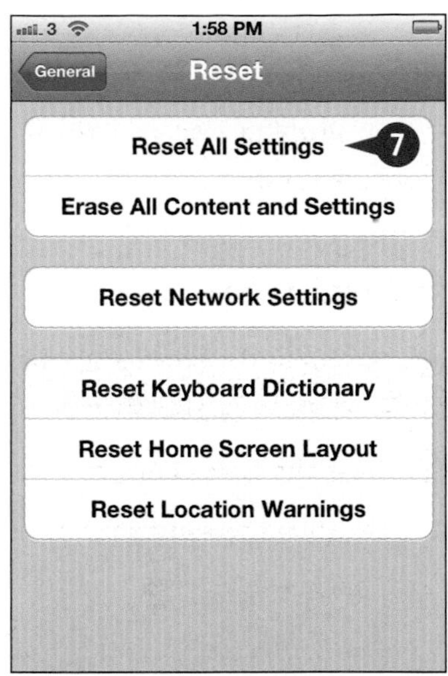

The Reset dialog box appears.

8 Tap **Reset All Settings**.

The iPhone resets all its settings.

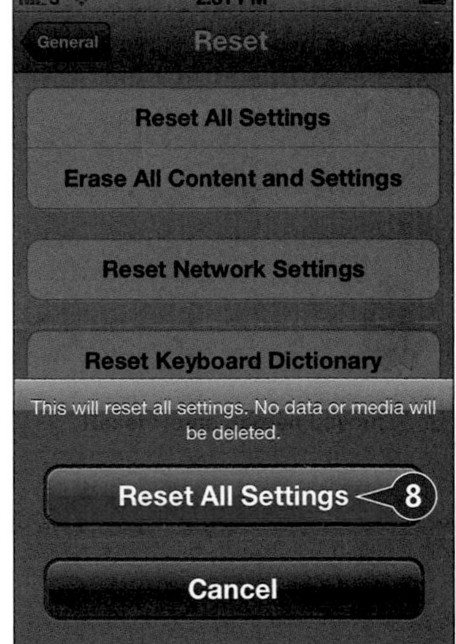

Does resetting all the iPhone's settings delete my data and my music files?

No, it does not. When you reset all the iPhone's settings, the settings go back to their defaults, but your data remains in place. But you will need to set the iPhone's settings again, either by restoring them using iTunes or by setting them manually, in order to get the iPhone working the same way again.

Troubleshoot Wi-Fi Connections

To get the most out of your iPhone without exceeding your data plan, use Wi-Fi networks whenever they are available.

Normally, the iPhone establishes and maintains Wi-Fi connections without problems. But you may sometimes need to request your iPhone's network address again, a process called renewing the lease on the IP address. You may also need to tell the iPhone to forget a network, and then rejoin the network manually, providing the password again.

Troubleshoot Wi-Fi Connections

Renew the Lease on Your iPhone's IP Address

1. Press the Home button.

   The Home screen appears.

2. Tap **Settings**.

   The Settings screen appears.

3. Tap **Wi-Fi**.

   The Wi-Fi Networks screen appears.

4. Tap ⊙ to the right of the network for which you want to renew the lease.

   The network's screen appears.

5. Tap and drag up to scroll down to the bottom.

6. Tap **Renew Lease**.

   The Renew Lease dialog box opens.

7. Tap **Renew Lease**.

8. Tap **Wi-Fi Networks**.

   The Wi-Fi Networks screen appears.

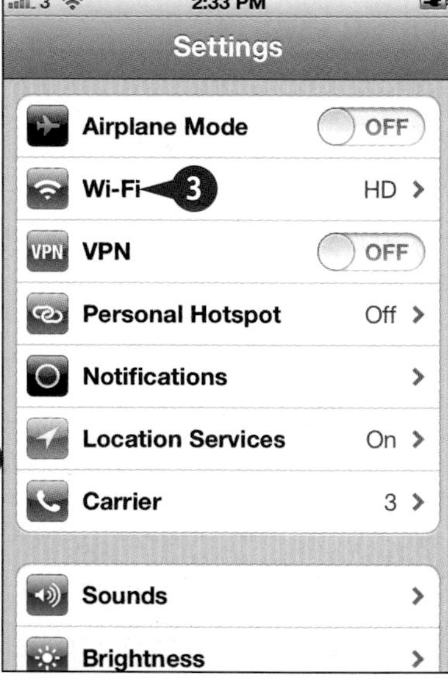

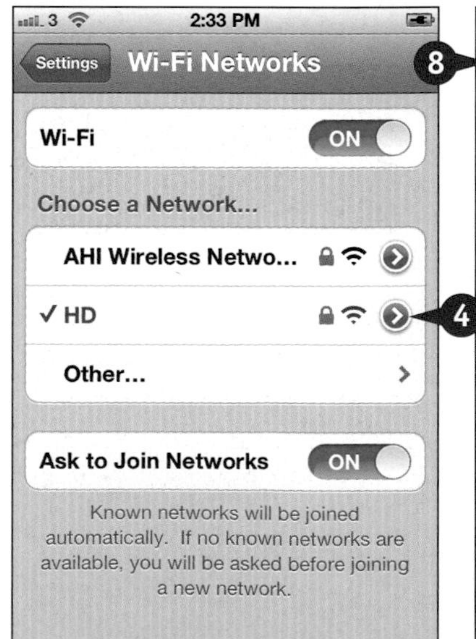

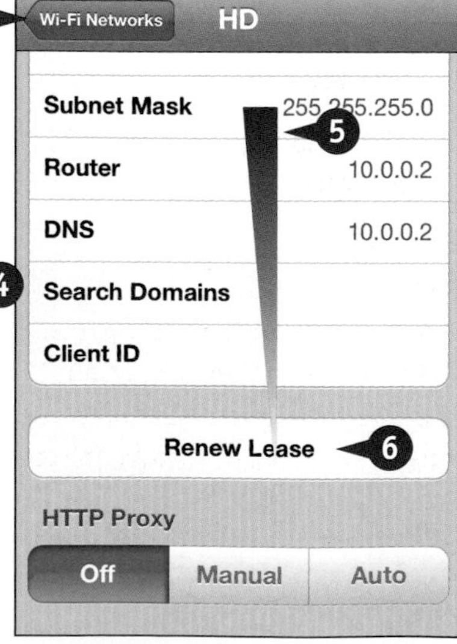

Forget a Network and Then Rejoin It

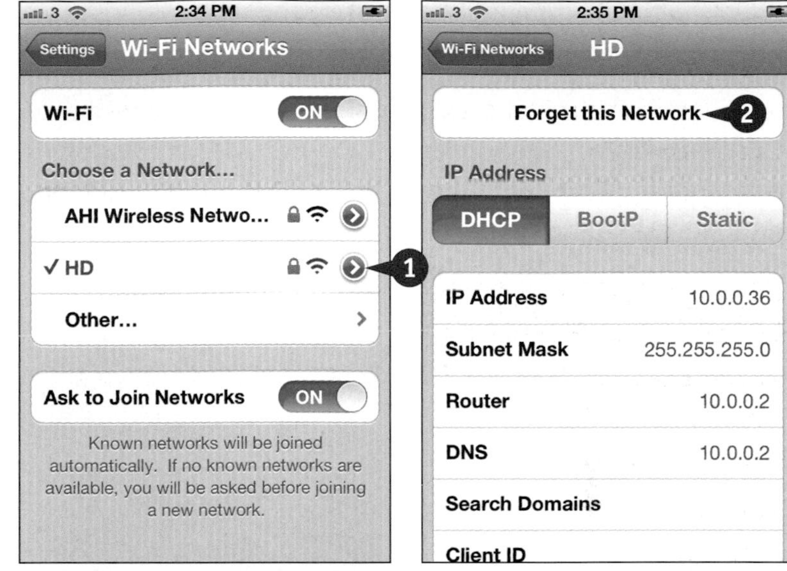

1. On the Wi-Fi Networks screen, tap ⊙ to the right of the network.

   The network's screen appears.

2. Tap **Forget this Network**.

   The Forget This Network dialog box opens.

3. Tap **Forget**.

   The iPhone removes the network's details.

4. Tap **Wi-Fi Networks**.

   The Wi-Fi Networks screen appears.

5. Tap the network's name.

   The password screen appears.

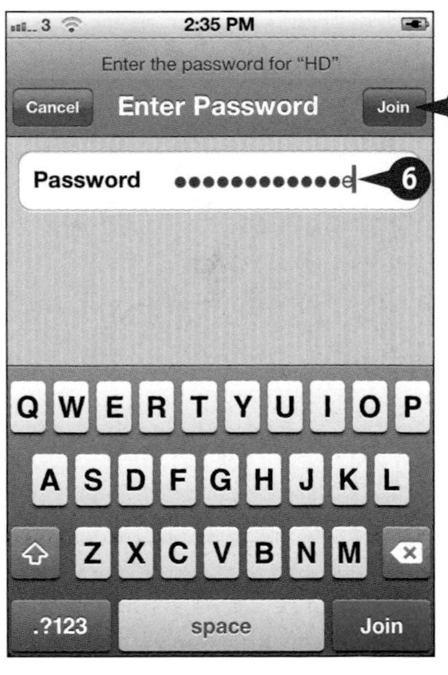

6. Type the password for the network.

7. Tap **Join**.

   The iPhone joins the network.

TIP

What else can I do to reestablish my Wi-Fi network connections?
If you are unable to fix your Wi-Fi network connections by renewing the IP address lease or by forgetting and rejoining the network, as described in this task, you may need to reset your network settings, as described earlier in this chapter. After resetting the network settings, set up each connection again manually.

Troubleshoot iTunes Sync Problems

To keep your iPhone charged and loaded with your current data and media files, you will need to connect it regularly to your computer and sync it using iTunes.

Connection and syncing are usually straightforward, but you may sometimes find that iTunes does not recognize your iPhone when you connect it. When this happens, you will have to troubleshoot the physical connection and iTunes' settings. If iTunes is not set to sync automatically with your iPhone, you must start the sync manually.

Troubleshoot iTunes Sync Problems

Check the USB Connection between Your Computer and Your iPhone

1. Check that the dock connector end of the cable is firmly plugged into the dock connector port on the iPhone. You may need to remove any case in order to make a good connection.

Note: Make sure the USB port you use is a full-power port rather than a low-power port. Use a USB port directly on your computer rather than a USB port on a hub or a peripheral device such as a keyboard.

2. Check that the USB end of the cable is firmly plugged into a USB port on your computer.

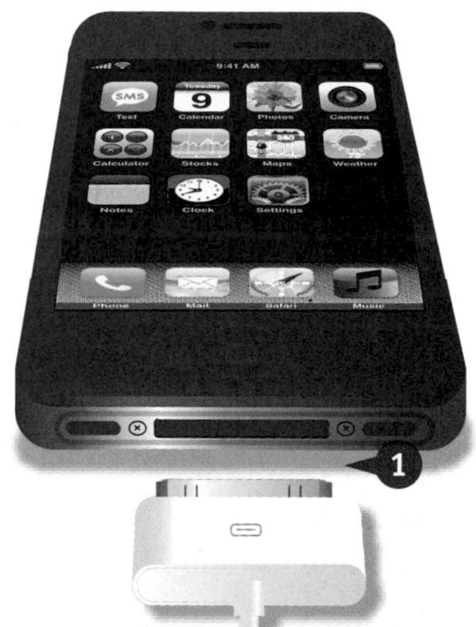

Restart the iPhone

1. Press and hold the Power button on the iPhone for several seconds.

2. On the shutdown screen, tap and drag the slider to the right.

   The iPhone turns off.

3. Press and hold the Power button for two seconds.

   The Apple logo appears on the screen, and the iPhone restarts.

4. Connect the iPhone to your computer via the USB cable.

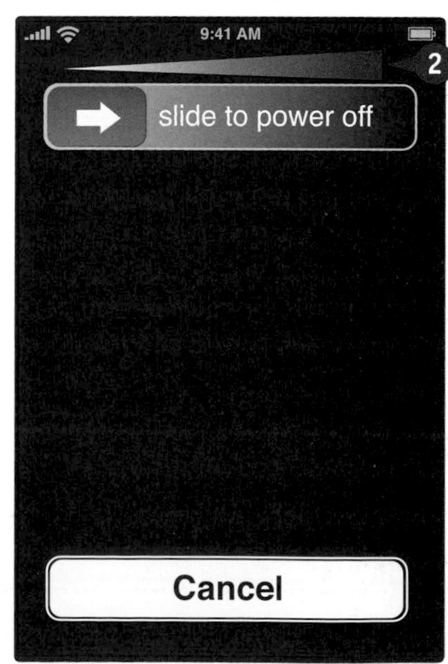

Restart iTunes

1. Close iTunes. In Windows, click **File** and then **Exit**. On a Mac, click **iTunes** and then click **Quit iTunes**.

Note: If neither restarting your iPhone nor restarting iTunes enables the two to communicate, try restarting your PC or Mac.

2. Restart iTunes. In Windows, click the **iTunes** icon on the Start menu. On a Mac, click the **iTunes** icon on the Dock.

3. Connect the iPhone to your computer via the USB cable.

Verify Automatic Syncing or Start a Sync Manually

1. If iTunes does not launch or become active when you connect your iPhone, launch or activate iTunes manually.

2. Click your iPhone in the Devices list.

3. On the iPhone's control screens, click **Summary**.

4. Click **Open iTunes when this iPhone is connected** (☐ changes to ☑).

5. Click **Apply**.

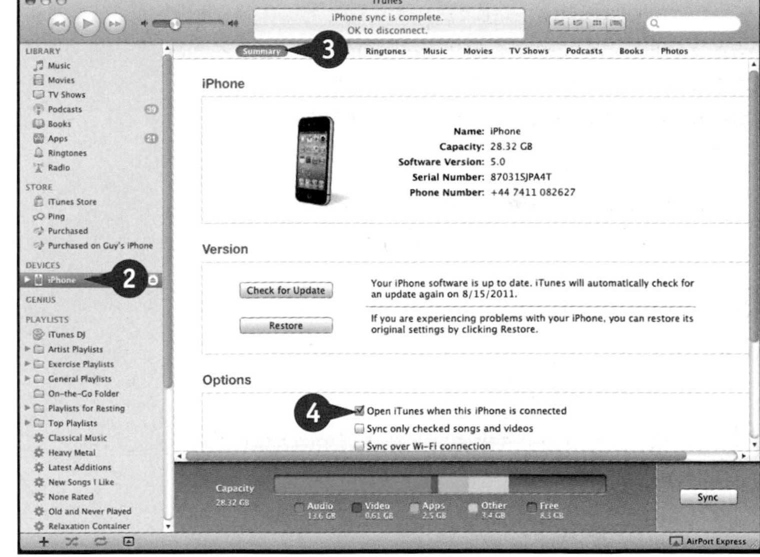

TIP

Why does nothing happen when I connect my iPhone to my computer?

If your iPhone's battery is exhausted, nothing happens for several minutes after you connect your iPhone to your computer. This is because the iPhone is charging its battery via the USB cable. After a few minutes, when the iPhone's battery has enough charge to power the screen, the screen comes on, and syncing begins as usual.

Locate Your iPhone with Find My iPhone

If you have an iCloud account or a MobileMe account, you can use the Find My iPhone feature to locate your iPhone when you have lost it or it has been stolen. You can also display a message on the iPhone — for example, to tell the person who has found the iPhone how to contact you — or remotely wipe the data on the iPhone.

To use Find My iPhone, you must first set up your iCloud account or MobileMe account on the iPhone, and then enable the Find My iPhone feature.

Locate Your iPhone with Find My iPhone

Turn On the Find My iPhone Feature

1. Set up your iCloud account or MobileMe account on the iPhone as discussed in Chapter 4.
2. Press the Home button.

   The Home screen appears.
3. Tap **Settings**.

   The Settings screen appears.
4. Tap and drag up to scroll down until the third group of buttons appears.
5. Tap **Mail, Contacts, Calendars**.

   The Mail, Contacts, Calendars screen appears.
6. Tap your iCloud account or MobileMe account.

   The screen for your iCloud account or MobileMe account appears.
7. Tap the **Find My iPhone** switch and move it to On.

   A confirmation dialog box appears.
8. Tap **Allow**.
9. Tap **Mail, Contacts, Calendars**.

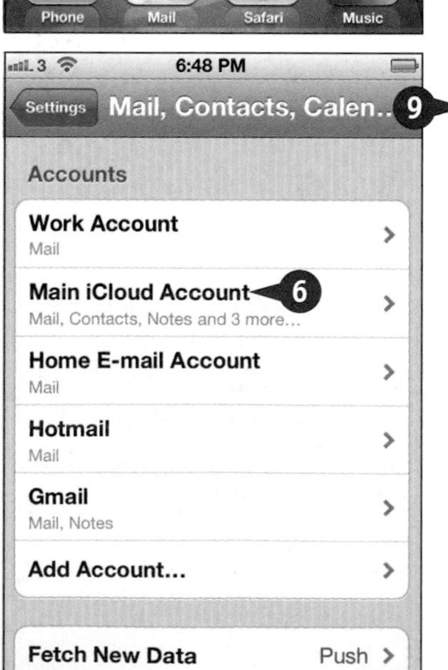

Locate Your iPhone Using Find My iPhone

1. Open a web browser, such as Internet Explorer or Safari.
2. Click the Address box.
3. Type **www.icloud.com** and press Enter in Windows or Return on a Mac.

   The iCloud Sign In web page appears.
4. Type your username.
5. Type your password.
6. Click **Sign In**.

   The iCloud site appears, displaying the page you last used.
7. Click **iCloud** (☁).

   The iCloud apps screen appears.
8. Click **Find My iPhone**.

   The Sign In Again to Access Find My iPhone dialog box appears.
9. Type your password.
10. Click **OK**.

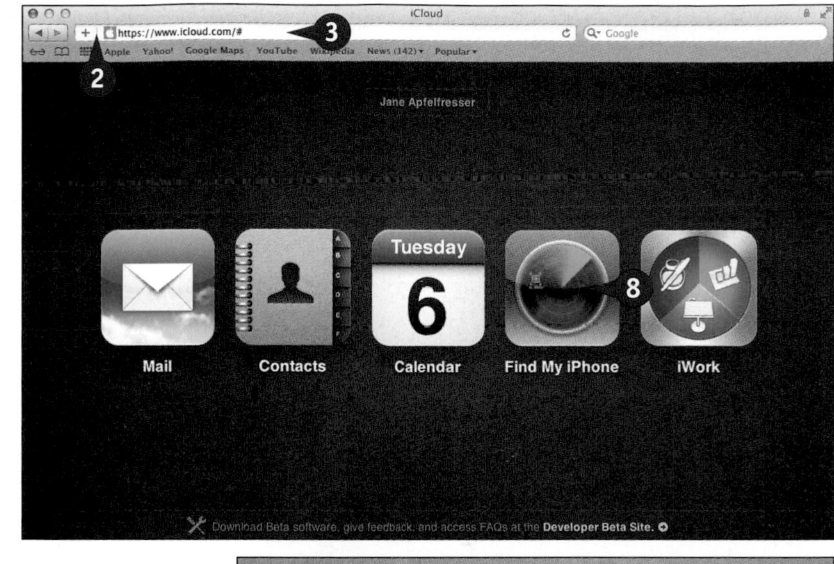

TIP

Is it worth displaying a message on my iPhone, or should I simply wipe it?
Almost always, it is definitely worth displaying a message on your iPhone. If you have lost your iPhone, and someone has found it, that person may be trying to return it to you. The chances are good that the finder is honest, even if he has not discovered that you have locked the iPhone with a passcode. That said, if you are certain someone has stolen your iPhone, you may prefer simply to wipe it, using the technique explained next.

continued ►

Find My iPhone is a powerful feature that you can use both when you have mislaid your iPhone accidentally and when someone has deliberately taken it from you.

If Find My iPhone reveals that someone else has taken your iPhone, you can wipe its contents to prevent whoever has taken it from hacking into your data. Be clear that wiping your iPhone prevents you from locating the iPhone again — ever. Wipe your iPhone only when you have lost it, you have no hope of recovering it, and you must destroy the data on it.

Locate Your iPhone with Find My iPhone (continued)

The iCloud Find My iPhone screen appears, showing the iPhone's location.

Ⓐ If you have multiple iPhones, iPads, or iPod touches registered with Find My iPhone, click the right device in the Devices list.

11 Click ⓘ.

The Info dialog box appears.

12 Click **Play Sound or Send Message.**

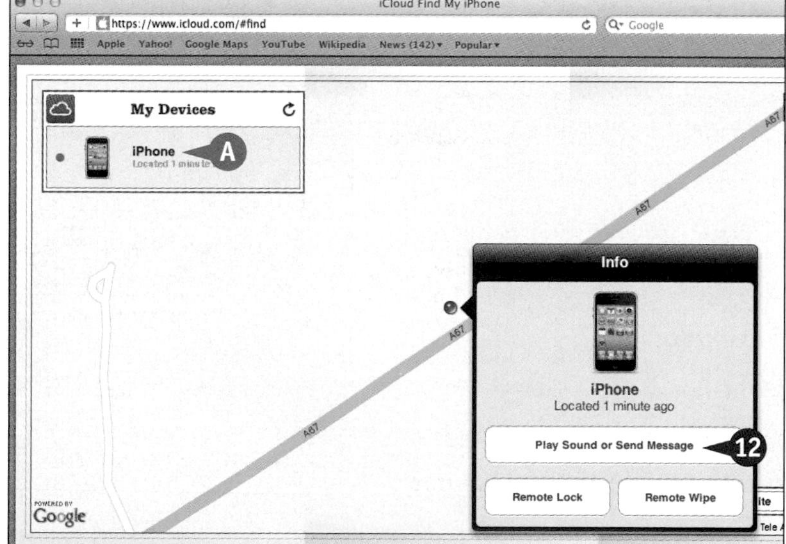

The Send Message dialog box opens.

13 Type the message you want to send.

14 Make sure the **Play Sound** switch is in the On position if you want the iPhone to play a sound.

15 Click **Send.**

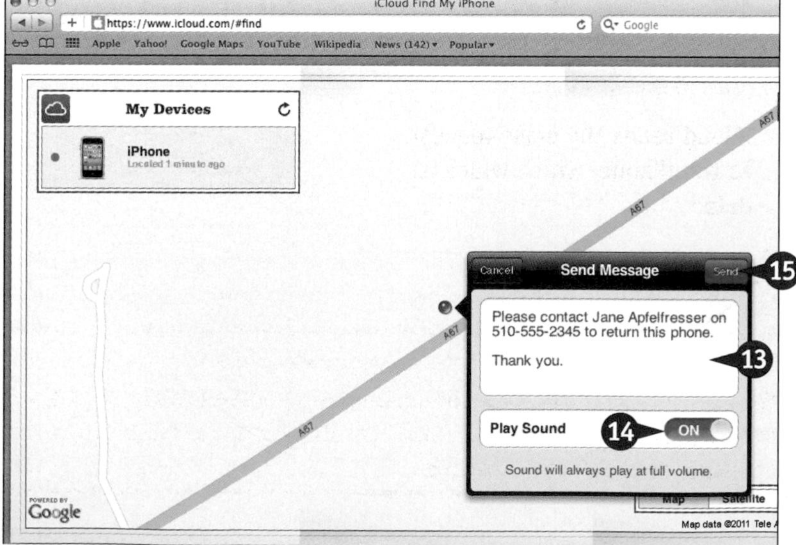

Lock the iPhone with a Passcode

1 Click **Remote Lock** in the Info dialog box.

The Remote Lock dialog box opens.

2 Click the numbers for a new passcode to apply to the iPhone.

The Remote Lock dialog box displays its Re-enter Passcode screen.

3 Click the passcode numbers again.

4 Click **Lock**.

iCloud sends the lock request to the iPhone, and then displays a dialog box telling you it sent the request.

5 Click **OK**.

Remotely Wipe the iPhone

1 Click **Remote Wipe** in the Info dialog box.

The Info dialog box displays controls for wiping the iPhone.

2 Click **Wipe iPhone**.

iCloud sends the erase request to the iPhone, which wipes its data.

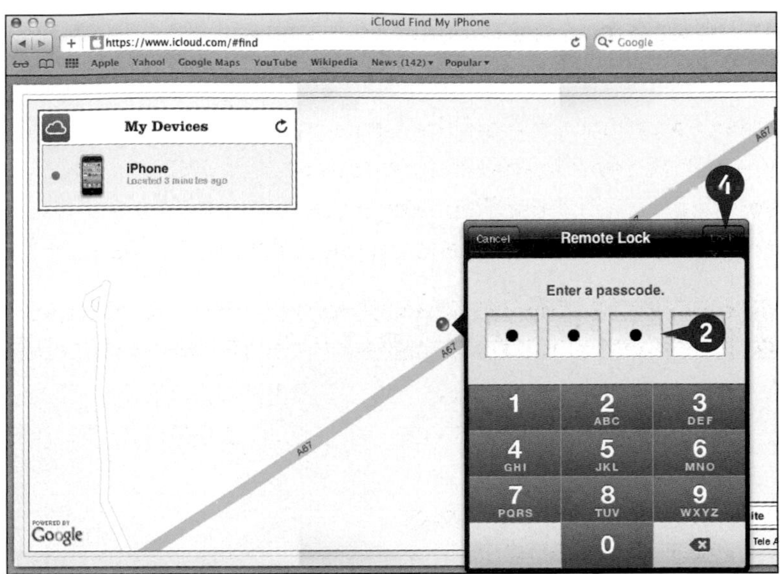

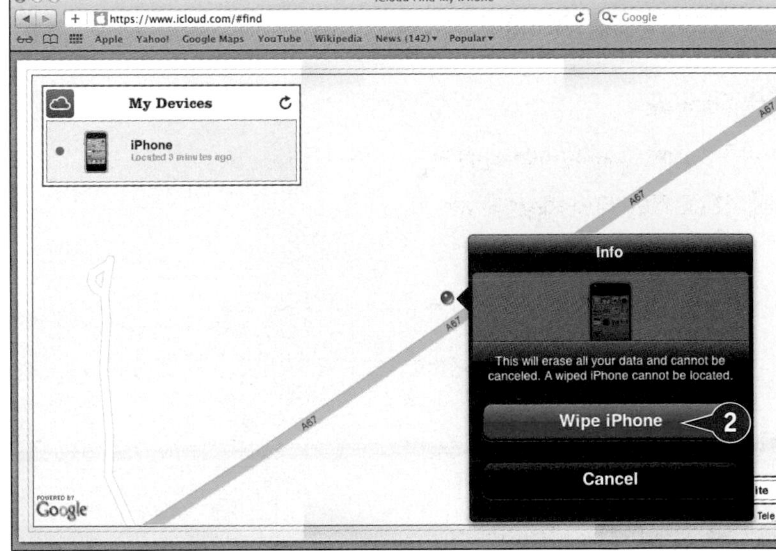

TIP

Can I remotely wipe the data on my iPhone if I do not have an iCloud account or a MobileMe account?

You can set a passcode for the iPhone as discussed in Chapter 3, and then move the **Erase Data** switch on the Passcode Lock screen to On. This setting makes the iPhone automatically erase its data after 10 failed attempts to enter the passcode.

Index

N

O

P

R

S

T

U

V

W

Y

Z

Read Less–Learn More®

Visual

There's a Visual book for every learning level...

Simplified®

The place to start if you're new to computers. Full color.

- Computers
- Creating Web Pages
- Digital Photography
- Excel
- Internet
- Laptops
- Mac OS
- Office
- PCs
- Windows
- Word

Teach Yourself VISUALLY™

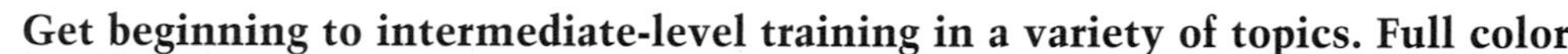

Get beginning to intermediate-level training in a variety of topics. Full color.

- Access
- Algebra
- Astronomy
- Bass Guitar
- Beadwork
- Bridge
- Car Care and Maintenance
- Chess
- Circular Knitting
- Collage & Altered Art
- Computers
- Crafting with Kids
- Crocheting
- Digital Photography
- Digital Video
- Dog Training
- Drawing
- Dreamweaver
- Excel
- Flash
- Golf
- Guitar
- Hand Dyeing
- Handspinning
- HTML
- iLife
- iPad
- iPhone
- iPhoto
- Jewelry Making & Beading
- Knitting
- Lightroom
- Macs
- Mac OS
- Office
- Outlook
- Photoshop
- Photoshop Elements
- Piano
- Poker
- PowerPoint
- Quilting
- Scrapbooking
- Sewing
- Web Design
- Windows
- Wireless Networking
- Word
- WordPress

Top 100 Simplified® Tips & Tricks

Tips and techniques to take your skills beyond the basics. Full color.

- Digital Photography
- eBay
- Excel
- Google
- Office
- Photoshop
- Photoshop Elements
- PowerPoint
- Windows

...all designed for visual learners—just like you!

Master VISUALLY®

Your complete visual reference. Two-color interior.

- 3ds Max
- Creating Web Pages
- Dreamweaver and Flash
- Excel
- iPod and iTunes
- Mac OS
- Office
- Optimizing PC Performance
- Windows
- Windows Server

Visual Blueprint™

Where to go for professional-level programming instruction. Two-color interior.

- ActionScript
- Ajax
- ASP.NET 2.0
- Excel Data Analysis
- Excel Pivot Tables
- Excel Programming
- HTML
- JavaScript
- Mambo
- Mobile App Development
- Perl and Apache
- PHP & MySQL
- SEO
- Ubuntu Linux
- Vista Sidebar
- Visual Basic
- XML

Visual™ Quick Tips

Shortcuts, tricks, and techniques for getting more done in less time. Full color.

- Beading
- Crochet
- Digital Photography
- Excel
- Golf
- Internet
- iPhone
- iPod & iTunes
- Knitting
- Mac OS
- Office
- Paper Crafts
- PowerPoint
- Quilting
- Sewing
- Windows
- Wire Jewelry

For a complete listing of Visual books, go to wiley.com/go/visual

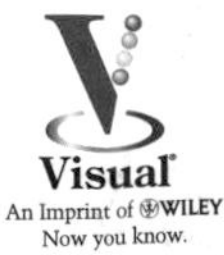